Bio-Inspired Algorithms

Bio-Inspired Algorithms

Guest Editors

Sándor Szénási
Gábor Kertész

MDPI

Basel • Beijing • Wuhan • Barcelona • Belgrade • Novi Sad • Cluj • Manchester

Guest Editors
Sándor Szénási
John von Neumann Faculty of Informatics
Óbuda University
Budapest
Hungary

Gábor Kertész
John von Neumann Faculty of Informatics
Óbuda University
Budapest
Hungary

Editorial Office
MDPI AG
Grosspeteranlage 5
4052 Basel, Switzerland

This is a reprint of the Special Issue, published open access by the journal *Algorithms* (ISSN 1999-4893), freely accessible at: https://www.mdpi.com/journal/algorithms/special_issues/bio_inspired_algo.

For citation purposes, cite each article independently as indicated on the article page online and as indicated below:

Lastname, A.A.; Lastname, B.B. Article Title. *Journal Name* **Year**, *Volume Number*, Page Range.

ISBN 978-3-7258-4373-2 (Hbk)
ISBN 978-3-7258-4374-9 (PDF)
https://doi.org/10.3390/books978-3-7258-4374-9

Contents

About the Editors

Sándor Szénási

Sándor Szénási received the Ph.D. degree from the Doctoral School of Applied Informatics and Applied Mathematics, Obuda University, Budapest, Hungary, in 2013. Currently, he is a professor at the John von Neumann Faculty of Informatics, Obuda University, and the Faculty of Economics and Informatics, J. Selye University. He is the leader of the High-Performance Computing Research Group at the John von Neumann Faculty of Informatics. His research interests include data-parallel algorithms, GPU programming, machine learning, and optimization with metaheuristics. He engages both in theoretical fundamentals and in algorithmic issues with respect to the realization of practical requirements and given constraints.

Gábor Kertész

Gábor Kertész received a Ph.D. in 2019 in Information Science and Technology; the main areas of his research were computer vision, parallel processing, and deep machine learning. His current research interests are metric learning and applied machine intelligence. He is an associate professor and the vice-dean for research at the John von Neumann Faculty of Informatics, Obuda University, Budapest, Hungary, and also a part-time research fellow at the HUN-REN SZTAKI (Institute for Computer Science and Control). He is the leader of the Applied Machine Learning Research Group at the John von Neumann Faculty of Informatics.

Preface

A Special Issue of the journal Algorithms called "Bio-Inspired Algorithms" was open for scientific papers related to its topic in 2024. A large number of manuscripts were submitted, 13 of which were suitable for the focus of the Special Issue and passed the rigorous and exhaustive review process. This reprint contains these excellent articles, which will hopefully reach an even wider audience.

The goal for this Special Issue was to seek original research papers about novel bio-inspired methods, analysis of already-existing techniques, or high-level practical applications from the field of computer science or any interdisciplinary field.

The accepted manuscripts discuss evolutional (Genetic Algorithms), swarm-intelligence-based (Ant Colony Optimization, Ant-Lion Optimizer, Grey Wolf Optimizer, Bat Algorithm, Moth Flame Optimization, etc.), or brain-inspired computing (Neural Networks, Deep Learning) methods. These were applied in several real-world research projects, including inverse kinematics of robot manipulations, optimization of biodiesel mixtures, and speech emotion recognition, as well as in purely theoretical contributions.

Sándor Szénási and Gábor Kertész
Guest Editors

algorithms

MDPI

Article

Inverse Kinematics of Robotic Manipulators Based on Hybrid Differential Evolution and Jacobian Pseudoinverse Approach

Jesus Hernandez-Barragan, Josue Plascencia-Lopez, Michel Lopez-Franco, Nancy Arana-Daniel and Carlos Lopez-Franco *

Computer Science Department, University of Guadalajara, 1421 Marcelino Garcia Barragan, Guadalajara 44430, Jalisco, Mexico; josed.hernandezb@academicos.udg.mx (J.H.-B.); josue.plascencia0154@alumnos.udg.mx (J.P.-L.); michel.lopez@academicos.udg.mx (M.L.-F.); nancy.arana@academicos.udg.mx (N.A.-D.)
* Correspondence: carlos.lfranco@academicos.udg.mx

Abstract: Robot manipulators play a critical role in several industrial applications by providing high precision and accuracy. To perform these tasks, manipulator robots require the effective computation of inverse kinematics. Conventional methods to solve IK often encounter significant challenges, such as singularities, non-linear equations, and poor generalization across different robotic configurations. In this work, we propose a novel approach to solve the inverse kinematics (IK) problem in robotic manipulators using a metaheuristic algorithm enhanced with a Jacobian step. Our method overcomes those limitations by selectively applying the Jacobian step to the differential evolution (DE) algorithm. The effectiveness and versatility of the proposed approach are demonstrated through simulations and real-world experimentation on a 5 DOF KUKA robotic arm.

Keywords: metaheuristic algorithms; manipulator robots; inverse kinematics (IK); differential evolution (DE); Jacobian matrix

1. Introduction

Manipulator robots, known for their unparalleled precision, efficiency, and safety, are revolutionizing industries across the globe. These versatile machines are pivotal in space applications, where they service satellites, remove orbital debris, and construct and maintain orbital assets, ensuring the sustainability of our extraterrestrial endeavors [1]. In the automotive industry, robotic manipulators excel in welding tasks, utilizing an electric arc and shielding gas to enhance manufacturing processes [2]. The healthcare sector has also benefited immensely, with robotic arms enabling minimally invasive surgeries that surpass traditional open surgery methods in terms of precision and recovery time [3]. By performing repetitive and hazardous tasks with consistent accuracy, these robotic systems not only improve operational efficiency but also ensure worker safety. Central to their functionality is the complex challenge of solving the inverse kinematics (IK) of the robotic manipulator, a crucial aspect that underpins their application in these diverse fields.

The inverse kinematics problem entails determining the joint variable configuration that corresponds to a specific position and orientation of the end-effector. This task is generally more complex than solving the forward kinematics problem for several reasons [4]:

- Equations to solve are generally non-linear, making it not always possible to find a closed-form solution.
- Multiple solutions may exist.
- Infinite solutions may exist.
- There might be no admissible solutions.

Conventional numerical methods based on differential kinematics rely on the Jacobian matrix to determine the relationship between joint variables and end-effector positions [5].

However, these methods encounter significant problems due to singularities in the Jacobian matrix, which can lead to undefined or infinite solutions [4,6]. Closed-form methods such as algebraic or geometric methods are commonly used for manipulators with simple geometric structures [7]. Due to these drawbacks, artificial intelligence methods are increasingly utilized to solve the inverse kinematics problem.

In recent years, although to a limited extent, the solution of inverse kinematics has been explored using Artificial Neural Networks (ANNs). Typically, the input to the network is the desired position and orientation of the end-effector and the output is the vector of generalized coordinates, representing the robot's joint configurations. However, this method faces challenges in generalizing across different kinematic structures or manipulators, as it requires a unique dataset for each specific manipulator. Due to the complexity of the problem, research has been limited to solving it within the three-dimensional Cartesian plane, with the additional necessity of identifying singularity zones [8,9]. Additionally, approaches that account for both position and rotation demand very large datasets and an optimization process for the candidate solution, often utilizing numerical methods such as the Newton–Raphson method [10].

For these reasons, this paper proposes solving the inverse kinematics problem using metaheuristic algorithms. In the past decade, metaheuristic algorithms have emerged as a viable alternative for addressing various challenges in robotics. These algorithms are particularly useful for solving problems that are difficult to tackle with conventional methods or for which no exact solution method exists [11]. In the literature we can find examples of the application of metaheuristic algorithms, such as their use for hyperparameter tuning in both machine learning algorithms and deep neural networks [12], and trajectory tracking optimization [13], as well as in robotic navigation [14].

A review of the state of the art in robotic applications, particularly addressing the inverse kinematics of manipulator robots, is presented in Table 1. This review highlights that differential evolution (DE) and particle swarm optimization (PSO) are the most commonly used metaheuristic algorithms for solving the inverse kinematics problem. Other algorithms, such as Artificial Bee Colony (ABC), bees algorithm (BA), Beta Salp Swarm Algorithm (β-SSA), Wild Geese Migration Optimization (GMO), Gray Wolf Optimization (GWO), and Firefly Algorithm (FA), have also been implemented. Most studies focus on a single manipulator, with only two cases [15,16] proposing more generalized methods. Typically, these studies address only the position problem, as incorporating orientation significantly increases the complexity of solving the inverse kinematics. Although joint limits are considered in all optimization processes, hard bounding is commonly applied to manage constraints, or candidate solutions are recalculated when they exceed the search space. This approach is necessary because metaheuristic algorithms are not inherently designed to handle constrained problems.

In this paper, we propose a novel method to solve inverse kinematics using a metaheuristic algorithm combined with a Jacobian step. Unlike traditional approaches, the Jacobian step is applied neither in each iteration nor to a subpopulation; it is used selectively when a deadlock is detected, and only to the global best solution. This strategy reduces the implementation complexity of the algorithm. Our method effectively addresses both position and orientation in inverse kinematics, formulating the problem as a constrained optimization task where joint limits are represented as constraints. Since metaheuristic algorithms are not inherently designed for constrained problems, we employ penalty functions to manage these constraints. Our approach is generalizable to redundant robots with n degrees of freedom. The applicability of the algorithm is demonstrated using a 5 DOF KUKA robotic arm, showcasing its effectiveness and versatility.

Table 1. State of the art related work.

Reference	Algorithm	DOFs	Orientation	Boundaries	Robot Application
[15]	PSO	5,6-DOF	✓	✓	✗
[16]	DE	6,7,8,9-DOF	✓	✓	✓
[17]	PSO, multi-PSP, imp PSO	6-DOF	✓	✓	✗
[18]	DE	5-DOF	✗	✓	✗
[19]	DE	6-DOF	✓	✓	✗
[20]	PSO	6-DOF	✓	✓	✗
[21]	ABC	6-DOF	✗	✓	✗
[22]	BA	6-DOF	✗	✓	✗
[23]	PSO	7-DOF	✗	✓	✗
[24]	FA	5-DOF	✗	✓	✗
[25]	β-SSA	6,8-DOF	✗	✓	✗
[26]	Modified DE	10-DOF	✗	✗	✗
[27]	GWO	6-DOF	✗	✓	✗
[28]	GMO	6-DOF	✓	✗	✗
Proposed Method	DE-H	5,6,7-DOF	✓	✓	✓

A comparative study is conducted using the following metaheuristic algorithms: the differential evolution algorithm "DE" proposed by storn et al. in 1997 [29], the particle swarm optimization algorithm "PSO" proposed by Kennedy and Heberhart in 1995 [30], the bees algorithm "BA" proposed by Pham et al. in 2006 [31], the invasive weed optimization algorithm "IWO" proposed by Mehrabian and Lucas in 2006 [32] and the imperialist competitive algorithm "ICA" proposed by Atashpaz-Gargari and Lucas in 2007 [33].

2. Robot Manipulator Kinematics

A robot manipulator consist of a series of links interconnected by joints, forming a kinematic chain. The beginning of the chain is fixed to a base and an end-effector tool is connected to the end of the chain. A joint variable $\mathbf{q}$ is defined as $\mathbf{q} = \begin{bmatrix} q_1 & q_2 & \cdots & q_n \end{bmatrix}^T$ where each joint q_j with $j = 1, 2, \cdots, n$, where n represents the total DOFs of the manipulator robot [4,34].

A manipulator kinematics model can be described based on the Denavit–Hartenberg convention (DH). Since each joint connects two links, a robot manipulator with n joints will have $n+1$ links. In the DH convention, joint i connects link $i-1$ to link i. Each link i is represented by a homogenous matrix ${}^{i-1}\mathbf{T}_i$ that transforms the frame attached to the link $i-1$ into the joint link i. The homogeneous matrix ${}^{i-1}\mathbf{T}_i$ is defined as

$$ {}^{i-1}\mathbf{T}_i = \begin{bmatrix} \cos\theta_i & -\sin\theta_i\cos\alpha_i & \sin\theta_i\sin\alpha_i & a_i\cos\theta_i \\ \sin\theta_i & \cos\theta_i\cos\alpha_i & -\cos\theta_i\sin\alpha_i & a_i\sin\theta_i \\ 0 & \sin\alpha_i & \cos\alpha_i & d_i \\ 0 & 0 & 0 & 1 \end{bmatrix}, \quad (1) $$

where the parameters θ_i, a_i, d_i, and α_i represent the joint angle, link length, link offset, and link twist, respectively. The parameter $\theta_i = q_i$ becomes the joint variable for revolute joints. In contrast, the parameter $d_i = q_i$ becomes the joint variable for prismatic joints. In both cases, the rest of the parameters remain constant.

The forward kinematics computes the end-effector pose ${}^0\mathbf{T}_n$ given the joint variable $\mathbf{q}$ which is

$$ {}^0\mathbf{T}_n(\mathbf{q}) = \prod_{i=1}^{n} {}^{i-1}\mathbf{T}_i(q_i). \quad (2) $$

The end-effector pose ${}^0\mathbf{T}_n$ contains the position $\mathbf{t}$ and orientation $\mathbf{R}$ of the tool in the following form:

$$ {}^0\mathbf{T}_n(\mathbf{q}) = \begin{bmatrix} \mathbf{R}(\mathbf{q}) & \mathbf{t}(\mathbf{q}) \\ \mathbf{0} & 1 \end{bmatrix} = \begin{bmatrix} r_{11} & r_{12} & r_{13} & t_x \\ r_{21} & r_{22} & r_{23} & t_y \\ r_{31} & r_{32} & r_{33} & t_z \\ 0 & 0 & 0 & 1 \end{bmatrix}. \tag{3} $$

The inverse kinematics computes the joint variable $\mathbf{q}$ given the end-effector pose ${}^0\mathbf{T}_n$. The iterative Jacobian pseudoinverse algorithm can solve the inverse kinematics as follows:

$$ \mathbf{q}_{k+1} = \mathbf{q}_k + \lambda \mathbf{J}^{\dagger}(\mathbf{q}_k)\mathbf{e}(\mathbf{q}_k), \tag{4} $$

where k represents the current iteration, λ is a positive scalar factor with $\lambda > 0$, $\mathbf{J} \in \mathbb{R}^{6\times n}$ is a Jacobian matrix, and $\mathbf{e}(\mathbf{q}_k)$ is an error between a desired and current end-effector pose. Moreover, the operation $\mathbf{J}^{\dagger}$ is the pseudoinverse of $\mathbf{J}$ also called the Moore–Penrose inverse. For manipulators of 6 DOF ($n = 6$), $\mathbf{J}^{-1}$ is rather used. The error $\mathbf{e}(\mathbf{q}_k)$ is defined as

$$ \mathbf{e}(\mathbf{q}_k) = \begin{bmatrix} \mathbf{e}_v(\mathbf{q}_k) & \mathbf{e}_\omega(\mathbf{q}_k) \end{bmatrix}^T, \tag{5} $$

where $\mathbf{e}_v(\mathbf{q}_k)$ is the translation error between the desired $\mathbf{t}_d$ and current $\mathbf{t}(\mathbf{q}_k)$ end-effector position. This error is defined as

$$ \mathbf{e}_v(\mathbf{q}_k) = \mathbf{t}_d - \mathbf{t}(\mathbf{q}_k). \tag{6} $$

Moreover, $\mathbf{e}_\omega(\mathbf{q}_k)$ is the orientation error between the desired $\mathbf{R}_d$ and current $\mathbf{R}(\mathbf{q}_k)$ orientation, that is,

$$ \mathbf{e}_\omega(\mathbf{q}_k) = \frac{1}{2}\left[\left(\mathbf{R}(\mathbf{q}_k) \begin{bmatrix} 1 \\ 0 \\ 0 \end{bmatrix} \times \mathbf{R}_d \begin{bmatrix} 1 \\ 0 \\ 0 \end{bmatrix} \right) + \left(\mathbf{R}(\mathbf{q}_k) \begin{bmatrix} 0 \\ 1 \\ 0 \end{bmatrix} \times \mathbf{R}_d \begin{bmatrix} 0 \\ 1 \\ 0 \end{bmatrix} \right) + \left(\mathbf{R}(\mathbf{q}_k) \begin{bmatrix} 0 \\ 0 \\ 1 \end{bmatrix} \times \mathbf{R}_d \begin{bmatrix} 0 \\ 0 \\ 1 \end{bmatrix} \right) \right]. \tag{7} $$

The forward kinematics always provide a solution for any joint variable $\mathbf{q}$. However, inverse kinematics may yield multiple solutions for the same end-effector pose ${}^0\mathbf{T}_n$. Additionally, the equations involved to solve the inverse kinematics are non-linear, and for that reason it is not always possible to find a closed-form solution. The iterative Jacobian pseudoinverse method is a commonly used approach for solving inverse kinematics. However, this method is prone to singularities, as it necessitates the inversion of a Jacobian matrix that can become rank deficient. To address these limitations, this work proposes solving the inverse kinematics problem using metaheuristic algorithms.

3. Differential Evolution

Differential evolution (DE) is a population-based algorithm employed for global optimization. In this algorithm, population members are called individuals and they represent potential solutions. These individuals are adjusted during an iterative process (generations) by performing three principal operations: mutation, crossover, and selection.

Initially, each individual $\mathbf{x}_i^G = \begin{bmatrix} x_{i,1}^G & x_{i,2}^G & \cdots & x_{i,D}^G \end{bmatrix}^T$ is randomly generated, where $i = 1, 2, 3, \cdots, N$ with N representing the total number of population members, D denoting the dimension of the problem, and G indicating the current generation.

The mutation operation generates a mutant vector $\mathbf{v}_i^G = \begin{bmatrix} v_{i,1}^G & v_{i,2}^G & \cdots & v_{i,D}^G \end{bmatrix}^T$ as follows:

$$ \mathbf{v}_i^G = \mathbf{x}_{r_1}^G + F\left(\mathbf{x}_{r_2}^G - \mathbf{x}_{r_3}^G\right), \tag{8} $$

where $\mathbf{x}_{r_1}^G$, $\mathbf{x}_{r_2}^G$, and $\mathbf{x}_{r_3}^G$ are individuals chosen randomly such that $r_1, r_2, r_3 \in \{1, N\}$ and $i \neq r_1 \neq r_2 \neq r_3$. Moreover, $F \in [0, 2]$ is called the amplification factor.

A trial vector $\mathbf{u}_i^G = \begin{bmatrix} u_{i,1}^G & u_{i,2}^G & \cdots & u_{i,D}^G \end{bmatrix}^T$ is created by the following crossover operation:

$$u_{i,j}^G = \begin{cases} v_{i,j}^G & \textbf{if } r \leq C_R \textbf{ or } j = r_j \\ x_{i,j}^G & \textbf{if } r > C_R \textbf{ and } j \neq r_j, \end{cases} \quad (9)$$

where $C_R \in [0,1]$ is the crossover constant, and $r \in [0,1]$ and $r_j \in \{1, D\}$ are random numbers.

In the selection operation, the trial vector $\mathbf{u}_i^G$ is compared to the current vector $\mathbf{x}_i^G$ according to the following scheme:

$$\mathbf{x}_i^{G+1} = \begin{cases} \mathbf{u}_i^G & \textbf{if } f(\mathbf{u}_i^G) < f(\mathbf{x}_i^G) \\ \mathbf{x}_i^G & \textbf{otherwise}, \end{cases} \quad (10)$$

where f is an objective function. Trial vector $\mathbf{u}_i^G$ replaces $\mathbf{x}_i^{G+1}$ if $\mathbf{u}_i^G$ yields a better solution; otherwise, $\mathbf{x}_i^G$ is retained in the next iteration. A detailed description of DE can be found in [29].

4. Approach Description

This section presents a comprehensive description of the objective function formulation and introduces the algorithm for solving inverse kinematics using a hybrid differential evolution approach.

4.1. Objective Function Formulation

This work proposes solving the inverse kinematics (IK) problem as a global constrained optimization task. The objective function is formulated to minimize the error between the desired end-effector pose $(\mathbf{R}_d, \mathbf{t}_d)$ and the current end-effector pose $(\mathbf{R}(\mathbf{q}), \mathbf{t}(\mathbf{q}))$, which can be computed using Equations (2) and (3).

The objective function f is defined as

$$f(\mathbf{q}) = k_t \|\mathbf{t}_d - \mathbf{t}(\mathbf{q})\| + k_R \|\mathbf{R}_d - \mathbf{R}(\mathbf{q})\|, \quad (11)$$

where $\|\mathbf{t}_d - \mathbf{t}(\mathbf{q})\|$ represents a Euclidean norm error between the desired and the current position, and $\|\mathbf{R}_d - \mathbf{R}(\mathbf{q})\|$ represents the Frobenius norm error between the desired and the current orientation. Additionally, k_t and k_R are positive weight factors.

The optimization problem is then defined as follows:

$$\arg\min_{\mathbf{q}} f(\mathbf{q}), \quad \text{subject to } \mathbf{q}_l < \mathbf{q} < \mathbf{q}_u, \quad (12)$$

where $\mathbf{q}_l$ and $\mathbf{q}_u$ are the lower and upper joint boundary, respectively. The joint boundary represents the joint limits. They are defined as

$$\begin{aligned} \mathbf{q}_l &= \begin{bmatrix} q_{l,1} & q_{l,2} & \cdots & q_{l,n} \end{bmatrix}^T, \\ \mathbf{q}_u &= \begin{bmatrix} q_{u,1} & q_{u,2} & \cdots & q_{u,n} \end{bmatrix}^T. \end{aligned}$$

The constrained optimization in (12) is reformulated as an unconstrained optimization problem using quadratic penalty functions. The proposed objective function $f'(\mathbf{q})$ is then defined as follows:

$$f'(\mathbf{q}) = f(\mathbf{q}) + \gamma \left[\sum_{j=1}^{n} \max\left(0,\, q_{l,j} - q_j\right)^2 + \sum_{j=1}^{n} \max\left(0,\, q_j - q_{u,j}\right)^2 \right], \quad (13)$$

where $\gamma > 0$ is a coefficient that scales the contribution of the penalty functions. By setting γ larger, constraints are penalized more severely. Moreover, when $q_{l,j} - q_j \leq 0$ and $q_j - q_{u,j} \leq 0$, the constraint in dimension j is satisfied.

Finally, the proposed optimization problem is given as

$$\arg\min_{\mathbf{q}} f'(\mathbf{q}). \tag{14}$$

Notice that the proposed objective function (13) incorporates the weighted error in both position and orientation, along with a penalty scheme. By minimizing the objective function, the joint configurations result in lower position and orientation errors while ensuring feasible joint solutions.

4.2. *Inverse Kinematics Using Hybrid Differential Evolution*

We propose enhancing the exploitation of differential evolution (DE) with Jacobian-based refinements, tracking the improvements of the best individuals over generations. If the position of the best individual stagnates, a Jacobian pseudoinverse step is performed to generate a candidate solution. This candidate solution replaces the current best individual if it provides a better solution. This operation enhances the local exploitation capabilities of DE with Jacobian-based refinements while preserving the exploration capabilities of DE.

The best individual is considered to be stagnating when there is not improvement after several generations. An l^G counter tracks the number of consecutive unsuccessful modifications at generation G. If l^G reaches a predefined stagnation limit L, a Jacobian-based refinement is performed. This process is called the Jacobian pseudoinverse step.

The Jacobian pseudoinverse step produces a candidate solution based on the conventional numerical method (4). The candidate solution $\mathbf{w}_g^G$ is generated as follows:

$$\mathbf{w}_g^G = \mathbf{x}_g^G + \mathbf{J}^{\dagger}(\mathbf{x}_g^G)\mathbf{e}(\mathbf{x}_g^G), \tag{15}$$

where $\mathbf{x}_g^G$ denotes the best individual at generation G. The candidate solution is then compared against the current best solution according to the following scheme:

$$\mathbf{x}_g^{G+1} = \begin{cases} \mathbf{w}_g^G & \textbf{if } f\left(\mathbf{w}_g^G\right) < f\left(\mathbf{x}_g^G\right) \\ \mathbf{x}_g^G & \textbf{otherwise,} \end{cases} \tag{16}$$

which is a selection operation. If candidate solution $\mathbf{w}_g^G$ produces a better solution than $\mathbf{x}_g^G$, $\mathbf{w}_g^G$ replaces the best individual for the next generation. Otherwise, $\mathbf{x}_g^G$ is retained.

4.3. *Proposed Algorithm*

The proposed inverse kinematics algorithm, based on hybrid differential evolution, is outlined in Algorithm 1. Initially, individuals are generated randomly based on the following operation:

$$x_{i,j} = q_{l,j} + r\left(q_{u,j} - q_{l,j}\right) \tag{17}$$

where $r \in [0,1]$ is a random number.

The algorithm performs the mutation, recombination, and selection operation on each individual in the population. Subsequently, the algorithm identifies the best individual $\mathbf{x}_g^G$. It then checks whether the best individual has stagnated, determined by whether the stagnation counter l^G exceeds the predefined limit L (i.e., $l^G > L$). If stagnation is detected, the proposed Jacobian pseudoinverse operation is performed. In this scenario, a candidate solution $\mathbf{w}_g^G$ is computed using the Jacobian pseudoinverse step. Local refinements are made if $\mathbf{w}_g^G$ proves to be a better solution than $\mathbf{x}_g^G$. Additionally, the stagnation counter $l^G > L$ increases when $f'\left(\mathbf{x}_g^{G+1}\right) < f'\left(\mathbf{x}_g^G\right)$, indicating an unsuccessful improvement. This process is repeated until the stopping criteria are met. Finally the algorithm returns the individual with the best fitness as the solution.

Algorithm 1 Proposed inverse kinematics based on hybrid differential evolution.

set objective function f' as in (13)
set $F \in [0,2]$ and $C_R \in [0,1]$ values
set joint boundary $\mathbf{q}_l$ and $\mathbf{q}_u$
set stagnation counter $l = 0$ and stagnation limit L
for each individual i **do**
for each dimension j **do**
randomly compute $r \in [0,1]$
$x_{i,j} = q_{l,j} + r\left(q_{u,j} - q_{l,j}\right)$
end
end
repeat
// Mutation, recombination, and selection operations on population:
for each individual i **do**
randomly choose r_1, r_2, r_3, such that $i \neq r_1 \neq r_2 \neq r_3$
$\mathbf{v}_i^G = \mathbf{x}_{r_1}^G + F(\mathbf{x}_{r_2}^G - \mathbf{x}_{r_3}^G)$
randomly compute $r_j \in \{1, D\}$
for each dimension j **do**
randomly compute $r \in [0,1]$
if r $\leq C_R$ **or** $j = r_j$ **then**
$u_{i,j}^G = v_{i,j}^G$
otherwise
$u_{i,j}^G = x_{i,j}^G$
end
end
if $f'(\mathbf{u}_i^G) < f'(\mathbf{x}_i^G)$ **then**
$\mathbf{x}_i^{G+1} = \mathbf{u}_i^G$
end
end
// Jacobian pseudoinverse operation:
find best individual g
if $l^G > L$ **then**
$\mathbf{w}_g^G = \mathbf{x}_g^G + \mathbf{J}^\dagger(\mathbf{x}_g^G)\mathbf{e}(\mathbf{x}_g^G)$
if $f'\left(\mathbf{w}_g^G\right) < f'\left(\mathbf{x}_g^G\right)$
$\mathbf{x}_g^{G+1} = \mathbf{w}_g^G$
otherwise
$\mathbf{x}_g^{G+1} = \mathbf{x}_g^G$
end
$l^G = 0$
end
if $f'\left(\mathbf{x}_g^{G+1}\right) < f'\left(\mathbf{x}_g^G\right)$ **then**
$l^{G+1} = 0$
otherwise
$l^{G+1} = l^G + 1$
end
until the stopping criteria are met
Return the individual with the best fitness as the solution

5. Simulation and Experimental Results

Experiments aim to test the proposed inverse kinematics algorithm under different manipulator structures. Simulations perform a comparison among metaheuristic algorithms. Moreover, real-world experiments validate the applicability of the proposal.

5.1. Simulation Experiments

The objective of these simulations is to compare the performance of various metaheuristic algorithms—BA (BA), differential evolution (DE), particle swarm optimization (PSO), invasive weed optimization (IWO), and the imperialist competitive algorithm (ICA)—in solving the inverse kinematics for both the position and orientation of the Puma 560 robot (6 DOF), Baxter robot (7 DOF), and KUKA iiwa robot (7 DOF). Moreover, simulations are performed using Matlab R2024b.

Each simulation consists of $G = 300$ iterations and a population of $N = 30$ individuals. The following parameters were defined: $k_t = 1.5$, $k_R = 0.8$, $\gamma = 1000$, $C_R = 0.9$, and $F = 0.6$; the Denavit–Hartenberg (DH) convention was used to describe the kinematic structure of the manipulators used in the simulations. Table 2 presents the DH parameters for the Puma-560 manipulator. Table 3 provides the DH parameters of the Baxter manipulator. Table 4 lists the DH parameters for the KUKA iiwa manipulator. Moreover, the illustrations in Figures 1–3 show the coordinate frames' assignment for the considered manipulators.

Table 2. Puma-560 manipulator DH parameters.

Joint	a [m]	α [rad]	d [m]	Θ [rad]
1	0	$\pi/2$	0	q_1
2	0.4318	0	0	q_2
3	0.0203	$-\pi/2$	0.15	q_3
4	0	$\pi/2$	0.4318	q_4
5	0	$-\pi/2$	0	q_5
6	0	0	0	q_6

Table 3. Baxter manipulator DH parameters.

Joint	a [m]	α [rad]	d [m]	Θ [rad]
1	0.069	$-\pi/2$	0.270	q_1
2	0	$\pi/2$	0	q_2
3	0.069	$-\pi/2$	0.364	q_3
4	0	$\pi/2$	0	q_4
5	0.01	$-\pi/2$	0.374	q_5
6	0	$\pi/2$	0	q_6
7	0	0	0.28	q_7

Table 4. KUKA iiwa manipulator DH parameters.

Joint	a [m]	α [rad]	d [m]	Θ [rad]
1	0	$-\pi/2$	0.360	q_1
2	0	$\pi/2$	0	q_2
3	0	$\pi/2$	0.420	q_3
4	0	$-\pi/2$	0	q_4
5	0	$-\pi/2$	0.400	q_5
6	0	$\pi/2$	0	q_6
7	0	0	0.126	q_7

The joint limits for the Puma-560 robot are as follows:

$$\mathbf{q}_l = \begin{bmatrix} -160 & -45 & -225 & -110 & -100 & -266 \end{bmatrix}^T$$

$$\mathbf{q}_u = \begin{bmatrix} 160 & 225 & 45 & 170 & 100 & 266 \end{bmatrix}^T$$

The joint limits for the Baxter robot are as follows:

$$\mathbf{q}_l = \begin{bmatrix} -97.5 & -123 & -175 & -3 & -175 & -90 & -175 \end{bmatrix}^T$$

$$\mathbf{q}_u = \begin{bmatrix} 97.5 & 60 & 175 & 150 & 175 & 120 & 175 \end{bmatrix}^T$$

The joint limits for the KUKA iiwa robot are as follows:

$$\mathbf{q}_l = \begin{bmatrix} -170 & -120 & -170 & -120 & -170 & -120 & -175 \end{bmatrix}^T$$

$$\mathbf{q}_u = \begin{bmatrix} 170 & 120 & 170 & 120 & 170 & 120 & 175 \end{bmatrix}^T$$

In all cases, the equivalent values in radians are used in the algorithms.

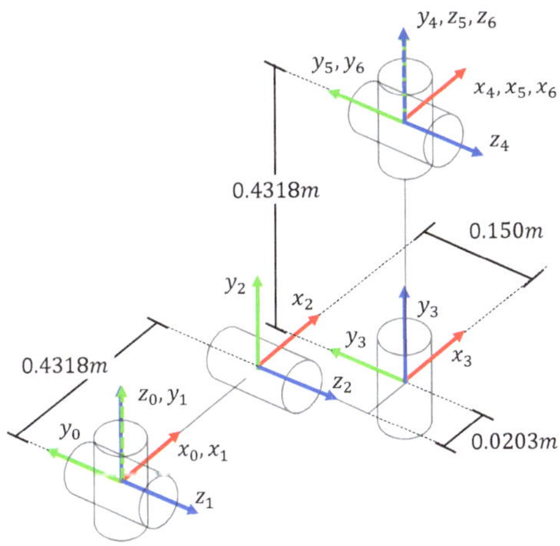

Figure 1. Coordinate frames' assignment for the Puma-560 manipulator.

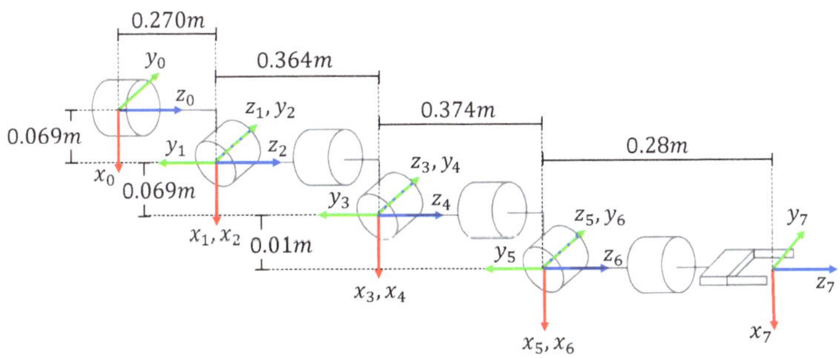

Figure 2. Coordinate frames' assignment for the Baxter manipulator.

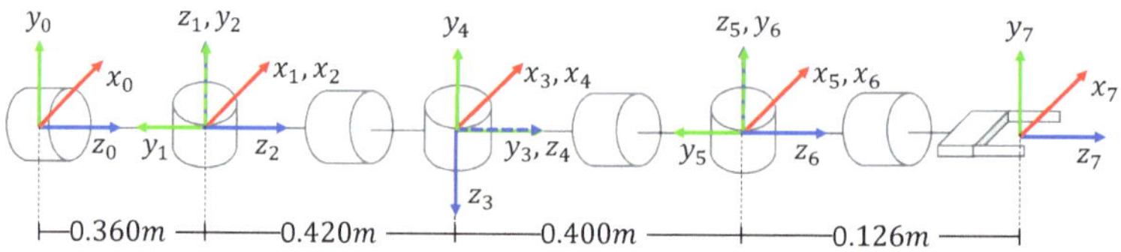

Figure 3. Coordinate frames' assignment for the KUKA iiwa manipulator.

The desired end-effector poses are defined with a set of 100 random positions and orientations generated in a valid workspace for the robotic manipulators, as shown in Figure 4. All random poses are reachable. Moreover, the proposed approach runs for every randomly desired pose independently. The best fitness value of each run is kept for statistical analysis.

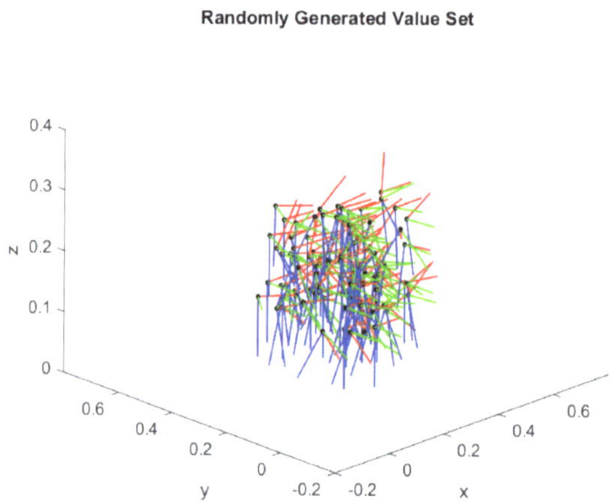

Figure 4. Randomly generated set of values.

Comparisons aim to analyze the statistical variation in the results of each algorithm. Boxplot graphics are used as a visual aid to identify the algorithm with the lowest variability, characterized by lower dispersion and lower fitness function values. A lower fitness value corresponds to smaller errors in both position and orientation. Moreover, lower fitness values indicate that joint values are feasible, as no penalties are applied. The results are presented using statistical measures such as mean, standard deviation, and the best and worst outcomes of each algorithm, all of which are summarized in tables.

In the following paragraphs, we consider the term 'standard algorithm' for algorithms that have been applied as described by their author, while the term 'hybrid algorithm' is used for algorithms that include the Jacobian pseudoinverse operations.

Figure 5 presents a comparison of data dispersion between standard and hybrid (H) algorithms using a boxplot. It is evident that the standard algorithms, Figure 5a, exhibit higher dispersion compared to the hybrid algorithms, Figure 5b. The DE and IWO hybrid algorithms demonstrate similar performance. Table 5 provides a comparison of the statistical measures obtained by the algorithms, showing that the DE hybrid algorithm (DE-H) achieves the best performance in solving the inverse kinematics of the Puma-560 robot.

Table 5. Comparison of the statistical performance of standard and hybrid algorithms in solving the inverse kinematics of the Puma-560 robot. Bold text indicates better fitness values.

	BA	BA-H	DE	DE-H	PSO	PSO-H	ICA	ICA-H	IWO	IWO-H
mean	0.05588	0.06406	0.30928	**5.8349×10^{-4}**	0.59901	0.10483	0.21649	0.21025	0.03125	0.02216
std	0.06336	0.08227	0.23273	**5.8348×10^{-3}**	0.13028	0.24129	0.1953	0.19845	0.06298	0.05877
best	5.55×10^{-8}	4.1748×10^{-9}	1.958×10^{-6}	**8.7469×10^{-17}**	0.26839	8.9099×10^{-17}	0.00637	0.00805	5.658×10^{-4}	1.0444×10^{-16}
worst	0.27954	0.3982	0.7387	**0.05835**	0.89976	0.90387	0.80264	0.91774	0.35721	0.39258

Figure 6 illustrates the simulation results for the 7 DOF Baxter robot. Figure 6a shows the data dispersion of standard algorithms, while Figure 6b demonstrates that the hybrid DE algorithm achieved the best result. Table 6 compares the statistical measures obtained by the algorithms in solving the inverse kinematics of the Baxter robot. Similar to the previous case, the hybrid DE algorithm (DE-H) exhibits the best performance.

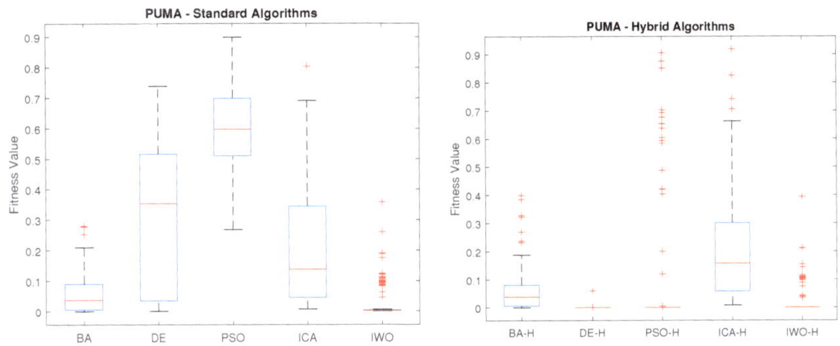

(a) (b)

Figure 5. Comparison of standard and hybrid algorithms in solving inverse kinematics of the Puma-560 robot. (**a**) Standard algorithms. (**b**) Hybrid algorithms.

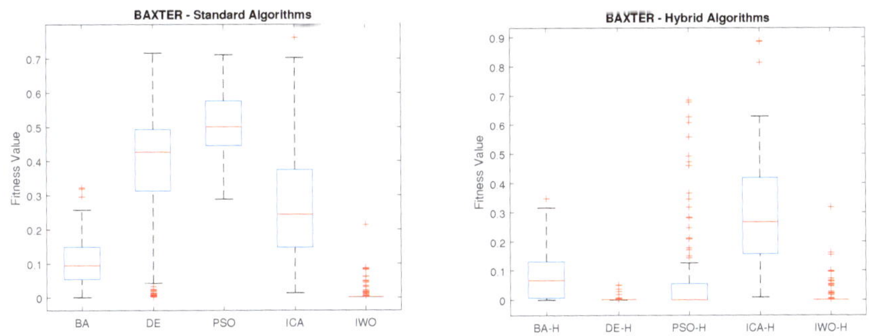

(a) (b)

Figure 6. Comparison of standard and hybrid algorithms in solving inverse kinematics of the Baxter robot. (**a**) Standard algorithms. (**b**) Hybrid algorithms.

Table 6. Comparison of the statistical performance of standard and hybrid algorithms in solving the inverse kinematics of the Baxter robot. Bold text indicates better fitness values.

	BA	BA-H	DE	DE-H	PSO	PSO-H	ICA	ICA-H	IWO	IWO-H
mean	0.10814	0.08995	0.37702	**2.2135×10^{-3}**	0.50789	0.08282	0.29066	0.28297	0.01056	0.01515
std	0.07306	0.09374	0.19066	**8.3733×10^{-3}**	0.09158	0.16858	0.17908	0.18431	0.02845	0.04382
best	6.277×10^{-5}	2.023×10^{-16}	0.00146	2.0507×10^{-15}	0.28868	1.182×10^{-16}	0.00925	0.01281	0.00052	**1.034×10^{-16}**
worst	0.32282	0.34745	0.71676	**0.05046**	0.71212	0.68462	0.88735	0.7619	0.21314	0.31733

Finally, Figure 7 presents the simulation results of KUKA iiwa robot. Figure 7a displays a boxplot of the error obtained by the standard algorithms, while Figure 7b shows a boxplot of the performance of the hybrid algorithms. The distribution comparison indicates that hybrid algorithms perform better, with DE and IWO demonstrating similar performance. Table 7 reveals that DE hybrid algorithm (DE-H) achieves the most significant improvement for the KUKA iiwa Robot.

Table 7. Comparison of the statistical performance of standard and hybrid algorithms in solving the inverse kinematics of the KUKA iiwa robot. Bold text indicates better fitness values.

	BA	BA-H	DE	DE-H	PSO	PSO-H	ICA	ICA-H	IWO	IWO-H
mean	0.070788	0.03839	0.54176	**1.713×10^{-3}**	0.58431	0.09882	0.24972	0.21884	3.777×10^{-3}	3.104×10^{-3}
std	0.06056	0.05618	0.14931	**9.085×10^{-3}**	0.10027	0.21386	0.17055	0.15758	0.01121	0.01208
best	2.514×10^{-7}	2.635×10^{-16}	0.00104	1.024×10^{-16}	0.28584	**7.124×10^{-17}**	0.00695	0.00343	0.00058	1.517×10^{-16}
worst	0.26805	0.23892	0.81966	**0.06788**	0.79564	0.80686	0.69871	0.79523	0.06801	0.06838

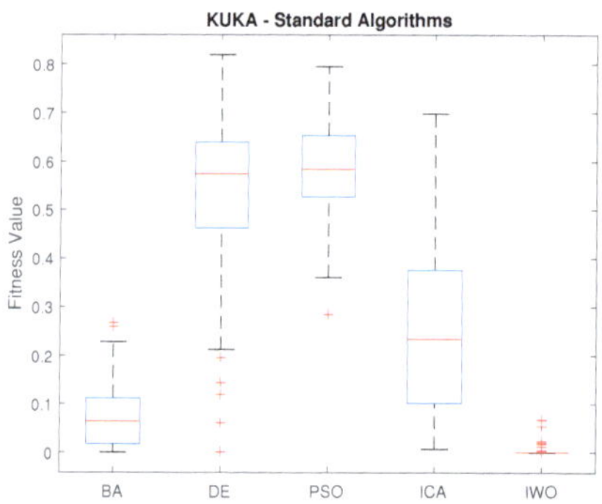

(a)

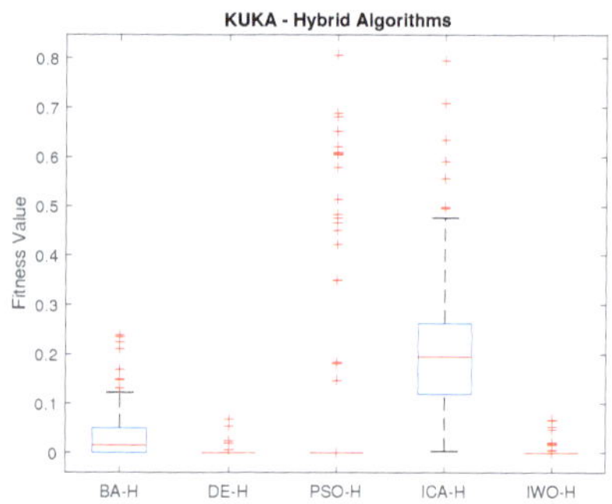

(b)

Figure 7. Comparison of standard and hybrid algorithms in solving inverse kinematics of the KUKA iiwa robot. (**a**) Standard algorithms. (**b**) Hybrid algorithms.

5.2. Second Simulation Experiment

In this part of the simulations, an edge-case experiment is conducted to evaluate the proposed approach. To solve the inverse kinematics, a desired end-effector position is proposed within the workspace to ensure it is reachable. However, some desired positions cannot be achieved with certain orientations. Therefore, appropriate orientation selection is crucial. This issue makes the inverse kinematics problem challenging to solve.

In these edge cases, gains k_t and k_R in Equation (11) can be adjusted to give priority to minimize the error between the desired and the current end-effector position, rather than orientation errors.

The edge-case experiments involve defining a reachable desired position with an unreachable desired orientation for the Baxter robot. The proposed approach is run independently 100 times for the same pose, and the best fitness value is retained for statistical analysis to compare all considered algorithms. Additionally, position and orientation errors between the desired and current end-effector poses are analyzed (see Equation (11)).

The experimental setup is conducted as follows: gains are set to $k_t = 1.5$ and $k_R = 0.25$ to give priority to minimize the position error. Moreover, $G = 300$, $N = 30$, $\gamma = 1000$, $C_R = 0.9$, and $F = 0.6$. Finally, the desired end-effector pose is defined as

$$\mathbf{T}_d = \begin{bmatrix} \mathbf{R}_d & \mathbf{t}_d \\ \mathbf{0} & 1 \end{bmatrix} = \begin{bmatrix} 0 & 0 & -1 & 0.5 \\ 0 & -1 & 0 & 0.4 \\ -1 & 0 & 0 & 0.6 \\ 0 & 0 & 0 & 1 \end{bmatrix}$$

Figure 8 presents the statistical results of the best fitness value achieved by each algorithm. As shown, DE-H outperformed the others, demonstrating a smaller data distribution and lower fitness values. It is worth noting that the best fitness values are around 0.15 due to the significant orientation error. Consequently, position and orientation errors are now compared independently for statistical analysis.

Table 8 presents the position error results. The DE-H algorithm outperformed the others, achieving the lowest mean and standard deviation (std) values. Even the worst position error obtained by DE-H is better than the mean errors of BA-H, PSO-H, and IWO-H. Although the best position error is achieved by ICA-H, its performance is considered an outlier due to the larger data distribution observed in Figure 8.

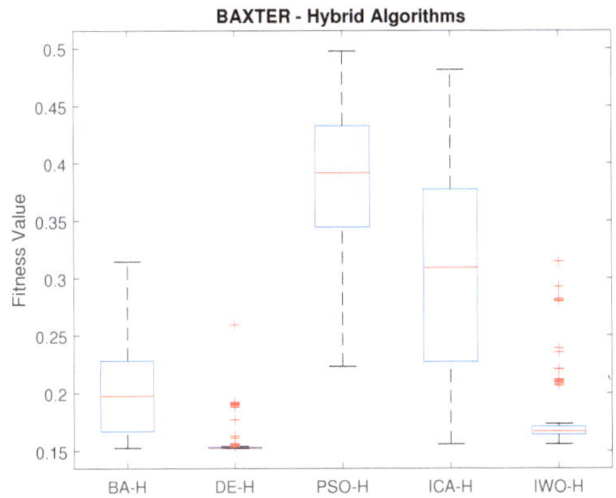

Figure 8. Comparison of hybrid algorithms for solving the inverse kinematics of the Baxter robot in an orientation-unreachable end-effector pose.

Table 8. Statistical comparison of the performance of hybrid algorithms in solving the inverse kinematics of the Baxter robot with an unreachable desired end-effector orientation. Bold text indicates superior position error values.

	BA-H	DE-H	PSO-H	ICA-H	IWO-H
mean	0.00125	**3.848×10^{-4}**	0.09077	3.921×10^{-3}	0.011339
std	0.00761	**0.00125**	0.04460	0.00144	0.00541
best	3.809×10^{-11}	3.706×10^{-6}	0.01205	**6.844×10^{-16}**	0.00190
worst	0.07373	**9.217×10^{-3}**	0.21037	0.01013	0.02502

In contrast to the position errors, the orientation errors reported in Table 9 are significantly higher, as the desired orientation is considered unreachable.

As expected, DE-H reported lower mean, standard deviation (std), and worst-case orientation error values compared to those in reachable poses. Although the best orientation error was achieved by PSO-H, its data distribution, as shown in Figure 8, is considerably larger than that of DE-H.

Table 9. Statistical comparison of the performance of hybrid algorithms in solving the inverse kinematics of the Baxter robot with an unreachable desired end-effector orientation. Bold text indicates lower orientation error values.

	BA-H	DE-H	PSO-H	ICA-H	IWO-H
mean	0.80584	**0.62786**	0.99834	1.2006	0.64396
std	0.1702	**0.05801**	0.32869	0.35645	0.11902
best	0.61119	0.59024	**0.37152**	0.62033	0.54221
worst	1.2591	**1.0353**	1.8244	1.9267	1.1768

We present another edge-case experiment involving four randomly selected unreachable desired positions, each with a corresponding reachable desired orientation, for the Baxter robot. Table 10 presents the position and orientation error results for each case, while Figure 9 illustrates the performance of the proposed approach in handling these unreachable poses. Coordinate frames in red represent the unreachable poses and coordinate frames in blue the achieved ones. Notice that all coordinate frames are adjusted with respect to orientation errors; however, position errors are not.

The results demonstrate that the proposed approach successfully solves the inverse kinematics problem by minimizing position errors, even when the desired orientation is unreachable.

Table 10. Position and orientation error results of unreachable poses in Baxter robot.

Random Pose	Position Error	Orientation Error
1	0.47979	3.1913×10^{-5}
2	0.73254	9.575×10^{-5}
3	0.71156	3.0564×10^{-4}
4	0.94969	3.2291×10^{-5}

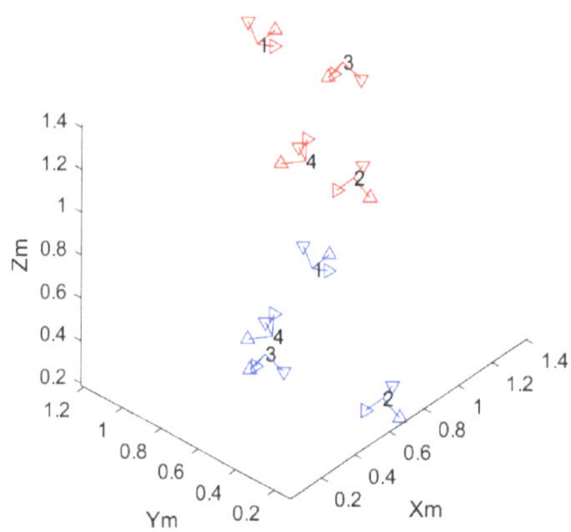

Figure 9. Unreachable pose experiment results. Coordinate frames in red represents the unreachable poses and coordinate frames in blue the achieved ones.

5.3. Real-World Experimental Results

Real-world experiments were conducted to demonstrate the applicability of the proposed approach. The optimal joint configuration computed by this method can serve as a reference for point-to-point motion planning. For the experiments, a cubic polynomial trajectory was used to compute the joint motion from an initial joint position $\mathbf{q}_i$ to the joint reference $\mathbf{q}_r$ at a desired run time T.

The experimentation consists of two phases. First, the proposed approach solves the inverse kinematics for a desired end-effector pose to estimate a joint reference $\mathbf{q}_r$. Then, the manipulator robot follows a cubic polynomial trajectory based on the initial joint configuration $\mathbf{q}_i$ and a run time T.

A 5 DOF KUKA YouBot was used for experimentation, as shown in Figure 10. The DH parameters are provided in Table 11 and the coordinate frame assignment is presented in Figure 11. The proposed algorithm was implemented using Matlab and the ROS environment. ROS components on the KUKA YouBot provide an internal PID controller in the joint space, which is convenient for the considered trajectory planning. A point-to-point trajectory planning is performed on an external computer with Matlab and the ROS toolbox.

Table 11. DH parameters of KUKA YouBot manipulator.

Joint	a [m]	α [rad]	d [m]	Θ [rad]
1	0.033	$\pi/2$	0.147	q_1
2	0.155	0	0	q_2
3	0.135	0	0	q_3
4	0	$\pi/2$	0	q_4
5	0	0	0.2174	q_5

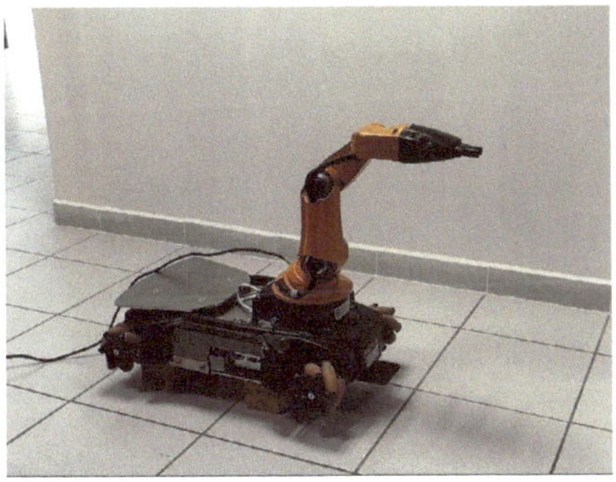

Figure 10. KUKA YouBot manipulator with 5 DOF.

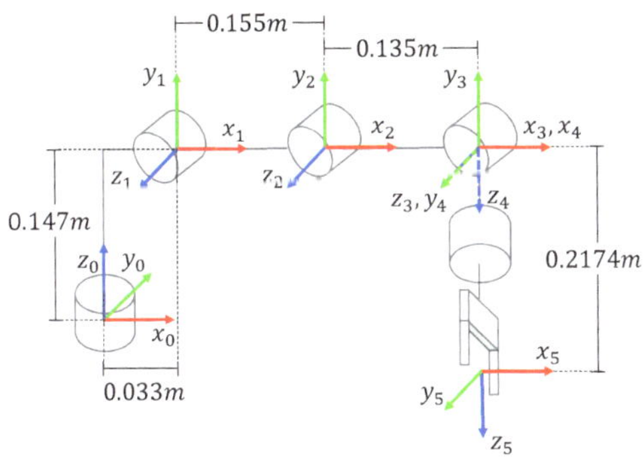

Figure 11. Coordinate frames' assignment for the KUKA YouBot manipulator.

The lower and upper joint limits are defined as

$$\begin{aligned} \mathbf{q}_l &= \begin{bmatrix} -169 & -65 & -150 & -102.5 & -167.5 \end{bmatrix}^T \\ \mathbf{q}_u &= \begin{bmatrix} 169 & 90 & 146 & 102.5 & 167.5 \end{bmatrix}^T \end{aligned}$$

In Experiment 1, a run time of $T = 8$ seconds is set, and the desired pose of the end-effector is specified as follows:

$$\mathbf{T}_d = \begin{bmatrix} \mathbf{R}_d & \mathbf{t}_d \\ \mathbf{0} & 1 \end{bmatrix} = \begin{bmatrix} 1 & 0 & 0 & 0.2 \\ 0 & -1 & 0 & -0.2 \\ 0 & 0 & 1 & 0 \\ 0 & 0 & 0 & 1 \end{bmatrix} \tag{18}$$

The inverse kinematics solution obtained through the proposed approach is

$$\mathbf{q}_r = \begin{bmatrix} 44.15 & 39.31 & -54.6 & 13.57 & 44.43 \end{bmatrix}^T$$

The initial joint configuration is selected as

$$\mathbf{q}_i = \begin{bmatrix} 0 & 90 & 0 & 90 & 0 \end{bmatrix}^T$$

The joint position and velocities for the motion planning in Experiment 1 are presented in Figure 12. Additionally, Figure 13 illustrates the final joint configuration along with the joint motion results as measured by the encoders.

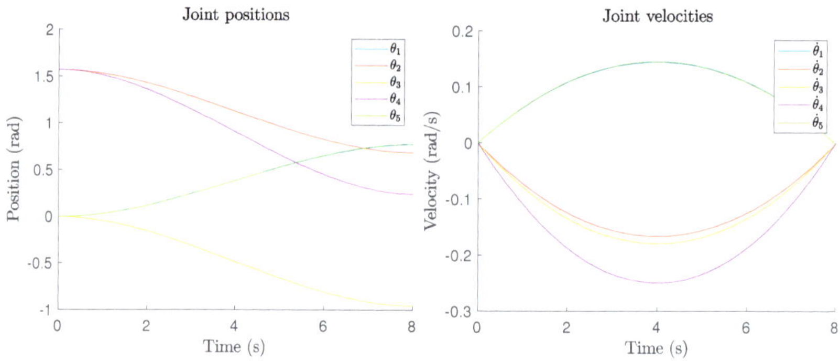

(**a**) (**b**)

Figure 12. Time history with a cubic polynomial timing law for Experiment 1. (**a**) Joint positions. (**b**) Joint velocities.

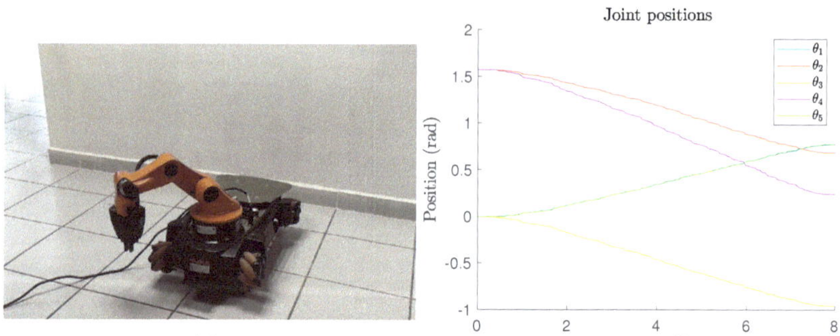

(**a**) (**b**)

Figure 13. KUKA YouBot final joint configuration for Experiment 1. (**a**) Real-world final joint configuration. (**b**) Joint motion results measured by encoders.

For Experiment 2, a run time of $T = 4$ seconds is set, and the desired pose of the end-effector is defined as

$$\mathbf{T}_d = \begin{bmatrix} \mathbf{R}_d & \mathbf{t}_d \\ \mathbf{0} & 1 \end{bmatrix} = \begin{bmatrix} 1 & 0 & 0 & 0.2 \\ 0 & -1 & 0 & 0.2 \\ 0 & 0 & 1 & 0 \\ 0 & 0 & 0 & 1 \end{bmatrix}$$

The inverse kinematics solution for Experiment 2, obtained through the proposed approach, is

$$\mathbf{q}_r = \begin{bmatrix} -44.10 & 40.46 & -50.10 & 13.97 & -45.37 \end{bmatrix}^T$$

and the considered initial joint configuration for this test is

$$\mathbf{q}_i = \begin{bmatrix} 0 & 90 & -45 & 45 & 0 \end{bmatrix}^T$$

The joint position and velocities of the motion planning for Experiment 2 are presented in Figure 14. Additionally, Figure 15 illustrates the final joint configuration along with the joint motion results measured by the encoders.

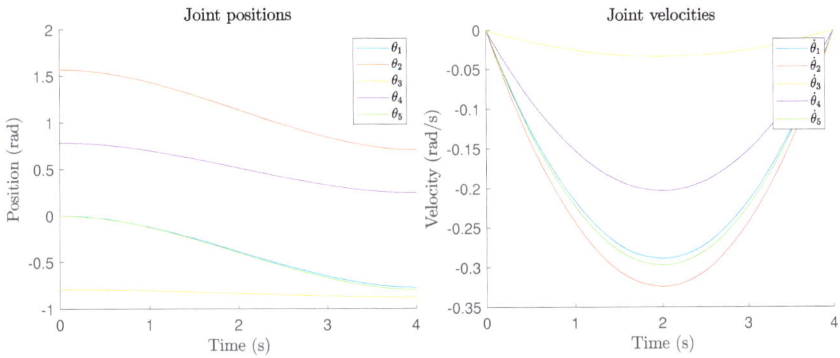

(a) (b)

Figure 14. Time history with a cubic polynomial timing law for Experiment 2. (**a**) Joint positions. (**b**) Joint velocities.

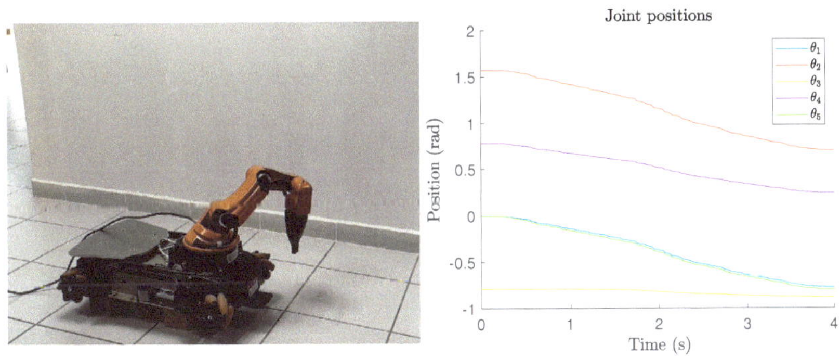

(a) (b)

Figure 15. KUKA YouBot final joint configuration for Experiment 2. (**a**) Real-world final joint configuration. (**b**) Joint motion results measured by encoders.

As observed in Figures 13b and 15b, the internal controller follows the given joint references given in Figures 12 and 14, respectively. This indicates that the manipulator reached the optimal joint configurations computed by the proposed approach. Furthermore, Figures 13 and 15 illustrate the real-world applicability of the proposed approach; the computed joint configurations are physically reachable.

For Experiment 3, a runtime of T = 4 s is set. In this case, a desired end-effector pose is defined with a reachable position but an unreachable orientation. The desired pose is specified as follows:

$$\mathbf{T}_d = \begin{bmatrix} \mathbf{R}_d & \mathbf{t}_d \\ \mathbf{0} & 1 \end{bmatrix} = \begin{bmatrix} 0 & 0 & 1 & 0.2 \\ 0 & -1 & 0 & 0.3 \\ 1 & 0 & 0 & 0.4 \\ 0 & 0 & 0 & 1 \end{bmatrix}$$

The inverse kinematics solution for experiment 3 is

$$\mathbf{q}_r = \begin{bmatrix}56.31 & 83.19 & -35.95 & 42.76 & 0.0028\end{bmatrix}^T$$

The initial joint configuration considered for the polynomial trajectory is as follows:

$$\mathbf{q}_i = \begin{bmatrix}0 & 90 & 0 & 90 & 0\end{bmatrix}^T$$

The joint positions and velocities for the motion planning are shown in Figure 16. Additionally, Figure 17 presents the final joint configuration along with the joint motion results measured by the encoders.

The achieved end-effector pose is

$$^0\mathbf{T}_n = \begin{bmatrix}0 & 0.832 & 0.554 & 0.2\\ 0 & -0.554 & 0.832 & 0.3\\ 1 & 0 & 0 & 0.4\\ 0 & 0 & 0 & 1\end{bmatrix}$$

As can be seen, the desired position is reached. The desired and current positions are practically the same. However, the desired and current orientations are only approximately aligned. As expected, the proposed approach prioritizes minimizing position errors over orientation errors, given that the desired orientation is not reachable. It is worth noting that the implementation in real-world experiments further demonstrates that the inverse kinematics solutions are physically feasible.

The proposed algorithm was executed on a computer with an Intel i7 processor and 16 GB of RAM. The inverse kinematics estimation took less than one second for each tested point. If further speed is required, the performance of metaheuristic algorithms can be enhanced using parallel architectures and dedicated hardware, such as NVIDIA CUDA.

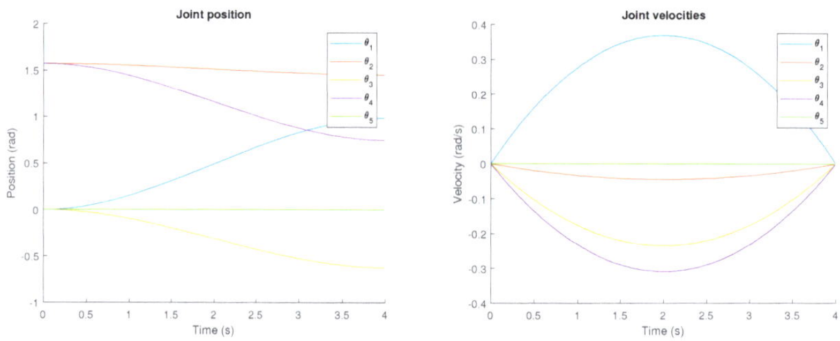

(**a**) (**b**)

Figure 16. Time history with a cubic polynomial timing law for Experiment 3. (**a**) Joint positions. (**b**) Joint velocities.

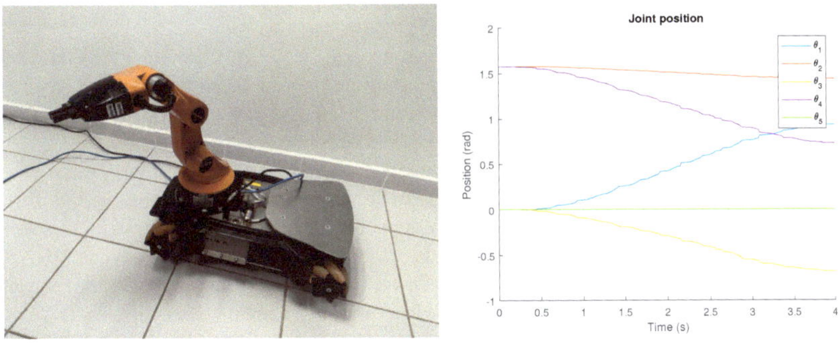

(**a**) (**b**)

Figure 17. KUKA YouBot final joint configuration for Experiment 3. (**a**) Real-world final joint configuration. (**b**) Joint motion results measured by encoders.

6. Discussion

The proposed approach was applied in three simulation experiments involving the Puma-560, Baxter, and KUKA iiwa robots. The inverse kinematics were successfully solved in each case, demonstrating the applicability of the system across different configurations. Among the tested algorithms, differential evolution (DE) consistently outperformed BA, PSO, and ICA. While the performance of DE and IWO exhibited similar performance across experiments, DE reported the lowest dispersion of the data.

When comparing the experimental results with and without hybridization, a significant improvement in the solution of the inverse kinematics is evident across all algorithms. The Jacobian step enhances the exploitation capabilities of the algorithm; algorithms like PSO, ICA, and BA exhibit stagnation, which indicates weak exploration capabilities, whereas DE and IWA demonstrate a strong exploration performance.

DE-H reported better fitness value results in all tests, achieving the lowest mean and standard deviation (std) values. This indicates that DE-H achieved the smallest error in both position and orientation with precision, along with the smallest data distribution, reflecting more consistent results. In contrast, ICA and PSO performed poorly in all tests, achieving the worst results in terms of mean and std values. Additionally, the performance of IWO-H was very similar to DE-H. However, DE-H outperformed all the other algorithms by achieving lower mean and std values.

The evaluation of the standard deviation (5.8348×10^{-3}) indicates that the method achieves sufficient precision in both position and orientation, making it suitable for applications such as medical procedures, where fine adjustments are critical.

The proposed approach was also applied in real-world experimentation, where the KUKA YouBot robot was considered as a case study. The application on the real robot demonstrates that the inverse kinematics results are acceptable, confirming that the constrained problem is solved despite the DE algorithm not being specifically designed for constrained problems.

A drawback of the conventional Jacobian pseudoinverse is that the inversion of J cannot always be guaranteed. Singular configurations cause J to become rank deficient, leading to system instability. In this work, a Jacobian pseudoinverse step is used to generate a candidate solution. In the presence of singularities, unfeasible solutions are avoided in the Jacobian pseudoinverse operation, as only improved joint solutions replace the current ones. This mechanism effectively prevents singularities.

Future work will focus on solving inverse kinematics for a mobile manipulator [16], incorporating the Jacobian step for fine-tuning. Additionally, we aim to extend the use of inverse kinematics to trajectory tracking and address grasping problems on platforms equipped with dual manipulators [35,36].

7. Conclusions

The hybrid metaheuristic algorithm approach proposed in this paper has demonstrated its applicability across different robotic manipulators by successfully solving inverse kinematics in two simulated experiments with six and seven degrees of freedom, as well as in an experiment with a real robot with five degrees of freedom.

Among the algorithms tested in this research, DE and IWO exhibited similar performance across the experiments. However, DE achieved the lowest scatter in the data, effectively solving both position and orientation with constraints, even though the algorithm was not designed to work with constraints.

The inclusion of the Jacobian matrix steps shows a significant improvement in the exploitation capabilities of the algorithms, However, algorithms with inherently poor exploration characteristics showed only marginal improvement.

Future work applying the methods proposed in this study promises favorable results for more complex problems, such as dual-arm systems and mobile manipulators. This work considers solving the inverse kinematics for manipulators with open kinematic chains. However, it is appealing to extend this work to solve the inverse kinematics of closed kinematics such as parallel manipulators.

Author Contributions: Conceptualization, C.L.-F.; methodology, C.L.-F., J.H.-B. and J.P.-L.; software, J.P.-L. and M.L.-F.; validation, J.P.-L. and M.L.-F.; formal analysis, C.L.-F. and N.A.-D.; investigation, C.L.-F., J.H.-B. and J.P.-L.; resources, J.H.-B. and M.L.-F.; writing, J.P-L; writing—review and editing, C.L.-F. and J.H.-B.; visualization, N.A.-D. and M.L.-F.; supervision, C.L.-F. and J.H.-B.; project administration, C.L.-F. and N.A.-D.; funding acquisition, C.L.-F. and N.A.-D. All authors have read and agreed to the published version of the manuscript.

Funding: This research received no external funding.

Data Availability Statement: Data can be made available upon request to interested researchers.

Acknowledgments: We thank the University of Guadalajara for supporting this work.

Conflicts of Interest: The authors declare no conflicts of interest.

References

1. Papadopoulos, E.; Aghili, F.; Ma, O.; Lampariello, R. Robotic manipulation and capture in space: A survey. *Front. Robot. AI* **2021**, *8*, 686723. [CrossRef] [PubMed]
2. Garriz, C.; Domingo, R. Development of trajectories through the kalman algorithm and application to an industrial robot in the automotive industry. *IEEE Access* **2019**, *7*, 23570–23578. [CrossRef]
3. Nisar, S.; Hameed, A.; Kamal, N.; Hasan, O.; Matsuno, F. Design and realization of a robotic manipulator for minimally invasive surgery with replaceable surgical tools. *IEEE/ASME Trans. Mechatronics* **2020**, *25*, 2754–2764. [CrossRef]
4. Siciliano, B.; Sciavicco, L.; Villani, L.; Oriolo, G. *Robotics: Modelling, Planning and Control*; Springer: London, UK, 2009.
5. Park, T. *Numerical Methods for Mixed Differential-Algebraic Equations in Kinematics and Dybamics (Constraints, Singularity, Nonholonomic, Holonomic, Condition Number)*; The University of Iowa: Iowa City, IA, USA, 1985.
6. Kucuk, S.; Bingul, Z. Inverse kinematics solutions for industrial robot manipulators with offset wrists. *Appl. Math. Model.* **2014**, *38*, 1983–1999. [CrossRef]
7. Bayro-Corrochano, E.; Zamora-Esquivel, J. Differential and inverse kinematics of robot devices using conformal geometric algebra. *Robotica* **2007**, *25*, 43–61. [CrossRef]
8. Almusawi, A.R.; Dülger, L.C.; Kapucu, S. A new artificial neural network approach in solving inverse kinematics of robotic arm (denso vp6242). *Comput. Intell. Neurosci.* **2016**, *2016*, 5720163. [CrossRef] [PubMed]
9. Aggarwal, L.; Aggarwal, K.; Urbanic, R.J. Use of artificial neural networks for the development of an inverse kinematic solution and visual identification of singularity zone (s). *Procedia Cirp* **2014**, *17*, 812–817. [CrossRef]
10. Lu, J.; Zou, T.; Jiang, X. A neural network based approach to inverse kinematics problem for general six-axis robots. *Sensors* **2022**, *22*, 8909. [CrossRef]
11. Hussain, K.; Mohd Salleh, M.N.; Cheng, S.; Shi, Y. Metaheuristic research: A comprehensive survey. *Artif. Intell. Rev.* **2019**, *52*, 2191–2233. [CrossRef]
12. Nematzadeh, S.; Kiani, F.; Torkamanian-Afshar, M.; Aydin, N. Tuning hyperparameters of machine learning algorithms and deep neural networks using metaheuristics: A bioinformatics study on biomedical and biological cases. *Comput. Biol. Chem.* **2022**, *97*, 107619. [CrossRef]

13. Lopez-Franco, C.; Diaz, D.; Hernandez-Barragan, J.; Arana-Daniel, N.; Lopez-Franco, M. A metaheuristic optimization approach for trajectory tracking of robot manipulators. *Mathematics* **2022**, *10*, 1051. [CrossRef]
14. Martinez-Soltero, E.G.; Hernandez-Barragan, J. Robot navigation based on differential evolution. *IFAC-PapersOnLine* **2018**, *51*, 350–354. [CrossRef]
15. Reyes, S.V.; Gardini, S.P. Inverse kinematics of manipulator robot using a PSO metaheuristic with adaptively exploration. In Proceedings of the 2019 IEEE XXVI International Conference on Electronics, Electrical Engineering and Computing (INTERCON), Lima, Peru, 12–14 August 2019; IEEE: Piscataway, NJ, USA, 2019; pp. 1–4.
16. López-Franco, C.; Hernández-Barragán, J.; Alanis, A.Y.; Arana-Daniel, N.; López-Franco, M. Inverse kinematics of mobile manipulators based on differential evolution. *Int. J. Adv. Robot. Syst.* **2018**, *15*, 1729881417752738. [CrossRef]
17. Yiyang, L.; Xi, J.; Hongfei, B.; Zhining, W.; Liangliang, S. A general robot inverse kinematics solution method based on improved PSO algorithm. *IEEE Access* **2021**, *9*, 32341–32350. [CrossRef]
18. Linh, T.; Nguyen, T.; Nguyen, T.; Hasegawa, H.; Watanabe, D. DE-based algorithm for solving the inverse kinematics on a robotic arm manipulators. *J. Phys. Conf. Ser.* **2021**, *1922*, 012008.
19. Gonzalez, C.; Blanco, D.; Moreno, L. Optimum robot manipulator path generation using Differential Evolution. In Proceedings of the 2009 IEEE Congress on Evolutionary Computation, Trondheim, Norway, 18–21 May 2009; IEEE: Piscataway, NJ, USA, 2009; pp. 3322–3329.
20. Almaghout, K.; Rezaee, A. PSO Based Solution for 6-DOF Serial Manipulator Inverse Kinematics Problem. *Int. J. Robot. Theory Appl.* **2023**, *9*, 20–25.
21. Dereli, S.; Köker, R. Simulation based calculation of the inverse kinematics solution of 7-DOF robot manipulator using artificial bee colony algorithm. *SN Appl. Sci.* **2020**, *2*, 27. [CrossRef]
22. Masajedi, P.; Heidari Shirazi, K.; Ghanbarzadeh, A. Verification of bee algorithm based path planning for a 6DOF manipulator using ADAMS. *J. Vibroeng.* **2013**, *15*, 805–815.
23. Huang, H.C.; Chen, C.P.; Wang, P.R. Particle swarm optimization for solving the inverse kinematics of 7-DOF robotic manipulators. In Proceedings of the 2012 IEEE International Conference on Systems, Man, and Cybernetics (SMC), Seoul, Republic of Korea, 14–17 October 2012; IEEE: Piscataway, NJ, USA, 2012; pp. 3105–3110.
24. Hernandez-Barragan, J.; Lopez-Franco, C.; Antonio-Gopar, C.; Alanis, A.Y.; Arana-Daniel, N. The inverse kinematics solutions for robot manipulators based on firefly algorithm. In Proceedings of the 2018 IEEE Latin American Conference on Computational Intelligence (LA-CCI), Gudalajara, Mexico, 7–9 November 2018; IEEE: Piscataway, NJ, USA, 2018; pp. 1–5.
25. Rokbani, N.; Mirjalili, S.; Slim, M.; Alimi, A.M. A beta salp swarm algorithm meta-heuristic for inverse kinematics and optimization. *Appl. Intell.* **2022**, *52*, 10493–10518. [CrossRef]
26. López-Muñoz, R.; Portilla-Flores, E.A.; Corona-Ramírez, L.G.; Vega-Alvarado, E.; Maya-Rodríguez, M.C. Inverse kinematics: An alternative solution approach applying metaheuristics. *Appl. Sci.* **2023**, *13*, 6543. [CrossRef]
27. Nyong-Bassey, B.E.; Epemu, A.M. Inverse kinematics analysis of novel 6-DOF robotic arm manipulator for oil and gas welding using meta-heuristic algorithms. *Int. J. Robot. Autom. Sci.* **2022**, *4*, 13–22.
28. Wu, H.; Zhang, X.; Song, L.; Zhang, Y.; Gu, L.; Zhao, X. Wild Geese Migration Optimization Algorithm: A New Meta-Heuristic Algorithm for Solving Inverse Kinematics of Robot. *Comput. Intell. Neurosci.* **2022**, *2022*, 5191758. [CrossRef] [PubMed]
29. Storn, R.; Price, K. Differential evolution—A simple and efficient heuristic for global optimization over continuous spaces. *J. Glob. Optim.* **1997**, *11*, 341–359. [CrossRef]
30. Kennedy, J.; Eberhart, R. Particle swarm optimization. In Proceedings of the ICNN'95-International Conference on Neural Networks, Perth, Australia, 7 November–1 December 1995; IEEE: Piscataway, NJ, USA, 1995; Volume 4, pp. 1942–1948.
31. Pham, D.T.; Ghanbarzadeh, A.; Koç, E.; Otri, S.; Rahim, S.; Zaidi, M. The bees algorithm—A novel tool for complex optimisation problems. In *Intelligent Production Machines and Systems*; Elsevier: Amsterdam, The Netherlands, 2006; pp. 454–459.
32. Mehrabian, A.R.; Lucas, C. A novel numerical optimization algorithm inspired from weed colonization. *Ecol. Inform.* **2006**, *1*, 355–366. [CrossRef]
33. Atashpaz-Gargari, E.; Lucas, C. Imperialist competitive algorithm: An algorithm for optimization inspired by imperialistic competition. In Proceedings of the 2007 IEEE Congress on Evolutionary Computation, Singapore, 25–28 September 2007; IEEE: Piscataway, NJ, USA, 2007; pp. 4661–4667.
34. Spong, M.; Hutchinson, S.; Vidyasagar, M. *Robot Dynamics and Control*; Wiley: Hoboken, NJ, USA, 2004.
35. Hernandez-Barragan, J.; Martinez-Soltero, G.; Rios, J.D.; Lopez-Franco, C.; Alanis, A.Y. A metaheuristic Optimization approach to solve inverse kinematics of mobile Dual-Arm robots. *Mathematics* **2022**, *10*, 4135. [CrossRef]
36. Wang, J.; Liu, S.; Zhang, B.; Yu, C. Inverse kinematics-based motion planning for dual-arm robot with orientation constraints. *Int. J. Adv. Robot. Syst.* **2019**, *16*, 1729881419836858. [CrossRef]

algorithms

MDPI

Article

Application of Evolutionary Computation to the Optimization of Biodiesel Mixtures Using a Nature-Inspired Adaptive Genetic Algorithm

Vasileios Vasileiadis, Christos Kyriklidis, Vayos Karayannis * and Constantinos Tsanaktsidis

Department of Chemical Engineering, University of Western Macedonia (UOWM), GR-50100 Kozani, Greece; vvasiliadis@uowm.gr (V.V.); c.kiriklidis@gmail.com (C.K.); ktsanaktsidis@uowm.gr (C.T.)
* Correspondence: vkarayannis@uowm.gr

Abstract: The present research work introduces a novel mixture optimization methodology for biodiesel fuels using an Evolutionary Computation method inspired by biological evolution. Specifically, the optimal biodiesel composition is deduced from the application of a nature-inspired adaptive genetic algorithm that first examines percentages of the ingredients in the optimal mixtures. The innovative approach's effectiveness lies in problem simulation with improvements in the evaluation of the specific function and the way to define and tune the genetic algorithm. Environmental imperatives in the era of climate change currently impose the optimized production of alternative environmentally friendly biofuels to replace fossil fuels. Biodiesel in particular, appears to be more attractive in recent years, as it originates from renewable bio-derived resources. The main ingredients of the specific biofuel mixture investigated in this research are diesel and biodiesel (100% from bioresources). The assessment of the new biodiesel examined was performed using a fitness function that estimated both the density and cost of the fuel. Beyond the evaluation criterion of cost, density also influences the suitability of this biofuel for commercial use and market sale. The outcomes from the modeling process can be beneficial in saving cost and time for new biodiesel production by using this novel decision-making tool in comparison with randomized laboratory experimentations.

Keywords: evolutionary computation; bio-inspired adaptive genetic algorithm; fuel mixture optimization; biodiesel production

1. Introduction

1.1. Literature Review

After a 4.5% decline in 2020 caused by COVID-19 restrictions, the Global Energy Consumption rose by 5% in 2021. The impact of societal development was estimated to be 3 points above the 2%/year average over the 2000–2019 period [1]. Because of Russia's reductions in gas supplies to Europe during the last years, along with increased global demands following the easing of COVID-19 restrictions, energy prices became significantly higher. Following the global economic downturn since 2010, coupled with the realization that conventional diesel fuel sources are finite and environmentally harmful, numerous research efforts focus on enhancing the performance of complex fuel and energy systems [2,3] and assessing alternative fuel options, including coal-bed methane, biofuel and lately hydrogen [4,5]. Biodiesel, in particular, emerges as a sustainable energy alternative, environmentally clean, boasting eco-friendly attributes. In fact, it lacks aromatic and toxic compounds, is biodegradable, and significantly reduces sulfur oxide, carbon monoxide, and unburned hydrocarbon emissions, as well as soot released by diesel engines, either produced by heterogeneous catalysis [6,7] or using supercritical methanol [8]. Although fossil fuels could be considered one of the most important development pillars for humanity, their emissions and the environmental issues they initiate restrict the appreciation towards them. Researchers nowadays are trying to propose good, feasible alternatives to traditional fossil fuels possessing nearly identical characteristics that have been sought after. Biodiesel appears to be a viable option, offering a clean and sustainable fuel source at competitive costs. Biodiesel is not only economical but also has important advantages, including non-toxicity, low pollution, and biodegradability, in comparison to conventional diesel. This ecological solution leads to an increasing high-quality fuel in abundant availability and biodiesel demand. Production principles [9,10] and recent needs in biomass oil analysis and final product specifications were outlined [11,12]. Strategies that can improve biodiesel-integrated processing, including reactive distillation [13–15], standards and testing methods [16], and sustainability issues [17,18], were also described. Europe stands out as the primary global producer of biodiesel, attributed to its environmental directives aimed at curbing greenhouse gas emissions (GHGs) alongside ensuring energy security [19]. EU goals for the year 2030 are the following:

1. From 1990, at least a 40% reduction in greenhouse gas emissions
2. Revision by 2023: 32% at least renewable energy apportion
3. Energy efficiency improvement at least 32.5%.

Biodiesel can be categorized into three groups based on the sources of ingredients:

- 1st Generation: Consumable Vegetable Oils
- 2nd Generation: Non-edible Oils and Animal Fats
- 3rd Generation: Microalgal Oils.

In contrast, traditional diesel fuel contains sulfur, a primary contributor to harmful emissions. Despite the lengthy and costly process of diesel desulfurization demanding substantial investments, the most effective means of reducing emissions lies in enhancing fuel quality using biodiesel blending. This approach not only lowers sulfur content but also upholds fuel quality standards. Moreover, fuel density is a crucial factor in determining the efficiency of different fuel mixtures containing diesel, biodiesel, and alkanols in compression ignition engines [20–22]. The labor-intensive and costly procedures involved in fuel mixture experimentation often result in extensive analyses to achieve optimal fuel quality and pricing [23,24]. This problem finds a solution using evolutionary computation that offers efficient solutions, decreasing the execution time and the cost of the necessary experiments in parallel.

A new decision-making approach involves the setup of a specific experimental procedure that can propose an optimized mixture composition with the lowest fuel price combined with the appropriate fuel density. Thus, the experiment process in the laboratory is more effective, concentrating the research interest around better results. Sophisticated methods drawing from natural phenomena, bio-inspired computational intelligence, algorithms in machine learning, and evolutionary computation strategies yield superior outcomes close to the optimal for intricate optimization challenges. Consequently, the practical applications of operational research rely on their utilization and advancement, i.e., on resource leveling and fuzzy clustering [25,26]. Machine Learning (ML) and Artificial Intelligence (AI) approach [27,28], and especially more than 100 studies were presented in recent years [29] focusing on the application of ML and AI on different aspects of renewable and sustainable energy [30,31], i.e., bioenergy [32] and low-carbon energy advancement [33], power dispatch systems [34], chemical process systems [35], and particularly biodiesel production [36] and conversion [37], as well as microalgal biofuel development [2,38], amplifying the design, handling, control, optimization, and monitoring. Specifically, relatively powerful methodologies employed include the following ML and AI algorithms evolved with deep learning:

- Linear Regression
- Principal component analysis (PCA),
- Genetic Algorithms (GA),
- K-Nearest Neighbors (KNN)
- Random Forest Regression (RF),
- Artificial Neural Networks (ANNs) or simulated neural networks (SNNs),

- Support Vector Machines (SVMs).
- Fuzzy Multi-Criteria methodologies

The algorithms discussed above can demonstrate superior predictive capabilities, boasting the highest levels of accuracy among methods utilized in Biodiesel production. Their effectiveness stems from the brain's inherent ability to learn and improve autonomously, tackling complex challenges posed by the survey. Consequently, these algorithms prove immensely valuable for modeling trans-esterification processes, studying physicochemical properties, real-time monitoring of biodiesel systems, analyzing emission composition, estimating temperatures, and assessing engine performance during the combustion phase. Some algorithms provide fatty methyl acid ester as an output, and they take different types of oil and catalyst as inputs, methanol-to-oil ratios, catalyst concentrations, reaction rates, domains, and frequencies. However, the aforementioned approaches concentrate on biodiesel mixture properties optimization via the prediction of the conversion into biodiesel under various conditions. Moreover, they do not suggest an optimal mixture on the basis of raw material availability, considering both cost and density, as achieved by the Genetic Algorithm for the optimal Fuel Mixture Problem presented hereunder.

1.2. Novel Contribution of the Research

The current research introduces a novel approach for biodiesel mixture optimization, employing an Evolutionary Computation method. The optimal Biodiesel Solution is a result of an adaptive genetic algorithm application.

It should be noticed that standard diesel emissions are high in sulfur oxides. As a result, desulfurization would have been an ideal process to achieve low sulfur oxide emissions. However, because of the high time and cost required for desulfurization, the approach of using mixtures of standard diesel and biodiesel was proposed. In the Environmental Technology Lab., Chemical Engineering Dept, UOWM, Greece, thorough experiments (approximately 3500) were conducted to develop a novel blend of Diesel and Biodiesel. These experiments yielded valuable insights into the characteristics of both components. Biodiesel, serving as the secondary ingredient, is derived from a combination of animal fat and vegetable sources. Specifically in this work, the key components of the optimal biodiesel blend are diesel and biodiesel, derived from a combination of animal fat (50%) and vegetable sources (50%), as determined by the experimental settings of the Laboratory of Environmental Technology.

So, the sequence in which cost and density affect the raw material percentages in optimal mixtures is investigated. More specifically, the higher the quality of a product is, the higher the price of the raw material. In parallel, the higher the density of a mixture is, the greater both power output and fuel economy are generated in a diesel engine. Those two properties (cost and density) are used as inputs in the genetic algorithm operation and the relevant experimental simulations. The mixture evaluation is implemented from a new mathematical function that combines the two parameters. The basic operators' Crossover and Mutation contribute to mixture improvement, producing the final bio-diesel fuel. When the Crossover operator creates biodiesel blending within the optimal solution range of the previous iteration, the Mutation process generates biodiesel combinations across the entire spectrum of feasibility, preventing potential entrapment in a localized optimal solution. The effectiveness of this approach revolves around:

(a) implementing innovative modeling techniques, including specific evaluations to enhance modeling.
(b) refining and defining the genetic algorithm.

Moreover, significant findings emerge from the experimental simulations conducted using this approach, including:

- Reducing Experiment Costs
- Minimizing Experiment Duration
- Improving Cost and Density using Enhanced Evaluation Functions

- Developing Environmentally Sustainable Fuels

This novel decision-making tool is now accessible to laboratory researchers, promoting the advancement of optimal fuel formulations. The genetic algorithm rapidly suggests the best mixture for experimentation within a vast pool of approximately 1.5×10^9 alternative combinations per experiment set. The benefits of this approach enhance the fuel production process, making the new Biodiesel more appealing compared to other competitive fuels.

This document is organized in the following parts: the mathematical representation of the Biofuel Blend Issue is presented, and the constraints in relation to ingredient accessibility are discussed in Section 2. Section 3 explores the principal methodological elements of the suggested methodology, aiming to enhance comprehension of the algorithm's fundamental workings. Lastly, the concluding segment provides a recapitulation of significant discoveries and emphasizes notable aspects.

2. Modeling of Biofuel Mixture

The Fuel Mixture Problem is a dynamic real-world problem explored by many researchers. Because of its high complexity, it does not facilitate the feasibility of all mixtures produced by laboratory experimentation due to the large set numbers demanded, implying high costs given a prolonged execution duration. Hence, the current method offers adaptable control over mixture production during the simulation phase. Utilizing the present Genetic Algorithm (GA), each mixture undergoes thorough evaluation, yielding precise and high-quality blends, thus expediting the identification of optimal solutions within a short experimental timeframe. The minimization of mixture function values arises from a multifaceted mathematical function that encompasses multiple objectives.

The objective is to minimize the Total Mixture Cost that is calculated for the ingredient as the weighted sum (w_1) of the product of the normalized cost/liter of the ingredient and the percentage of the ingredient in the mixture minus the weighted sum (w_2) of the product of the normalized density/liter of the ingredient and the percentage of the ingredient in the mixture:

$$TMFV = w_1 \times \sum_{i \in \{1,\ldots,n\}} \left(\frac{c_i}{c_{\max}} \times p_i \right) - w_2 \times \sum_{i \in \{1,\ldots,n\}} \left(\frac{d_i}{d_{\max}} \right)^4 \times p_i \quad (1)$$

The raw materials optimization problem lies in minimizing the function value of the new fuel mixture:

$$\min TMFV \quad (2)$$

Problem Restrictions:

- Min Ingredient Percentage% $\leq$ pi $\leq$ Max Ingredient Percentage%
- ci, where c1: diesel cost and c2: biodiesel cost
- di, where d1: diesel density and d2: biodiesel density
- wi, where weights: $w_1 + w_2 = 100\%$

i = 1: c1 = 2.000 EUR/L, d1 = 0.8191 g/mL and 1% $\leq$ pi $\leq$ 99%
i = 2: c2 = 0.7901 EUR/L, d2 = 0.8855 g/mL and 1% $\leq$ pi $\leq$ 30%
w_1 ($0\% \leq w_1 \leq 100\%$) and w_2 ($0\% \leq w_2 \leq 100\%$)

Restrictions on the percentage of ingredients help make chromosome development feasible. For instance, the second ingredient could range from 1% at the lowest to 30% at the most in the biodiesel blend. Values over 30% are then automatically rejected. 82% and 18% represent a feasible chromosome, including all the components.

The final mixture cost can be calculated using the raw material cost restrictions, where c1 = 2.000 EUR/L (diesel cost) and c2 = 0.7901 EUR/L (biodiesel cost).

Mixture Cost Calculation: 2.000 EUR/L × 82% + 0.7901 EUR/L × 18% = 1.7822 EUR/L.

The density of ingredients, d1 = 0.8191 g/mL (diesel density at 5 °C) and d2 = 0.8855 g/mL (biodiesel density at 5 °C) are applied to provide the final mixture density.

Mixture Density Calculation: 0.8191 g/mL × 75% + 0.8855 g/mL × 25% = 0.8357 g/mL.

The mixture function value evaluation uses weights w_1 and w_2, providing more significance either on mixture cost or mixture density. The research of these two characteristics provides the necessary information for the ingredient's participation in the optimal fuel mixture.

3. Algorithmic Framework

In various fields, genetic algorithms (GAs) employ nature-inspired methodologies to deliver superior outcomes. Initially proposed by Holland [39], genetic algorithms are rooted in evolutionary computation principles [40]. The current paper addresses the biodiesel mixture problem by introducing a novel evolutionary approach utilizing a Genetic Algorithm (GA) (Figure 1). Similar algorithms iteratively update population chromosomes over subsequent generations by utilizing selection, crossover, and mutation operators [26].

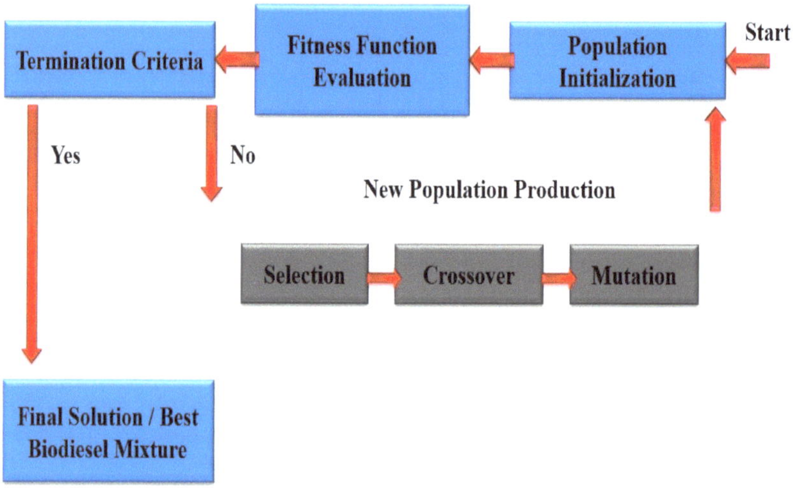

Figure 1. Genetic Algorithm Operation.

3.1. GA—Chromosome Representation

Example of Chromosome Representation: a random mixture made up of two ingredients, with percentages (w_1, w_2) always adding up to 100%. For instance, if Diesel is 78.22% and then Biodiesel is 21.78%.

The definitions and abbreviations of the main concepts that will be used hereunder are presented in Table 1.

Table 1. Abbreviations /Definition of Main Concepts.

Abbreviation	Concept Definition
Min (Max) Ingredient Percentage	Minimum (Maximum) Ingredient Percentage value.
InPer	Ingredient Percentage.
IPLS	Ingredient Percentage Local Search (in%).
I_1	Ingredient Percentage Local Search Bound created by minimum ingredient percentage.
I_2	Ingredient percentage Local Search Bound created by maximum ingredient percentage.
Max IPLS	Maximum IPLS value.
Min IPLS	Minimum IPLS value.

3.2. GA—Chromosome Representation

The process of generating generations involves two distinct phases. Initially, the first generation is established using the random creation of viable blends. Subsequently, in the subsequent phases, the formation of chromosomes for the generations follows a three-part process (also illustrated in Figure 2):

(a) Phase 1: A selection of the top-performing 10% of chromosomes from the current generation, known as the "TOP Mixtures," is carried over to the next generation.

(b) Phase 2: The next 60% of results are derived from the application of the Crossover operator, which produces new chromosomes.

(c) Phase 3: The remaining 30% of chromosomes are generated via mutation, utilizing the same method employed for the initial population's formation.

The creation of fuel mixtures involves determining the diesel and biodiesel proportions within each chromosome. Subsequently, a fitness function assesses each mixture based on criteria such as cost and density, thereby ordering all mixtures accordingly.

The solutions generated via crossover and mutation adhere to specified ingredient percentage ranges (minimum%–maximum%), ensuring that the sum of ingredient percentages always equals 100%. This approach guarantees the production of viable solutions, with no exclusion of feasible options during the evaluation process.

Following the establishment of the initial population, a framework is implemented, encompassing a range of ±IPLS (Incremental Percentage of the Last Solution) from the best chromosome percentages. This framework, suggested by Kyriklidis et al. [41], facilitates the optimization process by focusing on the optimal solution around the best chromosome from the previous generation. Each generation randomly selects a new IPLS value within a defined range (e.g., Generation 1, IPLS: 6%; Generation 2, IPLS: 9%; . . . Generation 100, IPLS: 10%).

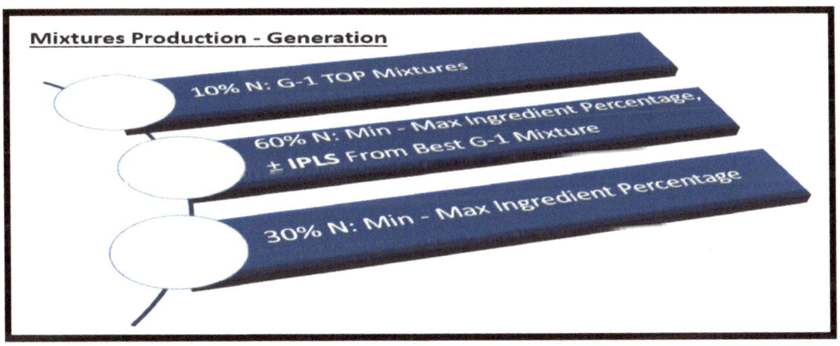

Figure 2. New generation mixtures production.

This method targets the prime solution domain from the preceding generation, acquiring values within the range of:

$$\{\min IPLS = 1\% : \max\text{IPLS} = \max InPer - (\min InPer + 1)\} \quad (3)$$

The decision-maker sets IPLS boundaries that meet the requirements of minimum and maximum ingredient percentages:

$$\begin{array}{c} for\ the\ \text{IPLSB}_1 : \text{IPLSB}_1 \geq \min InPer \\ and\ for\ the\ \text{IPLSB}_2 : \text{IPLSB}_2 \leq \max InPer \end{array} \quad (4)$$

The IPLSB1 and IPLSB2 limits derived from the process outlined above serve as the updated constraints for the new Biodiesel production. Enforcing these bounds ensures the creation of viable mixtures.

The present fuel mixture approach provides the following advantages:

- Focusing on last-generation best solutions (10% N) and leveraging them in next-generation production.
- The frame ± I, which leads to a faster optimal solution convergence, implements the local search method.
- Mutation operator prevents the GA from a premature convergence in a semi-optimal solution of moderate-quality fuel.

In summary, all GA parameters were carefully selected following thorough experimentation and the evaluation of over 100,000 simulations. Their efficacy remains on par with contemporary methods, yielding superior outcomes.

3.3. *GA—Chromosome Representation*

The effectiveness of the proposed GA methodology was assessed through two distinct sets of experiments categorized by mixture temperature: 5 °C, 10 °C, 15 °C, 20 °C, and 25 °C (referred to as sets henceforth):

(a) Set 1—Focused on Cost:

Within Evaluation Function TMFV, the weight value w_1 exceeds or equals 50%, denoted as $w_1 \geq 50\%$ (Table 2).

(b) Set 2—Focused on Density:

Within Evaluation Function TMFV, the weight value w_2 surpasses or equals 50%, denoted as $w_2 \geq 50\%$ (Table 2).

(c) Combination of Set 1 and Set 2:

The population size was fixed at 200, with 300 generations, and the costs of ingredients were set to diesel at 2.0000 EUR/L and biodiesel at 0.8091 EUR/L. The ingredient densities were diesel at 0.8191 g/mL and biodiesel at 0.8855 g/mL at 5 °C. Ingredient density varies based on temperatures between 5 and 25 °C (Table 3).

(d) The top 10% best-performing chromosomes from the preceding evaluated generation were directly carried over to the subsequent generation.

(e) The Crossover operator generated 70% of the population, adjusted by the IPLS value, randomly defined per generation within a range of ±5% to 10%.

(f) The Mutation operator was applied to the remaining 20% of chromosomes.

(g) Each experiment comprised 1000 independent simulations per Set and temperature (e.g., Set 1: 5 °C-1000 iterations, Set 1: 10 °C-1000 iterations, . . ., Set 2: 25 °C-1000 iterations).

In summary, comprehensive experimentation yielded the aforementioned configurations. The algorithm was implemented in the Matlab R2022a environment and executed on an AMD Ryzen 3 2200 G with Radeon Vega Graphics 3.50 GHz and 8.00 GB RAM. Biodiesel, as the secondary ingredient, is comprised of sources from 50% animal fat and 50% vegetable origin. The prices of vegetable origins (rap oil and sun oil) are globally available [42,43].

Table 2 categorizes the experimental sets according to temperature parameters ranging between 5 and 25 °C, distinguishing between sets emphasizing Cost (Set 1: $w_1 \geq 50\%$) and Density (Set 2: $w_2 \geq 50\%$). For instance, settings such as w_1 = 70% and w_2 = 30% prioritize Cost, as the cost criterion holds greater weight than the density criterion.

Table 2. W_1 and w_2 for Set 1 and Set 2 per Temperature between 5 °C–25 °C.

Experiment Temperatures	w_1/w_2 (Set 1)	w_1/w_2 (Set 2)
5 °C, 10 °C, 15 °C, 20 °C and 25 °C	50%/50%	50%/50%
	60%/40%	40%/60%
	70%/30%	30%/70%
	80%/20%	20%/80%
	90%/10%	10%/90%

Further experimental details are outlined in Table 3. Diesel and biodiesel are priced at 2.000 EUR/L and 0.8091 EUR/L, respectively, while their densities range from 0.8191 g/mL to 0.8915 g/mL, varying with temperature. Additionally, the proportions of ingredients in the mixtures are specified. Diesel percentage ranges from 1% to 99%, and biodiesel percentage ranges from 1% to 30%. The values presented in Table 3 reflect the availabilities and current prices observed during the laboratory experiments.

Table 3. Min and Max relative mixture composition (%), ingredient Cost and Density.

Fuel's Temperature	Min%	Max%	Cost EUR/L	Density g/mL
Diesel 5 °C	1	99	2.0000	0.8191
Biodiesel 5 °C	1	30	0.8091	0.8915
Diesel 10 °C	1	99	2.0000	0.8206
Biodiesel 10 °C	1	30	0.8091	0.8848
Diesel 15 °C	1	99	2.0000	0.8220
Biodiesel 15 °C	1	30	0.8091	0.8823
Diesel 20 °C	1	99	2.0000	0.8234
Biodiesel 20 °C	1	30	0.8091	0.8819
Diesel 25 °C	1	99	2.0000	0.8249
Biodiesel 25 °C	1	30	0.8091	0.8808

3.4. *Experimental Results*

Initially, the suggested GA approach was applied to Set 1, involving 25,000 individual simulations per temperature (ranging between 5 and 25 °C) and weight combinations (w_1 and w_2). This process spanned a duration of 3925.80 s (equivalent to approximately 65.43 min or approximately 1.09 h).

Table 4 presents these experimental results from temperatures 5 °C to 25 °C, with columns information: w_1 and w_2 weights combination, diesel ingredient percentage in the mixture, biodiesel ingredient percentage in the mixture, evaluation function value of mixture, mixture cost, and mixture density. Weights w_1 and w_2 always sum up to 100% and $w_1 \geq 50\%$ due to the Emphasis on Cost criterion. Diesel ingredient percentage ranges between 74.89% and 75.02%, while biodiesel ingredient percentage amounts to 24.98–25.11%. Evaluation Function values stand from −0.0771 to 0.7007.

A positive evaluation function value provides more influence on the cost criterion than the density criterion. On the other hand, a negative evaluation function value emphasizes the density criterion than the cost criterion. The Evaluation Function values in all groups are positive, except for w_1 = 50% and w_2 = 50%, which is negative but close to 0 value, which, as a result, provides a neutral criterion assessment. All the other groups offer clear priority to the cost criterion.

Regarding cost criterion values, the new fuel mixtures cost between 1.6976 EUR/L and 1.7386 EUR/L. The last information concerns density criterion values that range from 0.8340 g/mL–0.8395 g/mL, satisfying the ASTM D1298-99 limits: 0.8200 g/mL–0.8450 g/mL.

Each row in Table 4 provides details regarding the best mixture determined from 1000 independent simulations (totaling 25 optimal mixtures). The evaluation is centered around the minimum Total Mixture Function Value (TMFV). As the weight of w_1 increases, the TMFV value increases as well, signifying a greater emphasis on the cost criterion over the density criterion. There are slight variations in the percentages of ingredients, cost, and density among the optimal mixtures, as mentioned previously. Each experiment suggests an optimal solution—a biodiesel mixture (determined by temperature along with w_1 and w_2). The lowest TMFV value was achieved in Set 1 at a temperature of 5 °C with w_1 = 50% and w_2 = 50%.

A statistical analysis of the optimal solution in Set 1 follows.

Set 1 (temperature 5 °C, w_1 = 90%, w_2 = 10%) Optimal Mixture:

- Diesel percentage: 74.95%

- Biodiesel percentage: 25.05%
- TMFV: 0.6322
- Mixture Cost: 1.6976 EUR/L
- Mixture Density: 0.8378 g/mL

Table 4. Set 1 experiments for temperatures 5 °C–25 °C, Emphasis on Mixtures Cost, $w_1 \geq 50\%$.

Fuel's Temp.	w_1/w_2	Diesel%	Biodiesel%	TMFV	Cost	Density
5 °C	w_1: 50%, w_2: 50%	75.00%	25.00%	−0.0771	1.6988	0.8340
	w_1: 60%, w_2: 40%	75.00%	25.00%	0.1104	1.6985	0.8351
	w_1: 70%, w_2: 30%	74.98%	25.02%	0.2856	1.6978	0.8359
	w_1: 80%, w_2: 20%	74.97%	25.03%	0.4878	1.6978	0.8364
	w_1: 90%, w_2: 10%	74.95%	25.05%	0.6322	1.6976	0.8378
10 °C	w_1: 50%, w_2: 50%	75.01%	24.99%	−0.0727	1.7377	0.8349
	w_1: 60%, w_2: 40%	74.99%	25.01%	0.1134	1.7211	0.8355
	w_1: 70%, w_2: 30%	74.97%	25.03%	0.2987	1.7200	0.8363
	w_1: 80%, w_2: 20%	74.95%	25.05%	0.4881	1.6993	0.8376
	w_1: 90%, w_2: 10%	74.93%	25.07%	0.6781	1.6987	0.8379
15 °C	w_1: 50%, w_2: 50%	75.00%	25.00%	−0.0715	1.7379	0.8356
	w_1: 60%, w_2: 40%	74.98%	25.02%	0.1154	1.7216	0.8359
	w_1: 70%, w_2: 30%	74.96%	25.04%	0.2996	1.7222	0.8368
	w_1: 80%, w_2: 20%	74.95%	25.05%	0.4897	1.7077	0.8379
	w_1: 90%, w_2: 10%	74.93%	25.07%	0.6792	1.6991	0.8382
20 °C	w_1: 50%, w_2: 50%	75.01%	24.99%	−0.0704	1.7382	0.8367
	w_1: 60%, w_2: 40%	74.98%	25.02%	0.1155	1.7245	0.8371
	w_1: 70%, w_2: 30%	74.97%	25.03%	0.3011	1.7233	0.8377
	w_1: 80%, w_2: 20%	74.92%	25.08%	0.4954	1.7188	0.8385
	w_1: 90%, w_2: 10%	74.91%	25.09%	0.6808	1.6995	0.8389
25 °C	w_1: 50%, w_2: 50%	75.02%	24.98%	−0.0681	1.7386	0.8371
	w_1: 60%, w_2: 40%	75.01%	24.99%	0.1176	1.7248	0.8373
	w_1: 70%, w_2: 30%	74.95%	25.05%	0.3225	1.7254	0.8379
	w_1: 80%, w_2: 20%	74.91%	25.09%	0.5238	1.7195	0.8388
	w_1: 90%, w_2: 10%	74.89%	25.11%	0.7007	1.6999	0.8395

In a series of 1000 separate trials, the lowest Total Mixture Function Value (TMFV) recorded was 0.6322, while the highest TMFV reached was 0.6587. The difference between the minimum and maximum TMFV values is 0.0265. Meanwhile, the average TMFV across all trials stands at 0.6432, with a standard deviation of 0.0051 (refer to Figure 3a).

The performance of the approach is illustrated in Figure 3b, revealing that the majority of optimal solutions, comprising 764 mixtures (equivalent to 94.9% of the total), fall within the range of 0.6322 to 0.6484 TMFV (with 0.6322 being the minimum TMFV). This outcome underscores the effectiveness of the GA in generating solutions closely aligned with the Min fitness function within a short timeframe. Conversely, on the basis of the allocation of best solutions, only 51 mixtures (comprising 5.1% of the total) lie within the range of 0.6485 to 0.6607 TMFV (with 0.6587 being the maximum TMFV).

Regarding the cost of mixtures, a series of 1000 separate experiments suggest a 1.6976 EUR/L minimum and a 1.7457 EUR/L maximum mixture cost. The difference between the minimum and maximum costs is 0.0481. Meanwhile, the average mixture cost across all experiments stands at 1.7036 EUR/L, with a standard deviation of 0.0077 (as depicted in Figure 4a).

The allocation of Best Cost solutions is presented in Figure 4b. For most best solutions, 877 mixtures (951 = 504 + 245 + 129 + 73) or 95.1% are between 1.6976 EUR/L and 1.7219 EUR/L (minimum mixture cost 1.6976 EUR/L). The above results confirm the GA's effectiveness in providing fuel costs close to the minimum value. Based on the best solutions, the allocation of only (49 = 38 + 8 + 2 + 1) mixtures (4.9%) was between 1.7220 EUR/L and 1.7463 (maximum mixture cost 1.7457 EUR/L).

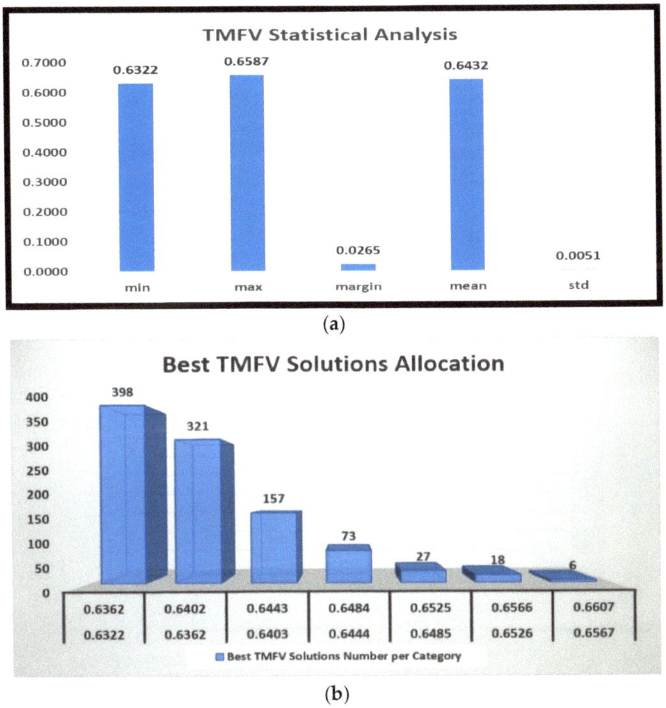

Figure 3. Set 1: (**a**) TMFV Statistical Analysis and (**b**) Best TMFV Solutions Allocation.

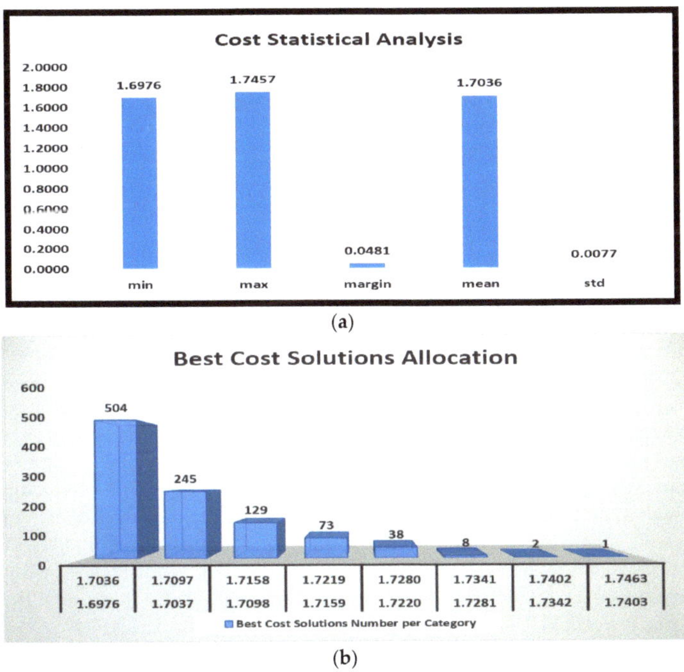

Figure 4. Set 1: (**a**) Cost Statistical Analysis and (**b**) Best Cost Solutions Allocation.

In terms of mixtures' density, a series of 1000 independent experiments indicate a minimum mixture density of 0.8378 g/mL and a maximum mixture density of 0.8537 g/mL. The difference between the minimum and maximum densities is 0.0159. The average mixture density across all experiments is 0.8390 g/mL, with a standard deviation of 0.0047 (as shown in Figure 5a).

The allocation of Best Density solutions is presented in Figure 5b. Most best solutions, 881 mixtures (881 = 452 + 234 + 121 + 74) or 88.1% is between 0.8378 g/mL and 0.8461 g/mL (minimum mixture density 0.8378 EUR/L), compared to the total 119 (344 = 59 + 34 + 22 + 4) mixtures or 11.9%, which were between 0.8462 g/mL and 0.8545 g/mL (maximum mixture density 0.8537 g/mL).

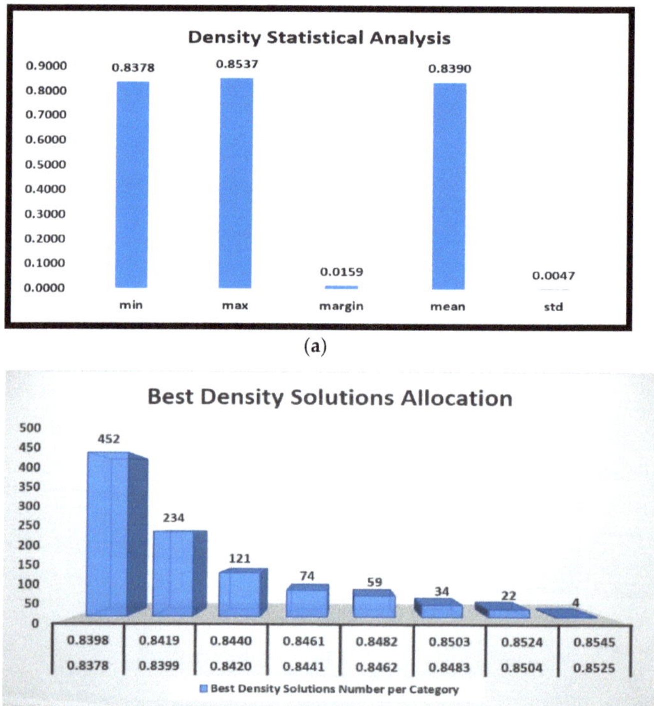

Figure 5. Set 1: (**a**) Density Statistical Analysis and (**b**) Best Density Solutions Allocation.

Subsequently, Set 2 underwent testing to assess the effectiveness of the proposed GA, involving 25,000 independent simulations per temperature (ranging from 5 °C to 25 °C) and various combinations of weights (w_1 and w_2). This testing phase lasted for a duration of 3645.34 s (approximately 60.76 min or approximately 1 h). Table 5 presents these experimental results from temperatures 5 °C to 25 °C, with columns information: w_1 and w_2 weights combination, diesel ingredient (%) in the mixture, biodiesel ingredient percentage in the mixture, evaluation function value of mixture, mixture cost, and mixture density.

Weights w_1 and w_2 always sum up to 100% and $w_2 \geq 50\%$ due to the Emphasis on Density criterion. Diesel ingredient percentage ranges between 74.89% and 75.02%, while biodiesel ingredient percentage amounts to 24.88–25.12%. Evaluation Function values range from −0.8852 to −0.0681.

The negative evaluation function value emphasizes the density criterion rather than the cost criterion.

The Evaluation Function values in all groups are negative but close to 0 value (w_1 = 50% and w_2 = 50%), which results in a neutral criterion assessment. All the other groups offer clear priority to the density criterion.

As regards cost criterion values, the new fuel mixtures cost between 1.6979 EUR/L and 1.7386 EUR/L. The last information concerns density criterion values range 0.8340 g/mL–0.8397 g/mL, satisfying the ASTM D1298-99 limits: 0.8200 g/mL–0.8450 g/mL.

Each row in Table 5 provides details regarding the best mixture identified from 1000 independent simulations (resulting in a total of 25 optimal mixtures). The evaluation is centered around the minimum Total Mixture Function Value (TMFV). As the value of w_2 rises, the TMFV value also increases, indicating a greater emphasis on the density criterion over the cost criterion. There are slight variations in the percentages of ingredients, optimal mixture cost, and density among the optimal mixtures, as previously discussed.

A statistical analysis of the optimal solution in Set 2 follows.

Optimal Mixture in Set 2 (temperature 20 °C, w_1 = 10%, w_2 = 90%):

- Diesel percentage: 74.88%
- Biodiesel percentage: 25.12%
- TMFV: −0.8852
- Mixture Cost: 1.7112 EUR/L
- Mixture Density: 0.8397 g/mL

Table 5. Set 2 experiments for temperatures 5 °C–25 °C, Emphasis on Mixtures Density, $w_2 \geq 50\%$.

Fuel's Temp.	w_1/w_2	Diesel%	Biodiesel%	TMFV	Cost	Density
5 °C	w_1: 50%, w_2: 50%	75.00%	25.00%	−0.0771	1.6988	0.8340
	w_1: 40%, w_2: 60%	74.99%	25.01%	−0.2267	1.6986	0.8355
	w_1: 30%, w_2: 70%	74.98%	25.02%	−0.4167	1.6984	0.8358
	w_1: 20%, w_2: 80%	74.96%	25.04%	−0.6378	1.6980	0.8366
	w_1: 10%, w_2: 90%	74.95%	25.05%	−0.8451	1.6979	0.8379
10 °C	w_1: 50%, w_2: 50%	75.01%	24.99%	−0.0727	1.7379	0.8349
	w_1: 40%, w_2: 60%	74.99%	25.01%	−0.2588	1.7222	0.8357
	w_1: 30%, w_2: 70%	74.96%	25.04%	−0.4506	1.7234	0.8364
	w_1: 20%, w_2: 80%	74.96%	25.04%	−0.6428	1.7056	0.8378
	w_1: 10%, w_2: 90%	74.93%	25.07%	−0.8322	1.6993	0.8381
15 °C	w_1: 50%, w_2: 50%	75.00%	25.00%	−0.0715	1.7379	0.8356
	w_1: 40%, w_2: 60%	74.98%	25.02%	−0.2684	1.7256	0.8361
	w_1: 30%, w_2: 70%	74.97%	25.03%	−0.4754	1.7237	0.8369
	w_1: 20%, w_2: 80%	74.94%	25.06%	−0.6682	1.7087	0.8380
	w_1: 10%, w_2: 90%	74.92%	25.08%	−0.8481	1.7023	0.8384
20 °C	w_1: 50%, w_2: 50%	75.01%	24.99%	−0.0704	1.7384	0.8367
	w_1: 40%, w_2: 60%	74.99%	25.01%	−0.2791	1.7268	0.8373
	w_1: 30%, w_2: 70%	74.96%	25.04%	−0.4984	1.7245	0.8379
	w_1: 20%, w_2: 80%	74.93%	25.07%	−0.6709	1.7198	0.8386
	w_1: 10%, w_2: 90%	74.91%	25.09%	−0.8687	1.7067	0.8390
25 °C	w_1: 50%, w_2: 50%	75.02%	24.98%	−0.0681	1.7386	0.8371
	w_1: 40%, w_2: 60%	75.00%	25.00%	−0.2981	1.7269	0.8375
	w_1: 30%, w_2: 70%	74.96%	25.04%	−0.5603	1.7258	0.8382
	w_1: 20%, w_2: 80%	74.92%	25.08%	−0.6991	1.7212	0.8389
	w_1: 10%, w_2: 90%	74.88%	25.12%	−0.8852	1.7112	0.8397

In a series of 1000 independent trials, the lowest Total Mixture Function Value (TMFV) recforded was −0.8852, while the highest TMFV reached was −0.8753. The difference between the minimum and maximum TMFV values is 0.0099. Meanwhile, the average TMFV across all trials stands at −0.8802, with a standard deviation of 0.0018 (as illustrated in Figure 6a).

The effectiveness of the method is illustrated in Figure 6b, where the majority of optimal solutions, totaling 936 mixtures (comprising 93.6% of the total), fall within the range of −0.8852 to −0.8793 TMFV (with −0.8852 being the minimum TMFV). This outcome validates the GA's capability to generate solutions closely aligned with the minimum fitness function within a brief timeframe. Based on best solutions allocation, only 64 (64 = 34 + 25 + 5) mixtures (6.4%) were between −0.8792 and −0.8748 (maximum mixture TMFV −0.8753).

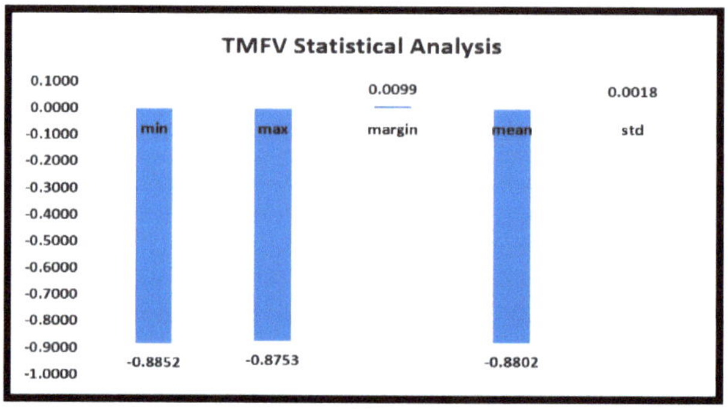

(a)

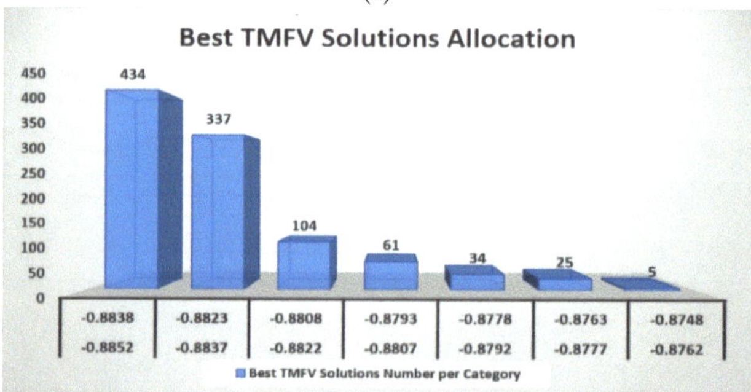

(b)

Figure 6. Set 2: (**a**) TMFV Statistical Analysis and (**b**) Best TMFV Solutions Allocation.

Regarding the cost of the mixtures, a set of 1000 independent experiments suggests a minimal mixture cost of 1.7112 EUR/L and a maximal mixture cost of 1.8598 EUR/L. The difference between the lowest and highest costs is 0.1486. Meanwhile, the average cost of the mixtures across all experiments stands at 1.7322 EUR/L, with a standard deviation of 0.0239 (as indicated in Figure 7a).

The allocation of Best Cost solutions is presented in Figure 7b. Most of the best solutions, 954 mixtures (954 = 523 + 227 + 132 + 72) or 95.4% are between 1.7112 EUR/L and 1.7963 EUR/L (minimum mixture cost 1.7112 EUR/L). The above results confirm the GA's effectiveness in providing fuel costs close to the minimum value. Based on the best solutions' allocation, only 46 (46 = 34 + 9 + 3) mixtures (4.6%) were between 1.7964 EUR/L and 1.8602 (maximum mixture cost 1.8598 EUR/L).

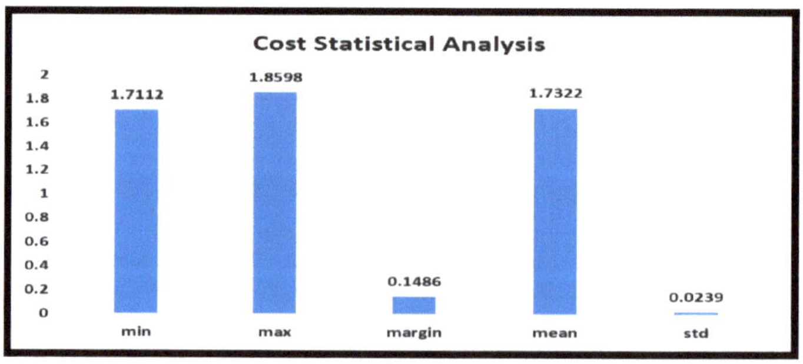

(a)

Figure 7. *Cont.*

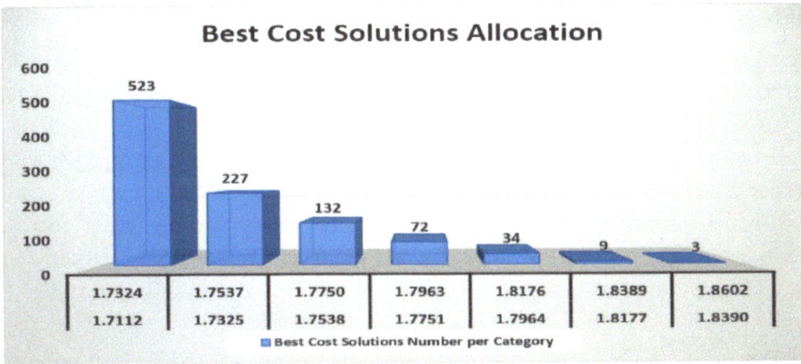

(**b**)

Figure 7. Set 2: (**a**) Cost Statistical Analysis and (**b**) Best Cost Solutions Allocation.

Regarding mixture density, a minimum mixture density of 0.8378 g/mL and a maximum mixture density of 0.8537 g/mL are suggested by 1000 separate trials. The mean mixture density is 0.8390 g/mL with a standard deviation of 0.0047, with a margin of 0.0159 between the minimum and maximum densities (Figure 8a).

Best Density solutions allocation are presented in Figure 8b. Most best solutions, 921 mixtures (921 = 532 + 234 + 91 + 64) or 92.1% is between 0.8397 g/mL and 0.8424 g/mL (minimum mixture density 0.8397 g/mL), compared to the total 79 (79 = 43 + 22 + 12 + 2) mixtures or 7.9%, which were between 0.8425 g/mL and 0.8452 g/mL (maximum mixture density 0.8537 g/mL).

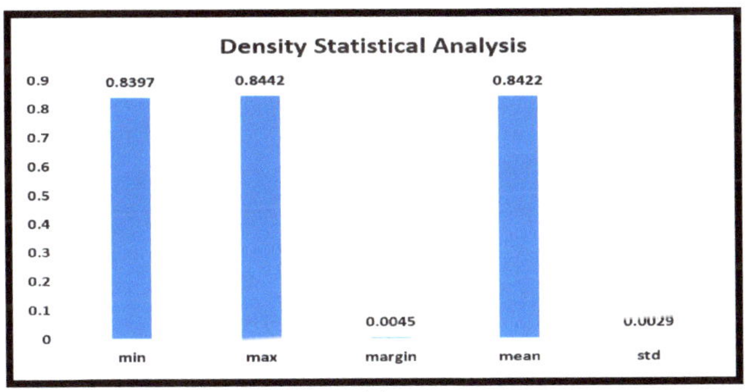

(**a**)

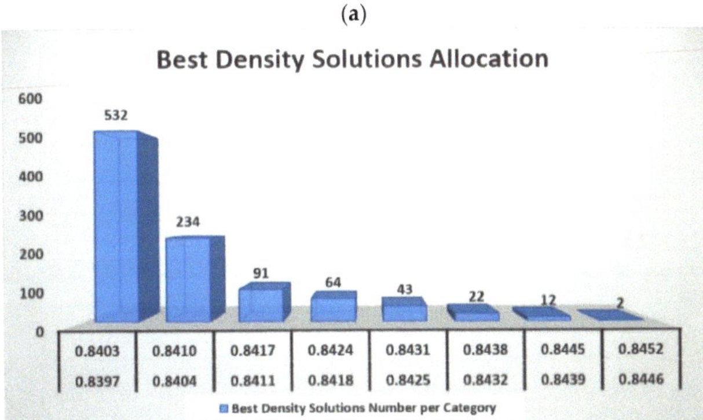

(**b**)

Figure 8. Set 2: (**a**) Density Statistical Analysis and (**b**) Best Density Solutions Allocation.

4. Combustion of Mixtures

After studying the changes in a very important property, mixture density, we considered it to be useful to see how these mixtures behave during their combustion so as to have an overall picture of the effect of the addition of biodiesel on the production of exhaust gases that are finally released into the atmosphere. Our goal was to see if the addition of biodiesel would reduce the exhaust gases and to what extent so that, based on the density analysis of the mixtures, we could also make conclusions about the exhaust gases produced upon combustion. For this purpose, a series of experiments were carried out directly on the gaseous phase of the exhaust emissions using an Optima 7 portable flue gas analyzer (MRU GmbH, Neckarsulm, Germany), and are shown in Table 6.

Measurements:

Mixture Composition: Diesel—Biodiesel 50% vegetable—50% animal sources.

Mixture Temperature: 25 °C.

Table 6. Mixture Relative Composition—Gaseous Pollutants.

	D–B (%)	Gaseous Pollutants					
		O_2	CO_2	CO	NO_X	C.P.	E.A.
1	100–0	3.9	12.6	130	69	94.9	22.9
2	95–5	3.9	12.5	132	69	94.8	23.3
3	90–10	4.0	12.6	133	69	94.9	23.7
4	85–15	4.1	12.5	135	70	94.9	24.2
5	80–20	4.1	12.7	137	70	94.9	24.2
6	75–25	4.2	12.7	139	71	95.0	24.5
7	70–30	4.2	12.6	142	71	95.2	24.9
8	65–35	4.3	12.6	147	71	95.1	25.5
9	60–40	4.3	12.6	152	72	95.2	26.2
10	55–45	4.5	12.7	158	72	95.3	26.8
11	50–50	4.5	12.7	162	73	95.4	27.4
12	45–55	4.5	12.7	165	73	95.3	27.4
13	40–60	4.4	12.6	168	71	95.4	27.2
14	35–65	4.4	12.6	170	70	95.4	27.0
15	30–70	4.5	12.7	172	69	95.4	26.8
16	25–75	4.5	12.6	174	68	95.0	26.6
17	20–80	4.5	12.5	179	68	95.1	26.4
18	15–85	4.5	12.5	184	69	95.2	26.0
19	10–90	4.6	12.5	194	69	95.1	25.7
20	5–95	4.6	12.6	204	69	95.0	25.4
21	0–100	4.6	12.6	216	68	95.2	25.1

O_2 = Oxygen, CO_2 = Carbon dioxide, CO = Carbon monoxide, NO_X = Nitrogen oxides, C.P. = Combustion performance, E.A. = Excess air.

It can be seen in Table 6 that the addition of biodiesel does not deteriorate the produced percentage of exhaust gases. Therefore, it can be used in the combustion technology to create environmentally friendly fuels and, in this particular work, does not cause a problem in terms of mixture density changes.

5. Concluding Remarks

Global communities are increasingly moving away from fossil fuels and seeking environmentally friendly alternatives. In recent years, biodiesel has garnered attention due to its production from renewable and eco-friendly sources. This study introduces a novel method for biodiesel production utilizing two ingredients: diesel and biodiesel derived entirely from vegetable sources. The implementation leverages the advantages of Genetic Algorithms (GA) within Evolutionary Computation.

Two specialized operators, namely crossover and mutation, support the GA's execution. The crossover operator explores a specific area near the optimal solution of the previous generation, while the mutation operator prevents premature convergence to suboptimal solutions or costlier fuels with lower density values.

Moreover, the Overall Mixture Performance Metric (OMPM) assesses the efficacy of novel biodiesel blends and the capability for the creation of competitive biofuel options in relation to ingredient availability. The OMPM underscores two key fuel attributes: expense and density, determined using factors w_1 and w_2, respectively, indicating the priority assigned to cost and density in the experimental fuel assessment process. The study entailed the exploration of optimal biodiesel blends through iterative experimentation (3×10^9 blends), segmented into two groups distinguished by temperatures spanning from 5 °C to 25 °C: Group 1—"Cost Priority" and Group 2—"Density Priority".

Tables 4 and 5 showcase the top 25 blends per group, with the two pinnacle blends as follows:

- Optimal Blend in Group 1 (5 °C, w_1 = 90%, w_2 = 10%): Diesel content: 74.95%, Biodiesel content: 25.05%, OMPM: 0.6322, Blend Cost: 1.6976 EUR/L, Blend Density: 0.8378 g/mL.
- Optimal Blend in Group 2 (20 °C, w_1 = 10%, w_2 = 90%): Diesel content: 74.88%, Biodiesel content: 25.12%, OMPM: −0.8852, Blend Cost: 1.7112 EUR/L, Blend Density: 0.8397 g/mL.

The new biodiesel costs less than 15.12% (Set 1) and 14.44% (Set 2) compared to diesel (priced at 2.0000 EUR/L), offering antagonistic prices, minimizing lower sulfur content, and reducing pollutant emissions.

Apart from the two optimal biodiesel fuels, the remaining fuels, recognized as best mixtures within their respective groups, present viable solutions with competitive costs and densities always within the standard limits ranging from 0.8200 g/mL to 0.8450 g/mL (ASTM D1298-99).

Additionally, the experiments yield several significant outcomes, including cost minimization, duration minimization, use of the EFM for improvements in both cost and density and the production of environmentally friendly fuel, showcasing the utility of this new decision-making in the production of optimized biodiesel mixture compositions.

In conclusion, the evolutionary GA approach demonstrates its capability to adequately address complex fuel mixture problems and can be recommended as a suitable and efficient approach for addressing new biodiesel production challenges.

Future research directions call for further GA algorithm evolvement and enhancement. Research on other factors that potentially may improve the quality of biodiesel is also under consideration. Moreover, the suggested technology can be applied to other biodiesel blends based on different components.

Author Contributions: Conceptualization, V.V., V.K. and C.T.; Data curation, C.K.; Formal analysis, V.V. and C.K.; Investigation, V.V.; Methodology, V.V. and C.K.; Project administration, V.V.; Resources, C.T.; Software, C.K.; Supervision, V.K. and C.T.; Validation, C.T.; Visualization, V.K.; Writing—original draft, C.K.; Writing—review and editing, V.K. All authors have read and agreed to the published version of the manuscript.

Funding: This research received no external funding.

Data Availability Statement: Data are not publicly available due to academic regulations, but they can be available upon request to interested researchers.

Conflicts of Interest: The authors declare no conflicts of interest.

References

1. Enerdata. Global Energy Trends—2022 Edition. In *World Energy & Climate Statistics—Yearbook 2022*; Enerdata: Paris, France, 2022.
2. Papapolymerou, G.; Karayannis, V.; Besios, A.; Riga, A.; Gougoulias, N.; Spiliotis, X. Scaling-up sustainable chlorella vulgaris microalgal biomass cultivation from laboratory to pilot-plant photobioreactor, towards biofuel. *Glob. Nest J.* **2019**, *21*, 37–42.
3. Pokushko, M.; Stupina, A.; Medina-Bulo, I.; Ezhemanskaya, S.; Kuzmich, R.; Pokushko, R. Algorithm for Application of a Basic Model for the Data Envelopment Analysis Method in Technical Systems. *Algorithms* **2023**, *16*, 460. [CrossRef]
4. Kokkinos, K.; Karayannis, V.; Samaras, N.; Moustakas, K. Multi-scenario analysis on hydrogen production development using PESTEL and FCM models. *J. Clean. Prod.* **2023**, *419*, 138251. [CrossRef]
5. Vasiliadou, I.A.; Semizoglou, Z.A.; Karayannis, V.G.; Tsanaktsidis, C.G. Extraction Study of Lignite Coalbed Methane as a Potential Supplement to Natural Gas for Enhancing Energy Security of Western Macedonia Region in Greece. *Appl. Sci.* **2024**, *14*, 174. [CrossRef]
6. Semwal, S.; Arora, A.K.; Badoni, R.P.; Tuli, D.K. Biodiesel production using heterogeneous catalysts. *Bioresour. Technol.* **2011**, *102*, 2151–2161. [CrossRef] [PubMed]
7. Roschat, W.; Kacha, M.; Yoosuk, B.; Sudyoadsuk, T.; Promarak, V. Biodiesel production based on heterogeneous process catalyzed by solid waste coral fragment. *Fuel* **2012**, *98*, 194–202. [CrossRef]
8. Lee, S.; Posarac, D.; Ellis, N. An experimental investigation of biodiesel synthesis from waste canola oil using supercritical methanol. *Fuel* **2012**, *91*, 229–237. [CrossRef]
9. Ma, F.; Hanna, M.A. Biodiesel production: A review. *Bioresour. Technol.* **1999**, *70*, 1–15. [CrossRef]
10. Kamm, B.; Kamm, M. Principles of biorefineries. *Appl. Microbiol. Biotechnol.* **2004**, *64*, 37–45. [CrossRef]
11. Tyson, K.S.; Bozell, J.; Wallace, R.; Petersen, E.; Moens, L. Biomass oil analysis: Research needs and recommendations. *NREL/Tech. Rep.* **2004**. [CrossRef]
12. Bezergianni, S.; Kalogeras, K.; Pilavachi, P.A. On maximizing biodiesel mixing ratio based on final product specifications. *Comput. Chem. Eng.* **2011**, *35*, 936–942. [CrossRef]
13. Gerpen, J.V.; Shanks, B.; Pruszko, R.; Clements, D.; Knothe, G. *Biodiesel Production Technology NREL/SR-510-36244*; National Renewable Energy Laboratory: Golden, CO, USA, 2004.
14. Balat, M.; Balat, H. Progress in biodiesel processing. *Appl. Energy* **2010**, *87*, 1815–1835. [CrossRef]
15. Pérez-Cisnerosa, E.S.; Mena-Espinoa, X.; Rodríguez-Lópezc, V.; Sales-Cruzb, M.; Viveros-Garcíaa, T.; Lobo-Oehmichen, R. An integrated reactive distillation process for biodiesel production. *Comput. Chem. Eng.* **2016**, *35*, 936–942. [CrossRef]
16. Burton, R. Biodiesel Standards and Testing Methods. In *Alternative Fuels Consortium*; Central Carolina Community College: Sanford, NC, USA, 2008.
17. Gomez, L.D.; Steele-King, C.G.; McQueen-Mason, S.J. Sustainable liquid biofuels from biomass: The writing's on the walls. *New Phytol.* **2008**, *178*, 473–485. [CrossRef] [PubMed]
18. Ramos, M.; Dias, A.P.S.; Puna, J.F.; Gomes, J.; Bordado, J.C. Review on biodiesel production processes and sustainable raw materials. *Energies* **2019**, *12*, 4408. [CrossRef]
19. Kavallari, A.; Smeets, E.; Tabeau, A. Land use changes from EU biofuel use: A sensitivity analysis. *Oper. Res.* **2014**, *14*, 261–281. [CrossRef]
20. Alptekin, E.; Canakci, M. Determination of the density and the viscosities of biodiesel–diesel fuel blends. *Renew. Energy* **2008**, *33*, 2623–2630. [CrossRef]
21. Tsanaktsidis, C.G.; Vasiliadis, V.; Itziou, A.; Petrakis, L.A.; Moisiadis, S.A. Application of factor analysis for the study of physicochemical properties in different blends of diesel fuel with biodiesel. *Int. J. Soft Comput. Eng.* **2013**, *3*, 42–46.
22. Malik, S.; Darolia, P.J.; Garg, S.K.; Sharma, V.K. Densities and excess molar volumes of mixtures containing diesel, biodiesel and alkanols at temperatures from 288.15 to 313.15 K. *Chin. J. Chem. Eng.* **2021**, *34*, 198–207. [CrossRef]
23. Tsanaktsidis, C.G.; Spinthiropoulos, K.G.; Guliyev, F.; Dimitriou, D.; Euthaltsidou, K.; Tzilantonis, G.T. Relation between quality and production cost for pure biodiesel bases on the mixes of raw materials. *IOP Conf. Ser. Earth Environ. Sci.* **2016**, *40*, 012048. [CrossRef]
24. Deya, P.; Raya, S.; Newarb, A. Defining a waste vegetable oil-biodiesel based diesel substitute blend fuel by response surface optimization of density and calorific value. *Fuel* **2021**, *283*, 118978. [CrossRef]
25. Valdez, F.; Castillo, O.; Melin, P. Bio-inspired algorithms and its applications for optimization in fuzzy clustering. *Algorithms* **2021**, *14*, 122. [CrossRef]
26. Kyriklidis, C.; Dounias, G. Evolutionary computation for resource leveling optimization in project management. In *Integrated Computer-Aided Engineering*; IOS Press: Amsterdam, The Netherland, 2016; Volume 23, pp. 173–184.
27. Samuel, A.L. Some studies in machine learning using the game of checkers. *IBM J. Res. Dev.* **1959**, *3*, 210–229. [CrossRef]
28. Russell, S.; Norvig, P. *Artificial Intelligence—A Modern Approach*, 3rd ed.; Hirsch, M., Ed.; Pearson Education Inc.: Hoboken, NJ, USA, 2010.

29. Xing, Y.; Zheng, Z.; Sun, Y.; Alikhani, M.A. A Review on Machine Learning Application in Biodiesel Production Studies. *Int. J. Chem. Eng.* **2021**, *2021*, 2154258. [CrossRef]
30. Kalogirou, S.A. Artificial neural networks in renewable energy systems applications: A review. *Renew. Sustain. Energy Rev.* **2001**, *5*, 373–401. [CrossRef]
31. Baños, R.; Manzano-Agugliaro, F.; Montoya, F.G.; Gil, C.; Alcayde, A.; Gómez, J. Optimization methods applied to renewable and sustainable energy: A review. *Renew. Sustain. Energy Rev.* **2011**, *15*, 1753–1766. [CrossRef]
32. Liao, M.; Yao, Y. Applications of artificial intelligence-based modeling for bioenergy systems: A review. *GCB Bioenergy* **2021**, *13*, 774–802. [CrossRef]
33. Kokkinos, K.; Karayannis, V. Supportiveness of low-carbon energy technology policy using fuzzy multicriteria decision-making methodologies. *Mathematics* **2020**, *8*, 1178. [CrossRef]
34. Zhou, Y.; Zhang, J.; Yang, X.; Ling, Y. Optimal reactive power dispatch using water wave optimization algorithm. *Oper. Res.* **2020**, *20*, 2537–2553. [CrossRef]
35. Mohd Ali, J.; Hussain, M.A.; Tade, M.O.; Zhang, J. Artificial Intelligence techniques applied as estimator in chemical process systems-a literature survey. *Expert. Syst. Appl.* **2015**, *42*, 5915–5931. [CrossRef]
36. Liu, Z.; Baghban, A. Application of LSSVM for biodiesel production using supercritical ethanol solvent. *Energy Sources Part A Recovery Util. Environ. Eff.* **2017**, *39*, 1869–1874. [CrossRef]
37. Mohadesi, M.; Rezaei, A. Biodiesel Conversion Modeling under Several Conditions Using Computational Intelligence Methods. *Environ. Prog. Sustain. Energy* **2018**, *37*, 562–568. [CrossRef]
38. Kokkinos, K.; Karayannis, V.; Moustakas, K. Optimizing Microalgal Biomass Feedstock Selection for Nanocatalytic Conversion Into Biofuel Clean Energy, Using Fuzzy Multi-Criteria Decision Making Processes. *Front. Energy Res.* **2021**, *8*, 622210. [CrossRef]
39. Holland, J.H. Genetic Algorithms. *Sci. Am.* **1992**, *267*, 66–72. [CrossRef]
40. Fuladi, S.K.; Kim, C.-S. Dynamic Events in the Flexible Job-Shop Scheduling Problem: Rescheduling with a Hybrid Metaheuristic Algorithm. *Algorithms* **2024**, *17*, 142. [CrossRef]
41. Kyriklidis, C.; Kyriklidis, M.-E.; Loizou, E.; Stimoniaris, A.; Tsanaktsidis, C.G. Optimal Bio Marine Fuel production evolutionary Computation: Genetic algorithm approach for raw materials mixtures. *Fuel* **2022**, *323*, 124232. [CrossRef]
42. Food and Agriculture Organization of the United Nations (FAOSTAT). Available online: https://www.fao.org/faostat/en/#data/PP (accessed on 1 February 2024).
43. Hellenic Statistical Authority, Greece (HSA). Available online: https://www.statistics.gr/ (accessed on 1 February 2024).

algorithms

MDPI

Article

Optimizing Speech Emotion Recognition with Deep Learning and Grey Wolf Optimization: A Multi-Dataset Approach

Suryakant Tyagi [1] and Sándor Szénási [2,3,*]

[1] Doctoral School of Applied Informatics and Applied Mathematics, Óbuda University, 1034 Budapest, Hungary; suryakant.tyagi@phd.uni-obuda.hu
[2] John von Neumann Faculty of Informatics, Óbuda University, 1034 Budapest, Hungary
[3] Faculty of Economics and Informatics, J. Selye University, 945 01 Komarno, Slovakia
* Correspondence: szenasi.sandor@nik.uni-obuda.hu or szenasis@ujs.sk

Abstract: Machine learning and speech emotion recognition are rapidly evolving fields, significantly impacting human-centered computing. Machine learning enables computers to learn from data and make predictions, while speech emotion recognition allows computers to identify and understand human emotions from speech. These technologies contribute to the creation of innovative human–computer interaction (HCI) applications. Deep learning algorithms, capable of learning high-level features directly from raw data, have given rise to new emotion recognition approaches employing models trained on advanced speech representations like spectrograms and time–frequency representations. This study introduces CNN and LSTM models with GWO optimization, aiming to determine optimal parameters for achieving enhanced accuracy within a specified parameter set. The proposed CNN and LSTM models with GWO optimization underwent performance testing on four diverse datasets—RAVDESS, SAVEE, TESS, and EMODB. The results indicated superior performance of the models compared to linear and kernelized SVM, with or without GWO optimizers.

Keywords: speech emotion recognition; neural network; deep learning; LSTM

1. Introduction

Speech emotion recognition (SER) is a research field aiming to develop systems that automatically recognize emotions from speech, with the potential to enhance user experiences in various applications like spoken dialogue systems, intelligent voice assistants, and computer games. However, the accuracy of current SER systems remains relatively low due to factors such as the intricate nature of human emotions, variability in human speech, and challenges in extracting reliable features from speech signals.

A typical SER system comprises two main components: feature extraction and classification. Feature extraction is tasked with capturing essential acoustic characteristics from the speech signal, including pitch and spectral features. Subsequently, the classification component assigns emotional labels to the speech signal based on extracted features.

In recent years, deep learning has emerged as a powerful tool for machine learning, finding success in domains like computer vision, speech recognition, and natural language processing. Deep learning is well suited for SER for several reasons. Firstly, deep learning models excel at capturing intricate relationships between features, crucial for accurately identifying emotions from speech. Secondly, deep learning models possess unique characteristics that enable them to efficiently leverage large speech datasets, a capability particularly advantageous in SER, where access to extensive annotated data facilitates model training and improves generalization to diverse speakers and emotional expressions. Additionally, while other models also claim the ability to generalize to new speakers and situations, deep learning models demonstrate a notable robustness and adaptability in handling variations, making them particularly effective in real-world SER applications.

Here are some other points to keep in mind before going forward with the research:

- The intricate nature of human emotions poses a challenge to developing accurate SER systems as emotions are complex and expressed in various ways. For instance, happiness may be conveyed through laughter, smiling, and a high-pitched voice, but also through tears, a frown, and a low-pitched voice.
- The variability in human speech further complicates SER systems, as individuals speak differently based on factors like age, gender, and accent. For example, a young woman from the United States may have a different speaking style than an older man from the United Kingdom.

In the dynamic landscape of speech emotion recognition (SER), marked by its rapid growth, this research aims to contribute to the evolution of computer interaction by leveraging deep learning advancements to advance real-time emotion recognition from speech. The primary objective involves extracting pivotal features from audio waveforms to construct a model that accurately predicts emotions. While Mel-frequency cepstral coefficients (MFCC) feature extraction was employed in this study, it is important to acknowledge that other feature extraction methods exist and could be explored in future research to potentially enhance performance. MFCC is widely used and has shown success in many SER applications due to its ability to capture spectral characteristics relevant to speech perception, it is essential to note that there is not a universally "best" technique. Different techniques may perform better in different contexts. Four datasets (RAVDESS, SAVEE, TESS, and EmoDB) were utilized to train and evaluate the model. The model underwent initial training with linear and kernelized support vector machines (SVMs), followed by comprehensive training with a convolutional neural network (CNN) model incorporating long short-term memory (LSTM). Further refinement of the datasets was achieved through the application of a Gray Wolf Optimizer, tailoring the parameters for optimal model fitting. It is important to clarify that, while the study contributed to refining the models and optimization techniques, the datasets themselves were not crafted by the authors. Despite the inherent challenges in doing so, the study underscores the potential of deep learning in enhancing the accuracy and efficiency of real-time emotion recognition systems.

2. Related Work

This section provides a concise overview of the speech emotion recognition (SER) research landscape, highlighting the importance of acoustic features [1,2]. Acoustic parameters play a crucial role in deciphering emotions, prompting studies to investigate emotion-specific profiles through these parameters. While the integration of diverse classifiers such as Bayesian, K-nearest neighbor (KNN), and decision trees has reshaped the research field, it's worth noting that models like Gaussian mixtures (GMMs) and hidden Markov models (HMMs) may lack insights into low-level feature distribution [3–14].

The introduction of deep learning in SER, particularly with end-to-end systems and deep neural networks (DNN), has led to significant accuracy improvements [15]. Explorations into feature fusion techniques integrating acoustic and lexical domains [16], breakthroughs like the RNN-ELM model addressing long-range context effects [17], and the preference for features like logarithmic Mel-frequency cepstral coefficients (logMel), MFCC, and extended Geneva Minimalistic Acoustic Parameter Set (eGeMAPS) over prosodic features [18] underscore the evolving landscape. The convolutional recurrent neural network for end-to-end emotion prediction from speech [19] and recent studies focusing on deep learning approaches utilizing spectrograms [20–27], including models with convolutional neural networks (CNNs) and long short-term memory (LSTM) networks, have demonstrated enhanced accuracy [21]. Ensemble models incorporating bagging and boosting techniques with support vector machines (SVMs) showcased significant accuracy gains [28].

Optimization algorithms for feature selection in SER, such as Cat Swarm Optimization (CSO), Grey Wolf Optimizer, and Enhanced Cat Swarm Optimization (ECSO), have shown promise in enhancing classification accuracy and reducing selected features [29,30]. The Whale-Imperialist Optimization algorithm (Whale-IpCA) introduced multiple support vector neural network (Multi-SVNN) classifiers for emotion identification [31], while feature selection methods employing metaheuristic search algorithms like Cuckoo Search and Non-dominated Sorting Genetic Algorithm-II (NSGA-II) demonstrated effective emotion classification with reduced features [32]. Comprehensive speech emotion recognition systems leverage diverse machine learning algorithms, including recurrent neural networks (RNNs), SVMs, and multivariate linear regression (MLR) [33]. Innovative feature selection approaches, such as the combination of Golden Ratio Optimization (GRO) and Equilibrium Optimization (EO) algorithms, have been explored [34–36].

Advanced architectures like dual-channel Long Short-Term Memory (LSTM) compressed capsule networks have been proposed for improved emotion recognition [37]. Furthermore, clustering-based Genetic Algorithm (GA) optimization techniques have been utilized to enhance feature sets for SER [38]. Recent research has also investigated the effectiveness of weighted binary Cuckoo Search algorithms for feature selection and emotion recognition from speech [39]. Moreover, the application of wavelet transform in SER has been explored for its potential in capturing relevant emotional features [40]. Ensemble methods like Bagged Support Vector Machines (SVMs) have shown promise in achieving robust emotion recognition from speech signals [41]. Convolutional Neural Networks (CNNs) have been employed to extract salient features for SER, leveraging their capability to capture hierarchical representations [42].

Additionally, novel methods for feature selection in SER, such as a hybrid metaheuristic approach combining Golden Ratio and Equilibrium Optimization algorithms, have been proposed [43]. Recent studies have explored the application of modulation spectral features for emotion recognition using deep neural networks [44]. Transfer learning frameworks, like EmoNet, have been developed to leverage multi-corpus data for improved SER performance [45–47]. Feature pooling techniques for modulation spectrum features have also been investigated to enhance SER accuracy, particularly in real-world scenarios [48,49].

3. Dataset

This study uses four different datasets, namely the Ryerson Audio-Visual Database of Emotional Speech and Song (RAVDESS), Toronto Emotional Speech Set (TESS), Emotional Database (EmoDB), and Surrey Audio-Visual Expressed Emotion (SAVEE). Details of the dataset and their limitations can be seen in Tables 1 and 2 respectively.

Table 1. The datasets used and their details.

Dataset	Description
RAVDESS	The Ryerson Audio-Visual Database of Emotional Speech and Song (RAVDESS) is a publicly available dataset designed for affective computing and emotion recognition research. It contains audio and video recordings of 24 actors performing eight different emotions in both speech and song. The dataset provides a diverse set of emotional expressions for study and is widely used in emotion recognition research.
TESS	The Toronto Emotional Speech Set (TESS) is a comprehensive and publicly available collection of 2803 audio recordings, featuring professional actors portraying seven distinct emotional categories. The dataset includes balanced representation from both male and female actors, making it valuable for developing and evaluating emotion recognition models.
SAVEE	The Surrey Audio-Visual Expressed Emotion (SAVEE) dataset is designed for research into speech emotion recognition, featuring 480 audio recordings with a single male actor portraying seven emotional states. The dataset provides a standardized resource for studying emotional speech and has been widely used in affective computing research.
EmoDB	The Emotional Database (EmoDB) is utilized for studying emotional speech recognition and consists of recordings from ten professional German actors portraying different emotions. The dataset, developed by the Technical University of Berlin, is valuable for developing and evaluating algorithms for automatic emotion classification from speech signals.

Table 2. Observations and considerations about datasets used.

Observations	Dataset-Specific Observations
Limited Actor Diversity	RAVDESS: 24 actors may not fully represent diverse vocal characteristics. SAVEE: Only four male actors may limit diversity and variability. EmoDB: Ten actors may not fully capture wide-ranging vocal characteristics.
Imbalanced Emotional Classes	RAVDESS, SAVEE, EmoDB: Some emotions have fewer instances, impacting model performance.
Controlled Recording Conditions	RAVDESS, SAVEE, EmoDB: Recordings in controlled studios lack natural variability, affecting generalizability to real-world scenarios.
Limited Contextual Information	RAVDESS, SAVEE, EmoDB: A lack of contextual cues in datasets may limit the applicability to real-world scenarios influenced by various factors.
Limited Language Representation	RAVDESS: Primarily English, limiting cross-lingual applications. EmoDB: Primarily German, affecting cross-lingual usability.
Limited Emotional Variability	SAVEE: Four basic emotions may restrict generalizability. EmoDB: Seven discrete emotions may not cover the full spectrum of human emotional experiences.
TESS Advantages	Diverse emotional expressions, large number of actors, naturalistic recording conditions, high-quality recordings, detailed metadata, and multimodal data: the TESS dataset stands out for its richness, naturalness, and comprehensive features, contributing to its reliability and robustness in emotional speech analysis.

Despite limitations in some datasets, they remain valuable for emotional speech analysis research. The TESS dataset, in particular, excels due to its diverse emotional expressions, large actor pool, natural recording conditions, high-quality data, detailed metadata, and multimodal features, making it a robust resource in emotional speech analysis research. Researchers should be aware of dataset-specific considerations when interpreting results and generalizing findings beyond a dataset's scope.

4. Experimental Setup

The experimental setup entails the development and evaluation of a recurrent neural network (RNN) with long short-term memory (LSTM) architecture for emotion recognition using audio datasets. Inspired by [20] work on CNNs for environmental sound recognition, this study extends their approach to emotion recognition. The LSTM model, comprising four LSTM layers, a dropout layer, and a dense layer, aims to effectively identify speech sections with relevant information. Additionally, the study introduces the Gray Wolf Optimizer (GWO) requiring optimization. In terms of model architecture, the CNN-LSTM ensemble incorporates both convolutional and recurrent layers to capture spatial and temporal dependencies in the audio data. Convolutional layers extract relevant features from the raw audio waveforms, while LSTM layers process sequences of features over time. Meanwhile, the SVM serves as a traditional yet robust classifier for emotion recognition tasks, leveraging its ability to find the optimal hyperplane to separate different emotion classes in the feature space.

Furthermore, the methodology unfolds in three main stages: feature extraction, feature selection (using GWO), and classification. Feature extraction involves extracting meaningful representations from the raw audio waveforms, such as Mel-frequency cepstral coefficients (MFCCs) or logMel features, to capture acoustic characteristics related to different emotions. Feature selection using GWO aims to identify the most discriminative features for emotion recognition, enhancing the model's performance. Subsequently, the selected features are fed into the classification stage, where SVM and CNNs handle the task of classifying emotions based on the extracted features. Specifically, GWO-SVM, GWO-CNN, and GWO-LSTM approaches are explored, each involving initialization, evaluation, updating the GWO population, and a stopping criterion. Key components include solution representation and fitness function, crucial for feature selection optimization. This comprehensive approach leverages both traditional and deep learning techniques, along with optimization algorithms, to optimize emotion recognition performance.

The GWO optimizer was introduced by Seyedali Mirjalili and Seyed Mohammad Mirjalili in 2014 [50]. GWO mimics wolf hunting strategies to solve optimization problems. It maintains a population of alpha, beta, delta, and omega wolves, updating their positions iteratively based on fitness and social interactions. GWO efficiently explores and exploits the search space through equations simulating hunting behavior. The methodology involves three steps: feature extraction, feature selection, and classification. Figure 1 displays the architecture of the conventional RNN-LSTM model for feature extraction and classification.

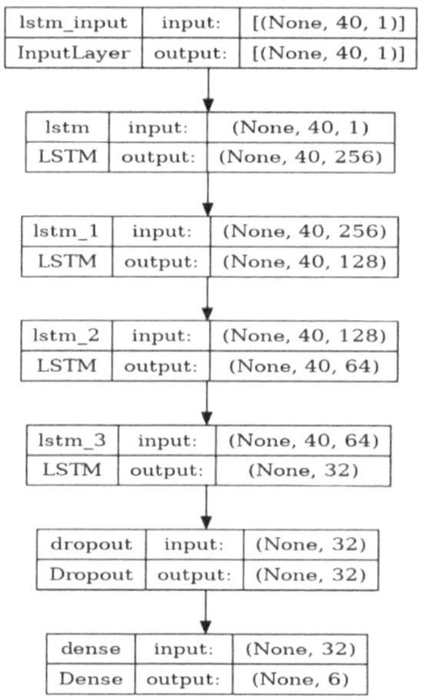

Figure 1. RNN-LSTM architecture.

GWO adapts as a feature selection method to identify crucial emotional features. Support vector machines (SVM) and convolutional neural networks (CNNs) handle the classification task. GWO-SVM, GWO-CNN, and GWO-LSTM approaches involve initializing, evaluating, and updating the GWO population and the stopping criterion. Key components include solution representation and fitness function, crucial for feature selection optimization.

This streamlined research methodology leverages GWO to optimize emotion feature selection, demonstrating its adaptability with SVM and CNNs to provide accurate classification. Figure 2 gives and abstract overview of proposed research.

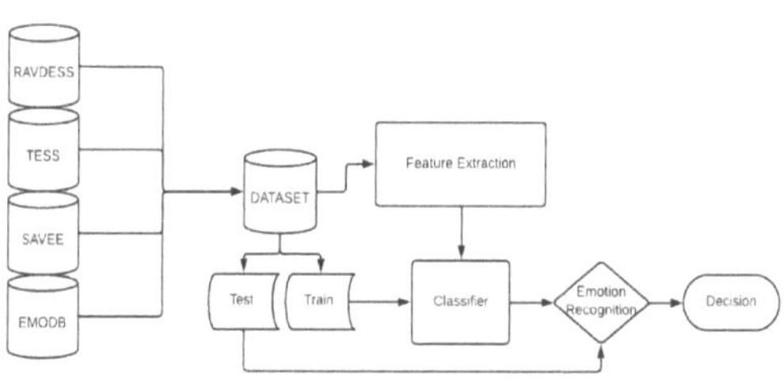

Figure 2. Methodology.

4.1. Social Hierarchy

In the social structure of gray wolves, a cohesive cultural dominance system is observed, comprising four distinct categories: alpha, beta, delta, and omega. The alpha, occupying the highest position, serves as the dominant authority and demonstrates superior intelligence in pack management. Assisting the alpha are the beta wolves, who play decision-making roles at the second level of the social order. The omega wolves make up the majority of the pack and are positioned at the lowest tier. Although not explicitly mentioned in the hierarchy levels, the delta wolves follow the beta wolves and function as leaders among the omega-level members. In the context of GWO solutions, they are classified based on the grey wolf social order, with the alpha wolf considered the most fit, followed by the beta and delta wolves. Figure 3 provides a visual representation of the social hierarchy within a wolf pack.

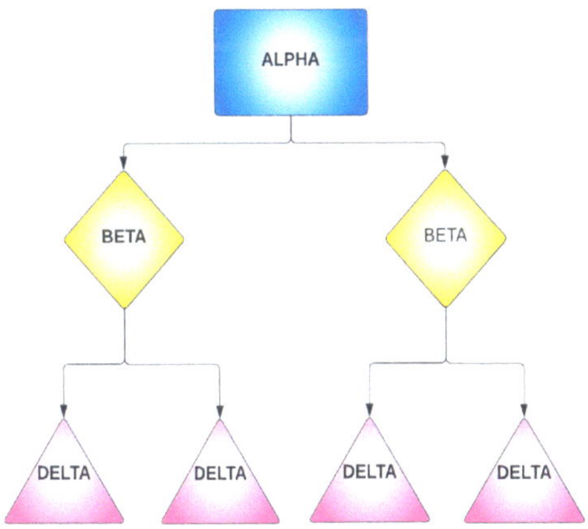

Figure 3. Social Hierarchy of the wolves within a pack.

4.2. Hunting Strategy

The hunting tactics utilized by a wolf pack entail a strategic process with three key stages: pursuit, encirclement, and assault. In the encirclement phase, a wolf exhibits the skill to tactically adjust its position, skillfully surrounding the prey within a defined area. This encircling behavior of gray wolves can be expressed mathematically as follows:

$$\mu = | v \times X'(i) - X(i) |, \tag{1}$$

$$X(i+1) - X'(i) - \eta \times \mu, \tag{2}$$

where η and v represent two controlling factors, X' represents the prey's location, X denotes the wolf's current location, and *i* indicates the present iteration. The values of the controllers η and v) are determined using the following calculations:

$$\eta = 2 \times \iota \times r_1 - \iota \tag{3}$$

$$v = 2 \times r_2 \tag{4}$$

where ι linearly decreases from 2 to 0 over the iterations, while the values r_1 and r_2 are random values within the range of [0, 1]. The range of the controller η is bounded by the interval $[-2\iota, 2\iota]$, which is determined by the value of ι.

4.3. Prey Search (Exploration)

The arrangement of alpha, beta, and delta wolves significantly influences the search behavior exhibited by other members of the pack as they pursue their prey. Throughout the prey search, the wolves disperse from one another and subsequently converge to encircle and launch an attack on their target. The wolves' dispersal is symbolized by the variable η, which assumes random values greater than 1 or less than −1, guiding the movement of search agents away from the prey's location. This process is designed to ensure thorough exploration and enhance the GWO capacity for a comprehensive global search to attain the most optimal solution. In the GWO algorithm, the variable v governs the exploration phase, comprising random values between 0 and 2. This enables the random emphasis or de-emphasis of the prey's significance, contingent on whether v exceeds or is less than 1, respectively. Unlike η, v does not undergo linear diminishment. The utilization of random values in GWO serves to emphasize both exploitation and exploration, extending to the final iteration. This feature proves crucial in scenarios where search agents may risk being confined to local optima, particularly in the later stages of the search process.

The mathematical model for encircling the prey involves a linear deduction of the value of ι. The fluctuation range of η is reduced to a similar degree by the parameter ι. In situations where η consists of random values between 1 and −1, the location of the search agent can be updated to a position near the prey's location, facilitating a more focused exploitation of the prey. In situations where η consists of random values between 1 and −1, the location of the search agent can be updated to a position near the prey's location, facilitating a more focused exploitation of the prey.

5. Results and Discussion

In this study, Python serves as the programming language for implementing our methodologies. Our central objective revolves around the integration of the Grey Wolf Optimizer (GWO) to optimize emotion features, thereby enhancing emotion recognition performance. To validate the efficacy of our approach, we conduct experiments across four distinct emotion datasets: Emotion Database, RAVDESS, TESS, and SAVEE. Our evaluation metrics encompass classification accuracy, precision, recall, and F1-score, providing comprehensive insights into the effectiveness of the proposed methodology.

It can be seen from Table 3 that the GWO optimizer, when used with classifiers like SVM, LSTM, and CNN, surpasses the conventional classification methods on all evaluation metrics. In EmoDB, the traditional Kernalized SVM shows a classification accuracy of only 55%, which is the worst among the six models. The use of GWO improved accuracy to 85%. The difference in accuracy is an improvement of 30% for EmoDB and RAVDESS, whereas the precision doubled for EmoDB and RAVDESS and improved 7× for SAVEE, which is a huge jump from that of traditional SVM classifiers. While the use of CNNs is not as accurate as SVMs, the GWO technique managed to improve all the measurement parameters of CNN as well.

Figure 4a,b display the confusion matrix representing a set of emotions comprising six categories: anger, happiness, neutral, fear, disgust, and sadness for RAVDESS. The proposed model achieved an overall accuracy of 53% when evaluated using this particular emotion set and an accuracy of 60% when evaluated with the GWO technique. Upon analyzing the confusion matrix (Figure 4a,b), it becomes apparent that the accuracy rates for the fear and neutral classes are relatively high compared to those of the other classes. In contrast, the angry class exhibits a lower classification accuracy. Additionally, there is a significant misclassification of neutral as sad and disgust as happy. Despite the underperformance of the angry class, the proposed model demonstrated effective distinction among the other emotions within this emotion set. Figure 4b displays the classification after using GWO, which, as can be seen, lowers the misclassifications by a small degree.

Figure 4c,d display the confusion matrix representing a set of emotions comprising six categories: anger, happiness, neutral, fear, disgust, and sadness for SAVEE. The proposed model achieved an accuracy of 57% when evaluated using this particular emotion set and an accuracy of 68% when evaluated with the Gray Wolf Optimization technique. Upon analyzing the confusion matrix (Figure 4c,d), it becomes apparent that the accuracy rates for the angry class are relatively high compared to the other classes, whereas the fear class exhibits the lowest classification accuracy. Despite the underperformance of all the classes, the proposed model demonstrated effective distinction among the other emotions within this emotion set. Figure 4d displays classification after using GWO, which, as can be seen, reduces the incidence of misclassifications by a small degree.

Figure 4e,f display the confusion matrix representing a set of emotions comprising six categories: anger, happiness, neutral, fear, disgust, and sadness for EmoDB. The proposed model achieved an overall accuracy of 75% when evaluated using this particular emotion set and an accuracy of 78% when evaluated with the Gray Wolf Optimization technique. Upon analyzing the confusion matrix, it becomes apparent that the accuracy rates for the disgust class are relatively high compared to the other classes, whereas the fear class exhibits a lower classification accuracy. The fear class is rarely classified accurately and is the lowest correctly identified class. Figure 4f shows the classification after using GWO, which, as can be seen, lowers the misclassifications by a small degree.

Table 3. Classification Performance of 6 classifiers on the four datasets.

Datasets	Measurements	Without GWO Optimizer SVM	K-SVM	CNN	LSTM	GWO Optimizer SVM	K-SVM	CNN	LSTM
EmoDB	Accuracy	0.74	0.55	0.75	0.76	0.85	0.85	0.78	0.83
	Precision	0.71	0.42	0.74	0.73	0.82	0.87	0.77	0.82
	Recall	0.70	0.45	0.69	0.71	0.82	0.84	0.77	0.87
	F1-Score	0.70	0.39	0.71	0.71	0.82	0.84	0.77	0.84
RAVDESS	Accuracy	0.74	0.55	0.53	0.73	0.85	0.87	0.60	0.73
	Precision	0.71	0.42	0.53	0.73	0.84	0.88	0.59	0.69
	Recall	0.70	0.45	0.52	0.82	0.83	0.85	0.56	0.71
	F1-Score	0.70	0.39	0.52	0.76	0.83	0.86	0.59	0.71
SAVEE	Accuracy	0.54	.35	0.57	0.62	0.76	0.75	0.68	0.71
	Precision	0.53	0.10	0.59	0.53	0.74	0.72	0.66	0.59
	Recall	0.51	0.25	0.51	0.57	0.75	0.68	0.64	0.72
	F1-Score	0.52	0.15	0.53	0.59	0.73	0.68	0.64	0.71
TESS	Accuracy	0.98	0.91	0.99	0.97	0.99	0.99	0.99	0.99
	Precision	0.98	0.93	0.99	0.96	0.99	0.99	0.99	0.99
	Recall	0.98	0.91	0.99	0.95	0.99	0.99	0.99	0.99
	F1-Score	0.98	0.91	0.99	0.96	0.99	0.99	0.99	0.99

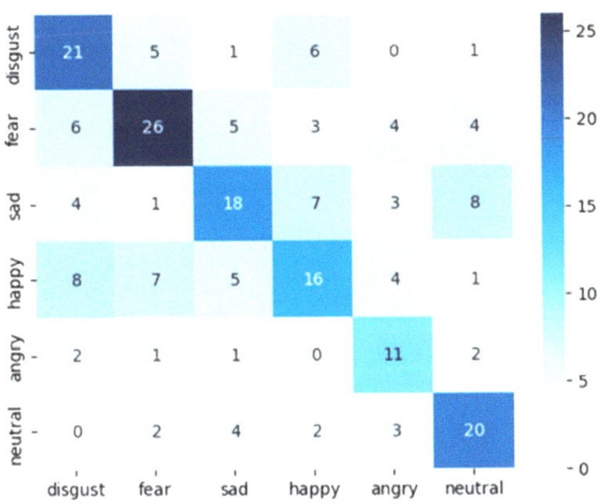

(**a**) Confusion Matrix for RAVDESS CNN

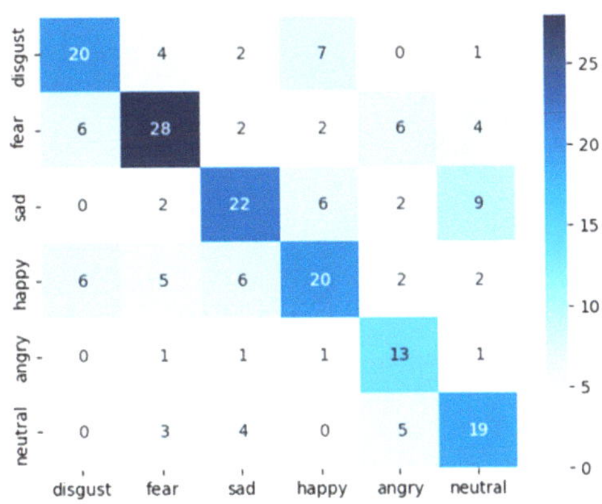

(**b**) Confusion Matrix for RAVDESS GWO-CNN

Figure 4. *Cont.*

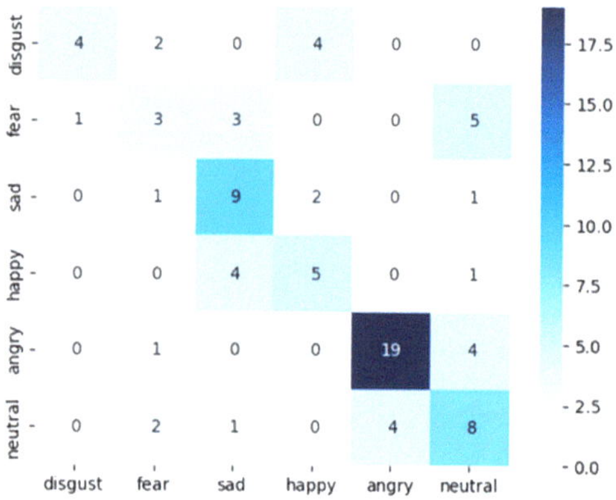

(**c**) Confusion Matrix for SAVEE CNN

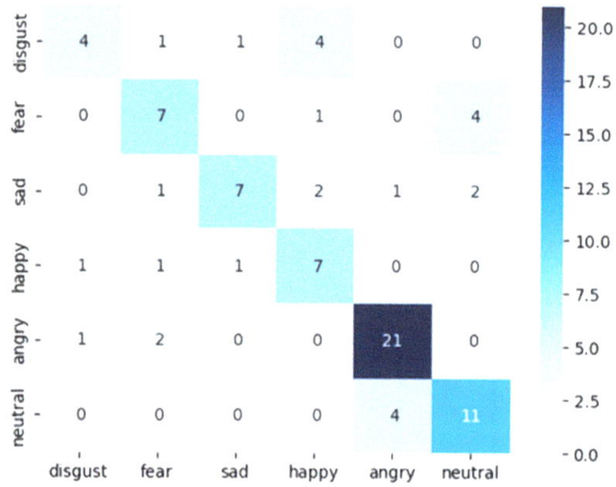

(**d**) Confusion Matrix for SAVEE GWO-CNN

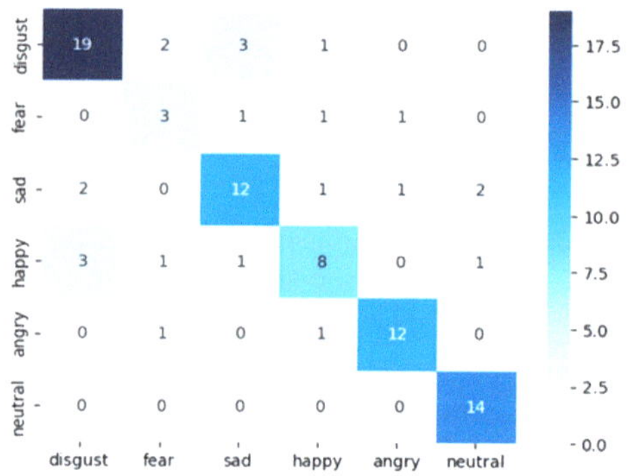

(**e**) Confusion Matrix for EmoDB-CNN

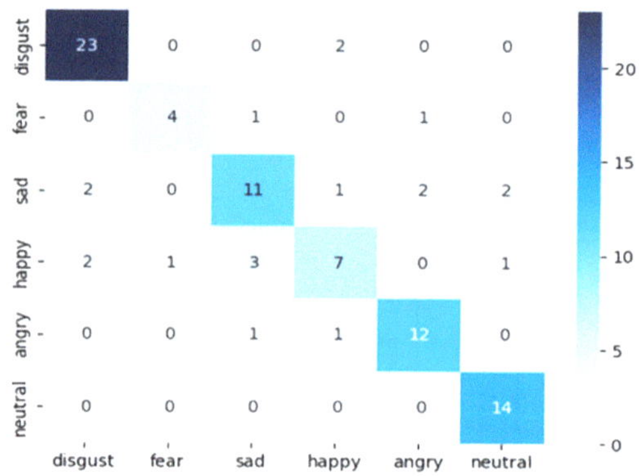

(**f**) Confusion Matrix for EmoDB GWO-CNN

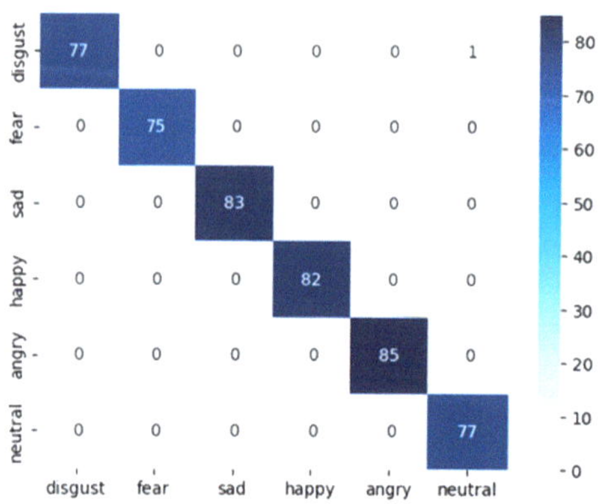

(**g**) Confusion Matrix for TESS CNN

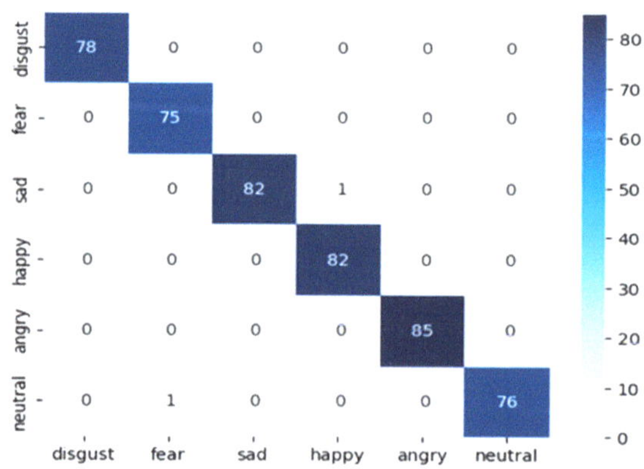

(**h**) Confusion Matrix for TESS GWO-CNN

Figure 4. The confusion matrix of GWO-CNN and CNN model was tested on four datasets—RAVDESS, SAVEE, TESS, and EMODB.

Figure 4g,h display the confusion matrix, representing a set of emotions comprising six categories: anger, happiness, neutral, fear, disgust, and sadness for TESS. The proposed model achieved an overall accuracy of 99% when evaluated using this particular emotion set and an accuracy of 100% when evaluated with the Gray Wolf Optimization technique. The TESS data are highly recommendable for speech emotion recognition as all the emotions are accurately classified by our model as well. The TESS dataset does not need Gray Wolf Optimization since it is already good enough to be used for accurate emotion classification via traditional methods.

In Figure 5a, the horizontal axis represents the number of epochs, and the vertical axis represents the accuracy and the validation accuracy through training. The accuracy peaks at nearly 90% once, while the validation accuracy rises with it to around 70% and then flattens. The model was set to train for 100 epochs with an Early Stopping Callback. This stopped the training at 61 epochs, denoting that training the model will no longer improve the results. As visible in Figure 5b, the horizontal axis represents the number of epochs, and the vertical axis represents the loss and the validation loss through training. The loss is relatively high at the beginning of training but decreases gradually. After a while, the validation loss starts to saturate and does not fall below the 0.11 mark. As visible in Figure 5c, the accuracy is relatively low at the beginning of training, but it increases gradually. The accuracy peaks at nearly 99% once, while the validation accuracy rises slower than that. The model was set to train for 100 epochs with an Early Stopping Callback. This stopped the training at 67 epochs, denoting that training the model will no longer improve the results. The testing accuracy is only 53%. As visible in Figure 5d, the x-axis represents the number of epochs, and the y-axis represents the loss and the validation loss through training. It is evident that the validation loss does not decrease and instead fluctuates between 0.14 and 0.12 at all times. This is why the testing accuracy and the validation accuracy are very low.

In Figure 5e, the horizontal axis represents the number of epochs, and the vertical axis represents the accuracy and the validation accuracy through training. The training accuracy climbs rapidly, whereas the callback stops the network after 56 epochs because further training will not yield useful results and will only result in overtraining. This is because the validation loss does not decrease. The model cannot accurately distinguish the emotions in the testing phase, and the validation loss always stays between 0.11 and 0.09.

Figure 5g shows the accuracy graph for the TESS dataset. There is again an exception to note, namely that the TESS dataset being balanced and great for SER produces excellent results. The accuracy climbs to greater than 95% within the first five epochs and then saturates around the 99% mark, ranging from 99.1% to 99.73% on training and validation. This is shown in the loss graph (Figure 5h) as well, which shows the loss nearing 0.01 as the epochs progress. The TESS dataset exhibits the highest values in all the parameters measured, with an average value of 99% in F1-score, precision, recall, and accuracy.

Table 4 shows a comparison of the proposed model with the existing studies conducted for the respective datasets. It can be seen that our proposed method outperforms the existing methods by good margins. Since TESS is a dataset that often displays an accuracy greater than 99%, there are not many comparisons for it. That is why RAVDESS, SAVEE, and EmoDB were given more emphasis during research and comparison. The average accuracy for the RAVDESS dataset lies between 60–75%, whereas our model achieved an accuracy of 87% with GWO optimization. The CNN and LSTM, however, underperformed for both RAVDESS and SAVEE datasets without the GWO optimizer. The GWO-SVM beat the traditional DNN frameworks and existing SVM models.

Table 4. Comparison with existing studies.

Reference	Dataset	Classifier Used	Accuracy
Bhavan et al. [44]	RAVDESS	Bagged ensemble of SVMs	75.69%
Zeng et al. [42]	RAVDESS	DNNs	64.52%
Shegokar and Sircar [43]	RAVDESS	SVMs	60.1%

Table 4. *Cont.*

Reference	Dataset	Classifier Used	Accuracy
This Work (Proposed Method)	SAVEE	GWO-SVM GWO-CNN	75% 65.47%
This Work (Proposed Method)	EmoDB	GWO-SVM GWO-CNN	85% 78%
This Work (Proposed Method)	TESS	GWO-SVM GWO-CNN	99.97% 99.93%

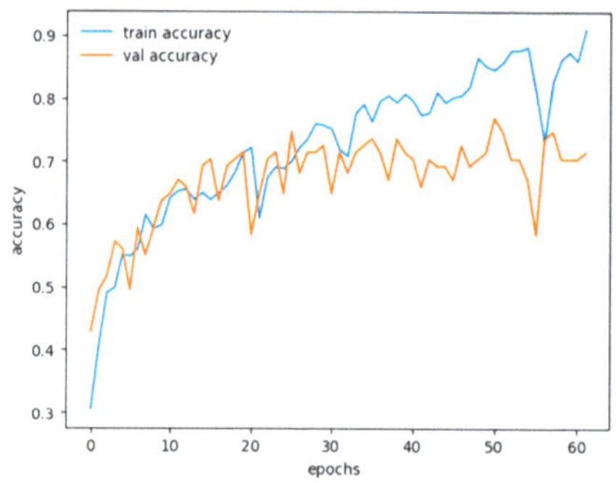

(**a**) Accuracy vs. Epochs for EmoDB

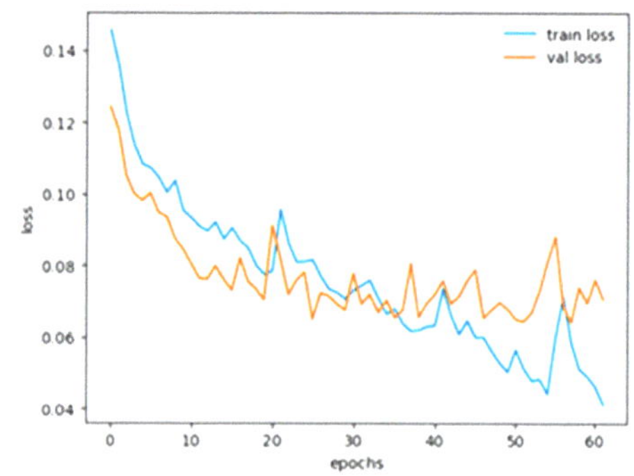

(**b**) Loss vs. Epochs for EmoDB

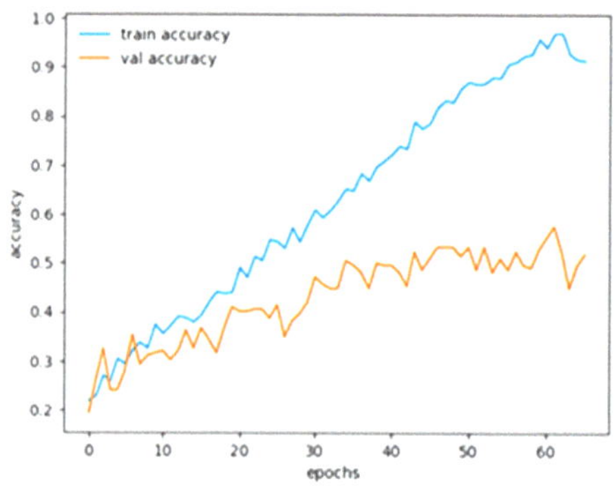

(**c**) Accuracy vs. Epochs for RAVDESS

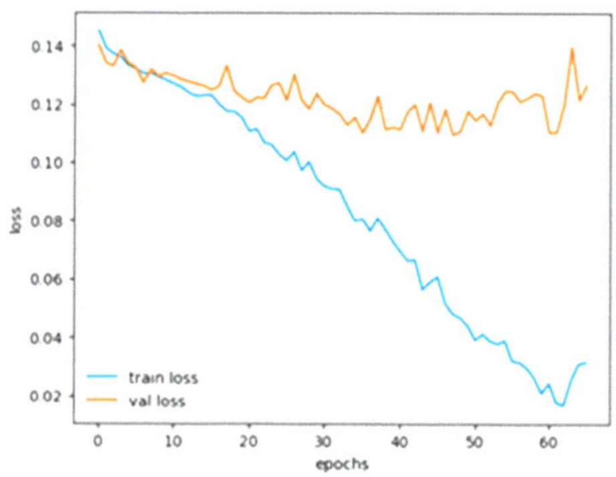

(**d**) Loss vs. Epochs for RAVDESS

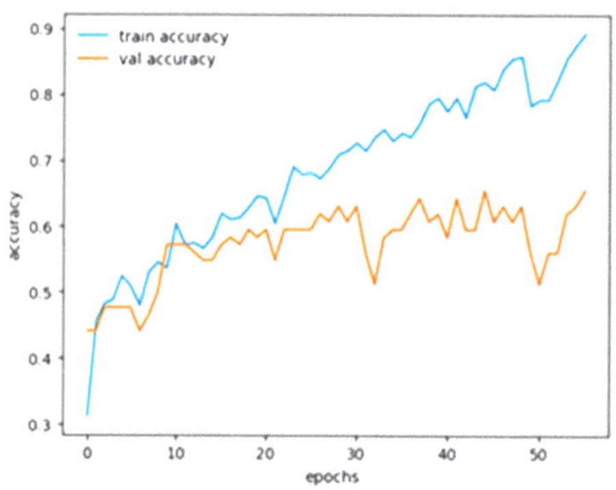

(**e**) Accuracy vs. Epochs for SAVEE

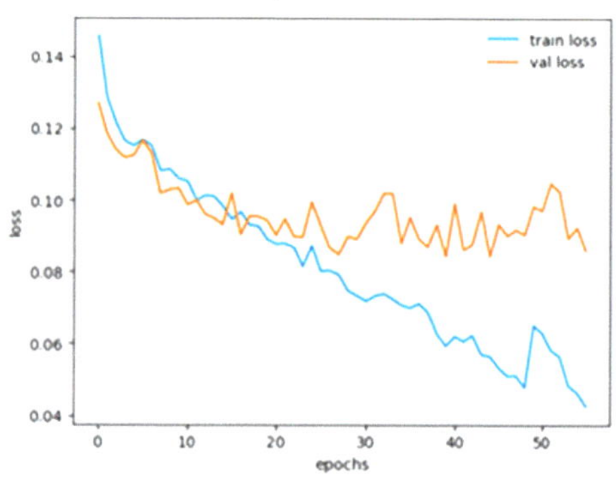

(**f**) Loss vs. Epochs for SAVEE

Figure 5. *Cont.*

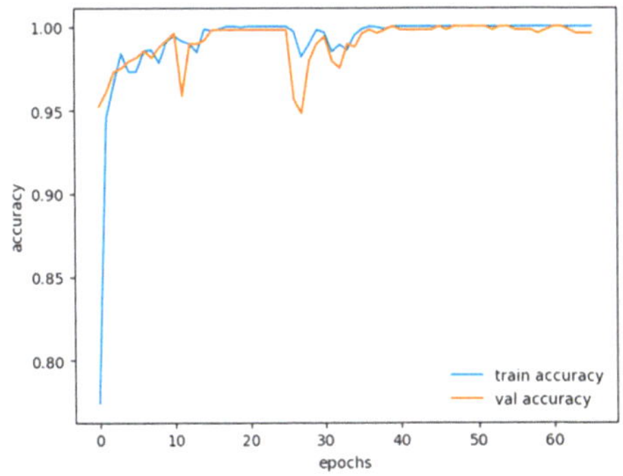

(**g**) Accuracy vs. Epochs for TESS

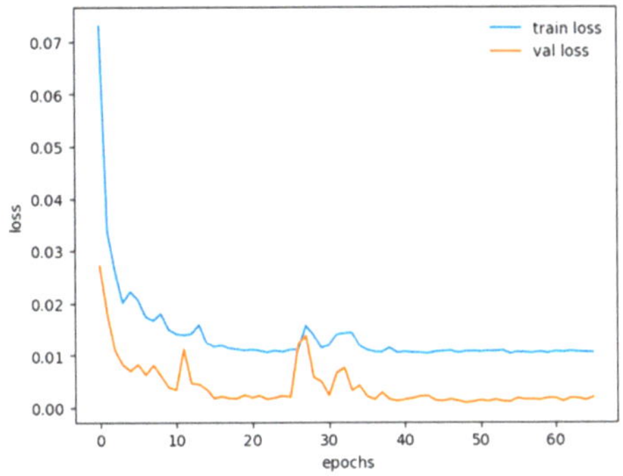

(**h**) Loss vs. Epochs for TESS

Figure 5. The accuracy and loss by epochs on four different datasets—RAVDESS, SAVEE, TESS, and EMODB, they should be listed as: (5 (**a**–**h**)).

6. Conclusions and Future Work

In this research study, a deep learning model was introduced for speech emotion recognition. The effectiveness of the proposed model was assessed using four datasets: EmoDB, RAVDESS, TESS, and SAVEE. The experimental findings demonstrated that the proposed model achieved better results with GWO, irrespective of the model used on the four datasets. The evaluations revealed that the results obtained were comparable to the accuracy of other convolutional neural networks (CNNs) utilizing spectrogram features. Consequently, it can be concluded that the proposed approach is highly suitable for emotion recognition.

It is recommended to evaluate the proposed approach further using additional emotion datasets. Additionally, the proposed model can be enhanced by utilizing large datasets to improve the recognition of all emotions. Another solution to increase the accuracy of the model could be to combine all four datasets present and extract common emotions from them. This will result in a more balanced dataset that will show promising results based on overall SER instead of individual datasets, with constraints being used for the same objective.

In the future, human assistance will no longer be necessary for speech recognition tasks as they transition into automated processes. Voice recognition is likely to become a seamless and automatic function. It would not be surprising if we are eventually all carrying earpieces like C-3PO that listen to our conversations. Ongoing research and development in deep learning are expanding the possibilities of speech recognition. Exciting advancements are being made, including the utilization of neural networks to analyze sound patterns, resulting in improved artificial intelligence algorithms. Speech recognition, a subset of deep learning, has been a subject of study for over five decades. Presently, speech recognition systems exhibit higher accuracy levels than ever before. The future holds even more promise for speech recognition as deep learning techniques enable training models on larger datasets and utilize increased computing power, enhancing the algorithms' data processing capabilities.

Author Contributions: Conceptualization, S.T.; methodology, S.T.; software, S.T.; validation, S.T. and S.S.; formal analysis, S.T.; writing—original draft preparation, S.T.; writing—review and editing, S.S.; visualization, S.T.; supervision, S.S. All authors have read and agreed to the published version of the manuscript.

Funding: This research received no external funding.

Data Availability Statement: Publicly available datasets were analyzed in this study. The datasets RAVDESS, TESS, SAVEE, and EmoDB might be available on Kaggle (https://www.kaggle.com) (5 November 2023).

Acknowledgments: The authors would like to thank the "Doctoral School of Applied Informatics and Applied Mathematics" and the "High Performance Computing Research Group" of Óbuda University for their valuable support. The authors would like to thank NVIDIA Corporation for providing graphics hardware for the experiments.

Conflicts of Interest: The authors declare no conflicts of interest.

References

1. Banse, R.; Scherer, K.R. Acoustic profiles in vocal emotion expression. *J. Personal. Soc. Psychol.* **1996**, *70*, 614–634. [CrossRef]
2. Mustafa, M.B.; Yusoof, A.M.; Don, Z.M.; Malekzadeh, M. Speech emotion recognition research: An analysis of research focus. *Int. J. Speech Technol.* **2018**, *21*, 137–156. [CrossRef]
3. Schuller, B.; Rigoll, G.; Lang, M. Hidden markov model-based speech emotion recognition. In Proceedings of the 2003 IEEE International Conference on Acoustics, Speech and Signal Processing (ICASSP), Hong Kong, China, 6–10 April 2003; Volume 2, p. II-1.
4. Hu, H.; Xu, M.-X.; Wu, W. GMM supervector based SVM with spectral features for speech emotion recognition. In Proceedings of the 2007 IEEE International Conference on Acoustics, Speech and Signal Processing (ICASSP), Honolulu, HI, USA, 15–20 April 2007; Volume 4, pp. IV-413–IV-416.
5. Lee, C.; Mower, E.; Busso, C.; Lee, S.; Narayanan, S. Emotion recognition using a hierarchical binary decision tree approach. *Speech Commun.* **2009**, *4*, 320–323.
6. Kim, Y.; Mower, E. Provost, Emotion classification via utterance level dynamics: A pattern-based approach to characterizing affective expressions. In Proceedings of the 2013 IEEE International Conference on Acoustics, Speech and Signal Processing (ICASSP), Vancouver, BC, Canada, 26–31 May 2013.
7. Eyben, F.; Wollmer, M.; Schuller, B. Openear—Introducing the munich open-source emotion and affect recognition toolkit. In Proceedings of the 2009 3rd International Conference on Affective Computing and Intelligent Interaction (ACII), Amsterdam, The Netherlands, 10–12 September 2009; pp. 1–6.
8. Mower, E.; Mataric, M.J.; Narayanan, S. A framework for automatic human emotion classification using emotion profiles. *IEEE Trans. Audio Speech Lang. Process.* **2011**, *19*, 1057–1070. [CrossRef]
9. Han, K.; Yu, D.; Tashev, I. Speech emotion recognition using deep neural network and extreme learning machine. In Proceedings of the INTERSPEECH 2014, Singapore, 7–10 September 2014; pp. 223–227.
10. Jin, Q.; Li, C.; Chen, S.; Wu, H. Speech emotion recognition with acoustic and lexical features. In Proceedings of the 2015 IEEE International Conference on Acoustics, Speech and Signal Processing (ICASSP), South Brisbane, QLD, Australia, 19–24 April 2015; pp. 4749–4753.
11. Lee, J.; Tashev, I. High-level feature representation using recurrent neural network for speech emotion recognition. In Proceedings of the INTERSPEECH 2015, Dresden, Germany, 6–10 September 2015; pp. 223–227.
12. Neumann, M.; Vu, N.T. Attentive convolutional neural network based speech emotion recognition: A study on the impact of input features, signal length, and acted speech. In Proceedings of the INTERSPEECH 2017, Stockholm, Sweden, 20–24 August 2017; pp. 1263–1267.
13. Trigeorgis, G.; Ringeval, F.; Brueckner, R.; Marchi, E.; Nicolaou, M.A.; Zafeiriou, S.; Schuller, B. Adieu features? End-to-end speech emotion recognition using a deep convolutional recurrent network. In Proceedings of the 2016 IEEE International Conference on Acoustics, Speech and Signal Processing (ICASSP), Shanghai, China, 20–25 March 2016; pp. 5200–5204.
14. Lim, W.; Jang, D.; Lee, T. Speech emotion recognition using convolutional and recurrent neural networks. In Proceedings of the 2016 Asia-Pacific Signal and Information Processing Association Annual Summit and Conference (APSIPA), Jeju, Republic of Korea, 13–16 December 2016; pp. 1–4.
15. Mirsamadi, S.; Barsoum, E.; Zhang, C. Automatic speech emotion recognition using recurrent neural networks with local attention. In Proceedings of the 2017 IEEE International Conference on Acoustics, Speech and Signal Processing (ICASSP), New Orleans, LA, USA, 5–9 March 2017; pp. 2227–2231.
16. Satt, A.; Rozenberg, S.; Hoory, R. Efficient emotion recognition from speech using deep learning on spectrograms. In Proceedings of the INTERSPEECH 2017, Stockholm, Sweden, 20–24 August 2017; pp. 1089–1093.
17. Ma, X.; Wu, Z.; Jia, J.; Xu, M.; Meng, H.; Cai, L. Emotion recognition from variable-length speech segments using deep learning on spectrograms. In Proceedings of the INTERSPEECH 2018, Hyderabad, India, 2–6 September 2018; pp. 3683–3687.
18. Yenigalla, P.; Kumar, A.; Tripathi, S.; Singh, C.; Kar, S.; Vepa, P. Speech emotion recognition using spectrogram phoneme embedding. In Proceedings of the INTERSPEECH 2018, Hyderabad, India, 2–6 September 2018; pp. 3688–3692.
19. Guo, L.; Wang, L.; Dang, J.; Zhang, L.; Guan, H. A feature fusion method based on extreme learning machine for speech emotion recognition. In Proceedings of the 2018 IEEE International Conference on Acoustics, Speech and Signal Processing (ICASSP), Calgary, AB, Canada, 15–20 April 2018; pp. 2666–2670.

20. Dai, W.; Dai, C.; Qu, S.; Li, J.; Das, S. Very deep convolutional neural networks for raw waveforms. In Proceedings of the 2017 IEEE International Conference on Acoustics, Speech and Signal Processing (ICASSP), New Orleans, LA, USA, 5–9 March 2017; pp. 421–425.
21. Burkhardt, F.; Paeschke, A.; Rolfes, M.; Sendlmeier, W.F.; Weiss, B. A database of German emotional speech. In Proceedings of the INTERSPEECH 2005, Libon, Portugal, 4–8 September 2005; pp. 1517–1520.
22. Busso, C.; Bulut, M.; Lee, C.-C.; Kazemzadeh, A.; Mower, E.; Kim, S.; Chang, J.N.; Lee, S.; Narayanan, S.S. IEMOCAP: Interactive emotional dyadic motion capture database. *Lang. Resour. Eval.* **2008**, *42*, 335–359. [CrossRef]
23. Shao, S.; Saleem, A.; Salim, H.; Pratik, S.; Sonia, S.; Abdessamad, M. AI-based Arabic Language and Speech Tutor. In Proceedings of the 2022 IEEE/ACS 19th International Conference on Computer Systems and Applications (AICCSA), Abu Dhabi, United Arab Emirates, 5–8 December 2022; IEEE: Piscataway, NJ, USA, 2022; pp. 1–8.
24. Wang, J.; Xue, M.; Culhane, R.; Diao, E.; Ding, J.; Tarokh, V. Speech emotion recognition with dual-sequence LSTM architecture. In Proceedings of the ICASSP 2020—2020 IEEE International Conference on Acoustics, Speech and Signal Processing (ICASSP), Barcelona, Spain, 4–8 May 2020; IEEE: Piscataway, NJ, USA, 2020; pp. 6474–6478.
25. Chernykh, V.; Sterling, G.; Prihodko, P. Emotion recognition from speech with recurrent neural networks. *arXiv* **2017**, arXiv:1701.08071.
26. Sathiyabhama, B.; Kumar, S.U.; Jayanthi, J.; Sathiya, T.; Ilavarasi, A.K.; Yuvarajan, V.; Gopikrishna, K. A novel feature selection framework based on grey wolf optimizer for mammogram image analysis. *Neural Comput. Appl.* **2021**, *33*, 14583–14602. [CrossRef]
27. Sreedharan, N.P.N.; Ganesan, B.; Raveendran, R.; Sarala, P.; Dennis, B.; Boothalingam, R.R. Grey wolf optimisation-based feature selection and classification for facial emotion recognition. *IET Biom.* **2018**, *7*, 490–499. [CrossRef]
28. Dey, A.; Chattopadhyay, S.; Singh, P.K.; Ahmadian, A.; Ferrara, M.; Sarkar, R. A hybrid meta-heuristic feature selection method using golden ratio and equilibrium optimization algorithms for speech emotion recognition. *IEEE Access* **2020**, *8*, 200953–200970. [CrossRef]
29. Shetty, S.; Hegde, S. Automatic classification of carnatic music instruments using MFCC and LPC. In *Data Management, Analytics and Innovation*; Springer: Berlin/Heidelberg, Germany, 2020; pp. 463–474.
30. Saldanha, J.C.; Suvarna, M. Perceptual linear prediction feature as an indicator of dysphonia. In *Advances in Control Instrumentation Systems*; Springer: Berlin/Heidelberg, Germany, 2020; pp. 51–64.
31. Mannepalli, K.; Sastry, P.N.; Suman, M. Emotion recognition in speech signals using optimization based multi-SVNN classifier. *J. King Saud Univ.-Comput. Inf. Sci.* **2018**, *34*, 384–397. [CrossRef]
32. Yildirim, S.; Kaya, Y.; Kılıç, F. A modified feature selection method based on metaheuristic algorithms for speech emotion recognition. *Appl. Acoust.* **2021**, *173*, 107721. [CrossRef]
33. Kerkeni, L.; Serrestou, Y.; Mbarki, M.; Raoof, K.; Mahjoub, M.A.; Cleder, C. Automatic speech emotion recognition using machine learning. In *Social Media and Machine Learning*; IntechOpen: London, UK, 2019.
34. Shen, P.; Changjun, Z.; Chen, X. Automatic speech emotion recognition using support vector machine. In Proceedings of the 2011 International Conference on Electronic & Mechanical Engineering and Information Technology, Harbin, China, 12–14 August 2011; IEEE: Piscataway, NJ, USA, 2011; Volume 2, pp. 621–625.
35. Issa, D.; Demirci, M.F.; Yazici, A. Speech emotion recognition with deep convolutional neural networks. *Biomed. Signal Process. Control* **2020**, *59*, 101894. [CrossRef]
36. Gomathy, M. Optimal feature selection for speech emotion recognition using enhanced cat swarm optimization algorithm. *Int. J. Speech Technol.* **2021**, *24*, 155–163. [CrossRef]
37. Daneshfar, F.; Kabudian, S.J. Speech emotion recognition using discriminative dimension reduction by employing a modified quantum-behaved particle swarm optimization algorithm. *Multimed. Tools Appl.* **2020**, *79*, 1261–1289. [CrossRef]
38. Shahin, I.; Hindawi, N.; Nassif, A.B.; Alhudhaif, A.; Polat, K. Novel dual-channel long short-term memory compressed capsule networks for emotion recognition. *Expert Syst. Appl.* **2022**, *188*, 116080. [CrossRef]
39. Kanwal, S.; Asghar, S. Speech emotion recognition using clustering based GA- optimized feature set. *IEEE Access* **2021**, *9*, 125830–125842. [CrossRef]
40. Zhang, Z. Speech feature selection and emotion recognition based on weighted binary cuckoo search. *Alex. Eng. J.* **2021**, *60*, 1499–1507. [CrossRef]
41. Wolpert, D.H. The lack of a priori distinctions between learning algorithms. *Neural Comput.* **1996**, *8*, 1341–1390. [CrossRef]
42. Zeng, Y.; Mao, H.; Peng, D.; Yi, Z. Spectrogram based multi-task audio classification. *Multimed. Tools Appl.* **2019**, *78*, 3705–3722. [CrossRef]
43. Shegokar, P.; Sircar, P. Continuous wavelet transform based speech emotion recognition. In Proceedings of the 2016 10th International Conference on Signal Processing and Communication Systems (ICSPCS), Surfers Paradise, QLD, Australia, 19–21 December 2016; IEEE: Piscataway, NJ, USA, 2016; pp. 1–8.
44. Bhavan, A.; Chauhan, P.; Shah, R.R.; Hitkul. Bagged support vector machines for emotion recognition from speech. *Knowl.-Based Syst.* **2019**, *184*, 104886. [CrossRef]
45. Mao, Q.; Dong, M.; Huang, Z.; Zhan, Y. Learning salient features for speech emotion recognition using convolutional neural networks. *IEEE Trans. Multimed.* **2014**, *16*, 2203–2213. [CrossRef]
46. Özseven, T. A novel feature selection method for speech emotion recognition. *Appl. Acoust.* **2019**, *146*, 320–326. [CrossRef]

47. Singh, P.; Sahidullah; Saha, G. Modulation spectral features for speech emotion recognition using deep neural networks. *Speech Commun.* **2023**, *146*, 53–69. [CrossRef]
48. Gerczuk, M.; Amiriparian, S.; Ottl, S.; Schuller, B.W. EmoNet: A transfer learning framework for multi-corpus speech emotion recognition. *IEEE Trans. Affect. Comput.* **2021**, *14*, 1472–1487. [CrossRef]
49. Avila, A.R.; Akhtar, Z.; Santos, J.F.; Oshaughnessy, D.; Falk, T.H. Feature pooling of modulation spectrum features for improved speech emotion recognition in the wild. *IEEE Trans. Affect. Comput.* **2021**, *12*, 177–188. [CrossRef]
50. Seyedali, M.; Mohammad, I.S.; Andrew, L. Grey Wolf Optimizer. *Adv. Eng. Softw.* **2014**, *69*, 46–61.

algorithms

MDPI

Article

CaAIS: Cellular Automata-Based Artificial Immune System for Dynamic Environments

Alireza Rezvanian [1,*], S. Mehdi Vahidipour [2] and Ali Mohammad Saghiri [3]

1 Department of Computer Engineering, University of Science and Culture, Tehran 1461968151, Iran
2 Computer Engineering Department, Faculty of Electrical and Computer Engineering, University of Kashan, Kashan 8731753153, Iran; vahidipour@kashanu.ac.ir
3 Department of Computer Science, William Paterson University, Wayne, NJ 07470, USA; saghiria@wpunj.edu
* Correspondence: rezvanian@usc.ac.ir

Abstract: Artificial immune systems (AIS), as nature-inspired algorithms, have been developed to solve various types of problems, ranging from machine learning to optimization. This paper proposes a novel hybrid model of AIS that incorporates cellular automata (CA), known as the cellular automata-based artificial immune system (CaAIS), specifically designed for dynamic optimization problems where the environment changes over time. In the proposed model, antibodies, representing nominal solutions, are distributed across a cellular grid that corresponds to the search space. These antibodies generate hyper-mutation clones at different times by interacting with neighboring cells in parallel, thereby producing different solutions. Through local interactions between neighboring cells, near-best parameters and near-optimal solutions are propagated throughout the search space. Iteratively, in each cell and in parallel, the most effective antibodies are retained as memory. In contrast, weak antibodies are removed and replaced with new antibodies until stopping criteria are met. The CaAIS combines cellular automata computational power with AIS optimization capability. To evaluate the CaAIS performance, several experiments have been conducted on the Moving Peaks Benchmark. These experiments consider different configurations such as neighborhood size and re-randomization of antibodies. The simulation results statistically demonstrate the superiority of the CaAIS over other artificial immune system algorithms in most cases, particularly in dynamic environments.

Keywords: artificial immune system; dynamic environment; dynamic optimization problem; hypermutation; cellular automata

1. Introduction

Real-world optimization problems often exhibit a dynamic nature, which leads to their modeling as Dynamic Optimization Problems (DOPs). In such problems, a model's parameters change over time due to the changing environment. Thus, finding an optimal solution is challenging because the objective function and constraints vary with time. As a result, although numerous successful optimization algorithms have been developed for static optimization problems, traditional optimization algorithms could not be effective at reaching an appropriate solution in such scenarios as they do not account for changes in real-time data. Thus, researchers tried to develop suitable algorithms to adapt to changes in dynamic environments.

Moreover, designing suitable optimization algorithms for solving real-world applications is not easy due to these environments' limitations and constraints. To name a few applications in dynamic environments, one can mention some examples of scheduling problems. These problems are in such a way that stochastic jobs may be inserted/deleted over time. Another example is routing problems, in which routers may fail or change status (from on to off or vice versa) in the whole routing network.

Time-based pricing [1] is a common problem in financial planning. In this problem, customers are divided into multiple groups based on their demand curves, and different prices are charged to each group at different times. This approach allows businesses to optimize their revenue by charging higher prices when demand is strong and lower prices when demand is weak. In channel assignment and multicast routing in multi-channel wireless mesh networks [2], these networks require dynamically efficient multicast routing protocols to ensure data delivery to multiple receivers simultaneously while minimizing network congestion and delay. Dynamic optimization techniques can be applied to address dynamic multicast problems in mobile ad hoc networks (MANETs) [3]. These networks are characterized by their dynamic topology and mobility, which makes multicast routing protocol optimization challenging. In dynamic multicast problems, the network topology is changed frequently due to node mobility or link failures. This requires an adaptive routing protocol to ensure reliable data delivery. Dynamic optimization techniques can improve multicast routing protocols' efficiency and adaptability in MANETs.

Dynamic optimization techniques can be applied to dynamic vehicle routing problems (VRPs) [4] to improve routing solutions' efficiency and adaptability. In dynamic VRPs, the number and routes of vehicles change dynamically over time due to various factors such as traffic conditions, weather, and customer demands. By using dynamic optimization techniques, it is possible to achieve more efficient and cost-effective routing solutions, reduce delivery times, and improve overall customer satisfaction. Dynamic job shop scheduling [5] is a scheduling problem in which jobs are processed on different machines in a factory. The goal is to determine the optimal sequence of jobs to be processed on each machine. This is carried out while considering some factors such as machine availability, job release times, and processing times. These problems are particularly challenging because the optimal schedule may change with time due to job requirements or machine availability changes. As a result, these problems require complex algorithms that adapt to changing conditions in real time. For more applications, it can be addressed in aerospace design [6], car distribution systems [7], object detection [8] and pollution control [7], electric vehicle dispatch optimization [9], cold chain logistics scheduling [10], and railway junction rescheduling [11].

The purpose of optimization in dynamic problems has shifted from simply identifying the stationary optimal solution(s) to precisely monitoring the trajectories of the optimal solution(s) over time [12–14]. As a result, it is crucial to adequately tackle the extra challenges presented by this scenario to achieve promising results. Reacting to changes is critical to maintaining optimization algorithms' performance in dynamic environments. The first step toward reacting to changes is to detect changes in the first place and then adopt a suitable strategy to deal with them. Richter [15] discussed two major change detection types: population based and sensor based. In population-based detection, statistical hypothesis testing is performed at each generation to see whether the alteration in the fitness of the individuals was not due to their convergence. In sensor-based detection, some measurements (so-called "fitness landscape sensors") are placed either randomly or regularly into the landscape. At every generation, the environment changes if any of the sensors detect an altered fitness value. Evolutionary algorithms (EAs) for addressing diverse applications characterized by dynamic behavior have received significant attention in recent years [3]. Conventional population-based algorithms can successfully solve static optimization problems but may fail in dynamic environments since they cannot recognize environmental changes. Different methods have been suggested to detect changes in the dynamic environment. Also, there is no prior knowledge or standard criteria for dealing with changing environments. A simple method can reset the optimization algorithm after detecting any environmental change, which can often be performed correctly [16]. Before reaching optimal regions, another change may occur through the evolution of an optimization algorithm. It is also possible to track the peaks around the optimal instead of locating the optimal using DOP algorithms as an alternative solution. Several techniques and improvements based on the characteristics of each EA are suggested for dynamic optimization [17–19], among which, the main approaches dealing with the dynamic environment can be categorized into several groups, including: (1) increasing diversity methods [13], (2) diversity maintenance methods [20], (3) memory-based methods [21], (4) predicting the next optimum solution, (5) self-adaptive mechanisms, (6) multi-population methods [22], and (7) hybridization of the methods [23,24]. This study uses diversity control with parameter adaptation by CAs for the distribution of parameters among the CA cells and their interaction.

A cellular automaton (CA) comprises numerous cells, each possessing a state that evolves through a set of feasible states according to a local rule. CA is especially appropriate for simulating natural systems that can be characterized as a vast collection of essential components interacting locally with one another. The cellular automata-based artificial immune system (CaAIS) proposed in this paper can be viewed as a stochastic cellular automaton [25], where the size of the state set corresponds to the number of points in the search space, and the cells update their states repeatedly until an appropriate predetermined criterion is met.

This paper presents a novel hybrid model of AIS using the cellular automata called cellular automata based on artificial immune system (CaAIS) for dynamic environments. Antibodies are distributed throughout a cellular grid of search space in the proposed model as nominal solutions. They are responsible for different solutions at different times. Based on the local interactions between cells and their local rules, the appropriate parameters and optimal solutions of cells are spread in the cell space. Due to CA properties, the CaAIS inherits the computational power of cellular automata [26] and AIS optimization capability.

In summary, our main contributions are highlighted as follows:

- We proposed a hybrid model of AIS and CA called cellular automata based on the artificial immune system (CaAIS) for dynamic environments.
- We proposed the CA local interactions in the CaAIS to adapt the parameters and increase diversity.
- As the environment changes, we propose a replacement mechanism that incorporates the near-best parameter of the cells and spreads to their neighbors.

The remainder of the paper is structured as follows: Section 2 provides an overview of related work on several studies on dynamic optimization problems. Section 3 introduces cellular automata in brief. The simple artificial immune algorithm is described in Section 4. The proposed algorithm (CaAIS) is described in detail in Section 5. Section 6 reports on the experimental results conducted on MPB and compares the CaAIS results with those of state-of-the-art and selected algorithms. Finally, Section 7 concludes this paper.

2. Related Work

In the literature, there are several studies on dynamic optimization problems. For example, Jin and Branke [27] tackled and deliberated on different forms of uncertainty in evolutionary optimization. Cruz et al. [16] have furthered the progress of the domain by achieving a dual objective, thereby enhancing its significance: (1) Their accomplishment involved the establishment of a vast collection of pertinent references on the subject matter from the previous ten years, which they then classified according to various criteria, including publication type, type of dynamism, dynamic optimization problem-solving approaches, performance metrics, applications, and year of publication. (2) Afterward, they conducted a comprehensive review of the research conducted on dynamic optimization problems using the compiled collection. Nguyen et al. [28] conducted a comprehensive investigation into the field of evolutionary optimization in dynamic environments, presenting an in-depth survey of the field. This research analyzed the latest advancements in the academic literature from four distinct perspectives, namely: (a) benchmark problems, (b) performance metrics, (c) methodologies, and (d) theories. Although their work is very valuable in studying and summarizing different methods for solving MPB, it does not provide categorical information on how different methods work and which mechanisms can improve the performance of different methods. In addition, it does not explain the reasons for specific approaches' superiority.

Yazdani et al. [29,30], in two parts of survey papers, presented a review of research studies regarding DOPs. Since an efficient dynamic optimization algorithm consists of several parts to cope with dynamic optimization problems, they tried to provide a comprehensive taxonomy to identify the parts of dynamic optimization algorithms. In the second part of this survey, they gave an overview of dynamic optimization problem benchmarks and performance measures. Moser et al. provide another study [31]. In this work, the authors surveyed the existing techniques in the literature for addressing MPB. They categorize the diverse methods into four groups: swarm intelligence algorithms, evolutionary algorithms, hybrid approaches, and other approaches.

In [22], Balckwell et al. introduced the concept of multi-swarms, which involves partitioning the population of particles into multiple subgroups, each with its own information sharing and exploration strategies. The researchers propose using an adaptive partitioning technique that dynamically adjusts the number and size of multi-swarms based on the characteristics of the problem and the environment. Then, they introduced the concept of exclusion, which allows individual particles to temporarily avoid regions of the search space that are not beneficial. By excluding certain areas, particles can avoid premature convergence and explore other areas of the search space. Additionally, the authors addressed the issue of anti-convergence, which occurs when all particles converge to a suboptimal solution. To mitigate this problem, the authors propose a re-initialization mechanism, which randomly disperses particles in the search space to encourage exploration.

In [32], Li et al. focused on improving particle swarm optimization (PSO) algorithms in dynamic environments by incorporating both speciation and adaptation mechanisms. Speciation is a process inspired by biological evolution, where particles are divided into different sub-populations or species based on their similarities. This helps maintain diversity and exploration, even in changing or dynamic environments. Adaptation, on the other hand, enables particles to adjust their behavior and parameters in response to environment changes. It allows particles to quickly react and update their positions and velocities to find better solutions. Nasiri et al. [33] proposed the integration of speciation, a concept from evolutionary biology, into the firefly algorithm. This is a widely used optimization algorithm inspired by fireflies' behavior. The algorithm partitions the population into different species based on their similar solutions. Fireflies within the same species closely cooperate and share information, while fireflies belonging to different species compete for resources. This division allows for both exploration and exploitation of the search space, improving the algorithm's ability to adapt to changing environments.

The authors in [34] focused on studying the effectiveness of a multi-population heuristic approach to solving non-stationary optimization tasks. The authors emphasize that real-world optimization problems often have non-stationary characteristics, meaning that the problem landscape changes over time. Thus, they introduced a multi-population heuristic approach, which involves multiple populations working in parallel. Each population adapts and evolves independently, making the approach suitable for solving non-stationary problems where the landscape changes unpredictably.

An appropriate candidate for a nature-inspired algorithm dealing with the changing environment components is an artificial immune system (AIS). An AIS [35] is an adaptive system inspired by vertebrate immune processes developed by researchers to solve complex real-world problems [36]. In this regard, some achievements have been made in AISs dealing with DOPs. Franca et al. have proposed modifications to the artificial immune network (AIN) algorithm for dynamic environments [37]. They utilize particular sub-populations for memory, linear search for parameter control, and novel operators for mutation in AIN. The multi-population strategy of the artificial immune algorithm in a dynamic environment has been suggested by Xhua et al., which obtained relatively successful results [38]. In [39], the authors focused on the improvement of adaptation in optimization problems subject to time-dependent changes. The authors propose a hybrid approach that combines genetic algorithms (GAs) and artificial immune systems (AIS) to enhance optimization. The proposed hybrid approach incorporates a multi-objective optimization framework, which combines exploration and exploitation objectives with AIS components. Specifically, the authors introduce an immune-inspired strategy for maintaining a diverse population of solutions and adaptively reacting to changes in the optimization landscape. The AIS components act as an additional mechanism for preserving diversity, increasing adaptability, and improving the algorithm's convergence rate.

Kelsey et al. [40] proposed a novel optimization technique called Immune-inspired Somatic Contiguous Hypermutation (ISCH). This technique is inspired by the immune system's somatic hypermutation process, which generates diverse antibodies to combat various pathogens. ISCH involves the creation of a population of candidate solutions, represented as individuals or antibodies. Each candidate solution corresponds to a specific state within the search space. The somatic contiguous hypermutation operator is then applied to these individuals to generate mutated offspring. Unlike traditional mutation operators, the contiguous hypermutation in ISCH selectively mutates contiguous regions within the candidate solutions. This approach allows for more focused exploration of the search space, potentially yielding better solutions in less time. In [41], De Castro et al. discussed the clonal selection algorithm (CSA) and its various applications in engineering. CSA is a computational optimization technique inspired by the immune system's clonal selection process. This algorithm mimics the immune system's ability to generate antibodies to combat infections, and it has been successfully applied to a wide range of engineering problems.

A comprehensive review and performance evaluation of some different mutation behaviors for the clonal selection algorithm, artificial immune network, and B-cell algorithm is reported in dynamic environments [42] by Trojanowski et al. There are some desirable results in a dynamic environment for adaptive operators using learning automata to increase diversity. This is developed for the immune algorithm immune network [13]. The dynamic T-cell algorithm, a novel immune algorithm inspired by the T-cell model, was developed for DOP based on four populations [43]. Another multi-population-based algorithm was introduced as an artificial immune algorithm for the dynamic environment based on the principle of biological immune response [44]. Nabizedeh et al. utilized a clonal selection algorithm as a local search for a search around the optima [45]. An adaptive version of the immune system algorithm utilizing learning automata is presented in [46], in which the hypermutation parameter is adjusted using learning automata as a successful reinforcement learning approach.

However, nature-inspired methods for dynamic optimization problems have certain limitations. One limitation is the exploration–exploitation trade-off. These algorithms may struggle to balance between exploring new regions of the search space to find better solutions and exploiting the current best solutions. In dynamic environments, where the optimal solution may change over time, this trade-off becomes even more challenging. Additionally, these methods may suffer from premature convergence, where they converge to suboptimal solutions too quickly and fail to adapt to changing environments. The lack of effective mechanisms to handle dynamic changes in the search space is another limitation, as these algorithms may struggle to quickly adapt and track the changing optimal solution. Overall, while nature-inspired methods have shown promise in solving optimization problems, their limitations in dynamic environments call for further research and development.

3. Cellular Automata

Cellular automata [47] is a dynamical system with discrete space and time. The CA is a mathematical model with an array of cells with local interactions for investigating sophisticated, complex phenomena. Each cell's behavior is determined based on its neighbor's behavior. CA is a decentralized, discrete, self-organized, and parallel system that enables one to create an ordered structure by starting from a random state. It is shown that the property of CA by applying a CA to a set of structures could not affect the set entropy. In this model, space is specified by a regular grid of cells, each representing a memory of states. In each step, the cell considers neighboring cells, and based on the communication rules, the next state is specified. In addition, each cell can work independently of the other cells.

Cellular automata consider different neighborhood configurations. Each set of cells is considered to be neighbors in a specific order. The two most well-known neighborhoods are the Von Neumann and Moore neighborhoods. The Von Neumann neighborhood includes four adjacent cells not diagonal to the central cell, while the Moore neighborhood includes all eight surrounding cells. Each cell in the Von Neumann neighborhood has an equal distance from the central cell. This model takes into account a wider range of neighboring cells, allowing for more complex interactions and patterns within the cellular automaton. These neighborhoods are commonly called the nearest neighbors and are illustrated in Figure 1 [48]. For the CaAIS, the Von Neumann model may be more suitable for scenarios where a more localized and restricted antibody spread is desired. In contrast, the Moore model allows for a more extensive spread of antibodies across cells.

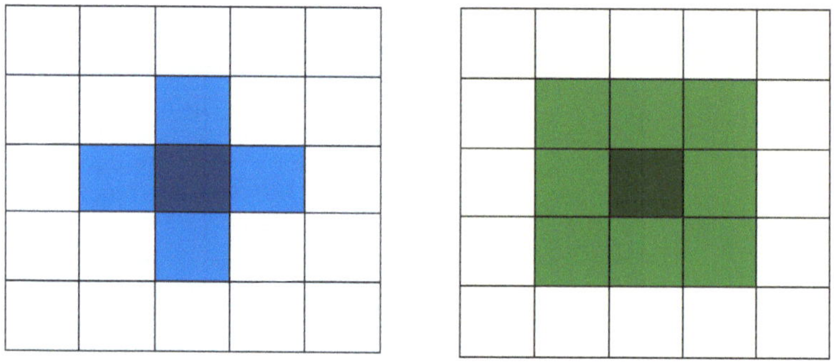

(**a**) (**b**)

Figure 1. The typical neighborhood model in a 2-D CA; (**a**) Von Neumann, (**b**) Moore.

The CaAIS is not the first evolutionary algorithm to use CA. In [49], CGA is a cellular evolutionary algorithm that utilizes a decentralized population approach. In this method, tentative solutions are introduced in overlapping neighborhoods. The hybrid CA with particle swarm optimization (PSO), called CPSO, is presented in a study to optimize functions [50]. The CPSO algorithm incorporates a CA mechanism into the velocity update process to modify particle trajectories. The CaAIS is similar to CGA and CPSO in that it is parameter dependent and hybridizes with CA. However, the CaAIS differs from CGA and CPSO models in several aspects. 1: The main evolutionary algorithm is based on AIS. 2: Unlike CGA, the CaAIS model does not use crossover and mutation operators. Based on the AIS algorithm, the CaAIS uses only hypermutation operators. 3: Unlike CGA, in the CaAIS, each antibody interacts only with its pre-defined neighboring antibodies. 4: the CaAIS focuses on optimization for dynamic environments.

Several hybridizations of CA and evolutionary algorithms are also reported in the literature, including CLA-EC [51], Cellular PSO [52,53], Cellular DE [19,54], CLA-DE [55], and Cellular fish swarm [56]. This paper proposes a hybrid model using cellular automata and an artificial immune system for optimization in dynamic optimization.

4. Artificial Immune Algorithm

An artificial immune system [35] is a branch of computational intelligence that draws inspiration from the natural immune system. It offers various algorithms for solving complex real-world problems [36]. Several applications of AIS algorithms have been reported by researchers, such as optimization [13], power systems [57], scheduling [58], pattern recognition, bioinformatics [59], data mining [60], psychometric technology [61], sensor networks [62], intrusion detection [63], mobile robot control [64], and clinical diagnostics [65]. Taking inspiration from human immune systems, many AIS algorithms are generated.

These algorithms include negative selection algorithms (NCA), clonal selection algorithms (CLONALG), bone marrow, artificial immune networks (AINE), toll-like receptors (TLR), danger theory, and dendritic cell algorithms (DCA) [36,60].

The immune network theory was presented by Jerne [66], while the artificial immune network (AIN) algorithm was developed for multi-model optimization by de Castro and Timmis [67]. This algorithm considers the immune cell as a population and its representation as a real value vector with Euclidian distance. One of the main properties of this algorithm is affinity maturation after random initialization, after which cells suffer mutation based on the affinity of cells to produce colonies according to Equation (1)

$$c' = c + \frac{\exp(-f^*)}{\beta} \times N(0,\ 1), \tag{1}$$

where c' is the mutated cell, β is a control parameter for the normalization of fitness value f^*, and $N(0,\ 1)$ specifies a Gaussian distribution by mean and variance 0 and 1, respectively. After the mutation of the clones, cells with maximum fitness values were retained, and cells with fitness values smaller than others were replaced with random cells [37]. Indeed, the AIN algorithm aims to attain a set of representations with the least redundancy. Although the AIN algorithm looks like a clonal selection algorithm, the main difference is attributed to the suppression mechanism for cell interaction. This eliminates certain sets of cells with less fitness than others. Algorithm 1 presents the artificial immune network algorithm pseudo-code [68].

Algorithm 1. Artificial immune network algorithm

1. **Initialize** the Ab population as antibodies, and β is a control parameter.
2. **Repeat** for each Ab.
3. Evaluate Ab.
4. Select the best Ab.
5. Clone and mutate Ab.
6. Retain the highest Ab as memories.
7. Remove weak memories.
8. Replace random Ab.
9. **Until** the termination condition is met

5. Proposed Model: Cellular Automata-Based on Artificial Immune System (CaAIS)

Parameters in the AIS algorithm play a critical role due to several parameters, such as hypermutation. These parameters affect the AIS algorithm's performance [35]. On the other hand, there are local interactions between *Ab*s in the immune system. Thus, in the proposed algorithm, a CA is used for enhancing the parameter adaptations of the algorithm. Each CA cell consists of antibodies denoted by Ab, and their parameters, such as β, are control parameters. This concept preserves diversity in the search space through CA local interaction. A general representation of the proposed model for CA deployment in a Von Neumann model is depicted in Figure 2.

After initialization, the proposed algorithm iterates in parallel for each cell. Each step is described in the following subsections. The pseudo-code of the proposed algorithm, the CaAIS, is presented in Algorithm 2.

Algorithm 2. Cellular automata-based artificial immune system (CaAIS)

1. (**Initialization**): Generate randomly the initial *Abs* population and initialize the parameters in each cell
2. Repeat for each cell in parallel
3. Evaluate the *Ab* population
4. (**Change Environment**) If changing the environment is detected, do the following operations on each *Ab*
5. (**Replacement**) Replace a set of *Abs* with the best of neighboring cells according to Equation (3), and
the remainder set reinitializes the parameters randomly.
6. Generate clones and then perform **Hypermutation** clones with equal probability to each clone according to the neighboring cells based on Equation (4).
7. Evaluate the fitness of every mutated clone, and select the best *Abs* using Equation (3) as a member of the new generation and remove the others.
8. (**CA Local interaction**) Interact between cells and run local rules transition in each cell for parameter selection value according to Equation (5).
9. Retain the best *ABs* as memory.
10. Remove a set of weak *Abs* and replace it with new *Abs* randomly.
11. Until (**Stopping criteria**) are met

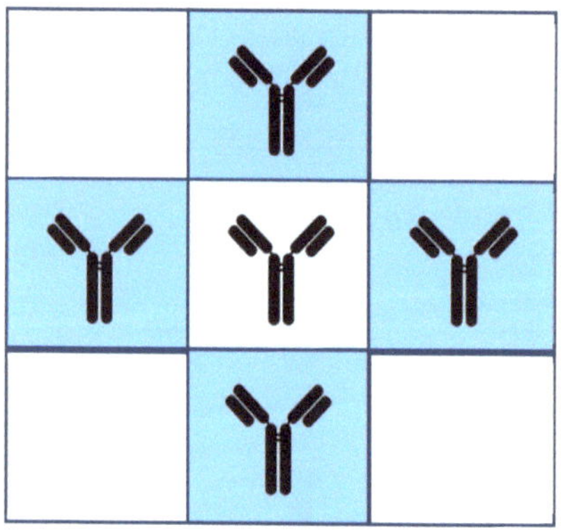

Figure 2. Deployment of schematic antibodies in a 2D cell space as Von Neumann model.

The description of each step of the CaAIS is given as follows.

5.1. Initialization

The initial *Ab* population was randomly generated using random distribution in the corresponding range in each cell as follows

$$Ab_{(i,j)} = lb + r(ub - lb), \tag{2}$$

where r is a random number distributed in $[0,\ 1]$, lb, ub are the lower and upper bound of the real variable $Ab_{(i,j)}$ for cell $(i,\ j)$, respectively. Additionally, in this step, the maximum iteration, mutation probability P_m, and other parameters, such as the control parameter β, are set.

5.2. Change the Environment

In the proposed algorithm, a change in environments is detected by re-evaluating the *BestAb* as the best *Ab* in the population. So, a change is detected if the fitness value of the *BestAb* has been changed since its last fitness evaluation. By detecting a change in the environment, the fitness value of each *Ab* also should be re-evaluated. A local search is performed around each individual as well. According to the proposed method, a local search is applied simply by interacting with neighbors. This idea helps Ab to track the previous best search attempts to find the new optimal position quickly.

5.3. Replacement

In a time of changing environment, a set of antibodies in each cell is replaced by the best neighbor. Other antibodies are reinitialized based on the last good neighbor in the memory as $CbestM_{(i,j)}$ for cell $(i,\ j)$, and the remaining are randomly initialized. Indeed, it provides a global search by random search and local search by replacing the cells and spreading in the neighbors. The replacement of antibodies is carried out using Equation (3).

$$Ab_{(i,j)} = \underset{i,j}{\operatorname{argmax}}\{ \underset{Ab_{(p,q)} \in N(Ab_{(i,j)})}{f(Ab)_{(p,q)}} \}, \tag{3}$$

where $Ab_{i,j}$ is the antibody in the central cell, $N(Ab_{(i,j)})$ returns the set of neighboring cells for $Ab_{i,j}$ in the central cell. Moreover, the best Ab of each cell as memory is considered as $CbestM_{(i,j)}$.

5.4. Hypermutation

Since cloning and hypermutation are the main operators of AIS, they are performed on the Ab population according to their fitness values. In this step, the Ab with a higher fitness value suffers more clones because the better Abs are closer to optimal. Then, hypermutation is applied as in Equation (4).

$$Ab_{(i,j)} = Ab_{(i,j)} + \frac{\exp(-f^*(Ab_{(i,j)}))}{\beta} \times N(0,\ 1), \tag{4}$$

where β is a control parameter for the normalization of fitness value $f^*(Ab_{(i,j)})$ for $Ab_{(i,j)}$ in cell $(i,\ j)$, $N(0,\ 1)$ specifies a Gaussian distribution by mean and variance 0 and 1, respectively.

5.5. CA Local Interactions

In the proposed algorithm, the Ab is an N-dimensional real vector, where N is the number of the dimensions of search space. In this discipline, the parameter of Ab is adjusted via local interaction between Abs in the CA in a parallel manner. The relation between Abs in a local grid in the Moore model is schematically presented in Figure 3.

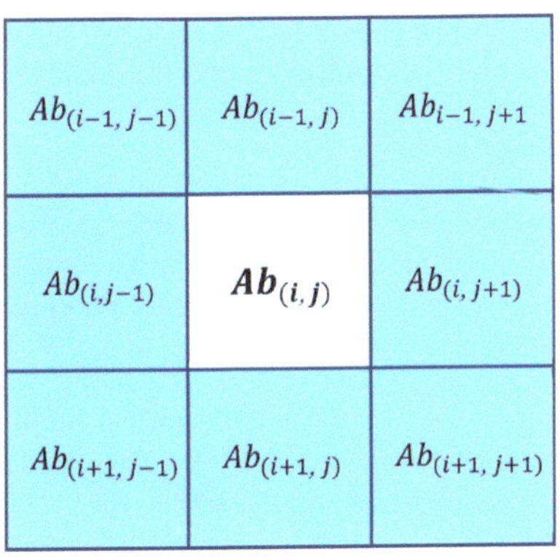

Figure 3. Representation of deployment of antibodies Ab in Moore model of CA.

In the case of a dynamic environment, the parameters of AIS become different with changing environments adaptively, and the diversity of population increases during the time based on CA. In this method, antibodies are distributed in the grid of cells so that each cell can access its neighboring information by interaction among the cells.

Since the immune algorithm's performance depends on mutation, values of β as the control parameter are chosen adaptively through the algorithm evolution. The first initialization of this parameter is randomly selected since there is no prior knowledge of the environment. When the algorithm proceeds, the value of β is updated based on the received feedback from the environment. While all antibodies in each cell are evaluated, information interactions between neighboring cells are performed, and the central cell for each window determines the best value of β using Equation (5),

$$\beta_{i,j} = \underset{i,j}{\text{argmax}}\{ \underset{\beta_{(p,q)} \in N(\beta_{(i,j)})}{f(Ab)_{(p,q)}} \}, \tag{5}$$

where $\beta_{(i,j)}$ and $\beta_{(p,q)}$ are the control parameters of mutated antibodies in the central cell and the control parameters of antibodies in neighboring cells, respectively.

The information interactions and the spread of parameters among cells in the *2D* model through the algorithm's evolution schematically are shown in Figure 4.

Figure 4. The representation of the local information interaction and its spread of parameters (i.e., control parameter β) among cells for the 2D model of Moore with s distance from the central cell.

5.6. Stopping Criteria

The process of evaluating the *Ab* population, detecting the change in environment and re-initialization and replacement, generating clones and hypermutation clones, evaluating the mutated clones, performing CA local interaction, retaining the best *Abs*, and removing the set of weak *Abs* is repeated until the stopping criteria are met. The proposed algorithm stops when the maximum number of iterations is met.

6. Experimental Study

First, this section introduces (1) the performance measure, (2) MPB as a popular dynamic environment benchmark [67], and (3) an experimental setup that allows the CaAIS to be evaluated. Then, the CaAIS experimental results compared to some well-known algorithms are reported in Section 5.3.

6.1. Performance Measure

Offline error (OE) has been used to evaluate the CaAIS, a popular measure in the literature for dynamic optimization. The average of the best value rather than the last change from optima is indicated in OE, which is defined by Equation (6):

$$OfflineError = \frac{1}{N_c}\sum_{j=1}^{N_c}\left(\frac{1}{N_{e(j)}}\sum_{i=1}^{N_e(j)}\left(f_j^* - f_{ji}^*\right)\right), \tag{6}$$

where N_c is the fitness evaluation of a changing environment, $N_e(j)$ is the fitness evaluation for the jth time of environment, f_j^* specifies the best value of the jth state (between j and $j+1$), and f_{ji}^* is the best current fitness value found up to now [16].

6.2. Dynamic Environment

Due to the dynamic nature of many real-world problems and the continuously changing environment, MPB, as a well-known dynamic environment, was developed as a means of algorithm evaluation [69]. MPBs are being presented in the n-dimensional environment with pre-defined peaks in X (location), H (height), W (weight). The peak functions are defined below as Equation (7), and the highest value obtained over all of them specifies the fitness landscape.

$$F\left(\vec{x},t\right) = \max_{i=1,\ldots N}\frac{H_i(t)}{1+W_i(t)\sum_{j=1}^{D}\left(x_j(t)-X_{ij}(t)\right)^2}, \tag{7}$$

where $X_{ij}(t)$ is the coordination related to the location, $W_i(t)$ is the width of the ith peak, $H_i(t)$ is the height of ith peak, all in time t. A uniform distribution is used to generate the height randomly ($H_i(t)$) in the range $[30,\ 70]$ and width ($W_i(t)$) in the range $[1,\ 12]$ of each peak.

The width $W_i(t)$ and height $H_i(t)$ are changed, respectively, as Equations (8) and (9)

$$W_i(t) = W_i(t-1) + width_{severity}.\delta, \tag{8}$$

$$H_i(t) = H_i(t-1) + height_{severity}.\delta, \tag{9}$$

where δ is a random number from a Gaussian distribution with a mean of 0 and variance of 1. The position of each peak is updated by vector $\vec{v_i}$ and it is formulated as follows:

$$\vec{X_i}(t) = \vec{X_i}(t)(t-1) + \vec{v_i}(t), \tag{10}$$

where $\vec{v_i}$ is defined as Equation (11)

$$\vec{v_i}(t) = \frac{s}{\left|\vec{r} + \vec{v_i}(t-1)\right|}\left((1-\lambda)\vec{r} + \lambda\vec{v_i}(t-1)\right), \tag{11}$$

where $\vec{v_i}(t)$ as the shift vector is a linear combination of a random vector $\vec{r} \in [0.0,\ 1.0]^D$ and the previous shift vector $\vec{v_i}(t)$ and is normalized by the length factor s. The severity of change is determined by parameter s, while the correlation between each peak's changes and the previous one is specified by λ. (i.e., $\lambda = 0$ specifies the change of peak is uncorrelated).

An example of the landscape generated by the MPB is illustrated in Figure 5. The peaks are distributed throughout the whole environment, while the peaks' location, weight, and height change over time.

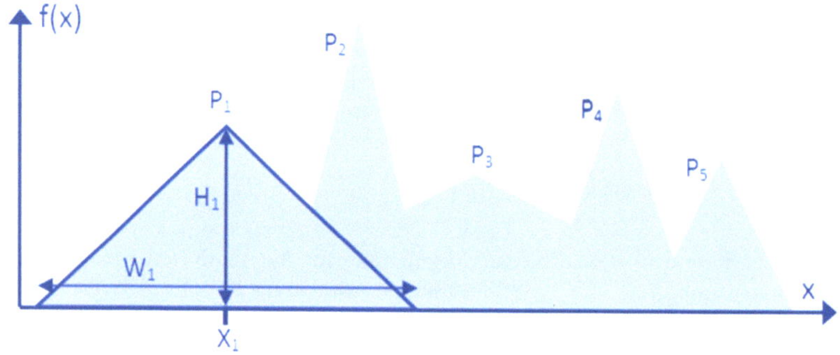

Figure 5. An example of a landscape generated by the MPB.

The default settings of MPB [70] to facilitate comparison with alternative algorithms are given in Table 1.

Table 1. The default settings of MPB for experimentation.

Setting	Default Value	Other Tested Values
Number of peaks (m)	10	5, 10, 20, 30, 40, 50, 100, 200
Number of dimensions (D)	5	10, 50
Frequency of change (f)	5000	1000, 2000, 3000
Height severity	7.0	
Width severity	1.0	
Peak shape	Cone	
Shift severity (s)	1	2, 3, 4, 5, 6
Search space range (A)	[0, 100]	
Height range (H)	[30, 70]	
Width range (W)	[1, 12]	
Correlation coefficient (λ)	[0.0, 1.0]	

6.3. *Experiments*

In this section, the CaAIS performance is studied in numerous experiments and compared with alternative algorithms reported in the literature. For each experiment, an average offline error over 30 independent runs with a 95% confidence level is presented. Moreover, each experiment contains its assumptions. Two groups of experiments are designed in this section. The first group considered various configurations of the proposed algorithm, and the other experiments employed comparisons with other algorithms with varying MPB scenarios.

6.3.1. Effect of Various Numbers of Initial Antibodies

A first set of experiments is conducted by OE to examine the effect of the initial antibody *Ab* size (initial population) on the MPB. Although the diversity values of antibody quantities can be considered for initialization, the population of AIS is increasing dynamically, so using multiple values would not be reasonable. Hence, 2–10, 20, and 50 antibodies are selected for initialization in this experiment. The effects of the number of initial antibodies in the proposed algorithm are depicted in Figure 6.

As evident from Figure 6, OE has been decreased by raising the initial *Ab* population to 5–6, and it shows relative improvement. Although it has been further increased, the result has been inversed, and the OE value has increased. By increasing the number of antibodies, it seems that more populations will cooperate to interact with each other and share the optimization solutions. In contrast, for the *Ab* population increased to more than six, the results are not promising. According to these results of OE for the *Ab* populations of five to six and with a shorter run time, the initial size of the *Ab* population is set to five antibodies for the rest of the experiments.

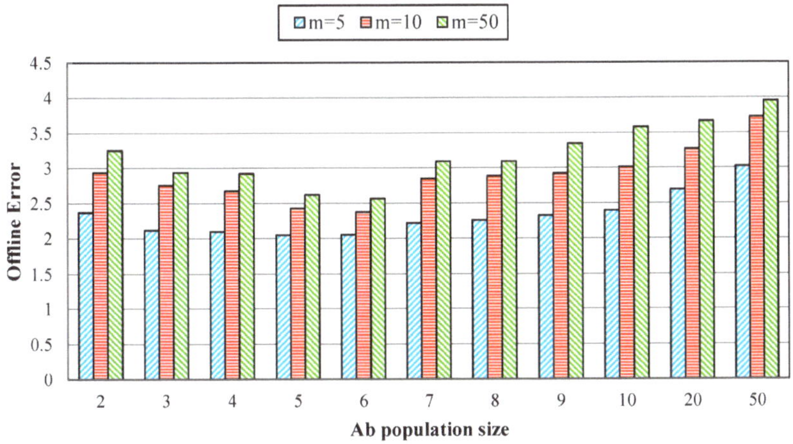

Figure 6. Offline error for various numbers of initial *Ab* population size.

6.3.2. Effect of Varying the Number of Neighborhood Sizes

Other experiments investigated the effects of several neighbor cells in CA. This experiment avoids large neighborhood structures to avoid additional computational challenges and a long run time. Therefore, the numbers of neighbor cells are studied from one to five for the effects of cell neighborhood sizes. The effects of the different cell neighborhood sizes are summarized in Figure 7.

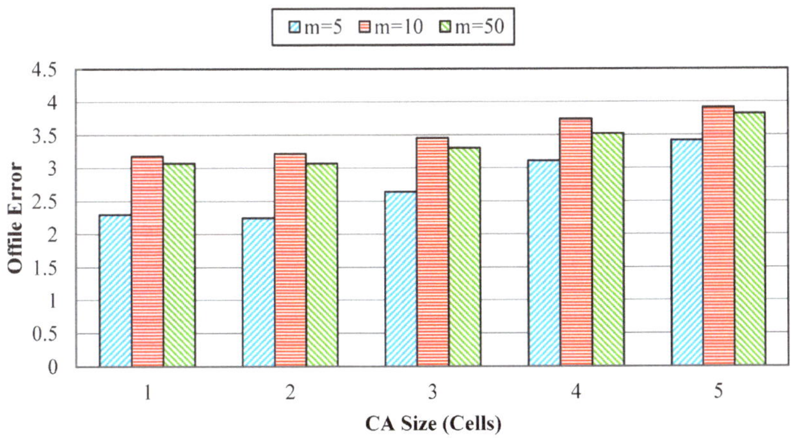

Figure 7. Effect of varying cell neighborhood sizes.

According to Figure 7, it can be observed that the cell neighborhood size has been increased until size two has relatively improved. However, no more than three to five values will be enhanced, and OE will be increased. Indeed, increasing the cell neighborhood size causes more complexity, and the advantage of local search deteriorates during the changing environment.

6.3.3. Effect of Varying the Re-Randomization of Antibodies

One reaction mechanism for changing the environment is re-randomizing a set of populations. The effects of varying the re-randomization of a set between 10 and 100% of the total population for the proposed algorithm can be seen in Figure 8. As reflected in Figure 8, the rate of re-randomization value replacement of the population has promising results between 30 and 60% of the population. It implies that a lower or higher rate of re-randomization would not be efficient. Smaller rates of replacement value (fewer than 30%) cause negligible effects on enhancing the results. It may due to a lack of diversity in the search space. In comparison, greater replacement values (over 60%) cause significant randomization, and the algorithm can not find a suitable solution, because it may be a candidate solution far from the optimal peaks. Therefore, due to the received proper results for the mid-range of the re-randomization rate, in the rest of the experiments, the rate of re-randomization is set to 50–60 percent of the *Ab* population.

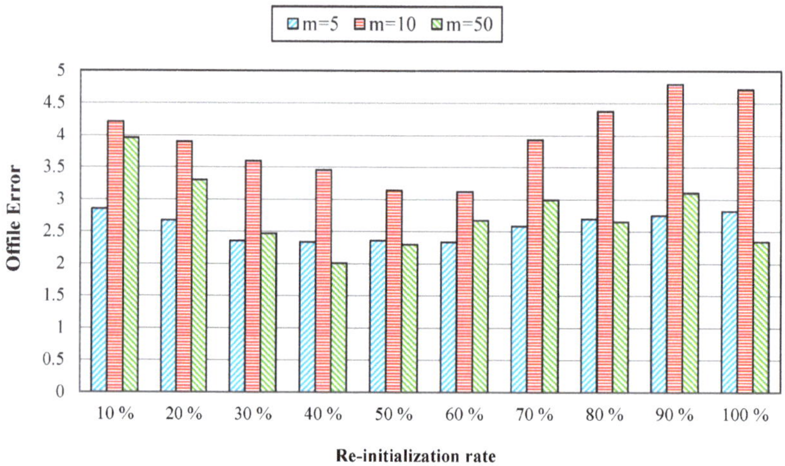

Figure 8. Comparison of different re-randomization for the CaAIS from 10 to 100%.

6.3.4. Comparison of the CaAIS with Peer Immune Algorithms

In this experiment, the performance of the CaAIS is compared with several algorithms, including the simple artificial immune system (SAIS) [39], artificial iterated immune algorithm (AIIA) [34], B-cell algorithm (BCA) [40], clonal selection algorithm (CLONALG) [41], artificial immune network (opt-aiNet) [67], learning automata-based immune algorithm (LAIA) [46], and the cellular PSO based on clonal selection algorithm (CPSOC) [45]. A statistical test is also applied to validate the significance of the results. The statistical test results of comparing algorithms by one-tailed *t*-test with 28 degrees of freedom at a 0.05 level of significance are reported in Table 2. Table 2 consists of two main columns for 5 peaks and 50 peaks as different environments. For each environment, the offline error and standard errors are given along with the results of the statistical significance test. The *t*-test result regarding the CaAIS with each alternative algorithm is shown as "+", "−", and "~" when the CaAIS is significantly better than, significantly worse than, and statistically equivalent to the alternative algorithm, respectively. According to Table 2, the results of the proposed method are statistically equivalent to those of BCA. They show better results than other general relativity algorithms. This is due to the cellular structure and immune properties that provide an adaptive balance between local and global search in changing environments.

Table 2. Comparison of OE ± standard error for the CaAIS versus other AIS algorithms with *t*-test results.

Algorithms	M = 5		M = 50	
	Offline Error	***t*-Test**	**Offline Error**	***t*-Test**
AIIA	2.6098 ± 0.43	+	3.7534 ± 0.31	+
SAIS	12.1631 ± 0.12	+	11.5783 ± 0.13	+
BCA	2.2566 ± 0.49	~	3.1245 ± 0.66	~
CLONALG	3.3376 ± 1.25	+	10.5300 ± 0.21	+
Opt-aiNet	2.3963 ± 0.05	+	4.7600 ± 0.06	+
LAIA	2.7813 ± 0.35	+	2.9497 ± 0.36	~
CPSOC	2.1923 ± 0.13	~	2.9546 ± 0.15	−
CaAIS	2.2979 ± 0.12	~	3.0707 ± 0.19	~

6.3.5. Effect of Various Severities of Shift

This experiment examines the effect of different values on shift severity. For comparison, it utilizes other methods, such as multi-swarm optimization methods [22], including mPSO, mCPSO, mQPSO [22], PSO with speciation (SPSO) [32], and SFA [33]. Figure 9 shows the average offline error for different algorithms. As seen in Figure 9, an increase in shift length leads to a corresponding increase in offline error across all algorithms. It means that longer shift lengths pose challenges for the environment and thus algorithms with less steep curves are preferred. Amongst these algorithms, the proposed algorithm outperforms other algorithms such as mQSO, mPSO, mCPSO, and SPSO, but not SFA due to its unique algorithm properties. It should be noted that all other methods are based on particle swarm optimization.

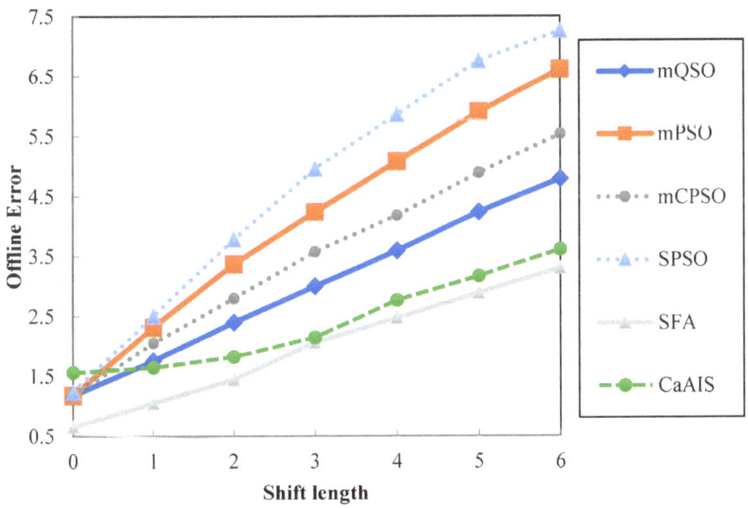

Figure 9. OE for different values of severity shift.

6.3.6. Effect of Various Numbers of Peaks

In an environment with moving peaks, the number of peaks is essential in determining the results. The numbers of different peaks indicate the algorithm's scalability in various states. This experiment is designed to examine the performance of the proposed algorithm when several peaks change. According to Table 1, the number of peaks changed within the range from 1 to 200. In this experiment, the proposed algorithm the CaAIS is compared with well-known algorithms such as multi-swarm optimization in two states, mCPSO and mQPSO [22], PSO with speciation (SPSO) [32], cellular differential evolution (CLDE) [54], fast multi-swarm optimization (FMSO) [71], dynamic population differential evolution (DynPopDE) [72], speciation-based firefly algorithm (SFA) [33], particle swarm optimization with composite (PSO-CP) [73], learning automata-based immune algorithm (LAIA) [46], cellular PSO (CLPSO) [53], multi-swarm cellular PSO with local search (CPSOL) [74], and multi-population differential evolution (DE) algorithm with learning automata (DynDE+LA) [75]. The effect of the varying number of peaks is listed in Table 3. It should be noted that the results of the compared algorithms are the same as those of their papers; therefore, in some cases, the results are not presented. According to Table 3, the CaAIS outperforms peer algorithms for 40 and 100 peaks, but for different numbers of peaks, another algorithm may have been the best. Table 3 shows that the CaAIS delivers marginally superior results for different numbers of peaks. The CaAIS produces better results as the number of peaks rises.

Table 3. Comparing offline error and standard error for varying numbers of peaks.

Peaks \ Algorithms	SPSO	CLPSO	CLDE	mQSO	mCPSO	FMSO	DynPopDE	PSO-CP	LAIA	CPSOL	DynDE+LA	CaAIS
1	2.64 ± 0.10	3.46 ± 0.22	**1.53 ± 0.07**	5.07 ± 0.17	4.93 ± 0.17	3.44 ± 0.11	-	3.41 ± 0.06	1.94 ± 0.19	1.02 ± 0.14	3.07 ± 0.12	2.24 ± 0.02
5	2.15 ± 0.07	1.79 ± 0.12	1.50 ± 0.04	1.81 ± 0.07	2.07 ± 0.08	2.94 ± 0.07	**1.03 ± 0.13**	-	2.09 ± 0.18	0.99 ± 0.15	1.41 ± 0.08	2.28 ± 0.02
10	2.51 ± 0.09	1.84 ± 0.08	1.64 ± 0.03	1.80 ± 0.06	2.08 ± 0.07	3.11 ± 0.06	1.39 ± 0.07	**1.31 ± 0.06**	2.14 ± 0.15	1.75 ± 0.10	1.32 ± 0.06	2.24 ± 0.02
20	3.21 ± 0.07	2.63 ± 0.11	2.46 ± 0.05	2.42 ± 0.07	2.64 ± 0.07	3.36 ± 0.06	-	-	2.97 ± 0.21	**1.93 ± 0.11**	2.60 ± 0.07	2.51 ± 0.03
30	3.64 ± 0.07	2.91 ± 0.10	2.62 ± 0.05	2.48 ± 0.07	2.63 ± 0.08	3.28 ± 0.05	-	**2.02 ± 0.07**	2.98 ± 0.23	2.28 ± 0.10	3.05 ± 0.10	2.63 ± 0.03
40	3.85 ± 0.08	3.16 ± 0.11	2.76 ± 0.05	2.55 ± 0.07	2.67 ± 0.07	3.26 ± 0.04	-	-	3.07 ± 0.29	2.62 ± 0.09	3.34 ± 0.07	**2.28 ± 0.02**
50	3.86 ± 0.08	3.23 ± 0.11	2.75 ± 0.05	2.50 ± 0.06	2.65 ± 0.06	3.22 ± 0.05	**2.10 ± 0.06**	-	2.93 ± 0.27	2.74 ± 0.10	3.56 ± 0.09	2.32 ± 0.02
100	4.01 ± 0.07	3.43 ± 0.10	2.73 ± 0.03	2.36 ± 0.04	2.49 ± 0.04	3.06 ± 0.4	2.34 ± 0.05	2.14 ± 0.08	3.06 ± 0.24	2.84 ± 0.12	3.88 ± 0.11	**1.67 ± 0.03**

Table 3. *Cont.*

Peaks \ Algorithms	SPSO	CLPSO	CLDE	mQSO	mCPSO	FMSO	DynPopDE	PSO-CP	LAIA	CPSOL	DynDE+LA	CaAIS
200	3.82 ± 0.05	3.38 ± 0.09	2.61 ± 0.02	2.26 ± 0.03	2.44 ± 0.04	2.84 ± 0.03	2.44 ± 0.05	**2.04 ± 0.07**	2.95 ± 0.23	2.69 ± 0.08	3.71 ± 0.09	2.64 ± 0.03

7. Conclusions

This paper presents a hybrid method using cellular automata and an artificial immune system. Unlike conventional AIS algorithms for dynamic environments, antibodies are distributed through a grid of cells in the proposed algorithm. They try to find environmental peaks by local interaction with antibodies in neighbor cells. The information interaction is implemented in two ways: one, the best value of control parameters and memory in neighbor cells totally after the evaluation of antibodies is replaced in the central cell; and later, during the changing environment, a set of the population is replaced with neighbors' antibodies. The proposed methods are enforced by both local and global search due to the characteristics of AIS and CA. The results of experiments on the proposed algorithm on MPB compared with well-known algorithms reveal relative improvements in dynamic environments. The simulation results show the superiority of the CaAIS statistically in comparison with peer artificial immune system algorithms in most cases in dynamic environments. To address the potential applications of the CaAIS to real-world dynamic optimization problems, one can optimize the allocation of resources in dynamic environments, such as transportation logistics or energy management systems, or optimize investment portfolios by adapting to changing market conditions and adjusting asset allocations accordingly, to name a few. Finally, for future research directions, techniques should be developed to improve the algorithm's ability to adapt to rapidly changing environments and handle complex dynamic scenarios. In addition, strategies should be developed to enhance the scalability of the algorithm, particularly for large-scale dynamic optimization problems to be considered.

Author Contributions: Conceptualization, A.R.; methodology, A.R.; software, A.R.; validation, A.R. and S.M.V.; formal analysis, A.R. and S.M.V.; investigation, A.R. and S.M.V.; resources, A.R., S.M.V. and A.M.S.; data curation, A.R., S.M.V. and A.M.S.; writing—original draft preparation, A.R.; writing—review and editing, A.R., S.M.V. and A.M.S.; visualization, A.R., S.M.V. and A.M.S.; supervision, A.R.; project administration, A.R., S.M.V. and A.M.S. All authors have read and agreed to the published version of the manuscript.

Funding: This research received no external funding.

Data Availability Statement: Data is contained within the article.

Conflicts of Interest: The authors declare no conflicts of interest.

References

1. Kim, S.-K.; Kim, J.-Y.; Cho, K.-H.; Byeon, G. Optimal Operation Control for Multiple BESSs of a Large-Scale Customer under Time-Based Pricing. *IEEE Trans. Power Syst.* **2017**, *33*, 803–816. [CrossRef]
2. Cheng, H.; Yang, S. Joint QoS Multicast Routing and Channel Assignment in Multiradio Multichannel Wireless Mesh Networks Using Intelligent Computational Methods. *Appl. Soft Comput.* **2011**, *11*, 1953–1964. [CrossRef]
3. Cheng, H.; Yang, S. Genetic Algorithms with Immigrants Schemes for Dynamic Multicast Problems in Mobile Ad Hoc Networks. *Eng. Appl. Artif. Intel.* **2010**, *23*, 806–819. [CrossRef]
4. Khouadjia, M.R.; Sarasola, B.; Alba, E.; Jourdan, L.; Talbi, E.G. A Comparative Study between Dynamic Adapted PSO and VNS for the Vehicle Routing Problem with Dynamic Requests. *Appl. Soft Comput.* **2012**, *12*, 1426–1439. [CrossRef]
5. Adibi, M.A.; Zandieh, M.; Amiri, M. Multi-Objective Scheduling of Dynamic Job Shop Using Variable Neighborhood Search. *Expert Syst. Appl.* **2010**, *37*, 282–287. [CrossRef]

6. Mack, Y.; Goel, T.; Shyy, W.; Haftka, R. Surrogate Model-Based Optimization Framework: A Case Study in Aerospace Design. In *Evolutionary Computation in Dynamic and Uncertain Environments*; Yang, S., Ed.; Studies in Computational Intelligence; Springer: Berlin/Heidelberg, Germany, 2007; Volume 51, pp. 323–342.
7. Michalewicz, Z.; Schmidt, M.; Michalewicz, M.; Chiriac, C.; Yang, S. Adaptive Business Intelligence: Three Case Studies. In *Evolutionary Computation in Dynamic and Uncertain Environments*; Studies in Computational Intelligence; Springer: Berlin/Heidelberg, Germany, 2007; Volume 51, pp. 179–196.
8. Hossain, M.; Dewan, M.; Chae, O. A Flexible Edge Matching Technique for Object Detection in Dynamic Environment. *Int. J. Appl. Intell.* **2012**, *36*, 638–648. [CrossRef]
9. Shi, L.; Zhan, Z.-H.; Liang, D.; Zhang, J. Memory-Based Ant Colony System Approach for Multi-Source Data Associated Dynamic Electric Vehicle Dispatch Optimization. *IEEE Trans. Intell. Transp. Syst.* **2022**, *23*, 17491–17505. [CrossRef]
10. Wu, L.-J.; Shi, L.; Zhan, Z.-H.; Lai, K.-K.; Zhang, J. A Buffer-Based Ant Colony System Approach for Dynamic Cold Chain Logistics Scheduling. *IEEE Trans. Emerg. Top. Comput. Intell.* **2022**, *6*, 1438–1452. [CrossRef]
11. Eaton, J.; Yang, S.; Mavrovouniotis, M. Ant Colony Optimization with Immigrants Schemes for the Dynamic Railway Junction Rescheduling Problem with Multiple Delays. *Soft Comput.* **2016**, *20*, 2951–2966. [CrossRef]
12. Kordestani, J.K.; Rezvanian, A.; Meybodi, M.R. An Efficient Oscillating Inertia Weight of Particle Swarm Optimisation for Tracking Optima in Dynamic Environments. *J. Exp. Theor. Artif. Intell.* 2015; *in press*. [CrossRef]
13. Kordestani, J.K.; Mirsaleh, M.R.; Rezvanian, A.; Meybodi, M.R. *Advances in Learning Automata and Intelligent Optimization*; Springer: Berlin/Heidelberg, Germany, 2021.
14. Kordestani, J.K.; Rezvanian, A.; Meybodi, M.R. CDEPSO: A Bi-Population Hybrid Approach for Dynamic Optimization Problems. *Appl. Intell.* **2014**, *40*, 682–694. [CrossRef]
15. Richter, H. Detecting Change in Dynamic Fitness Landscapes. In Proceedings of the IEEE Congress on Evolutionary Computation, Trondheim, Norway, 18–21 May 2009; pp. 1613–1620.
16. Cruz, C.; González, J.R.; Pelta, D.A. Optimization in Dynamic Environments: A Survey on Problems, Methods and Measures. *Soft Comput.* **2010**, *15*, 1427–1448. [CrossRef]
17. Nickabadi, A.; Ebadzadeh, M.; Safabakhsh, R. A Competitive Clustering Particle Swarm Optimizer for Dynamic Optimization Problems. *Swarm Intell.* **2012**, *6*, 177–206. [CrossRef]
18. Ayvaz, D.; Topcuoglu, H.R.; Gurgen, F. Performance Evaluation of Evolutionary Heuristics in Dynamic Environments. *Int. J. Appl. Intell.* **2012**, *37*, 130–144. [CrossRef]
19. Noroozi, V.; Hashemi, A.B.; Meybodi, M.R. Alpinist CellularDE: A Cellular Based Optimization Algorithm for Dynamic Environments. In Proceedings of the Fourteenth International Conference on Genetic and Evolutionary Computation Conference Companion (GECCO 2012), Philadelphia, PA, USA, 7–11 July 2012; ACM: New York, NY, USA, 2012; pp. 1519–1520.
20. Yang, S. Genetic Algorithms with Memory-and Elitism-Based Immigrants in Dynamic Environments. *Evol. Comput.* **2008**, *16*, 385–416. [CrossRef] [PubMed]
21. Yang, S.; Cheng, H.; Wang, F. Genetic Algorithms With Immigrants and Memory Schemes for Dynamic Shortest Path Routing Problems in Mobile Ad Hoc Networks. *IEEE Trans. Syst. Man. Cybern Part. C Appl. Rev.* **2010**, *40*, 52–63. [CrossRef]
22. Blackwell, T.; Branke, J. Multiswarms, Exclusion, and Anti-Convergence in Dynamic Environments. *IEEE Trans. Evol. Comput.* **2006**, *10*, 459–472. [CrossRef]
23. González, J.R.; Masegosa, A.D.; García, I.J. A Cooperative Strategy for Solving Dynamic Optimization Problems. *Memetic Comput.* **2011**, *3*, 3–14. [CrossRef]
24. Yu, X.; Tang, K.; Chen, T.; Yao, X. Empirical Analysis of Evolutionary Algorithms with Immigrants Schemes for Dynamic Optimization. *Memetic Comput.* **2009**, *1*, 3–24. [CrossRef]
25. Giacobini, M.; Alba, E.; Tomassini, M. Selection Intensity in Asynchronous Cellular Evolutionary Algorithms. In Proceedings of the Genetic and Evolutionary Computation—GECCO 2003, Chicago, IL, USA, 12–16 July 2003; Lecture Notes in Computer Science. Springer: Berlin/Heidelberg, Germany, 2003; Volume 2723, pp. 955–966.
26. Wolfram, S. *Theory and Applications of Cellular Automata*; World Scientific Publication: Singapore, 1986.
27. Jin, Y.; Branke, J. Evolutionary Optimization in Uncertain Environments-a Survey. *IEEE Trans. Evol. Comput.* **2005**, *9*, 303–317. [CrossRef]
28. Nguyena, T.T.; Yangb, S.; Brankec, J. Evolutionary Dynamic Optimization: A Survey of the State of the Art. *Swarm Evol. Comput.* **2012**, *6*, 1–24. [CrossRef]
29. Yazdani, D.; Cheng, R.; Yazdani, D.; Branke, J.; Jin, Y.; Yao, X. A Survey of Evolutionary Continuous Dynamic Optimization over Two Decades—Part A. *IEEE Trans. Evol. Comput.* **2021**, *25*, 609–629. [CrossRef]
30. Yazdani, D.; Cheng, R.; Yazdani, D.; Branke, J.; Jin, Y.; Yao, X. A Survey of Evolutionary Continuous Dynamic Optimization over Two Decades—Part B. *IEEE Trans. Evol. Comput.* **2021**, *25*, 630–650. [CrossRef]
31. Moser, I.; Chiong, R. Dynamic Function Optimization: The Moving Peaks Benchmark. In *Metaheuristics for Dynamic Optimization*; Springer: Berlin/Heidelberg, Germany, 2013; pp. 35–59.
32. Li, X.; Branke, J.; Blackwell, T. Particle Swarm with Speciation and Adaptation in a Dynamic Environment. In Proceedings of the 8th Annual Conference on Genetic and Evolutionary Computation (GECCO '06), Seattle, DC, USA, 2–12 July 2006; pp. 51–58.
33. Nasiri, B.; Meybodi, M.R. Speciation Based Firefly Algorithm for Optimization in Dynamic Environments. *Int. J. Artif. Intell.* **2012**, *8*, 118–132.

34. Trojanowski, K.; Wierzchon, S.T. Studying Properties of Multipopulation Heuristic Approach to Non-Stationary Optimisation Tasks. In *Intelligent Information Processing and Web Mining*; Springer: Berlin/Heidelberg, Germany, 2003; Volume 22, pp. 23–32.
35. Timmis, J.; Neal, M. A Resource Limited Artificial Immune System for Data Analysis. *Knowl.-Based Syst.* **2001**, *14*, 121–130. [CrossRef]
36. Zheng, J.; Chen, Y.; Zhang, W. A Survey of Artificial Immune Applications. *Artif. Intell. Rev.* **2010**, *34*, 19–34. [CrossRef]
37. de Franca, F.O.; Von Zuben, F.J.; de Castro, L.N. An Artificial Immune Network for Multimodal Function Optimization on Dynamic Environments. In Proceedings of the 2005 Conference on Genetic and Evolutionary Computation (GECCO '05), Washington, DC, USA, 25–29 June 2005; ACM: New York, NY, USA, 2005; pp. 289–296.
38. Xuhua, S.; Feng, Q. An Optimization Algorithm Based on Multi-Population Artificial Immune Network. In Proceedings of the Fifth International Conference on Natural Computation (ICNC '09), Tianjin, China, 14–16 August 2009; pp. 379–383.
39. Gasper, A.; Collard, P. From GAs to Artificial Immune Systems: Improving Adaptation in Time Dependent Optimization. In Proceedings of the 1999 Congress on Evolutionary Computation, (CEC 99), Washington, DC, USA, 6–9 July 1999; Volume 3.
40. Kelsey, J.; Timmis, J. Immune Inspired Somatic Contiguous Hypermutation for Function Optimisation. In Proceedings of the Genetic and Evolutionary Computation—GECCO 2003, Chicago, IL, USA, 12–16 July 2003; Lecture Notes in Computer Science. Springer: Berlin/Heidelberg, Germany, 2003; Volume 2723, pp. 207–218.
41. De Castro, L.N.; Von Zuben, F.J. The Clonal Selection Algorithm with Engineering Applications. In Proceedings of the GECCO00 Workshop on Artificial Immune Systems and Their Applications, Las Vegas, NV, USA, 8 July 2000; Volume 3637, pp. 36–39.
42. Trojanowski, K.; Wierzchon, S.T. Immune-Based Algorithms for Dynamic Optimization. *Inf. Sci.* **2009**, *179*, 1495–1515. [CrossRef]
43. Aragón, V.S.; Esquivel, S.C.; Coello Coello, C.A. A T-Cell Algorithm for Solving Dynamic Optimization Problems. *Inf. Sci.* **2011**, *181*, 3614–3637. [CrossRef]
44. Shi, X.; Qian, F. Immune Response-Based Algorithm for Optimization of Dynamic Environments. *J. Cent. South Univ.* **2011**, *18*, 1563–1571. [CrossRef]
45. Nabizadeh, S.; Rezvanian, A.; Meybodi, M.R. A Multi-Swarm Cellular PSO Based on Clonal Selection Algorithm in Dynamic Environments. In Proceedings of the 2012 International Conference on Informatics, Electronics & Vision (ICIEV), Dhaka, Bangladesh, 18–19 May 2012; pp. 482–486.
46. Rezvanian, A.; Meybodi, M.R.; Kim, T. Tracking Extrema in Dynamic Environments Using a Learning Automata-Based Immune Algorithm. In *Grid and Distributed Computing, Control and Automation*; Communications in Computer and Information Science; Springer: Berlin/Heidelberg, Germany, 2010; Volume 121, pp. 216–225.
47. Ceccherini-Silberstein, T.; Coornaert, M. *Cellular Automata and Groups*; Springer: Berlin/Heidelberg, Germany, 2010.
48. Kroc, J.; Hoekstra, A.; Sloot, P.M.A. *Simulating Complex Systems by Cellular Automata*; Springer: New York, NY, USA, 2010.
49. Alba, E.; Dorronsoro, B. *Cellular Genetic Algorithms*; Springer: Berlin/Heidelberg, Germany, 2008; Volume 42.
50. Shi, Y.; Liu, H.; Gao, L.; Zhang, G. Cellular Particle Swarm Optimization. *Inf. Sci.* **2011**, *181*, 4460–4493. [CrossRef]
51. Rastegar, R.; Meybodi, M.R.; Hariri, A. A New Fine-Grained Evolutionary Algorithm Based on Cellular Learning Automata. *Int. J. Hybrid Intell. Syst.* **2006**, *3*, 83–98. [CrossRef]
52. Hashemi, A.B.; Meybodi, M.R. A Multi-Role Cellular PSO for Dynamic Environments. In Proceedings of the 14th International CSI Computer Conference, Tehran, Iran, 20–21 October 2009; pp. 412–417.
53. Hashemi, A.; Meybodi, M.R. Cellular PSO: A PSO for Dynamic Environments. In *Advances in Computation and Intelligence*; Cai, Z., Ed.; Lecture Notes in Computer Science; Springer: Berlin/Heidelberg, Germany, 2009; pp. 422–433.
54. Noroozi, V.; Hashemi, A.; Meybodi, M.R. CellularDE: A Cellular Based Differential Evolution for Dynamic Optimization Problems. In *Adaptive and Natural Computing Algorithms*; Dobnikar, A., Ed.; Lecture Notes in Computer Science; Springer: Berlin/Heidelberg, Germany, 2011; pp. 340–349.
55. Vafashoar, R.; Meybodi, M.R.; Momeni Azandaryani, A.H. CLA-DE: A Hybrid Model Based on Cellular Learning Automata for Numerical Optimization. *Appl. Intell.* **2012**, *36*, 735–748. [CrossRef]
56. Yazdani, D.; Golyari, S.; Meybodi, M.R. A New Hybrid Algorithm for Optimization Based on Artificial Fish Swarm Algorithm and Cellular Learning Automata. In Proceedings of the 2010 5th International Symposium on Telecommunications (IST), Tehran, Iran, 4–6 December 2010; pp. 932–937.
57. Basu, M. Artificial Immune System for Dynamic Economic Dispatch. *Int. J. Electr. Power Energy Syst.* **2011**, *33*, 131–136. [CrossRef]
58. Wu, S.S.; Li, B.Z.; Yang, J.G. A Three-Fold Approach to Solve Dynamic Job Shop Scheduling Problems by Artificial Immune Algorithm. *Adv. Mater. Res.* **2010**, *139*, 1666–1669. [CrossRef]
59. Zhang, Y.; Wang, S.; Wu, L.; Huo, Y. Artificial Immune System for Protein Folding Model. *J. Converg. Inf. Technol.* **2011**, *6*, 55–61.
60. Dasgupta, D.; Yu, S.; Nino, F. Recent Advances in Artificial Immune Systems: Models and Applications. *Appl. Soft Comput.* **2011**, *11*, 1574–1587. [CrossRef]
61. Chang, T.-Y.; Shiu, Y.-F. Simultaneously Construct IRT-Based Parallel Tests Based on an Adapted CLONALG Algorithm. *Int. J. Appl. Intell.* **2012**, *36*, 979–994. [CrossRef]
62. Wallenta, C.; Kim, J.; Bentley, P.J.; Hailes, S. Detecting Interest Cache Poisoning in Sensor Networks Using an Artificial Immune Algorithm. *Int. J. Appl. Intell.* **2010**, *32*, 1–26. [CrossRef]
63. Zeng, J.; Liu, X.; Li, T.; Li, G.; Li, H.; Zeng, J. A Novel Intrusion Detection Approach Learned from the Change of Antibody Concentration in Biological Immune Response. *Int. J. Appl. Intell.* **2011**, *35*, 41–62. [CrossRef]

64. Fernandez-Leon, J.A.; Acosta, G.G.; Mayosky, M.A. From Network-to-Antibody Robustness in a Bio-Inspired Immune System. *Biosystems* **2011**, *104*, 109–117. [CrossRef]
65. Zhao, W.; Davis, C.E. A Modified Artificial Immune System Based Pattern Recognition Approach–An Application to Clinical Diagnostics. *Artif. Intell. Med.* **2011**, *52*, 1–9. [CrossRef] [PubMed]
66. Jerne, N.K. Towards a Network Theory of the Immune System. *Ann. Immunol.* **1974**, *125C*, 373–389.
67. de Castro, L.N.; Timmis, J. An Artificial Immune Network for Multimodal Function Optimization. In Proceedings of the 2002 Congress on Evolutionary Computation, (CEC '02), Honolulu, HI, USA, 12–17 May 2002; pp. 699–704.
68. Timmis, J.; Hone, A.; Stibor, T.; Clark, E. Theoretical Advances in Artificial Immune Systems. *Theor. Comput. Sci.* **2008**, *403*, 11–32. [CrossRef]
69. Branke, J. Memory Enhanced Evolutionary Algorithms for Changing Optimization Problems. In Proceedings of the 1999 Congress on Evolutionary Computation, Washington, DC, USA, 6–9 July 1999; pp. 1875–1882.
70. The Moving Peaks Benchmark. Available online: http://www.aifb.unikarlsruhe.de/~jbr/MovPeaks/ (accessed on 1 May 2010).
71. Li, C.; Yang, S. Fast Multi-Swarm Optimization for Dynamic Optimization Problems. In Proceedings of the Fourth International Conference on Natural Computation, 2008, (ICNC'08), Jinan, China, 18–20 October 2008; Volume 7, pp. 624–628.
72. du Plessis, M.C.; Engelbrecht, A.P. Differential Evolution for Dynamic Environments with Unknown Numbers of Optima. *J. Glob. Optim.* **2013**, *55*, 73–99. [CrossRef]
73. Liu, L.; Wang, D.; Tang, J. Composite Particle Optimization with Hyper-Reflection Scheme in Dynamic Environments. *Appl. Soft Comput.* **2011**, *11*, 4626–4639. [CrossRef]
74. Nabizadeh, S.; Rezvanian, A.; Meybodi, M.R. Tracking Extrema in Dynamic Environment Using Multi-Swarm Cellular PSO with Local Search. *Int. J. Electron. Inf.* **2012**, *1*, 29–37.
75. Kordestani, J.K.; Ranginkaman, A.E.; Meybodi, M.R.; Novoa-Hernández, P. A Novel Framework for Improving Multi-Population Algorithms for Dynamic Optimization Problems: A Scheduling Approach. *Swarm Evol. Comput.* **2019**, *44*, 788–805. [CrossRef]

algorithms

MDPI

Article

Carousel Greedy Algorithms for Feature Selection in Linear Regression

Jiaqi Wang [1,*], Bruce Golden [2,*] and Carmine Cerrone [3]

1 Department of Mathematics, University of Maryland, College Park, MD 20742, USA
2 Robert H. Smith School of Business, University of Maryland, College Park, MD 20742, USA
3 Department of Economics and Business Studies, University of Genoa, 16126 Genoa, Italy; carmine.cerrone@unige.it
* Correspondence: jqwang@umd.edu (J.W.); bgolden@umd.edu (B.G.)

Abstract: The carousel greedy algorithm (CG) was proposed several years ago as a generalized greedy algorithm. In this paper, we implement CG to solve linear regression problems with a cardinality constraint on the number of features. More specifically, we introduce a default version of CG that has several novel features. We compare its performance against stepwise regression and more sophisticated approaches using integer programming, and the results are encouraging. For example, CG consistently outperforms stepwise regression (from our preliminary experiments, we see that CG improves upon stepwise regression in 10 of 12 cases), but it is still computationally inexpensive. Furthermore, we show that the approach is applicable to several more general feature selection problems.

Keywords: carousel greedy; feature selection; linear regression

1. Introduction

The carousel greedy algorithm (CG) is a generalized greedy algorithm that seeks to overcome the traditional weaknesses of greedy approaches. A generalized greedy algorithm uses a greedy algorithm as a subroutine in order to search a more expansive set of solutions with a small and predictable increase in computational effort. To be more specific, greedy algorithms often make poor choices early on and these cannot be undone. CG, on the other hand, allows the heuristic to correct early mistakes. The difference is often significant.

In the original paper, Cerrone et al. (2017) [1] applied CG to several combinatorial optimization problems such as the minimum label spanning tree problem, the minimum vertex cover problem, the maximum independent set problem, and the minimum weight vertex cover problem. Its performance was very encouraging. More recently, it has been applied to a variety of other problems; see Table 1 for details.

CG is conceptually simple and easy to implement. Furthermore, it can be applied to many greedy algorithms. In this paper, we will focus on using CG to solve the well-known linear regression problem with a cardinality constraint. In other words, we seek to identify the k most important variables, predictors, or features out of a total of p. The motivation is quite straightforward. Stepwise regression is a widely used greedy heuristic to solve this problem. However, the results are not as near-optimal as we would like. CG can generate better solutions within a reasonable amount of computing time.

In addition to the combinatorial optimization problems studied in Cerrone et al. (2017) [1], the authors also began to study stepwise linear regression. Their experiments were modest and preliminary. A pseudo-code description of their CG stepwise linear regression approach is provided in Algorithm 1. For the problem to be interesting, we assume that the number of explanatory variables to begin with (say, p) is large and the number of these variables that we want in the model (say, k) is much smaller.

Table 1. Recent applications of CG.

Year	Problem	Authors
2023	Knapsack Problem with Forfeits	D'Ambrosio et al. [2]
2022	Knapsack Problem with Forfeits	Capobianco et al. [3]
2022	Maximum Network Lifetime Problem with Time Slots and Coverage Constraints	Cerulli et al. [4]
2021	Grocery Distribution Plans in Urban Networks with Street Crossing Penalties	Cerrone et al. [5]
2021	Finding Minimum Positive Influence Dominating Sets in Social Networks	Shan et al. [6]
2020	Knapsack Problem with Forfeits	Cerulli et al. [7]
2020	Remote Sensing with Unmanned Aerial Vehicles (UAVs)	Hammond et al. [8]
2020	Close-Enough Traveling Salesman Problem	Carrabs et al. [9]
2019	Community Detection in Complex Networks	Kong et al. [10]
2019	Strong Generalized Minimum Labeling Spanning Tree Problem	Cerrone et al. [11]
2019	Sentiment Analysis	Hadi et al. [12]
2018	A Distribution Problem	Cerrone et al. [13]
2017	Maximum Network Lifetime Problem with Interference Constraints	Carrabs et al. [14]

Algorithm 1 Pseudo-code of carousel greedy for linear regression from [1].

Input I (I is the set of explanatory variables)
Input n (n is the number of explanatory variables you want in the model)
Let $S \leftarrow$ model containing all the explanatory variables in I
$R \leftarrow$ partial solution produced by removing from S, $|S| - n$ elements according to the backward selection criteria
for αn iterations **do**
  remove from tail of R an explanatory variable
  according to the forward selection criteria, add an element to head of R
    $\triangleright$ R is an ordered sequence, where its head is the side for adding and the tail for removing
end for
return R

The experiments were limited, but promising. The purpose of this article is to present a more complete study of the application of CG to linear regression with a constraint on the number of explanatory variables. In all of the experiments in this paper, we assume a cardinality constraint. Furthermore, in the initial paper on CG, Cerrone et al. (2017) [1] worked with two datasets for linear regression and also assumed a target number of explanatory/predictor variables. This is an important variant of linear regression and it ensures that different subsets of variables can be conveniently compared using RSS.

2. Linear Regression and Feature Selection

The rigorous mathematical definition of the problem is:

$$\min_{\theta} RSS = \sum_{i=1}^{n} (\sum_{j=1}^{p} X_{ij}\theta_j - y_i)^2, \tag{1}$$

$$\text{subject to } \sum_{j=1}^{p} I_{\theta_j \neq 0} \leq k, \tag{2}$$

where the following notation applies:

RSS: the residual sum of squares,
$X \in \mathbb{R}^{n \times p}$: the independent variables,
X_{ij}: the ith row and j^{th} column of X,
$y \in \mathbb{R}^n$: the dependent variable,
y_i: the ith element of y,

$\theta \in \mathbb{R}^p$: the coefficient vector of explanatory variables,
θ_j: the jth element of θ,
n: the number of observations,
p: the total number of explanatory variables (features),
k: the number of explanatory variables we want in the model, and
$I_{\theta_j \neq 0}$: equals 1 if $\theta_j \neq 0$ is true and 0 otherwise.

While we use RSS (i.e., OLS or ordinary least squares) as the objective function, other criteria, such as AIC [15], C_p [16], BIC [17], and RIC [18], are possible. We point out that our goal in this paper is quite focused. We do not consider the other criteria mentioned above. In addition, we do not separate the data into training, test, and validation sets as is commonly the case in machine learning models. Rather, we concentrate on minimizing RSS over the training set. This is fully compatible with the objective in linear regression and best subset selection.

There are three general approaches to solving the problem in (1) and (2). We summarize them below.

1. Best subset selection. This direct approach typically uses mixed integer optimization (MIO). It has been championed in articles by Bertsimas and his colleagues [19,20]. Although MIO solvers have become very powerful in the last few decades and they can solve problems much faster than in the past, running times can still become too large for many real-world datasets. Zhu et al. [21] has recently proposed a polynomial time algorithm, but it requires some mild conditions on the dataset and it works with high probability, but not always.
2. Regularization. This approach was initially used to address overfitting in unconstrained regression so that the resulting model would behave in a *regular* way. In this approach, the constraints are moved into the objective function with a penalty term. Regularization is a widely used method because of its speed and high performance in making predictions on test data. The most famous regularized model, lasso [22], uses the L^1-penalty as shown below:

$$\min_{\theta} \sum_{i=1}^{n} (\sum_{j=1}^{p} X_{ij}\theta_j - y_i)^2 + \lambda \sum_{j=1}^{p} |\theta_j| \tag{3}$$

   As λ becomes larger, it will prevent θ from having a large L^1-norm. At the same time, the number of nonzero θ_i values will also become smaller. For any k, there exists a λ such that the number of nonzero θ_i values is roughly k, but the number can sometimes jump sharply. This continuous optimization model is very fast, but there are some disadvantages. Some follow-up papers using ideas such as adaptive lasso [23], L0Learn [24], trimmed lasso [25], elastic net [26], and MC+ [27] appear to improve the model by modifying the penalty term. Specifically, L0Learn [24] uses the L^0-penalty as shown below:

$$\min_{\theta} \sum_{i=1}^{n} (\sum_{j=1}^{p} X_{ij}\theta_j - y_i)^2 + \lambda \sum_{j=1}^{p} I_{\theta_j \neq 0}. \tag{4}$$

   For sparse high-dimensional regression, some authors [28,29] use L^2 regularization without removing the cardinality constraint.
3. Heuristics. Since the subset selection problem is hard to solve optimally, a compromise would be to find a very good solution quickly using a heuristic approach. Stepwise regression is a widely used heuristic for this problem. An alternating method that can achieve a so-called partial minimum is presented in [30]. SparseNet [31] provides a coordinate-wise optimization algorithm. CG is another heuristic approach. One idea is to apply CG from a random selection of predictor variables. An alternative is to apply CG to the result of stepwise regression in order to improve the solution. We might expect the latter to outperform MIO in terms of running time, but not in terms

of solution quality. In our computational experiments, we will compare approaches with respect to RSS on training data only.

There are different variants of the problem specified in (1) and (2). We can restrict the number of variables to be at most k, as in (1) and (2). Alternatively, we can restrict the number of variables to be exactly k. Finally, we can solve an unrestricted version of the problem. We point out that when we minimize RSS over training data only, it always helps to add another variable. Therefore, when the model specifies there will be at most k variables, the solution will involve exactly k variables.

In response to the exciting recent work in [19,20] on the application of highly sophisticated MIO solvers (e.g., Gurobi) to solve the best subset regression problem posed in (1) and (2), Hastie et al. [32] have published an extensive computational comparison in which best subset selection, forward stepwise selection, and lasso are evaluated on synthetic data. The authors used both a training set and a test set in their experiments. They implemented the mixed integer quadratic program from [20] and made the resulting R code available in [32]. They found that best subset selection and lasso work well, but neither dominates the other. Furthermore, a relaxed version of lasso created by Meinshausen [33] is the overall winner.

Our goal in this paper is to propose a smart heuristic to solve the regression problem where k is fixed in advance. The heuristic should be easy to understand, code, and use. It should have a reasonably fast running time, although it will require more time than stepwise regression. We expect that for large k, it will be faster than best subset selection.

In this paper, we will test our ideas on the three real-world datasets from the UCI ML Repository (see https://archive.ics.uci.edu/, accessed on 11 April 2023) listed below:

1. CT (Computerized Tomography) Slice Dataset: n = 10,001, $p = 384$;
2. Building Dataset: $n = 372$, $p = 107$; and
3. Insurance Dataset: $n = 9822$, $p = 85$.

Since we are most interested in the linear regression problem where k is fixed, we seek to compare the results of best subset selection, CG, and stepwise regression. We will use the R code from [32], our CG code, and the stepwise regression code from (http://www.science.smith.edu/~jcrouser/SDS293/labs/lab8-py.html, accessed on 11 September 2022) in our experiments. For now, we can say that best subset selection takes much more time than stepwise regression and it typically obtains much better solutions. Our goal will be to demonstrate that CG represents a nice compromise approach. We expect CG solutions to be better than stepwise regression solutions and the running time to be much faster than it is for the best subset selection solutions.

We use the following hardware: CPU 11th Gen Intel(R) Core(TM) i7-11700F @ 2.50 GHz 2.50 GHz. The algorithms in this paper are implemented in Python 3.9.12, unless otherwise mentioned. CG is implemented in Python 3.9.12 without parallelization, unless otherwise mentioned. On the other hand, when Gurobi 10.0.0 is used, all of the 16 threads are utilized (in parallel).

3. Algorithm Description and Preliminary Experiments

3.1. Basic Algorithm and Default Settings

In contrast to the application of CG to linear regression in [1], shown in Algorithm 1, we present a general CG approach to linear regression with a cardinality constraint in Algorithm 2.

Algorithm 2 Pseudo-code of carousel greedy for linear regression with a cardinality constraint.

Input $I, k, S, \beta, \alpha, \gamma$
Output R
$R \leftarrow S$ with $\beta|S|$ variables dropped from head ▷ $\beta|S|$ rounded to the nearest integer
REC $\leftarrow R$
RECRSS $\leftarrow$ RSS of R
for $\alpha(1-\beta)|S|$ iterations **do**
    Remove γ variables from the tail of R
    Add γ variables from $I - R$ to the head of R one by one according to forward selection criterion
    if RSS of $R <$ REC **then**
        REC $\leftarrow R$
        RECRSS $\leftarrow$ RSS of R
    end if
end for
R $\leftarrow$ Use forward selections to add elements to REC one by one until k variables are selected
return R

Here, the inputs are:
I: the set of explanatory variables,
k: the number of variables we want in the model,
S: the initial set of variables with $|S| = k$,
β: the percentage of variables we remove initially,
α: the number of carousel loops where we have $(1-\beta)|S|$ carousel steps in each loop, and
γ: the number of variables we remove/add in each carousel step.

The starting point of Algorithm 2 is a feasible variable set S with order. We drop a fraction of β from S. Then, we start our α carousel loops of removing and adding variables. In each carousel step, we remove γ variables from the tail of R and add γ variables to the head of R one by one according to forward selection. The illustration of head and tail is shown in Figure 1. Each time we finish a carousel step, the best set of variables in terms of RSS is recorded. When carousel loops are finished, we add variables to the best recorded set according to the forward selection criterion one by one until a feasible set of k variables is selected.

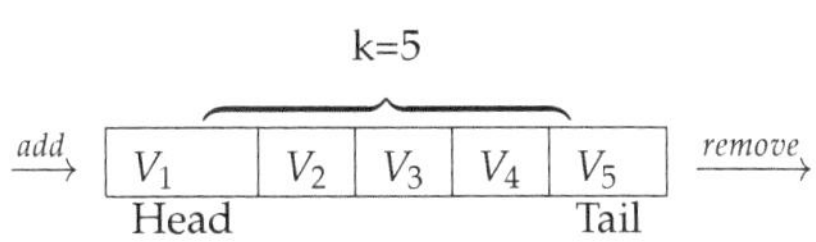

Figure 1. An illustration of head and tail for $k = 5$, $\beta = 0$.

For a specific linear regression problem, I and k are fixed. S, β, α, γ are the parameters which must be set by the user. In general, the best values may be difficult to find and they may vary widely from one problem/dataset to another.

As a result, we start with a default set of parameter values and run numerous experiments. These parameter values work reasonably well across many problems. We present the pseudo-code and flowchart for this simple implementation of a CG approach in Algorithm 3 and Figure 2.

Algorithm 3 Pseudo-code of the default version of carousel greedy we recommend for linear regression with a cardinality constraint.

Input I, k
Output R
$S \leftarrow$ the solution produced by forward stepwise regression $\triangleright$ In the order of selection
$R \leftarrow S$
$LastImpro = 0$
$RECRSS =$ RSS of R
while $LastImpro < k$ **do**
    $LastImpro = LastImprove + 1$
    Remove 1 variable from the tail of R
    Add 1 variable to the head of R according to forward selection
    if RSS of $R < RECRSS$ **then**
        $LastImpro = 0$
    end if
end while
return R

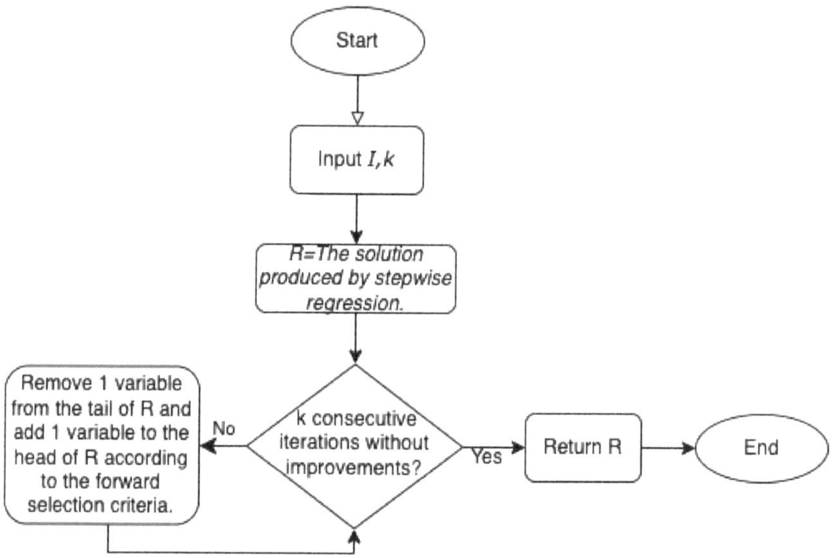

Figure 2. Flowchart of default CG.

In other words, the default parameters are:
$S =$ the result of stepwise regression with k variables,
$\beta = 0$,
α is set in an implicit way such that we have k consecutive carousel steps without improvement of RSS, and
$\gamma = 1$.

3.2. Properties

There are a few properties for this default setting:

1. The RSS of the output will be at least as good as the RSS from stepwise regression.
2. The RSS of the incumbent solution is always monotonically decreasing.
3. When the algorithm stops, it is impossible to achieve further improvements of RSS by running additional carousel greedy steps.

4. The result is a so-called full swap inescapable (FSI(1)) minimum [24], i.e., no interchange of an inside element and an outside element can improve the RSS.

3.3. Preliminary Experiments

The following experiments show how CG evolves the solution from stepwise regression. As shown in Figure 3, CG consistently improves the RSS of the stepwise regression solution gradually in the beginning and stabilizes eventually. A final horizontal line segment of length 1 indicates that no further improvements are possible.

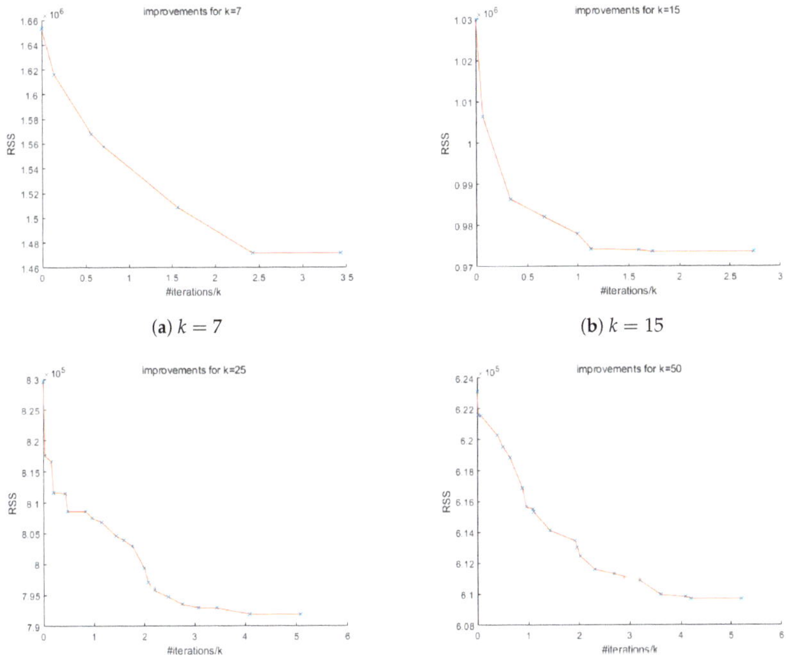

(**a**) $k = 7$ (**b**) $k = 15$ (**c**) $k = 25$ (**d**) $k = 50$

Figure 3. Improvements from carousel greedy with stepwise initialization for the CT slice dataset. The RSS of stepwise regression is at $x = 0$.

For the CT slice dataset we are using, the best subset selection cannot completely solve the problems in a reasonable time. When we limit the time of the best subset selection algorithm to a scale similar to CG, the RSS of its output is not as good as CG. Even if we give best subset selection more than twice as much time, the result is still not as good. The results are shown in Table 2 (the best results in Table 2 for each k are indicated in bold).

From Figures 4 and 5, some improvements from stepwise regression solutions can be observed. However, as the number of observations (n) and the number of variables (p) in the dataset become smaller, the model itself becomes simpler, in which case there will be less room for CG to excel and the number of improvements also becomes smaller. Figure 5b,c show no improvements from stepwise regression. This might mean the stepwise regression solution is already relatively good. In that case, we may want to use other initializations to see if we can find better solutions.

Table 2. Comparisons of stepwise regression, CG, and best subset with different time limits.

	$k = 7$ RSS	Time (s)	$k = 15$ RSS	Time (s)
Stepwise regression	1,653,208	5.55	1,029,899	16.08
CG with stepwise initialization	**1,471,932**	28.45	**973,695**	97.82
Best subset (warm start + MIP)	1,570,721	28.35	1,015,076	97.69
Best subset (warm start + MIP)	1,570,681	100.00	999,294	250.00
	$k = 25$ RSS	Time (s)	$k = 50$ RSS	Time (s)
Stepwise regression	829,608	38.45	623,118	132.24
CG with stepwise initialization	**791,960**	440.14	**609,722**	1409.88
Best subset (warm start + MIP)	819,911	441.75	611,207	1413.88
Best subset (warm start + MIP)	807,925	1000.00	610,542	3600.00

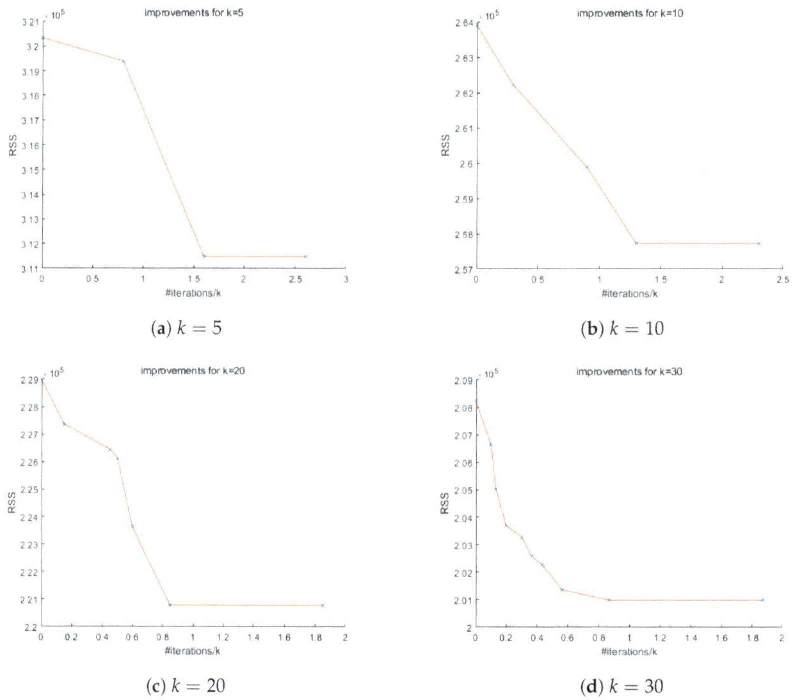

Figure 4. Improvements from carousel greedy with stepwise initialization for the Building dataset.

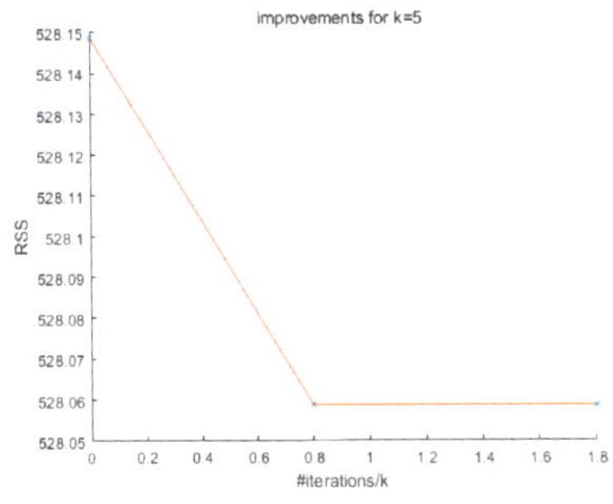

(**a**) $k = 5$

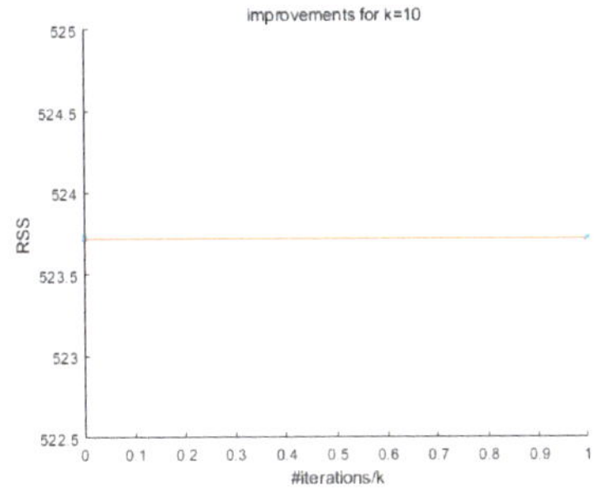

(**b**) $k = 10$

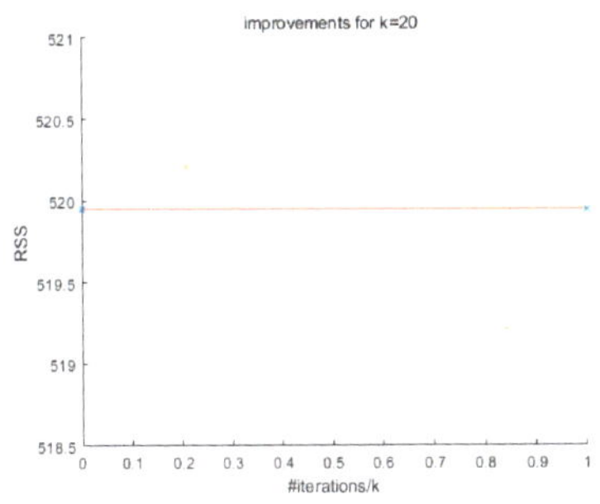

(**c**) $k = 20$

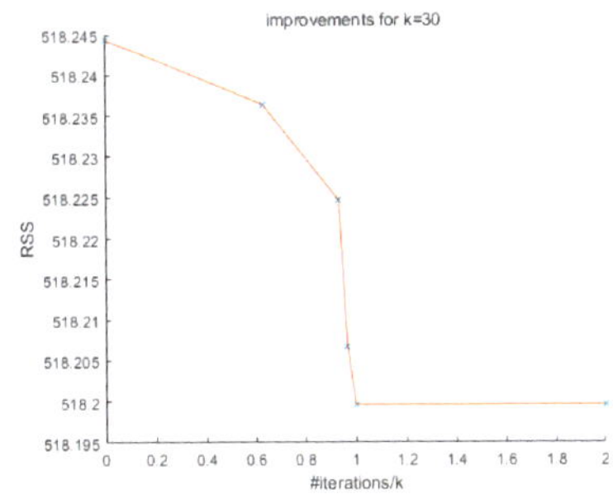

(**d**) $k = 30$

Figure 5. Improvements for carousel greedy with stepwise initialization for the Insurance dataset.

3.4. Stepwise Initialization and Random Initialization

As shown in Algorithm 2, there can be different initializations in a general CG algorithm. We might be able to find other solutions by choosing other initializations. A natural choice would be a complete random initialization.

We run the experiments for CG with stepwise initialization and random initialization for the CT slice dataset. For random initialization, we run 10 experiments and look at the average or minimum among the first 5 and among all 10 experiments.

From Table 3, we can see that the average RSS of random initialization is similar to that of stepwise initialization and usually takes slightly less time. The results are also quite close between different random initializations for most cases. However, if we run random initialization multiple times, for example, 5∼10 times, the best output will very likely be better than for stepwise initialization.

We now look back at the cases of Figure 5b,c using random initializations. We run 10 experiments on the Insurance dataset for $k = 10$ and 10 for $k = 20$ and plot the best, in terms of the final RSS, out of 10 experiments.

As shown in Figure 6, although we are able to find better solutions using random initialization than stepwise initialization, the improvements are very small. In this case, we are more confident that the stepwise regression solution is already good, and CG provides a tool to verify this.

In practice, if time permits or parallelization is available, we would suggest running CG with both stepwise initialization and multiple random initializations and taking the best result. Otherwise, stepwise initialization would be a safe choice.

Table 3. CG with stepwise initialization and random initialization for the CT slice dataset.

	$k = 7$ RSS	Time (s)	$k = 15$ RSS	Time (s)
Stepwise regression	1,653,208	5.55	1,029,899	16.08
CG with stepwise initialization	1,471,932	28.45	973,695	97.82
CG with random initialization (average over 10 experiments)	1,471,932	13.52	972,886	100.44
(min RSS over 10 experiments)	1,471,932		970,712	
CG with random initialization (average over 5 experiments)	1,471,932	16.88	972,674	96.32
(min RSS over 5 experiments)	1,471,932		970,712	
	$k = 25$ RSS	Time (s)	$k = 50$ RSS	Time (s)
Stepwise regression	829,608	38.45	623,118	132.24
CG with stepwise initialization	791,960	440.14	609,722	1409.88
CG with random initialization (average over 10 experiments)	791,581	300.25	612,304	1057.20
(min RSS over 10 experiments)	788,836		606,865	
CG with random initialization (average over 5 experiments)	791,380	273.90	612,404	1120.17
(min RSS over 5 experiments)	788,836		606,865	

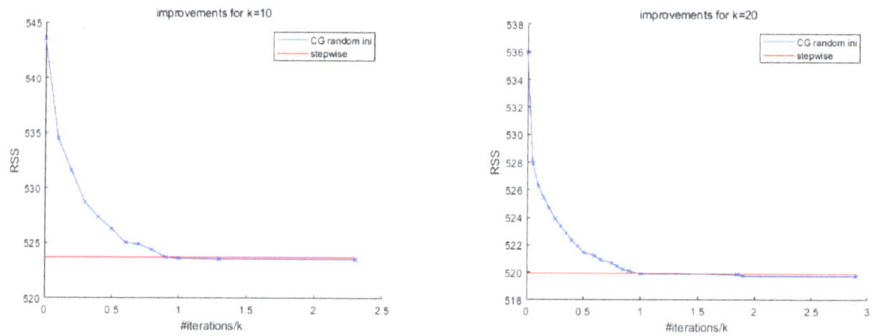

(**a**) $k = 10$ (**b**) $k = 20$

Figure 6. Improvements from carousel greedy with random initialization for the Insurance dataset.

3.5. Gurobi Implementation of Best Interchange to Find an FSI(1) Minimum

An alternative approach to Algorithm 3 is the notion of an FSI(1) minimum. This is a local minimum as described in Section 3.2. The original method for finding an FSI(1) minimum in [24] was to formulate the best interchange as the following best interchange MIP (BI-MIP) and apply it iteratively as in Algorithm 4. We will show that CG obtains results comparable to those from FSI(1), but without requiring the use of sophisticated integer programming software.

$$\text{BI-MIP: } \min \sum_{i=1}^{n} \left(\sum_{j=1}^{p} X_{ij}\theta_j - y_i\right)^2, \tag{5}$$

$$\text{subject to } -Mz_i \le \theta_i \le Mz_i, \quad \forall i \in [p], \tag{6}$$

$$z_i \le w_i, \quad \forall i \in S, \tag{7}$$

$$\sum_{i \in S^c} z_i \le 1, \tag{8}$$

$$\sum_{i \in S} w_i \le |S| - 1, \tag{9}$$

$$\theta_i \in \mathbb{R}, \quad \forall i \in [p], \tag{10}$$

$$z_i \in \{0, 1\}, \quad \forall i \in [p], \tag{11}$$

$$w_i \in \{0, 1\}, \quad \forall i \in S. \tag{12}$$

Here, we start from an initial set S and try to find a best interchange between a variable inside S and a variable outside S. The decision variables are θ, w, and z. z_is indicate the nonzeros in θ, i.e., if $z_i = 0$, then $\theta_i = 0$. w_i's indicate whether we remove variable i from

S, i.e., if $w_i = 0$, then variable i is removed from S. $[p]$ is defined to be the set $\{1, 2, \ldots, p\}$. In (5), we seek to minimize RSS. In (6), for every $i \in [p]$, $z_i = 1$ if θ_i is nonzero and M is a sufficiently large constant. From (7), we see that if variable i is removed, then θ_i must be zero. Inequality (8) means that the number of selected variables outside S is at most 1, i.e., we add at most 1 variable to S. From (9), we see that we remove at least 1 variable from S (the optimal solution removes exactly 1 variable).

In Algorithm 4 for finding an FSI(1) minimum, we solve BI-MIP iteratively until an iteration does not yield any improvement. The pseudo-code is as follows:

Algorithm 4 Pseudo-code of finding an FSI(1) local minimum by Gurobi.

```
Initialize |S| = k by forward stepwise regression with coefficients θ
while TRUE do
    S' ← Apply BI-MIP to S
    if RSS of S' ≥ RSS of S then
        Break
    end if
    S = S'
end while
return S
```

Recall that our default version of CG also returns an FSI(1) local minima. The solutions of the two methods are expected to return equally good solutions on average. We begin with a comparison on the CT slice dataset.

As shown in Table 4, the final RSS by Gurobi is very close to CG (the best results in Table 4 for each k are indicated in bold), but the running time is much longer for small k and not much faster for larger k. This is the case even though Gurobi uses all of the 16 threads by default while CG uses only one thread by default in Python. Therefore, our algorithm is simpler and does not require a commercial solver like Gurobi. It is also more efficient than the BI-MIP by Gurobi in terms of finding a local optima when k is small.

The circumstance can be different for an "ill-conditioned" instance. We tried to apply Algorithm 4 to the Building dataset, but it is a very simple model where $k = 1$ cannot be solved. Meanwhile, CG can solve it without any difficulty. The source of the issue is the quadratic coefficient matrix. The objective of BI-MIP is quadratic. When Gurobi solves quadratic programming, a very large difference between the largest and smallest eigenvalues of the coefficient matrix can bring about a substantial numerical issue. For the Building dataset, the largest eigenvalue is of order 10^{15}, the smallest eigenvalue is of order 10^{-10}. That's intractable for Gurobi. Therefore, CG is numerically more stable than Algorithm 4 using Gurobi.

Table 4. Iterated BI-MIPs by Gurobi (Algorithm 4) for the CT slice dataset (using up to 16 threads).

	k = 5		k = 7	
	RSS	Time (s)	RSS	Time (s)
Stepwise regression	2,129,794	3.41	1,653,208	5.55
CG with stepwise initialization	**2,104,917**	10.03	**1,471,932**	28.45
Iterated BI-MIPs by Gurobi with stepwise initialization	2,106,992	59.89	**1,471,932**	99.64
	k = 10		k = 15	
	RSS	Time (s)	RSS	Time (s)
Stepwise regression	1,307,711	8.22	1,029,899	16.08
CG with stepwise initialization	**1,198,650**	47.63	973,695	97.82
Iterated BI-MIPs by Gurobi with stepwise initialization	**1,198,650**	161.9	**970,712**	286.43

Table 4. *Cont.*

	k = 20 RSS	Time (s)	k = 25 RSS	Time (s)
Stepwise regression	911,080	25.99	829,608	38.45
CG with stepwise initialization	**870,346**	214.43	**791,960**	440.14
Iterated BI-MIPs by Gurobi with stepwise initialization	**870,346**	303.65	792,731	566.38
	k = 30 RSS	Time (s)	k = 35 RSS	Time (s)
Stepwise regression	767,448	52.70	723,472	68.81
CG with stepwise initialization	**741,317**	437.13	700,462	566.73
Iterated BI-MIPs by Gurobi with stepwise initialization	751,680	406.33	**699,196**	457.45
	k = 40 RSS	Time (s)	k = 45 RSS	Time (s)
Stepwise regression	685,136	85.31	651,250	107.74
CG with stepwise initialization	**666,991**	453.45	**638,087**	493.93
Iterated BI-MIPs by Gurobi with stepwise initialization	**666,991**	416.42	643,517	353.18
	k = 50 RSS	Time (s)		
Stepwise regression	623,118	132.24		
CG with stepwise initialization	609,722	1409.88		
Iterated BI-MIPs by Gurobi with stepwise initialization	**609,478**	768.68		

3.6. Running Time Analysis

Each time we add a variable, we need to run the least squares procedure (computing $(X_S^T X_S)^{-1} X_S^T y$, where X_S is the $n \times k$ submatrix of X whose column is indexed by S) a total of p times. For each addition of a variable, from basic numerical linear algebra, the complexity is $O(k^2(k+n))$. Therefore, for each new variable added, the complexity is $O(pk^2(k+n))$. If n is much larger than k, which is often the case, the complexity is about $O(npk^2)$. From the structure of Algorithm 2, we will add a variable $\alpha(1-\beta)\gamma k$ times. As a result, the complexity of CG is $O(\alpha(1-\beta)\gamma npk^3)$. We can treat α, β, γ as constants because they are independent of k, n, p. Therefore, the complexity of CG is still $O(npk^3)$.

4. Generalized Feature Selection

In this section, we will discuss two generalized versions of feature selection. Recall the feature selection problem that we discussed is

$$\min_{\theta} \sum_{i=1}^{n} (\sum_{j=1}^{p} X_{ij}\theta_j - y_i)^2, \tag{13}$$

$$\text{subject to } \sum_{j=1}^{p} I_{\theta_j \neq 0} \leq k. \tag{14}$$

This can be reformulated (big-M formulation) as the following MIP (for large enough $M > 0$):

$$\min_{\theta,z} \sum_{i=1}^{n} (\sum_{j=1}^{p} X_{ij}\theta_j - y_i)^2, \tag{15}$$

$$\text{subject to } -Mz_i \leq \theta_i \leq Mz_i, \quad \forall i \in [p], \tag{16}$$

$$\sum_{i \in [p]} z_i \leq k, \tag{17}$$

$$z_i \in \{0,1\}, \quad \forall i \in [p]. \tag{18}$$

Here, z_i is the indicator variable for θ_i, where $z_i = 1$ if θ_i is nonzero and $z_i = 0$ otherwise.

The problem can be generalized by adding some constraints.

Case A: Suppose we have sets of variables that are highly correlated. For example, if variables i, j, and k are in one of these sets, then we can add the following constraint:

$$z_i + z_j + z_k \leq 1. \tag{19}$$

If l and m are in another set, we can add

$$z_l + z_m \leq 1. \tag{20}$$

Case B: Suppose some of the coefficients must be bounded if the associated variables are selected. Then we can add the following constraints:

$$l_i z_i \leq \theta_i \leq u_i z_i, \quad \forall i \in [p]. \tag{21}$$

In (21), we allow $l_i = -\infty$ or $u_i = \infty$ for some i to include the case where the coefficients are unbounded from below or above.

CG can also be applied to Cases A and B. Let us restate CG and show how small modifications to CG can solve Cases A and B.

Recall that, in each carousel step of feature selection, we delete one variable and add one. Assume S_d is the set of variables *after* deleting one variable in a step. Then, the problem of adding one becomes: Solve unconstrained linear regression problems on the set $S_d \cup \{l\}$ for each $l \notin S_d$ and return the l with the smallest RSS. Expressed formally, this is

$$\text{argmin}_{l \notin S_d} f(l, S_d). \tag{22}$$

Here $f(l, S_d)$ indicates the RSS we obtain by adding l to S_d. It can be found from the following problem:

$$f(l, S_d) = \min_{\theta} \sum_{i=1}^{n} \Big(\sum_{j \in S_d \cup \{l\}} X_{ij}\theta_j - y_i \Big)^2. \tag{23}$$

In (23), only a submatrix of X with size $n \times (|S_d| + 1)$ is involved. That is, we solve a sequence of smaller size unconstrained linear regression problems for each $l \notin S_d$ and compare the results.

Following this idea, by using CG, we solve a sequence of smaller size unconstrained linear regression problems where the cardinality constraint is no longer in any subproblem.

For generalized feature selection, CG has the same framework. The differences are that the candidate variables to be added are limited by the notion of correlated sets for Case A, and the sequence of smaller size linear regression problems become constrained, as in (21), for Case B. The term we designate for the new process of adding a variable is the "generalized forward selection criterion." Let us start with Case A.

Case A: The addition of one variable is almost the same as for Algorithms 1–3, but the candidate variables should be those not highly correlated with any current variables, instead of any $l \notin S_d$. As an example, suppose variables i, j, and k are highly correlated. (For the sake of clarity, we point out that the data for variable i is contained in $X_{.i}$.) We want no more than one of these in our solution. At the l-th carousel step before adding a variable, we check whether one of these three is in S_d or not. If i is in S_d, we cannot add i or k. If i is not in S_d, we can add i, j, k or any other variable.

Case B: We can add variables as usual, but the coefficients corresponding to some of these variables are now bounded. We will need to solve a sequence of bounded variable least squares (BVLS) problems of the form

$$\text{argmin}_{l \notin S_d} f(l, S_d). \tag{24}$$

Here, $f(l, S_d)$ can be obtained from the following problem:

$$f(l,S_d) = \min_{\theta} \sum_{i=1}^{n} (\sum_{j \in S_d \cup \{l\}} X_{ij}\theta_j - y_i)^2, \tag{25}$$

$$\text{subject to } l_i \leq \theta_i \leq u_i, \quad \forall i \in S_d \cup \{l\}. \tag{26}$$

We extract the general subproblem of BVLS from the above:

$$\min_{\theta} \sum_{i=1}^{n} (\sum_{j \in S} X_{ij}\theta_j - y_i)^2, \tag{27}$$

$$\text{subject to } l_i \leq \theta_i \leq u_i, \quad \forall i \in S. \tag{28}$$

This is a quadratic (convex) optimization problem within a bounded and convex region (a p-dim box), which can be solved efficiently. There are several algorithms available without the need for any commercial solver. For example, a free and open-source Python library "Scipy" can solve it efficiently. The pseudo-codes for the application of CG and MIP to generalized feature selection can be found in Appendix A.

5. Conclusions and Future Work

In this paper, we propose an application of CG to the feature selection problem. The approach is straightforward and does not require any commercial optimization software. It is also easy to understand. It provides a compromise solution between the best subset selection and stepwise regression. The running time of CG is usually much shorter than that of the best subset selection and a few times longer than that of stepwise regression. The RSS of CG is always at least as good as for stepwise regression, but is typically not as good as for best subset. Therefore, CG is a very practical method for obtaining (typically) near-optimal solutions to the best subset selection problem.

With respect to the practical implications of our work, we point to the pervasiveness of greedy algorithms in the data science literature. Several well-known applications of the greedy algorithm include constructing a minimum spanning tree, implementing a Huffman encoding, and solving graph optimization problems (again, see [1]). In addition, numerous greedy algorithms have been proposed in the machine learning literature over the last 20 years for a wide variety of problems (e.g., see [34–38]). CG may not be directly applicable in every case, but we expect that it can be successfully applied in many of these cases.

We also show that the result of our CG can produce a so-called FSI(1) minimum. Finally, we provide some generalizations to more complicated feature selection problems in Section 4.

The implementation of CG still has some room for improvement. We leave this for future work, but here are some ideas. The computational experiments in this paper are based mainly on Algorithm 3, which includes a set of default parameter values. However, if we work from Algorithm 2, there may be a better set of parameter values, in general, or there may be better values for specific applications. Extensive computational experiments would have to focus on running time and accuracy in order to address this question. Furthermore, we think there are some more advanced results from numerical linear algebra that can be applied to improve the running time of the sequence of OLS problems that must be solved within CG. In addition, we think our approach can be applied to other problems in combinatorial optimization and data science. For example, we are beginning to look into the integration of neural networks and CG. The key idea is to replace the greedy selection function with a specifically trained neural network. CG could be employed to enhance the decisions recommended by the neural network. Again, we hope to explore this in future work.

Author Contributions: Conceptualization, B.G.; methodology, J.W., B.G. and C.C.; software, J.W.; validation, J.W., B.G. and C.C.; formal analysis, J.W.; investigation, J.W.; resources, B.G. and C.C.; data curation, J.W.; writing—original draft preparation, J.W.; writing—review and editing, B.G.; visualization, J.W.; supervision, B.G. and C.C.; project administration, B.G. All authors have read and agreed to the published version of the manuscript.

Funding: This research received no external funding.

Data Availability Statement: The datasets presented in this study are available in UCI ML Repository at https://archive.ics.uci.edu/ (accessed on 11 April 2023).

Conflicts of Interest: The authors declare no conflict of interest.

Appendix A. Pseudo-Code of Algorithms for Generalized Feature Selection

For generalized feature selection, all we need to do is to replace all of the forward selection steps in Algorithms 1–4 by generalized forward selection steps. For example, steps 1 and 8 for Algorithm A1 vs. Algorithm 3 reflect this change. Similarly, steps 1 and 3 for Algorithm A2 vs. Algorithm 4 reflect this change. Generalized forward selection includes both Case A and Case B. We provide the pseudo-codes of the generalizations of Algorithms 3 and 4 in Algorithms A1 and A2. The pseudo-codes of the generalizations of Algorithms 1 and 2 are left for the readers to deduce.

Algorithm A1 Pseudo-code of the default version of carousel greedy that we recommend for generalized feature selection.

Input I, k
Output R
1: $S \leftarrow$ the solution produced by generalized forward stepwise regression ▷ In the order of selection
2: $R \leftarrow S$
3: $LastImpro = 0$
4: $RECRSS$ = RSS of R
5: **while** $LastImpro < k$ **do**
6: $\quad LastImpro = LastImprove + 1$
7: $\quad$ Remove 1 variable from the tail of R
8: $\quad$ Add 1 variable to the head of R according to generalized forward selection
9: $\quad$ **if** RSS of $R < RECRSS$ **then**
10: $\quad\quad LastImpro = 0$
11: $\quad$ **end if**
12: **end while**
13: return R

In Algorithm A2, to apply generalized forward selection, best interchange MIP (BI-MIP) in Algorithm 4 should be replaced by generalized best interchange MIP (GBI-MIP) in Algorithm A2. Also, forward stepwise regression is replaced by generalized forward stepwise regresssion in step 1. The other parts of Algorithm 4 and Algorithm A2 are the same. GBI-MIP generalizes BI-MIP by introducing two additional constraints, one for Case A and the other for Case B, which means we can also incorporate both cases. The formulation of GBI-MIP is provided below:

$$\begin{aligned}
\text{GBI-MIP: min} \sum_{i=1}^{n}(\sum_{j=1}^{p} X_{ij}\theta_j - y_i)^2, && \text{(A1)}\\
\text{subject to } -Mz_i \leq \theta_i \leq Mz_i, \quad \forall i \in [p], && \text{(A2)}\\
\sum_{i \in HC_j} z_i \leq 1, \quad j = 1, ..., m, && \text{(A3)}\\
l_i z_i \leq \theta_i \leq u_i z_i, \quad \forall i \in [p], && \text{(A4)}\\
z_i \leq w_i, \quad \forall i \in S, && \text{(A5)}\\
\sum_{i \in S^c} z_i \leq 1, && \text{(A6)}\\
\sum_{i \in S} w_i \leq |S| - 1, && \text{(A7)}\\
\theta_i \in \mathbb{R}, \quad \forall i \in [p], && \text{(A8)}\\
z_i \in \{0,1\}, \quad \forall i \in [p], && \text{(A9)}\\
w_i \in \{0,1\}, \quad \forall i \in S. && \text{(A10)}
\end{aligned}$$

Here (A3) and (A4) are the two additional constraints for Case A and Case B, respectively. $HC_j, j = 1, \ldots, m$ are the sets of highly correlated variables. To exclude Case A, we can let each HC_j include only one variable. That is, each variable is only highly correlated with itself, and no other variables are highly correlated with it. To exclude Case B, we can let $l_i = -M, u_i = M$ for any $i \in [p]$ in (A4).

Algorithm A2 Pseudo-code of finding an FSI(1) local minimum for generalized feature selection by Gurobi.

Initialize $|S| = k$ by generalized forward stepwise regression with coefficients θ
while TRUE **do**
  $S' \leftarrow$ Apply GBI-MIP to S
  if RSS of $S' \geq$ RSS of S **then**
    Break
  end if
  $S = S'$
end while
return S

References

1. Cerrone, C.; Cerulli, R.; Golden, B. Carousel greedy: A generalized greedy algorithm with applications in optimization. *Comput. Oper. Res.* **2017**, *85*, 97–112. [CrossRef]
2. D'Ambrosio, C.; Laureana, F.; Raiconi, A.; Vitale, G. The knapsack problem with forfeit sets. *Comput. Oper. Res.* **2023**, *151*, 106093. [CrossRef]
3. Capobianco, G.; D'Ambrosio, C.; Pavone, L.; Raiconi, A.; Vitale, G.; Sebastiano, F. A hybrid metaheuristic for the knapsack problem with forfeits. *Soft Comput.* **2022**, *26*, 749–762. [CrossRef]
4. Cerulli, R.; D'Ambrosio, C.; Iossa, A.; Palmieri, F. Maximum network lifetime problem with time slots and coverage constraints: Heuristic approaches. *J. Supercomput.* **2022**, *78*, 1330–1355. [CrossRef]
5. . Cerrone, C.; Cerulli, R.; Sciomachen, A. Grocery distribution plans in urban networks with street crossing penalties. *Networks* **2021**, *78*, 248–263. [CrossRef]
6. Shan, Y.; Kang, Q.; Xiao, R.; Chen, Y.; Kang, Y. An iterated carousel greedy algorithm for finding minimum positive influence dominating sets in social networks. *IEEE Trans. Comput. Soc. Syst.* **2021**, *9*, 830–838. [CrossRef]
7. Cerulli, R.; D'Ambrosio, C.; Raiconi, A.; Vitale, G. The knapsack problem with forfeits. In *Combinatorial Optimization. ISCO 2020*; Lecture Notes in Computer Science; Baïou, M., Gendron, B., Günlük, O., Mahjoub, A.R., Eds.; Springer International Publishing: Cham, Switzerland, 2020; Volume 12176, pp. 263–272.
8. Hammond, J.E.; Vernon, C.A.; Okeson, T.J.; Barrett, B.J.; Arce, S.; Newell, V.; Janson, J.; Franke, K.W.; Hedengren, J.D. Survey of 8 UAV set-covering algorithms for terrain photogrammetry. *Remote Sens.* **2020**, *12*, 2285. [CrossRef]

9. Carrabs, F.; Cerrone, C.; Cerulli, R.; Golden, B. An adaptive heuristic approach to compute upper and lower bounds for the close-enough traveling salesman problem. *INFORMS J. Comput.* **2020**, *32*, 1030–1048. [CrossRef]
10. Kong, H.; Kang, Q.; Li, W.; Liu, C.; Kang, Y.; He, H. A hybrid iterated carousel greedy algorithm for community detection in complex networks. *Phys. A Stat. Mech. Its Appl.* **2019**, *536*, 122124. [CrossRef]
11. Cerrone, C.; D'Ambrosio, C.; Raiconi, A. Heuristics for the strong generalized minimum label spanning tree problem. *Networks* **2019**, *74*, 148–160. [CrossRef]
12. Hadi, K.; Lasri, R.; El Abderrahmani, A. An efficient approach for sentiment analysis in a big data environment. *Int. J. Eng. Adv. Technol. (IJEAT)* **2019**, *8*, 263–266.
13. Cerrone, C.; Gentili, M.; D'Ambrosio, C.; Cerulli, R. An efficient and simple approach to solve a distribution problem. In *New Trends in Emerging Complex Real Life Problems*; ODS: Taormina, Italy, 2018; pp. 151–159.
14. Carrabs, F.; Cerrone, C.; D'Ambrosio, C.; Raiconi, A. Column generation embedding carousel greedy for the maximum network lifetime problem with interference constraints. In Proceedings of the Optimization and Decision Science: Methodologies and Applications: ODS, Sorrento, Italy, 4–7 September 2017; Springer: Berlin/Heidelberg, Germany, 2017; pp. 151–159.
15. Akaike, H. Information theory and an extension of the maximum likelihood principle. In *Selected Papers of Hirotugu Akaike*; Springer: Berlin/Heidelberg, Germany, 1998; pp. 199–213.
16. Mallows, C.L. Some comments on Cp. *Technometrics* **2000**, *42*, 87–94.
17. Schwarz, G. Estimating the dimension of a model. *Ann. Stat.* **1978**, *6*, 461–464. [CrossRef]
18. Foster, D.P.; George, E.I. The risk inflation criterion for multiple regression. *Ann. Stat.* **1994**, *22*, 1947–1975. [CrossRef]
19. Bertsimas, D.; King, A. OR forum—An algorithmic approach to linear regression. *Oper. Res.* **2016**, *64*, 2–16. [CrossRef]
20. Bertsimas, D.; King, A.; Mazumder, R. Best subset selection via a modern optimization lens. *Ann. Stat.* **2016**, *44*, 813–852. [CrossRef]
21. Zhu, J.; Wen, C.; Zhu, J.; Zhang, H.; Wang, X. A polynomial algorithm for best-subset selection problem. *Proc. Natl. Acad. Sci. USA* **2020**, *117*, 33117–33123. [CrossRef] [PubMed]
22. Tibshirani, R. Regression shrinkage and selection via the lasso. *J. R. Stat. Soc. Ser. B (Methodol.)* **1996**, *58*, 267–288. [CrossRef]
23. Zou, H. The adaptive lasso and its oracle properties. *J. Am. Stat. Assoc.* **2006**, *101*, 1418–1429. [CrossRef]
24. Hazimeh, H.; Mazumder, R. Fast best subset selection: Coordinate descent and local combinatorial optimization algorithms. *Oper. Res.* **2020**, *68*, 1517–1537. [CrossRef]
25. Bertsimas, D.; Copenhaver, M.S.; Mazumder, R. The trimmed lasso: Sparsity and robustness. *arXiv* **2017**, arXiv:1708.04527.
26. Zou, H.; Hastie, T. Regularization and variable selection via the elastic net. *J. R. Stat. Soc. Ser. B Stat. Methodol.* **2005**, *67*, 301–320. [CrossRef]
27. Zhang, C.H. Nearly unbiased variable selection under minimax concave penalty. *Ann. Stat.* **2010**, *38*, 894–942. [CrossRef] [PubMed]
28. Bertsimas, D.; Van Parys, B. Sparse high-dimensional regression: Exact scalable algorithms and phase transitions. *Ann. Stat* **2020**, *48*, 300–323. [CrossRef]
29. Atamturk, A.; Gomez, A. Safe screening rules for L0-regression from perspective relaxations. In Proceedings of the 37th International Conference on Machine Learning, Virtual Event, 13–18 July 2020; Volume 119, pp. 421–430.
30. Moreira Costa, C.; Kreber, D.; Schmidt, M. An alternating method for cardinality-constrained optimization: A computational study for the best subset selection and sparse portfolio problems. *INFORMS J. Comput.* **2022**, *34*, 2968–2988. [CrossRef]
31. Mazumder, R., Friedman, J.H.; Hastie, T. SparseNet: Coordinate descent with nonconvex penalties. *J. Am. Stat. Assoc.* **2011**, *106*, 1125–1138. [CrossRef] [PubMed]
32. Hastie, T.; Tibshirani, R.; Tibshirani, R. Best subset, forward stepwise or lasso? Analysis and recommendations based on extensive comparisons. *Stat. Sci.* **2020**, *35*, 579–592. [CrossRef]
33. Meinshausen, N. Relaxed lasso. *Comput. Stat. Data Anal.* **2007**, *52*, 374–393. [CrossRef]
34. Mannor, S.; Meir, R.; Zhang, T. Greedy algorithms for classification–consistency, convergence rates, and adaptivity. *J. Mach. Learn. Res.* **2003**, *4*, 713–742.
35. Tewari, A.; Ravikumar, P.; Dhillon, I.S. Greedy algorithms for structurally constrained high dimensional problems. In Proceedings of the the 24th International Conference on Neural Information Processing Systems, Granada, Spain, 12–15 December 2011; Curran Associates Inc.: Red Hook, NY, USA, 2011; pp. 882–890.
36. Barron, A.R.; Cohen, A.; Dahmen, W.; DeVore, R.A. Approximation and learning by greedy algorithms. *Ann. Stat.* **2008**, *36*, 64–94. [CrossRef]
37. Painter-Wakefield, C.; Parr, R. Greedy algorithms for sparse reinforcement learning. In Proceedings of the the 29th International Coference on International Conference on Machine Learning, Edinburgh, UK, 26 June–1 July 2012; pp. 867–874.
38. Shafique, K.; Shah, M. A noniterative greedy algorithm for multiframe point correspondence. *IEEE Trans. Pattern Anal. Mach. Intell.* **2005**, *27*, 51–65. [CrossRef] [PubMed]

algorithms

MDPI

Article

A Comparative Study of Swarm Intelligence Metaheuristics in UKF-Based Neural Training Applied to the Identification and Control of Robotic Manipulator

Juan F. Guerra, Ramon Garcia-Hernandez *, Miguel A. Llama and Victor Santibañez

Tecnologico Nacional de Mexico, Instituto Tecnologico de La Laguna, Torreon 27000, Mexico; m.jfguerrac@correo.itlalaguna.edu.mx (J.F.G.); mllama@lalaguna.tecnm.mx (M.A.L.); vasantibanezd@lalaguna.tecnm.mx (V.S.)
* Correspondence: rgarciah@lalaguna.tecnm.mx

Abstract: This work presents a comprehensive comparative analysis of four prominent swarm intelligence (SI) optimization algorithms: Ant Lion Optimizer (ALO), Bat Algorithm (BA), Grey Wolf Optimizer (GWO), and Moth Flame Optimization (MFO). When compared under the same conditions with other SI algorithms, the Particle Swarm Optimization (PSO) stands out. First, the Unscented Kalman Filter (UKF) parameters to be optimized are selected, and then each SI optimization algorithm is executed within an off-line simulation. Once the UKF initialization parameters P_0, Q_0, and R_0 are obtained, they are applied in real-time in the decentralized neural block control (DNBC) scheme for the trajectory tracking task of a 2-DOF robot manipulator. Finally, the results are compared according to the criteria performance evaluation using each algorithm, along with CPU cost.

Keywords: swarm intelligence; neural networks; robot control; unscented Kalman filter

1. Introduction

Metaheuristics can be classified into various categories based on their natural inspiration [1]. One prominent category is swarm intelligence-based algorithms, which draw inspiration from the collective behavior of social insect colonies, bird flocks, or animal herds. Swarm intelligence (SI) algorithms simulate the cooperative and self-organizing behavior observed in natural swarms to solve complex optimization problems [2,3].

SI, inspired by the collective behavior of social insect colonies, encompasses a diverse range of algorithms that facilitate efficient problem-solving through cooperation and self-organization. These algorithms simulate the collaboration and information exchange observed in natural swarms, enabling them to achieve global optimization. By harnessing the collective intelligence exhibited by swarm systems, SI metaheuristics offer promising avenues for optimizing neural network training and enhancing the identification and control capabilities of robotic systems.

To conduct a comprehensive analysis, we selected four state-of-the-art SI algorithms known for their unique characteristics and optimization strategies. Ant Lion Optimization (ALO), drawing inspiration from the hunting behavior of ant lions, employs a powerful search mechanism to explore and exploit the solution space efficiently. Bat Algorithm (BA) mimics the echolocation behavior of bats, utilizing frequency tuning and pulse emission concepts to achieve effective optimization. Grey Wolf Optimizer (GWO) emulates the social hierarchy and hunting dynamics of grey wolves, employing three fundamental types of wolf-inspired operators to strike a balance between exploration and exploitation. Moth Flame Optimization (MFO), inspired by the moth's phototaxis behavior toward flames, incorporates attraction and repulsion mechanisms to guide the optimization process effectively. Finally, we compare these algorithms against the well-established Particle Swarm Optimization (PSO), which draws inspiration from the social behavior of bird flocking, enabling particles to adaptively search the solution space based on individual and swarm experience.

Overall, SI algorithms offer powerful optimization techniques that leverage the collective intelligence and self-organization observed in natural swarms. Their robustness, global exploration capabilities, self-adaptation, parallelism, scalability, and bio-inspired concepts make them well-suited for addressing a wide range of optimization problems in various domains. By mimicking the behavior of swarms, these algorithms provide effective solutions and insights for solving complex optimization challenges [4,5].

Furthermore, the nature-inspired characteristics of SI optimization methods introduce robustness and adaptability to different problem domains. They can be readily applied to robotic systems, including those with complex dynamics and uncertain environments [6]. By employing metaheuristic optimization techniques, the Unscented Kalman Filter (UKF) initialization parameters can be tailored to specific robotic platforms and tasks, leading to an improved estimation and control performance.

By integrating SI algorithms with UKF-based neural training, we aim to improve the accuracy of identification and control in a two-degrees-of-freedom (DOF) robot manipulator.

To elaborate further, let us delve into the distinguishing features and underlying principles of ALO, BA, GWO, and MFO algorithms. ALO utilizes a population of artificial ant lions to mimic hunting behaviors, where each ant lion represents a potential solution in the search space [7]. The algorithm employs pride update and position update mechanisms to perform efficient exploration and exploitation. BA, on the other hand, emulates the echolocation behavior of bats to optimize solutions. Bats navigate through a combination of random flight, frequency tuning, and pulse emission, allowing them to find optimal solutions in dynamic environments [8]. GWO, inspired by the cooperative hunting dynamics of grey wolves, utilizes three types of wolf operators (alpha, beta, and delta) to balance exploration and exploitation. The alpha wolf coordinates exploration, while the beta and delta wolves perform local exploitation and global exploration, respectively [9]. MFO draws inspiration from the attraction of moths to flame, employing attraction and repulsion mechanisms to guide the optimization process effectively. Moths are attracted to the light source but are also repelled by other moths, leading to a balanced exploration–exploitation trade-off [10].

To compare these algorithms against the widely used PSO, we consider PSO ability to adaptively search the solution space based on individual and swarm experience. PSO employs velocity updates and position adjustments to explore and exploit the search space efficiently [1,11,12]. By contrasting the unique characteristics and optimization strategies of ALO, BA, GWO, and MFO with the PSO algorithm, we can gain valuable insights into their relative strengths and weaknesses by applying them to our proposed identification and control scheme. We selected these algorithms mainly because of the following advantages: their small numbers of tuning parameters, low CPU time costs, the ability to maintain joint torque limits, and a better overall performance than other SI algorithms, such as Artificial Bee Colony (ABC), Ant Colony Optimization (ACO), Cuckoo Search (CS), Accelerated Particle Swarm Optimization (APSO), and Whale Optimization Algorithm (WOA).

The structure of this work is as follows. In Section 2, we mentioned some main characteristics of the SI algorithms employed. Section 3 describes the methodology of neural identification and control scheme. The simulation and real-time results for trajectory tracking are presented in Section 4. Discussions of the results are reflected in Section 5. Finally, concluding remarks are given in Section 6.

2. Swarm Intelligence Algorithms

Metaheuristics are a family of optimization algorithms designed to find suitable solutions for complicated optimization problems. In contrast to traditional optimization methods, which aim to find the global optimal, metaheuristic algorithms obtain acceptable results quickly, even in the presence of multiple local optima.

In summary, metaheuristics are fantastic tools for finding good solutions to a wide variety of optimization problems. They are especially useful in situations where traditional methods are not effective, such as problems with high dimensionality, non-convex, noise, or incomplete data.

Bio-inspired algorithms are unique metaheuristic methods inspired by natural processes, phenomena, concepts, and systems mechanisms. Each has features and strengths that provide interpretability and inspiration for solving real-world problems in diverse fields, such as engineering, computer science, economics, and biology. These algorithms mimic the behavior of systems in nature, such as evolutionary computation and swarm behavior [1].

SI is a subfield of bio-inspired algorithms that draws inspiration from collective behavior in nature and focuses on the emergent behavior of decentralized populations through local interactions and self-organization. Figure 1 shows the flow chart of the proposed methodology, which is described as follows: firstly, the UKF parameters to be optimized are selected; then, each SI optimization algorithm is executed within an off-line simulation. Once the UKF initialization parameters P_0, Q_0, and R_0 are obtained, they are applied in real-time in the decentralized neural block control (DNBC) scheme for the trajectory tracking task of a 2-DOF robot manipulator. Finally, the results are compared according to the objective function evaluation.

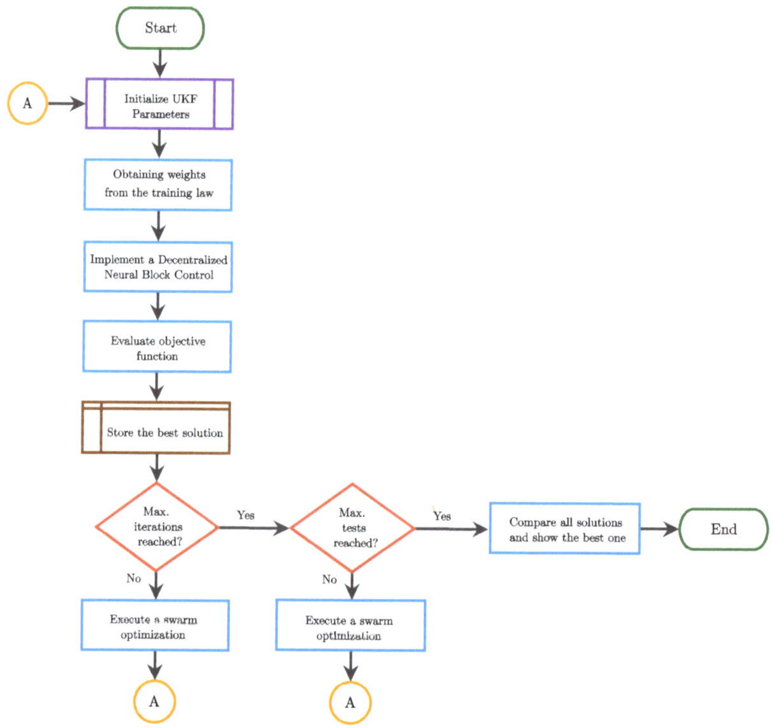

Figure 1. Proposed methodology flowchart.

Although there is an endless number of SI algorithms, which have multiple modifications, in the proposed approach, we use algorithms in their original versions, of which a brief description is presented below.

2.1. Particle Swarm Optimization (PSO)

Particle Swarm Optimization (PSO) is a widely used metaheuristic algorithm inspired by the collective behavior of bird flocks or fish schools. It has demonstrated remarkable success in solving various optimization problems [11]. PSO operates on the principle of iteratively adjusting the positions and velocities of particles in a multidimensional search space. Algorithm 1 shows the implementation of PSO [12].

Algorithm 1 PSO Pseudocode

```
Require:
n: number of particles
d: dimension of the search space
t_max: maximum number of iterations
w: inertia weight
φ1: cognitive acceleration coefficient
φ2: social acceleration coefficient
x_i: position of particle i
v_i: velocity of particle i
pbest_i: best position of particle i
gbest: global best position
Ensure:
x*: optimal solution
f*: optimal fitness
Function PSO( )
  for i = 1 to n do
    Initialize x_i and v_i randomly
  end for
  while t < t_max do
    for i = 1 to n do
      Update velocity: v_i ← w v_i + φ1(pbest_i − x_i) + φ2(gbest − x_i)
      Update position: x_i ← x_i + v_i
    end for
    for i = 1 to n do
      if f(x_i) < f(pbest_i) then
        pbest_i ← x_i
      end if
      if f(x_i) < f(gbest) then
        gbest ← x_i
      end if
    end for
    t ← t + 1
  end while
  x* ← gbest
  f* ← f(gbest)
end Function
```

2.2. Ant Lion Optimizer (ALO)

The Ant Lion Optimizer (ALO) is a potent metaheuristic algorithm inspired by the predatory behavior of ant lions. It has gained significant attention in optimization engineering due to its ability to deal with complex problems effectively. ALO displays unique characteristics that distinguish it from other metaheuristics, such as PSO [7].

ALO emulates the hunting strategy employed by ant lions to capture their prey, which consists of building conical pits in sandy areas. For optimization problems, ALO capitalizes on this natural behavior to explore and exploit the solution space efficiently. Algorithm 2 shows the implementation of ALO [13].

Algorithm 2 ALO Pseudocode

Require:
p: number of antlions
u: upper bounds of variables
l: lower bounds of variables
$alpha$: evaporation rate
$beta$: attractiveness rate
t_{max}: maximum number of iterations
x_i: position of antlion i
$f(x_i)$: fitness of antlion i
x_i^*: best position of antlion i
$f(x_i^*)$: best performance of antlion i

Ensure:
x^*: optimal solution
f^*: optimal fitness
Function ALO( )
  for $i = 1$ to p **do**
    Initialize x_i randomly
  end for
  while $t < t_{max}$ **do**
    for $i = 1$ to p **do**
      Generate a new position x_i'
      Calculate the fitness of x_i'
      if $f(x_i') < f(x_i)$ **then**
        $x_i \leftarrow x_i'$
      end if
    end for
    for $i = 1$ to p **do**
      Evaporation: $x_i \leftarrow x_i + \alpha(x_i^* - x_i)$
      Attractiveness: $x_i \leftarrow x_i + \beta(x_i - x_{best})$
    end for
    $t \leftarrow t + 1$
  end while
  $x^* \leftarrow x_{best}$
  $f^* \leftarrow f_{best}$
end Function

2.3. *Bat Algorithm (BA)*

The Bat Algorithm (BA) is an SI algorithm inspired by the echolocation behavior of bats. The BA demonstrates unique characteristics that set it apart from other metaheuristic algorithms [8].

The algorithm begins by initializing a population of bats, where each bat represents a potential solution to the optimization problem. Bats fly through the search space, continuously adjusting their positions and velocities based on their knowledge. BA implementation is illustrated in Algorithm 3 [1].

Algorithm 3 BA Pseudocode

Require:
n: number of bats
d: dimension of the search space
t_{max}: maximum number of iterations
A: loudness
r: pulse rate
α: cooling factor
γ: wavelength
x_i: position of bat i
$f(x_i)$: fitness of bat i
x_i^*: best position of bat i
$f(x_i^*)$: best fitness of bat i
Ensure:
x^*: optimal solution
Function BA()
  for $i = 1$ to n **do**
    Initialize x_i randomly
  end for
  while $t < t_{max}$ **do**
    for $i = 1$ to n **do**
      Generate a new position x_i'
      Calculate the fitness of x_i'
      if $f(x_i') < f(x_i)$ **then**
        $x_i \leftarrow x_i'$
      end if
      Update loudness: $\alpha_i \leftarrow \alpha_i - 1$
      Update pulse rate: $\beta_i \leftarrow \beta_i + 1$
    end for
    for $i = 1$ to n **do**
      Probability of loudness: $p_i = \frac{1}{\alpha_i}$
      Probability of pulse rate: $q_i = \frac{1}{\beta_i}$
      if $p_i > q_i$ **then**
        $x_i \leftarrow x_i + \gamma(x_i^* - x_i)$
      else
        $x_i \leftarrow x_i - \gamma(x_i - x_{best})$
      end if
    end for
    $t \leftarrow t + 1$
  end while
  $x^* \leftarrow x_{best}$
  $f^* \leftarrow f(x_{best})$
end Function

2.4. Grey Wolf Optimizer (GWO)

The Grey Wolf Optimizer (GWO) is an SI algorithm inspired by the hunting behavior of grey wolves in nature. The GWO imitates the social hierarchy and cooperative hunting strategies observed in wolf packs to guide the search for optimal solutions [9].

In the GWO, a population of candidate solutions, represented as grey wolves, explores the search space by adjusting their positions and mimicking the hunting behaviors of alpha, beta, and delta wolves. GWO implementation is shown in Algorithm 4 [14].

Algorithm 4 GWO Pseudocode

Require:

n: number of wolves
d: dimension of the search space
t_{max}: maximum number of iterations
a: alpha coefficient
b: beta coefficient
c: delta coefficient
x_i: position of wolf i
$f(x_i)$: fitness of wolf i
x_i^*: best position of wolf i
$f(x_i^*)$: best fitness of wolf i

Ensure:

x^*: optimal solution
Function GWO( )
    for $i = 1$ to n **do**
        Initialize x_i randomly
    end for
    while $t < t_{max}$ **do**
        for $i = 1$ to n **do**
            Calculate a, b, and c
            Update position: $x_i \leftarrow x_i + a(x_i^* - x_i) + b(x_i^b - x_i) + c(x_i^c - x_i)$
        end for
        for $i = 1$ to n **do**
            if $f(x_i) < f(x_i^*)$ **then**
                $x_i^* \leftarrow x_i$
            end if
        end for
        $t \leftarrow t + 1$
    end while
    $x^* \leftarrow x_{best}$
    $f^* \leftarrow f(x_{best})$
end Function

2.5. Moth Flame Optimization (MFO)

The Moth Flame Optimization (MFO) is an SI algorithm inspired by the navigation behavior of moths in nature. The MFO mimics the attraction of moths toward artificial light sources to guide the search for optimal solutions [10]. Algorithm 5 displays MFO implementation [15].

Algorithm 5 MFO Pseudocode

Require:
n: number of moths
d: dimension of the search space
t_{max}: maximum number of iterations
a: absorption coefficient
r: random number
x_i: position of moth i
$f(x_i)$: fitness of moth i
x_i^*: best position of moth i
$f(x_i^*)$: best fitness of moth i
Ensure:
x^*: optimal solution
Function MFO()
  for $i = 1$ to n **do**
    Initialize x_i randomly
  end for
  while $t < t_{max}$ **do**
    for $i = 1$ to n **do**
      Generate a new position x_i'
      Calculate the fitness of x_i'
      if $f(x_i') < f(x_i)$ **then**
        $x_i \leftarrow x_i'$
      end if
      Absorption: $x_i \leftarrow x_i - a(x_i^* - x_i)$
      Random walk: $x_i \leftarrow x_i + r(x_{best} - x_i)$
    end for
    $t \leftarrow t + 1$
  end while
  $x^* \leftarrow x_{best}$
  $f^* \leftarrow f(x_{best})$
end Function

3. Decentralized Neural Block Control (DNBC-UKF)

This section shows the proposed SI optimization approach for UKF learning of decentralized neural block control (DNBC-UKF) [16] applied to a 2-DOF robot manipulator.

For this purpose, we take the system to the following form

$$\begin{aligned} \boldsymbol{\mathcal{X}}^1_{\mathrm{i},k+1} &= f^1_{\mathrm{i}}\left(\boldsymbol{\mathcal{X}}^1_{\mathrm{i}}\right) + B^1_{\mathrm{i}}\left(\boldsymbol{\mathcal{X}}^1_{\mathrm{i}}\right)\boldsymbol{\mathcal{X}}^2_{\mathrm{i}} + \Gamma^1_{i\ell}, \\ &\vdots \\ \boldsymbol{\mathcal{X}}^r_{\mathrm{i},k+1} &= f^r_{\mathrm{i}}\left(\boldsymbol{\mathcal{X}}^1_{\mathrm{i}}, \cdots, \boldsymbol{\mathcal{X}}^r_{\mathrm{i}}\right) + B^r_{\mathrm{i}}\left(\boldsymbol{\mathcal{X}}^1_{\mathrm{i}}, \cdots, \boldsymbol{\mathcal{X}}^j_{\mathrm{i}}\right)u_{\mathrm{i}} + \Gamma^r_{i\ell} \end{aligned} \tag{1}$$

where $\mathrm{i} = 1, \ldots, N$, $j = 1, \ldots, r-1$, $l = 1, \ldots, m_{ij}$. N is the number of subsystems and $u_i \in \mathbb{R}^{m_{\mathrm{i}}}$ is the input vector. f^j_{i}, B^j_{i}, and Γ^j_{i} are assumed smooth and bounded functions, with $f^j_{\mathrm{i}}(0) = 0$, and $B^j_{\mathrm{i}}(0) = 0$; in addition, the structures of the subsystems are expressed by $m_{\mathrm{i}1} \leq m_{i2} \leq \cdots \leq m_{\mathrm{i}j} \leq p_{\mathrm{i}}$. On the other hand, the interconnection terms Γ^j_{i} are described by reflecting the relation between the i-th subsystem and the other ones.

The following RHONN structure is used in order to identify the behavior of system (1)

$$
\begin{aligned}
\boldsymbol{x}^1_{i,k+1} &= \boldsymbol{w}^1_{i,k} S\left(\boldsymbol{\mathcal{X}}^1_{i,k}\right) + \boldsymbol{w}'^1_{i} \boldsymbol{\mathcal{X}}^2_{i,k}, \\
&\vdots \\
\boldsymbol{x}^r_{i,k+1} &= \boldsymbol{w}^r_{i,k} S\left(\boldsymbol{\mathcal{X}}^1_{i,k}, \cdots, \boldsymbol{\mathcal{X}}^r_{i,k}\right) + \boldsymbol{w}'^r_{i} \boldsymbol{u}_{i,k}
\end{aligned}
\tag{2}
$$

where $\boldsymbol{x}^j_{i,k+1} = \begin{bmatrix} x^1_i & x^2_i & \cdots & x^r_i \end{bmatrix}^\top$ is the j-th block neuron state with $i = 1, \dots, N$ and $j = 1, \dots, r-1$; $\boldsymbol{w}'^j_{i,k}$ are fixed parameters with $rank(\boldsymbol{w}'^j_i) = m_{ij}$. $S(\bullet)$ is the activation function and $\boldsymbol{u}_{i,k}$ represents the input vector.

The NN training task consists of finding values of $w^{j,k}_i$ that minimize the identification error. For this reason, we propose to use a learning method using only the identification error information, such as the UKF described in Figure 2.

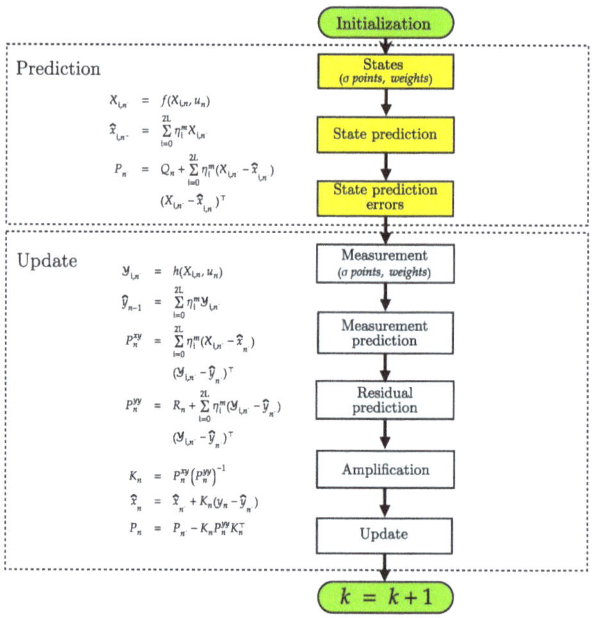

Figure 2. UKF framework.

The UKF is a powerful estimation and control tool: with wide applications in control theory; for the identification of nonlinear systems; and for the training of neural networks. Its versatility lies in its ability to handle nonlinear dynamics, non-Gaussian distributions, and uncertainties associated with real-world systems.

In the context of control theory, the UKF serves as an efficient means for state estimation in nonlinear systems. It allows for the real-time estimation of the system's internal states, which are often unobservable or difficult to measure directly [17]. By incorporating nonlinear models and the measured system outputs, the UKF provides accurate and reliable estimates of the system's states, enabling effective control strategies to be devised. The estimated states obtained from the UKF can then be utilized for feedback control, trajectory tracking, and system stabilization in a wide range of dynamic systems [18,19].

The UKF also plays a significant role in the identification of nonlinear systems. Identification refers to the process of determining the mathematical models or parameters that represent the underlying dynamics of a system based on observed input–output data. Nonlinear systems pose significant challenges in identification due to their complex dynamics. The UKF addresses these challenges by iteratively updating the system model parameters, enabling an accurate estimation of the nonlinear system's behavior. By leveraging the filtering and estimation capabilities of the UKF, researchers and engineers can effectively identify the dynamics, parameters, and structure of complex nonlinear systems, leading to an improved understanding and control of such systems [20].

Additionally, the UKF is employed in the training of neural networks, specifically in the context of Recurrent Neural Networks (RNNs). RNNs are powerful architectures for modeling sequential data and time series. It is possible to use the UKF in the training process to optimize the internal states, weights, and biases of the network in order to improve its learning capability and prediction accuracy [21]. By incorporating the UKF within the training process, the neural network can effectively capture and model the complex nonlinear dependencies present in the data, leading to an improved performance in tasks such as time series forecasting, speech recognition, and natural language processing [22,23].

The initialization of a UKF involves determining the initial state estimate, the covariance matrix and the process noise covariance matrix, which can make the selection of these initialization parameters a complex task, especially when using heuristic techniques [18]. The challenge arises because these parameters significantly impact the filter's performance and are often problem-specific, requiring domain expertise and careful tuning. The manual selection of these parameters can be time-consuming, and may not guarantee optimal performance.

In such scenarios, employing metaheuristic optimization methods proves to be a promising approach for selecting these initialization parameters. Metaheuristic optimization methods offer several advantages when applied to the selection of UKF initialization parameters. Firstly, these methods provide a systematic and automated approach to parameter tuning, relieving the burden of manual parameter selection. They can efficiently explore the vast parameter space, searching for the optimal combination that minimizes the error or maximizes a performance metric. By leveraging the search mechanisms inherent in metaheuristic algorithms, such as exploration and exploitation, the initialization parameters can be fine-tuned to enhance the convergence and accuracy of the UKF.

Secondly, metaheuristic optimization methods can handle nonlinearity, multimodality, and non-convexity in the optimization landscape, which are common challenges in parameter selection for UKF initialization. These algorithms possess the flexibility to adapt and explore diverse regions of the parameter space, avoiding local optima and finding near-optimal or globally optimal solutions.

3.1. SI Optimization for UKF Learning

Using the UKF to estimate the NN weights, and correcting for identification errors, the filter is updated at each step. Usually, P_i^j, Q_i^j, and R_i^j are initialized as diagonal matrices with entries $P_i^j(0)$, $Q_i^j(0)$, and $R_i^j(0)$, respectively. Given that, typically, these entries are defined heuristically, we propose employing SI methods to improve the UKF training algorithm.

According to the optimal control theory [24], it is common to use error-based performance measures such as those described in Table 1. On the other hand, in (3), the Bolza form [25] is described and used as an objective function to evaluate the overall performance, including information from the control input of the system.

$$J = \overbrace{\underbrace{\mathbf{e}_{kf}^{\top} L \mathbf{e}_{kf} T}_{\text{Mayer form}} + \underbrace{\sum_{k_0}^{k_f} \left[\mathbf{e}_k^{\top} Q \mathbf{e}_k + \mathbf{u}_k^{\top} R \mathbf{u}_k \right] T}_{\text{Lagrange form}}}^{\text{Bolza form}} \tag{3}$$

where k_0 is the initial iteration; k_f is the final iteration; T is the sampling time; $\mathbf{e}_k$ is the error vector; $\mathbf{u}_k$ is the control input vector; and L, Q, and R are gain matrices with appropriate dimensions.

Table 1. Performance criteria.

Criteria	Formula
Integral Absolute Error (IAE)	$\sum_{k=0}^{\frac{t}{T}} \lvert\mathbf{e}_k\rvert$
Integral Squared Error (ISE)	$\sum_{k=0}^{\frac{t}{T}} \mathbf{e}_k^2$
Integral Time-weighted Absolute Error (ITAE)	$\sum_{k=0}^{\frac{t}{T}} k\lvert\mathbf{e}_k\rvert$
Integral Time-weighted Squared Error (ITSE)	$\sum_{k=0}^{\frac{t}{T}} k\mathbf{e}_k^2$

Although the Bolza form is a good performance criterion, it presents a serious disadvantage for this work. The final value of the error vector is not very useful for our methodology because it does not significantly represent the system identification and trajectory tracking; in other words, we need to know how it behaves throughout the simulation. For this reason, we propose an objective function, based on that found in [26], for the SI algorithms as follows:

$$f_{obj} = \varrho_1 \mathrm{MSE}(e_{i,k}) + \varrho_2 \mathrm{MSE}(z_{i,k}) + \sum_{k=0}^{\frac{t}{T}} [\varrho_3 (u_{i,k-1} - u_{i,k})] \tag{4}$$

where MSE represents the mean square error; t is the total time of the simulation; $e_{i,k}$ represents the identification error; $z_{i,k}$ is the tracking error; $u_{i,k}$ represents the input control; and ϱ_1, ϱ_2, and ϱ_3 are scaling factors to bring all the terms of the objective function to a similar order.

3.2. DNBC-UKF Controller Design

Once the RHONN training has been defined, we design a controller based on the tracking error z_i as follows:

$$\mathbf{z}^j_{i,k} = \boldsymbol{x}^j_{i,k} - \boldsymbol{x}^{1j}_{id,k} \tag{5}$$

where $\boldsymbol{x}^j_{id,k}$ is the desired trajectory signal and $\boldsymbol{x}^j_{i,k}$ is the NN state [27].

The new value is obtained as:

$$\mathbf{z}^j_{i,k+1} = \boldsymbol{w}^j_{i,k} S(\boldsymbol{\mathcal{X}}^1_{i,k}, \ldots, \boldsymbol{\mathcal{X}}^j_{i,k}) + \boldsymbol{w}'^j_i \boldsymbol{u}_{i,k} - \boldsymbol{x}^j_{id,k+1}. \tag{6}$$

Then, system (2) should be expressed as a function of variables $\mathbf{z}^j_{i,k}$ as:

$$\mathbf{z}^j_{i,k+1} = k^j_i \mathbf{z}^j_{i,k} + \boldsymbol{w}'^j_i \boldsymbol{u}_{i,k} - \boldsymbol{x}^j_{id,k+1} \tag{7}$$

When a sliding mode control strategy is implemented, the control input must be limited by u_{0i} as:

$$|\boldsymbol{u}_{i,k}| \leq \boldsymbol{u}_{0i}. \tag{8}$$

The sliding surface is designed as $S_{D_i,k} = \mathbf{z}^r_{i,k} = 0$; then, system (7) is rewritten as follows:

$$S_{D_i,k+1} = \boldsymbol{w}^r_{i,k} S(\boldsymbol{\mathcal{X}}^1_{i,k}, \ldots, \boldsymbol{\mathcal{X}}^r_{i,k}) + \boldsymbol{w}'^r_i \boldsymbol{u}_{i,k} - \boldsymbol{x}^r_{id,k+1}. \tag{9}$$

The proper selection of the sliding manifold [28] presents the possibility of finding a bounded control law by u_{0i}; the control $u_{i,k}$ is composed as

$$u_{i,k} = \begin{cases} u_{eq_i,k} & \text{for} \left\| u_{eq_i,k} \right\| \leq u_{0i}, \\ u_{0i} \dfrac{u_{eq_i,k}}{\| u_{eq_i,k} \|} & \text{for} \left\| u_{eq_i,k} \right\| > u_{0i}, \end{cases} \tag{10}$$

where $u_{eq_i,k}$ is calculated from $S_{D_i,k+1} = 0$ as

$$u_{eq_i,k} = \frac{1}{w_i'^r} \left[-w_{i,k}^r S(\mathcal{X}_{i,k}^1, \ldots, \mathcal{X}_{i,k}^r) + x_{id,k+1}^r \right]. \tag{11}$$

Figure 3 illustrates the block diagram of the proposed SI optimization approach.

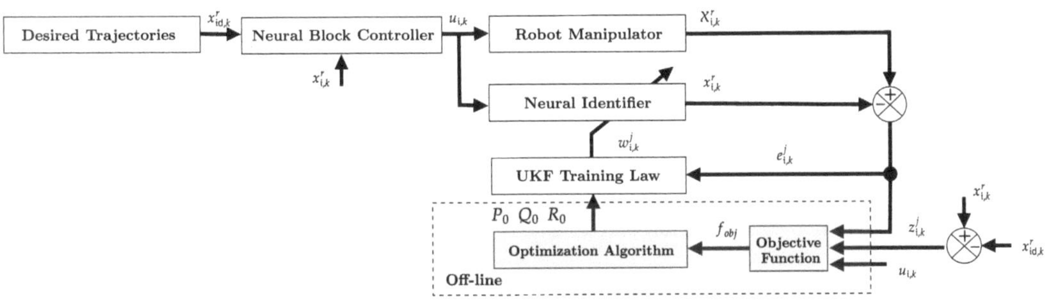

Figure 3. Decentralized neural identification and control scheme with SI optimization approach.

4. Results

The performance of the proposed approach was analyzed and compared using the following SI algorithms: ABC, ACO, ALO, BA, CS, GWO, MFO, PSO, APSO, and WOA. The comparisons were performed to find the algorithm that best minimizes the trajectory tracking error without exceeding the limits of the input torques.

This last condition of not surpassing the torque bounds is necessary for algorithm selection in real-time experiments. The experiments were performed on a 2-DOF vertical direct-drive robot manipulator, which is located at the Tecnologico Nacional de Mexico/Instituto Tecnologico de La Laguna, Mexico.

4.1. Prototype Description

To illustrate the implementation of the proposed scheme, we used the robot manipulator shown in Figure 4, which consists of two rigid links articulated by high-torque brushless direct-drive servos that present a reduced backlash and a significantly lower joint friction to drive the joints. The robot actuators act as torque sources and receive analog voltage as a torque reference signal. Joint positions are obtained using incremental encoders that send information to a DAQ [16].

The numerical values for the 2-DOF robot manipulator parameters alongside the dynamic model can be found in [29].

In order to prove the proposed approach, the discrete-time trajectories [27] were chosen as

$$x_{1d,k}^1 = b_1(1 - e^{d_1 kT^3}) + c_1(1 - e^{d_1 kT^3}) \sin(\omega_1 kT) [\text{rad}],$$
$$x_{2d,k}^1 = b_2(1 - e^{d_2 kT^3}) + c_2(1 - e^{d_2 kT^3}) \sin(\omega_2 kT) [\text{rad}]$$

where $b_1 = \pi/4$, $c_1 = \pi/18$, $d_1 = -2.0$, and $\omega_1 = 5$ [rad/s] are used for the first joint, while $b_2 = \pi/3$, $c_2 = 25\pi/36$, $d_2 = -1.8$, and $\omega_2 = 1$ [rad/s] are used for the second joint.

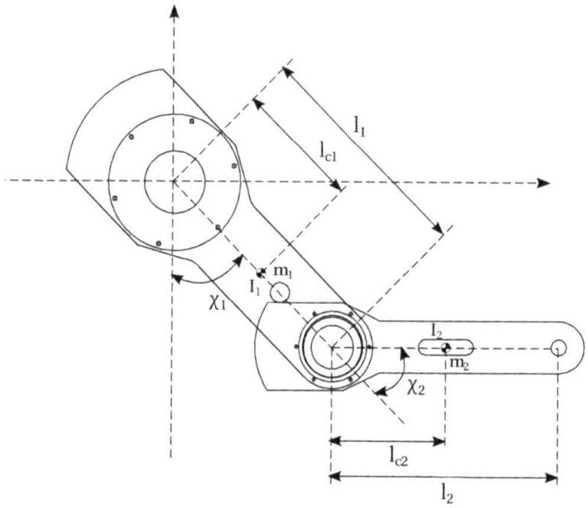

Figure 4. Diagram of the 2-DOF robot manipulator.

4.2. Simulation Results

For the simulations, the parameter settings of the SI algorithms considered are summarized as follows: starting with the common parameters, the number of iterations, which was 15; the population size was 30; the variables were 54; and the simulation time was 10 s. The particular parameter settings are given in Table 2.

Table 2. Parameter settings for SI algorithms.

Reference	Algorithm	Parameter Values
[30]	ABC	Limit: 100, F_l: 0.1, F_u: 0.9, p: 0.5
[31]	ACO	α: 1.0, β: 3.0, Evaporation Rate: 0.5
[32]	ALO	Probabilistic Switch: 0.1, Random Walk Length: 1.5, Levy Flight a: 1.0, b: 1.0
[33]	BA	A: 0.25, r: 0.5, α: 1.0, γ: 0.1, f_{min}: 0.0, f_{max}: 2.0
[34]	CS	Discover Rate p_a: 0.25, Levy Flight a: 0.1, b: 0.9
[35]	GWO	a_0: 2.0
[36]	MFO	a: 1.0, b: 1.0
[37]	PSO	φ_1: 2.0, φ_1: 2.0, w: 0.7, $v_{\max}$: 0.1
[37]	APSO	φ_1: 1.5, φ_2: 1.5, w: 0.7, $v_{\max}$: 0.1, p_a: 0.1, p_r: 0.1
[38]	WOA	a_1: 2.0, a_2: −1.0

SI algorithms presented in Table 2 were considered for comparison purposes because they have been employed previously in the state-of-the-art for neural network training, as reported in [39–48].

In all simulations, the specifications of the test machine were an AMD Ryzen 9 4900HS® (AMD Ryzen is a registered trademark of Advanced Micro Devices, Inc., Santa Clara, CA, USA) CPU 3.0 GHz and 16 GB of RAM. Moreover, the experiments were performed in the MATLAB R2015a environment® (MATLAB is a registered trademark of MathWorks, Inc., Natick, MA, USA).

For comparative purposes, we tested each SI algorithm 50 times independently. To qualify the results, we calculated statistical data of the mean, standard deviation (SD), and the best and worst results for different performance indices and the proposed objective function. The performance of the algorithms is reflected in a small mean value with a low standard distribution, implying a small difference between the best and worst results. Table 3 shows the performance measures.

Table 3. Simulation results performance.

	ABC							ACO					
	IAE	ISE	ITAE	ITSE	BOLZA	F_{obj}		IAE	ISE	ITAE	ITSE	BOLZA	F_{obj}
Best	1.6659	2.0687	1.9251	3.1455	1.2122	1.4809	**Best**	1.1065	7.0311	1.9234	0.7806	1.3876	1.7014
Worst	4.9574	17.3234	4.4748	14.6351	2.9154	2.5511	**Worst**	8.4880	55.0904	3.7347	7.7709	4.0725	2.8205
Mean	3.0176	8.3139	3.3381	6.4803	1.9728	1.7846	**Mean**	2.1222	19.0324	2.4459	3.2221	2.7406	1.9049
SD	0.6569	3.5723	0.4139	1.9143	0.2121	0.0855	**SD**	0.5998	6.9280	0.3136	0.8942	0.4055	0.1137
Avg. CPU time	385.6374	382.4414	377.5315	388.1568	329.2899	327.3551	**Avg. CPU time**	319.4551	270.9993	273.8600	285.6364	271.8496	271.7896
	ALO							BA					
	IAE	ISE	ITAE	ITSE	BOLZA	F_{obj}		IAE	ISE	ITAE	ITSE	BOLZA	F_{obj}
Best	0.4117	0.8757	0.1221	0.0297	0.4798	0.7722	**Best**	0.4622	0.6824	0.2282	0.0778	0.8319	0.7865
Worst	2.4396	8.0046	1.6833	1.7144	2.3748	2.4519	**Worst**	3.0243	6.5020	1.7291	5.6521	2.5186	2.1805
Mean	0.9106	2.1424	0.5598	0.4147	0.9967	1.4478	**Mean**	0.9396	2.2031	0.6312	1.6451	1.4602	1.5367
SD	0.4119	0.9296	0.3396	0.3418	0.4452	0.1835	**SD**	0.4535	1.3601	0.3055	1.2372	0.2681	0.1425
Avg. CPU time	195.2782	193.8541	188.2104	195.6159	199.8425	193.8247	**Avg. CPU time**	162.2854	251.0991	173.2529	172.2656	234.0957	188.7852
	CS							GWO					
	IAE	ISE	ITAE	ITSE	BOLZA	F_{obj}		IAE	ISE	ITAE	ITSE	BOLZA	F_{obj}
Best	1.1682	8.6384	1.9009	2.2488	2.1922	2.2349	**Best**	0.5485	0.8409	0.2685	0.1061	0.9654	1.0775
Worst	7.6640	26.8575	5.1201	17.8572	4.8216	3.7666	**Worst**	4.0810	13.8469	6.0435	11.2769	4.6651	2.7274
Mean	3.3023	17.9493	2.9659	6.2737	3.5290	2.9180	**Mean**	1.1522	2.2295	2.2620	1.5815	2.1502	1.7703
SD	1.2205	3.2834	0.7816	2.6353	0.4599	0.2444	**SD**	0.8178	2.8493	1.0776	1.8125	0.8949	0.2275
Avg. CPU time	317.7669	313.6375	312.7115	313.0690	312.2985	313.7871	**Avg. CPU time**	197.7674	199.4584	200.7393	200.1622	225.8913	199.8676
	MFO							PSO					
	IAE	ISE	ITAE	ITSE	BOLZA	F_{obj}		IAE	ISE	ITAE	ITSE	BOLZA	F_{obj}
Best	0.5013	0.6742	0.2346	0.0871	0.6720	1.0254	**Best**	1.5053	4.6942	0.5468	1.5487	1.4258	1.4388
Worst	4.4130	10.5064	5.7266	7.2781	4.6758	2.7274	**Worst**	6.4121	29.8629	3.3398	11.8439	4.6686	3.8913
Mean	2.0395	3.5393	2.7144	1.1115	2.8113	1.7599	**Mean**	2.5117	14.8761	2.2052	5.0699	2.3209	2.1410
SD	0.9656	1.8749	1.1719	1.4426	0.9352	0.2437	**SD**	0.7388	6.2862	0.3225	2.2650	0.7198	0.4797
Avg. CPU time	196.3359	193.7482	196.1711	195.6669	194.9560	195.0981	**Avg. CPU time**	205.5427	204.3713	205.1566	204.0309	204.3103	203.5299

Table 3. *Cont.*

	APSO							WOA					
	IAE	ISE	ITAE	ITSE	BOLZA	F_{obj}		IAE	ISE	ITAE	ITSE	BOLZA	F_{obj}
Best	1.2219	9.6568	1.0353	2.0965	1.3454	1.3019	**Best**	0.7574	0.9207	0.9669	0.3357	1.0693	1.3655
Worst	7.5709	89.5887	5.9703	21.9045	12.5607	5.9705	**Worst**	4.3771	45.0806	4.9312	8.2819	4.7169	4.7380
Mean	3.2289	36.6708	2.3626	11.7262	2.2305	3.4699	**Mean**	2.0837	2.5373	1.8365	1.9530	2.3689	1.9793
SD	0.9328	15.0780	0.7621	3.7311	1.2944	0.8019	**SD**	0.5674	3.6982	0.6706	1.2024	0.5636	0.3771
Avg. CPU time	195.5655	194.8540	195.7047	195.3598	228.1618	203.4104	**Avg. CPU time**	171.9729	163.0374	163.3186	162.5492	155.6390	155.6390

4.3. Experimental Results

The selection of the ALO, BA, GWO, MFO, and PSO algorithms for real-time experiments was because they show a balanced performance with low computational costs. However, the main reason was that during the entire simulation, none of them exceeded the torque limits.

Real-time experiments were implemented using Ansi C on WinMechLab, a real-time platform running on an Intel Pentium 4 PC with real-time Windows XP, with a 2.5 ms sampling period, and using a MultiQ-PCI data acquisition board from Quanser Consulting Inc., Markham, ON, CAN [49].

Figures 5 and 6 show the tracking trajectories for each link obtained in the simulation using the SI algorithms compared to the non-optimized UKF, we include in Table 4 and Figure 7 the values of the performance of the algorithms by evaluating the objective function and $\mathcal{L}_2$-norm, described by

$$\mathcal{L}_2\text{-norm} = \sqrt{\frac{T}{t}\sum_{i=0}^{n}||z_{i,k}||^2}$$

where T is the sampling time and t is the total time of the simulation, which, for this case is 20 s. In addition, Table 5 includes the RMS of the joint input torques comparing each algorithm with the UKF with non-optimized parameters. Moreover, the input pairs for each link are shown in Figures 8a to 9e.

Table 4. Objective function evaluation for real-time experimentation.

Algorithm UKF	f_{obj}
non-optimized	2.0023
ALO	1.2678
BA	1.3529
GWO	1.4797
MFO	1.3948
PSO	1.7829

Table 5. RMS for joint input torques of SI algorithms.

Algorithm UKF	RMS($u_{1,k}$)	RMS($u_{2,k}$)
non-optimized	30.6562	2.5715
ALO	30.5262	2.5931
BA	30.3053	2.6880
GWO	30.7568	3.2744
MFO	30.3398	2.8736
PSO	30.5262	2.5931

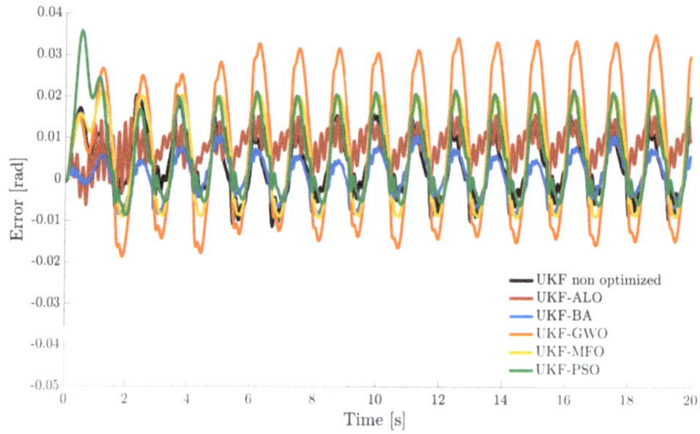

Figure 5. Trajectory tracking position error link 1.

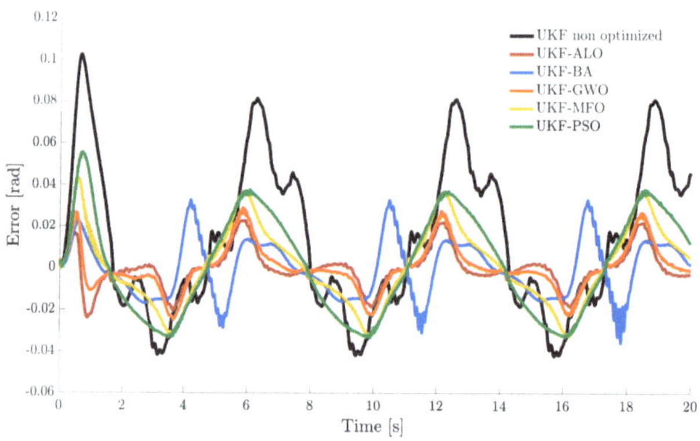

Figure 6. Trajectory tracking position error link 2.

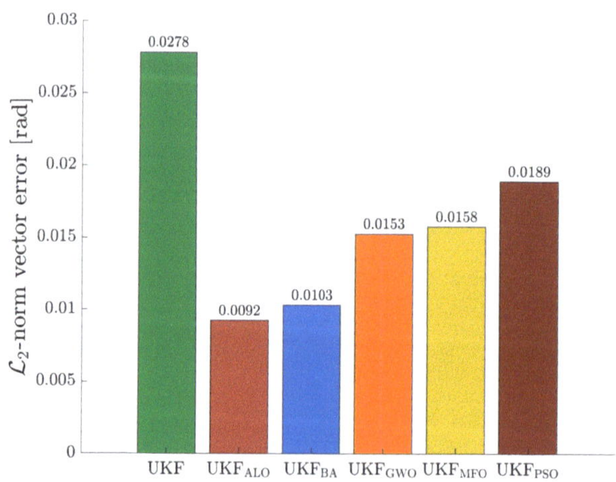

Figure 7. $\mathcal{L}_2$-norm for SI algorithms.

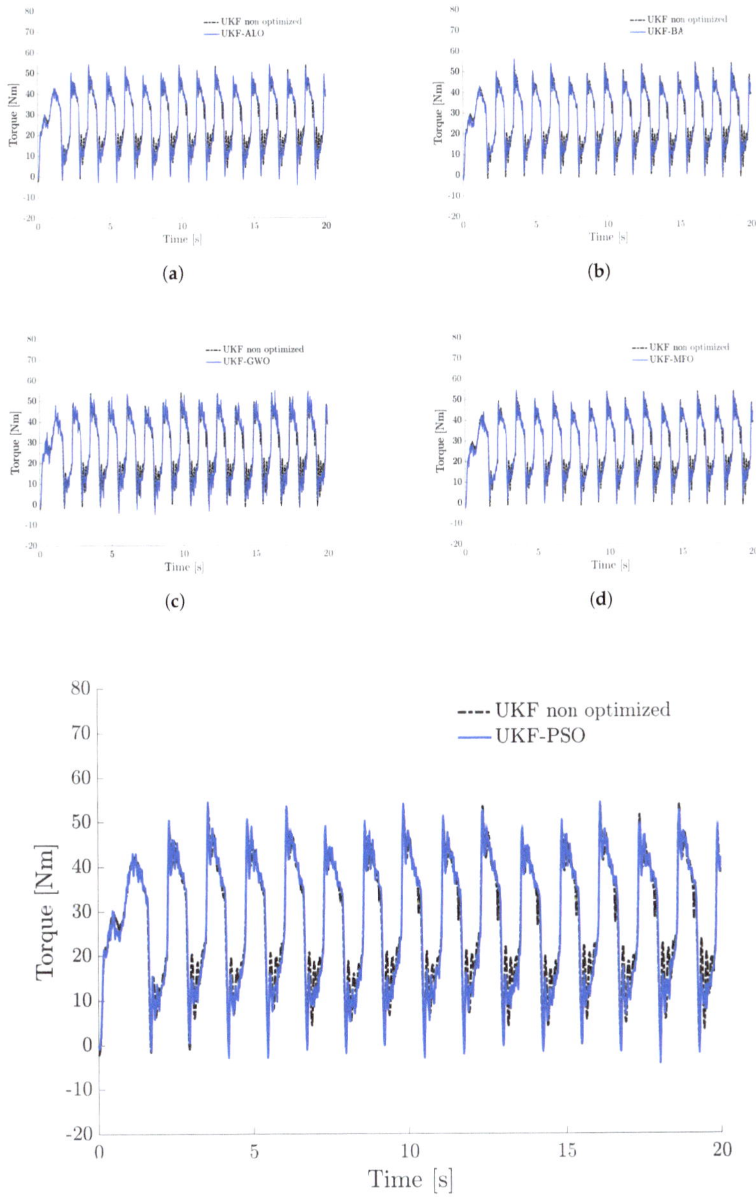

Figure 8. Input torque link 1 with SI optimization. (**a**) Input torque link 1 ALO. (**b**) Input torque link 1 BA. (**c**) Input torque link 1 GWO. (**d**) Input torque link 1 MFO. (**e**) Input torque link 1 PSO.

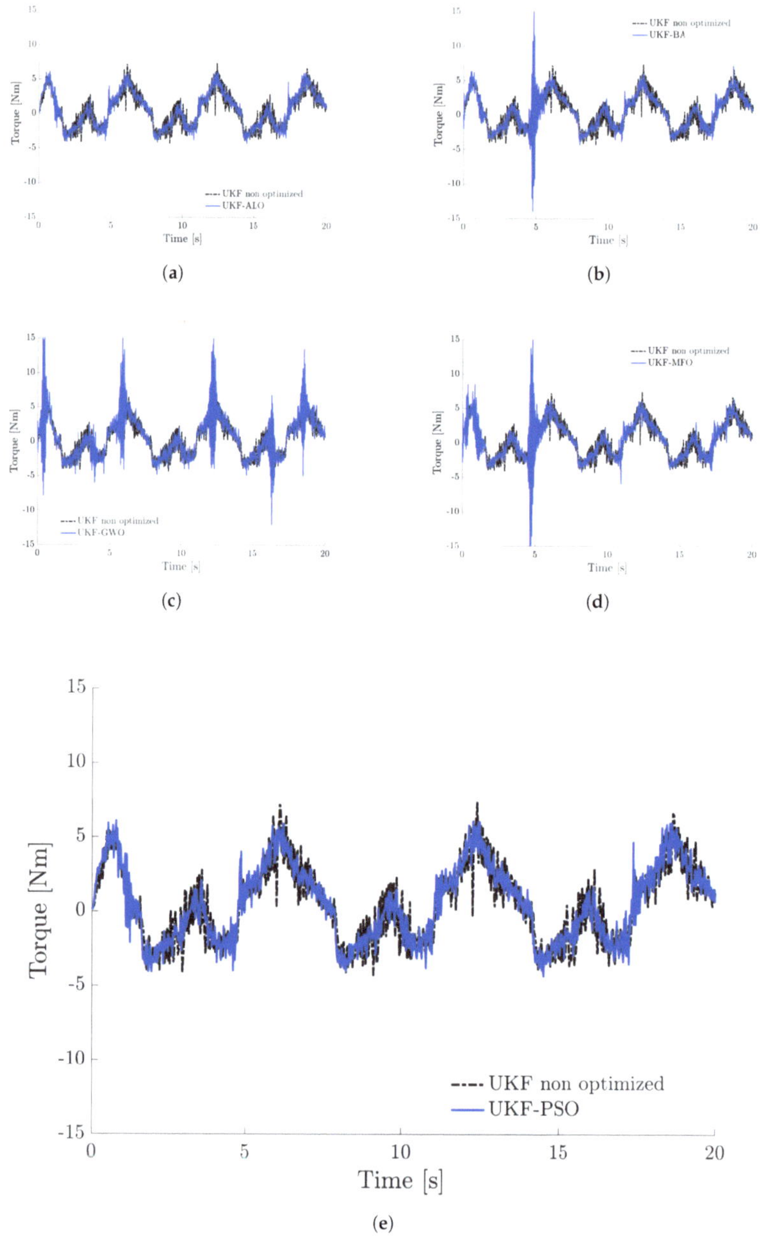

Figure 9. Input torque link 2 with SI optimization. (**a**) Input torque link 2 ALO. (**b**) Input torque link 2 BA. (**c**) Input torque link 2 GWO. (**d**) Input torque link 2 MFO. (**e**) Input torque link 2 PSO.

5. Discussion

For the tracking control problem of a 2-DOF robot manipulator, we proposed a DNBC controller, which does not require any knowledge of the system since it uses a UKF-trained neural identifier, whose added value presents an optimization tuning via SI algorithms. Everyone tuned the initial filter parameters in an off-line simulation subsequently used in real-time experiments.

The selection of SI algorithms employed in this work is due to the following criteria:

1. Few tuning parameters.
2. Good exploitation–exploration balance.
3. Low computational cost concerning their performance.

The computational cost is the factor that we consider to be most important when carrying out the proposed optimization task, at least for the off-line simulation. Since the stochastic nature of both the UKF filter and the algorithms must be taken into account, in addition to the added cost of the controller, this translates into an increase in the number of attempts to achieve acceptable results. For this reason, Table 3 shows the average CPU time for each SI algorithm utilized.

Interpreting the results obtained in the off-line simulation, we can highlight the following:

1. According to Tables 2 and 3, all algorithms meet the selection criteria, have few parameters, acceptable performance, and relatively low CPU time.
2. All performance indices show similar average CPU time for each algorithm. The algorithm with the lowest average CPU time was BA, while the highest was ABC.
3. Based on the statistical mean and standard deviation, the best-performing algorithm overall was ALO, followed by BA, GWO, and MFO, in that order.

In the case of real-time experiments, the principal selection criterion is to maintain joint torque limits. Only the Bolza form (3) and the objective function (4) of all performance measures consider the joint torques. Although Table 3 shows that all algorithms perform well, input torque signals in the simulation of the ABC, ACO, CS, APSO, and WOA algorithms exceeded the joint torque limits. For this reason, they were discarded from being used in real-time experiments.

Interpreting the results obtained in real-time, we can reach the following final remarks:

1. According to Figures 5–7, all algorithms perform better than the UKF without optimization. This demonstrates the advantages of using the proposed methodology. Table 4 shows the values of the objective function (4) evaluated in all used algorithms; the performance of these algorithms is reflected by minimizing the value of the objective function since it is described in terms of tracking and identification errors. As we can observe, the one with the best performance is the ALO, which we can also contrast in Figure 7. The controller performance shows a notorious improvement concerning a previous heuristic tuning.
2. Concerning Figure 5, the performance of the GWO for the first link is not up to par. However, according to Figure 6, this algorithm on the second link performs better than the other algorithms. Figure 9c exhibits this in the noise of the input torque signal, which is reflected in the RMS value in Table 5.

6. Conclusions

In this work, we have presented the implementation of SI-inspired algorithms in the selection of UKF initialization parameters and their real-time application in a discrete-time decentralized neural block control scheme. We proposed a new objective function that effectively utilizes information from trajectory tracking and identification errors paired with the slopes of the input torques. This function allows us to meet minimizing tracking errors without overshooting the bounds on the control input signals. We performed in simulation a comparative experimental study of the performance of the following SI algorithms: ABC, ACO, ALO, BA, CS, GWO, MFO, PSO, APSO, and WOA. For this analysis, we used five performance indices in addition to our proposed objective function. The real-time experiments were carried out on a 2-DOF robot manipulator, showing ALO, BA, GWO, MFO, and PSO performance, which were the best in our comparative study.

In summary, the main contribution of this work is the implementation of the use of SI-inspired algorithms in the selection of UKF initialization parameters and its real-time implementation in a discrete-time decentralized neural block control; moreover, an experimental comparative study of performance was carried out between the ALO, BA, GWO, MFO, and PSO.

Author Contributions: Conceptualization, J.F.G., R.G.-H., M.A.L. and V.S; methodology, J.F.G., R.G.-H., M.A.L. and V.S; software, J.F.G. and V.S; validation, J.F.G., R.G.-H., M.A.L. and V.S.; formal analysis, J.F.G., R.G.-H., M.A.L. and V.S.; investigation, J.F.G., R.G.-H., M.A.L. and V.S.; resources, J.F.G., R.G.-H., M.A.L. and V.S.; writing—original draft preparation, J.F.G. and R.G.-H.; writing—review and editing, J.F.G., R.G.-H., M.A.L. and V.S.; visualization, J.F.G., R.G.-H., M.A.L. and V.S.; supervision, R.G.-H., M.A.L. and V.S.; project administration, R.G.-H.; funding acquisition, R.G.-H., M.A.L. and V.S. All authors have read and agreed to the published version of the manuscript.

Funding: This research was funded by financial support of the research projects of the Tecnológico Nacional de México/I. T. La Laguna and CONACYT.

Data Availability Statement: Data sharing not applicable.

Acknowledgments: The authors would like to thank to all the staff in División de Estudios de Posgrado e Investigación del Tecnológico Nacional de México/I. T. de La Laguna.

Conflicts of Interest: The authors declare no conflict of interest.

Abbreviations

The following abbreviations are used in this manuscript:

ABC	Artificial Bee Colony
ACO	Ant Colony Optimization
ALO	Ant Lion Optimizer
APSO	Accelerated Particle Swarm Optimization
BA	Bat Algorithm
CS	Cuckoo Search
DOF	Degrees of Freedom
EKF	Extended Kalman filter
GWO	Grey Wolf Optimizer
IAE	Integral Absolute Error
ISE	Integral Squared Error
ITAE	Integral Time-weighted Absolute Error
ITSE	Integral Time-weighted Squared Error
MFO	Moth Flame Optimization
MSE	Mean Square Error
NBC	Nonlinear Block Control
NN	Neural network
PSO	Particle Swarm Optimization
RHONN	Recurrent High Order Neural Networks
RMS	Root Mean Square
SD	Standard Deviation
SI	Swarm Intelligence
UKF	Unscented Kalman filter
WOA	Whale Optimization Algorithm

References

1. Yang, X.S.; Karamanoglu, M. Nature-inspired computation and swarm intelligence: A state-of-the-art overview. In *Nature-Inspired Computation and Swarm Intelligence*; Elsevier: Amsterdam, The Netherlands, 2020; pp. 3–18.
2. Tang, J.; Liu, G.; Pan, Q. A review on representative swarm intelligence algorithms for solving optimization problems: Applications and trends. *IEEE/CAA J. Autom. Sin.* **2021**, *8*, 1627–1643. [CrossRef]
3. Alanis, A.Y. Bioinspired Intelligent Algorithms for Optimization, Modeling and Control: Theory and Applications. *Mathematics* **2022**, *10*, 2334. [CrossRef]
4. Degas, A.; Islam, M.R.; Hurter, C.; Barua, S.; Rahman, H.; Poudel, M.; Ruscio, D.; Ahmed, M.U.; Begum, S.; Rahman, M.A.; et al. A survey on artificial intelligence (AI) and eXplainable AI in air traffic management: Current trends and development with future research trajectory. *Appl. Sci.* **2022**, *12*, 1295. [CrossRef]

5. Cao, X.; Yan, H.; Huang, Z.; Ai, S.; Xu, Y.; Fu, R.; Zou, X. A multi-objective particle swarm optimization for trajectory planning of fruit picking manipulator. *Agronomy* **2021**, *11*, 2286. [CrossRef]
6. Malik, A.; Henderson, T.; Prazenica, R. Multi-objective swarm intelligence trajectory generation for a 7 degree of freedom robotic manipulator. *Robotics* **2021**, *10*, 127. [CrossRef]
7. Mirjalili, S. The ant lion optimizer. *Adv. Eng. Softw.* **2015**, *83*, 80–98. [CrossRef]
8. Yang, X.S.; He, X. Bat algorithm: Literature review and applications. *Int. J. Bio-Inspired Comput.* **2013**, *5*, 141–149. [CrossRef]
9. Mirjalili, S.; Mirjalili, S.M.; Lewis, A. Grey wolf optimizer. *Adv. Eng. Softw.* **2014**, *69*, 46–61. [CrossRef]
10. Mirjalili, S. Moth-flame optimization algorithm: A novel nature-inspired heuristic paradigm. *Knowl.-Based Syst.* **2015**, *89*, 228–249. [CrossRef]
11. Eberhart, R.; Kennedy, J. Particle swarm optimization. In Proceedings of the IEEE International Conference on Neural Networks, Perth, WA, Australia, 27 November–1 December 1995; IEEE: New York, NY, USA, 1995; Volume 4, pp. 1942–1948.
12. Rao, S.S. *Engineering Optimization: Theory and Practice*; John Wiley & Sons: Hoboken, NJ, USA, 2019.
13. Oliveira, J.; Oliveira, P.M.; Boaventura-Cunha, J.; Pinho, T. Evaluation of hunting-based optimizers for a quadrotor sliding mode flight controller. *Robotics* **2020**, *9*, 22. [CrossRef]
14. Panda, M.; Das, B. Grey wolf optimizer and its applications: A survey. In *Proceedings of the Third International Conference on Microelectronics, Computing and Communication Systems: MCCS 2018*; Springer: Singapore, 2019; pp. 179–194.
15. William, M.V.A.; Ramesh, S.; Cep, R.; Kumar, M.S.; Elangovan, M. MFO Tunned SVR Models for Analyzing Dimensional Characteristics of Cracks Developed on Steam Generator Tubes. *Appl. Sci.* **2022**, *12*, 12375. [CrossRef]
16. Guerra, J.F.; Garcia-Hernandez, R.; Llama, M.A.; Santibañez, V. UKF-Based Neural Training for Nonlinear Systems Identification and Control Improvement. *IEEE Access* **2022**, *10*, 114501–114513. [CrossRef]
17. Wan, E.A.; Van Der Merwe, R. The unscented Kalman filter for nonlinear estimation. In Proceedings of the Adaptive Systems for Signal Processing, Communications, and Control Symposium 2000, AS-SPCC, the IEEE 2000, Lake Louise, AB, Canada, 4 October 2000; IEEE: New York, NY, USA, 2000; pp. 153–158.
18. Julier, S.J.; Uhlmann, J.K. Unscented filtering and nonlinear estimation. *Proc. IEEE* **2004**, *92*, 401–422. [CrossRef]
19. Simon, D. *Optimal State Estimation: Kalman, H Infinity, and Nonlinear Approaches*; John Wiley & Sons: Hoboken, NJ, USA, 2006.
20. Särkkä, S. *Bayesian Filtering and Smoothing*; Cambridge University Press: Cambridge, UK, 2013.
21. Zhang, G.; Qi, Y. Neural network-based nonlinear dynamic modeling for process control. *Control Eng. Pract.* **2005**, *13*, 185–192.
22. Zhang, Z. Neural networks for nonlinear dynamic system modeling and identification. In *Proceedings of the Advances in Neural Networks*; Springer: Berlin/Heidelberg, Germany, 2008; pp. 268–272.
23. Alanis, A.Y.; Arana-Daniel, N.; Lopez-Franco, C. *Bio-Inspired Algorithms for Engineering*; Butterworth-Heinemann: Oxford, UK, 2018.
24. Kirk, D.E. *Optimal Control Theory: An Introduction*; Courier Corporation: North Chelmsford, MA, USA, 2004.
25. Sethi, S.P.; Sethi, S.P. *What Is Optimal Control Theory?* Springer: Berlin/Heidelberg, Germany, 2019.
26. Llama, M.; Flores, A.; Garcia-Hernandez, R.; Santibañez, V. Heuristic global optimization of an adaptive fuzzy controller for the inverted pendulum system: Experimental comparison. *Appl. Sci.* **2020**, *10*, 6158. [CrossRef]
27. Garcia-Hernandez, R.; Lopez-Franco, M.; Sanchez, E.N.; Alanis, A.Y.; Ruz-Hernandez, J.A. *Decentralized Neural Control: Application to Robotics*; Studies in Systems, Decision and Control; Springer: Cham, Switzerland, 2017; Volume 96.
28. Utkin, V.; Guldner, J.; Shi, J. *Sliding Mode Control in Electro-Mechanical Systems*; CRC Press: Boca Raton, FL, USA, 2009.
29. Kelly, R.; Davila, V.S.; Perez, J.A.L. *Control of Robot Manipulators in Joint Space*; Springer Science & Business Media: Berlin/Heidelberg, Germany, 2005.
30. Camarena, O.; Cuevas, E.; Pérez-Cisneros, M.; Fausto, F.; González, A.; Valdivia, A. Ls-II: An improved locust search algorithm for solving optimization problems. *Math. Probl. Eng.* **2018**, *2018*, 1–15. [CrossRef]
31. Deif, D.S.; Gadallah, Y. An ant colony optimization approach for the deployment of reliable wireless sensor networks. *IEEE Access* **2017**, *5*, 10744–10756. [CrossRef]
32. Abualigah, L.; Shehab, M.; Alshinwan, M.; Mirjalili, S.; Elaziz, M.A. Ant lion optimizer: A comprehensive survey of its variants and applications. *Arch. Comput. Methods Eng.* **2021**, *28*, 1397–1416. [CrossRef]
33. Chakri, A.; Ragueb, H.; Yang, X.S. Bat algorithm and directional bat algorithm with case studies. In *Nature-Inspired Algorithms and Applied Optimization*; Springer: Cham, Switzerland, 2018; pp. 189–216.
34. Hernandez-Barragan, J.; Martinez-Soltero, G.; Rios, J.D.; Lopez-Franco, C.; Alanis, A.Y. A Metaheuristic Optimization Approach to Solve Inverse Kinematics of Mobile Dual-Arm Robots. *Mathematics* **2022**, *10*, 4135. [CrossRef]
35. Mirjalili, S.; Gandomi, A.H. *Comprehensive Metaheuristics: Algorithms and Applications*; Elsevier: Amsterdam, The Netherlands, 2023.
36. Mirjalili, S. *Handbook of Moth-Flame Optimization Algorithm: Variants, Hybrids, Improvements, and Applications*; CRC Press: Boca Raton, FL, USA, 2022.
37. Mirjalili, S. Evolutionary algorithms and neural networks. In *Studies in Computational Intelligence*; Springer: Cham, Switzerland, 2019; Volume 780.
38. Mirjalili, S.; Dong, J.S.; Lewis, A. Nature-inspired optimizers. *Stud. Comput. Intell.* **2020**, *811*, 7–20.
39. Abdolrasol, M.G.; Hussain, S.S.; Ustun, T.S.; Sarker, M.R.; Hannan, M.A.; Mohamed, R.; Ali, J.A.; Mekhilef, S.; Milad, A. Artificial neural networks based optimization techniques: A review. *Electronics* **2021**, *10*, 2689. [CrossRef]

40. Na, Q.; Yin, G.; Liu, A. A novel heuristic artificial neural network model for urban computing. *IEEE Access* **2019**, *7*, 183751–183760. [CrossRef]
41. Heidari, A.A.; Faris, H.; Mirjalili, S.; Aljarah, I.; Mafarja, M. Ant lion optimizer: Theory, literature review, and application in multi-layer perceptron neural networks. In *Nature-Inspired Optimizers: Theories, Literature Reviews and Applications*; Springer: Cham, Switzerland, 2020; pp. 23–46.
42. Bangyal, W.H.; Ahmad, J.; Rauf, H.T. Optimization of neural network using improved bat algorithm for data classification. *J. Med. Imaging Health Inform.* **2019**, *9*, 670–681. [CrossRef]
43. Tran-Ngoc, H.; Khatir, S.; De Roeck, G.; Bui-Tien, T.; Wahab, M.A. An efficient artificial neural network for damage detection in bridges and beam-like structures by improving training parameters using cuckoo search algorithm. *Eng. Struct.* **2019**, *199*, 109637. [CrossRef]
44. Zhang, X.; Hou, J.; Wang, Z.; Jiang, Y. Joint SOH-SOC estimation model for lithium-ion batteries based on GWO-BP neural network. *Energies* **2022**, *16*, 132. [CrossRef]
45. Pham, V.D.; Nguyen, Q.H.; Nguyen, H.D.; Pham, V.M.; Bui, Q.T. Convolutional neural network—Optimized moth flame algorithm for shallow landslide susceptible analysis. *IEEE Access* **2020**, *8*, 32727–32736. [CrossRef]
46. Liu, X.h.; Zhang, D.; Zhang, J.; Zhang, T.; Zhu, H. A path planning method based on the particle swarm optimization trained fuzzy neural network algorithm. *Clust. Comput.* **2021**, *24*, 1901–1915. [CrossRef]
47. Khan, A.; Bukhari, J.; Bangash, J.I.; Khan, A.; Imran, M.; Asim, M.; Ishaq, M.; Khan, A. Optimizing connection weights of functional link neural network using APSO algorithm for medical data classification. *J. King Saud-Univ.-Comput. Inf. Sci.* **2022**, *34*, 2551–2561. [CrossRef]
48. Brodzicki, A.; Piekarski, M.; Jaworek-Korjakowska, J. The whale optimization algorithm approach for deep neural networks. *Sensors* **2021**, *21*, 8003. [CrossRef]
49. Pizarro-Lerma, A.; Santibañez, V.; Garcia-Hernandez, R.; Villalobos-Chin, J. Sectorial fuzzy controller plus feedforward for the trajectory tracking of robotic arms in joint space. *Mathematics* **2021**, *9*, 616. [CrossRef]

algorithms

MDPI

Article

Model Predictive Evolutionary Temperature Control via Neural-Network-Based Digital Twins

Cihan Ates *,†, Dogan Bicat †, Radoslav Yankov, Joel Arweiler, Rainer Koch and Hans-Jörg Bauer

Institute of Thermal Turbomachinery, Karlsruhe Institute of Technology (KIT), 76137 Karlsruhe, Germany; rainer.koch@kit.edu (R.K.); hans-joerg.bauer@kit.edu (H.-J.B.)

* Correspondence: cihan.ates@kit.edu; Tel.: +49-72160844703

† These authors contributed equally to this work.

Abstract: In this study, we propose a population-based, data-driven intelligent controller that leverages neural-network-based digital twins for hypothesis testing. Initially, a diverse set of control laws is generated using genetic programming with the digital twin of the system, facilitating a robust response to unknown disturbances. During inference, the trained digital twin is utilized to virtually test alternative control actions for a multi-objective optimization task associated with each control action. Subsequently, the best policy is applied to the system. To evaluate the proposed model predictive control pipeline, experiments are conducted on a multi-mode heat transfer test rig. The objective is to achieve homogeneous cooling over the surface, minimizing the occurrence of hot spots and energy consumption. The measured variable vector comprises high dimensional infrared camera measurements arranged as a sequence (655,360 inputs), while the control variable includes power settings for fans responsible for convective cooling (3 outputs). Disturbances are induced by randomly altering the local heat loads. The findings reveal that by utilizing an evolutionary algorithm on measured data, a population of control laws can be effectively learned in the virtual space. This empowers the system to deliver robust performance. Significantly, the digital twin-assisted, population-based model predictive control (MPC) pipeline emerges as a superior approach compared to individual control models, especially when facing sudden and random changes in local heat loads. Leveraging the digital twin to virtually test alternative control policies leads to substantial improvements in the controller's performance, even with limited training data.

Keywords: model predictive control; digital twin; neural network; deep learning; genetic programming; evolutionary algorithm; heat transfer; temperature control; data driven control; data-driven engineering

1. Introduction

Model Predictive Control (MPC) represents an advanced control method that distinguishes itself by employing a mathematical system model to anticipate future system behavior and makes proactive decisions in response to expected deviations from a set point. Unlike traditional control methods that reactively rely on past and present system behavior, MPC combines the principles of feedback control and numerical optimization to achieve optimal control outcomes. By continuously optimizing the system model in real-time, MPC determines an optimal trajectory for the manipulated variable.

The essential constituents of MPC encompass three fundamental elements: (i) a predictive model capturing the dynamics of the controlled system, (ii) a trajectory to be tracked and (iii) an optimal controller achieved through continuous optimization. Notably, only the initial value of the optimized output trajectory is implemented in the system, with the prediction and optimization process being repeated at each time step. This adaptive approach enables MPC to dynamically respond to changing conditions and deliver accurate control by considering future system behavior.

As the MPC revolves around the iterative solution of an optimization problem, it necessitates a system model, as well as a mathematical description of the corresponding control law [1]. These models are traditionally derived from first principles or obtained through system identification techniques using measured data [2]. However, an attractive alternative approach is to directly implement an MPC controller using solely measured data, without relying on prior knowledge of an accurate model [3]. The data-driven approach particularly offers practical advantages in scenarios where (i) obtaining a precise model may be challenging, time-consuming and/or expensive to evaluate; (ii) the process is ill-defined; (iii) the process is time-variant or stochastic in nature. Herein, recent advancements in machine learning facilitates the creation of input–output-based digital twin models (DT) that do not require a thorough mathematical description of the process [4], enabling the implementation of intelligent controllers that can adapt to the system dynamics and change their control policies in real time. These techniques allow for treating the system and the physical process within itself as a black box [5], while maintaining good accuracy, by approximating the mapping from the input to the output space [6].

Examples of using machine learning in MPC cover a broad range of applications. In one of the early works, Liu and Atkeson combined the linear quadratic regulator with unsupervised clustering (k-nearest neighbor) [7]. Other shallow learning applications include Gaussian process modeling for the safe exploration of dynamical systems [8], the optimal energy management in commercial building micro-grids [9], heating, ventilation and air-conditioning (HVAC) control of a hospital surgery center [10]; Bayesian regression for safe predictive learning control [11], statistical time series modeling (ARIMA) for optimal energy management [9], random forests for HVAC systems [12] and support vector machines for milling [13]. Feed-forward neural network (NN) applications within an MPC framework can also be found in various disciplines. Piche et al. [14] implemented an NN to regulate set point changes in a polyethylene reactor, resulting in a 30% improvement in transition speed and a significant reduction in controlled variable fluctuations. The work of Mu and Rees [15] is another early example combining NNs with MPC to control the shaft speed of a gas turbine engine. Gas turbine models were created via a nonlinear autoregressive moving average model with exogenous inputs (NARMAX) and neural networks, enabling an improved control performance compared to PID controllers through various step tests. Afram et al. [16] employed NNs to develop a supervisory MPC for residential heating, ventilation, and air conditioning(HVAC) systems. Their approach successfully reduced the operating costs of the equipment, while ensuring that thermal comfort constraints were not compromised. In comparison to the fixed set-point (FSP) approach, the NN-augmented MPC achieved cost savings ranging from 6% to 73%, depending on the season. Similarly, Li et al. [17] investigated the application of an NN in the context of MPC, focusing on temperature control in a stirred tank reactor. Maddalena et al. [18] used NNs to generate control laws for MPC of voltage-current regulation in DC-DC converters. Similarly, Nubert et al. [19] demonstrated that the computation time of MPC can be drastically reduced with an NN controller for real-world robotic systems. In another study, Shin et al. [20] employed an NN in conjunction with MPC to control a simulated depropanizer in Aspen HYSYS, achieving a remarkable 60% reduction in settling time compared to a traditional PID controller. Nunez et al. [21] utilized a recurrent neural network (RNN) along with a particle swarm optimization (PSO) to model an industrial paste thickening process. The RNN-based MPC successfully maintained the desired concentration of the paste thickener, even in the presence of severe pump failures. Other RNN-based applications include solving a generic nonconvex control problem [22], optimal policy selection [23], fault diagnosis for HVAC systems [24], theory [25] and application [26] of a generic nonlinear system for open-loop simulations, multi-mode process control of a generic system [27], chemical reactor control [28], crystallization processes [29] annealing furnaces [30], N-tank problems [31] and corn production [32]. Achirei et al. [33] very recently introduced a model-based predictive controller that utilized the object map obtained from the convolutional neural network (CNN) detector and light detection and ranging (LIDAR) data to guide an omnidirectional robot to specific positions in a warehouse environment. For a more comprehensive understanding of recent advancements in model predictive control, we recommend consulting several key papers. Sand [34] offers a detailed comparison of different predictive control methods. In the realm of autonomous systems, Rosolia et al. [35] delve into the realm of data-driven control. For those interested in chemical process systems, Rawlings and Maravelias [36] provide a comprehensive exploration. Schwenzer et al. [37] present a holistic view of model predictive control, while Schweidtmann et al. [38] explore the integration of machine learning techniques in this context.

The literature review on NN-augmented MPC reveals the successful utilization of neural networks as effective approximators in MPC. Recent advancements in deep learning, such as neural networks with memory functions (RNNs) and specialized architectures capable of handling spatial information (CNNs), have further enhanced the representational power of data-driven models. Our contribution introduces a noteworthy progression within the domain of intelligent control strategies, stemmed from the strategic utilization of *ConvLSTM-based* digital twins' spatiotemporal pattern extraction abilities, enabling the successful implementation of a real-time population-based MPC in systems with many controlled variables. In particular, we propose a data-driven intelligent controller that leverages NN-based digital twins for hypothesis testing. Initially, a diverse set of control laws is generated using genetic programming with the digital twin of the system, facilitating a robust response to unknown disturbances. During inference, the trained digital twin is utilized to virtually test alternative control actions for a multi-objective optimization task associated with each control action. Subsequently, the best policy is applied to the system. To evaluate the proposed intelligent control pipeline, experiments are conducted on a multi-mode heat transfer test rig. The measured variable vector comprises high-dimensional infrared camera measurements arranged in a sequence (i.e., 655,360 inputs), while the control variable includes power settings for three fans responsible for convective cooling. Disturbances are induced by randomly altering the set point of local heat loads. The objective is to achieve homogeneous cooling over the surface, minimizing the occurrence of hot spots and energy consumption.

The structure of this paper is outlined below. Section 2 begins by providing an explanation of the experimental setup. Next, the model architecture of the NN-based digital twin is detailed. Then, the genetic programming implementation for generating a diverse control law population is described. Lastly, the design of the experiment used to evaluate the performance of MPC is presented. In Section 3, the predictive capabilities of the digital twin are assessed, followed by an evaluation of the MPC performance in real time test experiments. The paper concludes with a discussion about the current limitations of the approach, and the future directions.

2. Materials and Methods

2.1. Experimental Setup

This case study is motivated by the significant impact that high-temperature technical processes can have on the degradation of components. Accordingly, the proposed approach seeks to develop an intelligent controller using machine learning techniques to enable predictive cooling. The main objective is to generate control laws that facilitate a uniform temperature distribution, thereby minimizing the stresses and deformations arising from the formation of hot spots in the presence of unknown disturbances, or sudden changes in the thermal load.

The physical setup is designed as a multi-mode cooling problem. It consists of the following components (Figure 1):

- A copper plate—selected due to its high thermal conductivity in order to reduce the duration of the experiments;
- The copper plate is coated with a high-emissivity black paint (Nextel Velvet Coating 811-21) for improved signal-to-noise ratio;
- Three heating strips on the backside of the plate arranged in a "Z"-like pattern—310 mm × 17 mm, 24 V, 36 W;
- Three fans located on the perimeter of the plate—SUNON, 12 V, 1.62 W;

- A data acquisition module (myDAQ, NI) with an in-house built control unit;
- A mid-wave infrared camera—FLIR SC5000, (512 × 640) pixels;
- A LabVIEW interface for the real-time control of the system.

The infrared camera detects thermal radiation emitted by the copper plate and other components. The detected radiation is dependent on the plate surface temperature only for constant ambient conditions. This is achieved by conducting the tests in an air-conditioned room. This way, changes in the camera signal can be directly attributed to changes in the plate surface temperature.

A single experiment begins from an initial steady state s_0. A heating disturbance is then introduced through the strips and the fan loads are adjusted. The experiment lasts until a new steady state s_1 is reached. Figure 2 depicts the recordings of two experiments (top row and bottom row) from the training dataset. The first six frames show the steady-state temperature distribution reached at the end of the previous operating point, while the final two frames illustrate the new steady state under the new thermal loads and cooling configuration. There are two options for s_0. We either start with the system completely shut down (no heating or cooling), or we carry on with the steady state reached in the previous operating point.

Figure 1. The physical setup is devised as a multi-mode cooling problem, depicted in the upper section. The arrangement of fans around the copper plate is illustrated in the lower left corner, while the configuration of heating strips at the back of the plate, along with randomly placed thermal insulators, is shown in the lower right corner.

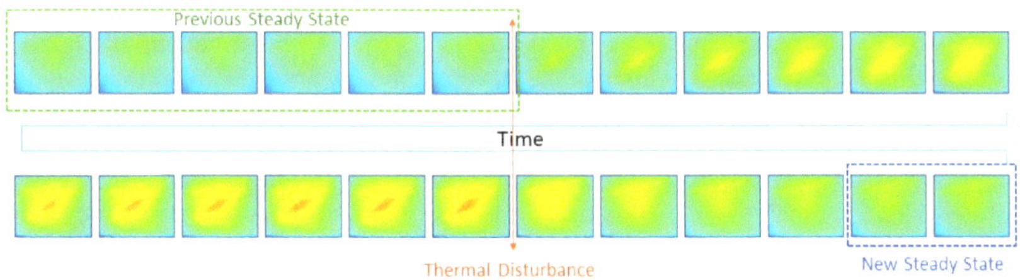

Figure 2. Visualization of two experiments from the dataset.

The following conditions are used to define the second steady state s_1 (Figure 3):

1. The per pixel percentage difference of consecutive frames after 16×16 max filter is less than 1.5%. The application of this max filter is required for two reasons. First, due to thermal inertia, the difference between consecutive frames can be small, and thus we increase the rigidity of the steady-state condition. Second, we reduce the impact of objects that have the same temperature in all frames (e.g., the frame around the plate).
2. The pixels with a 3% deviation in consecutive frames are less than 1% of the total pixels in a frame after a 16×16 max filter.

It is important to highlight that thermal insulation is absent at the slab edges as well as behind the resistance heating strips. The experimental configuration, illustrated in Figure 1, was executed in this manner. Once the system attains a steady state, it does so due to the interplay of forced and natural convection, conduction, and radiative heat transfer processes. In other words, the system was deliberately rendered more susceptible to environmental disturbances and fluctuations.

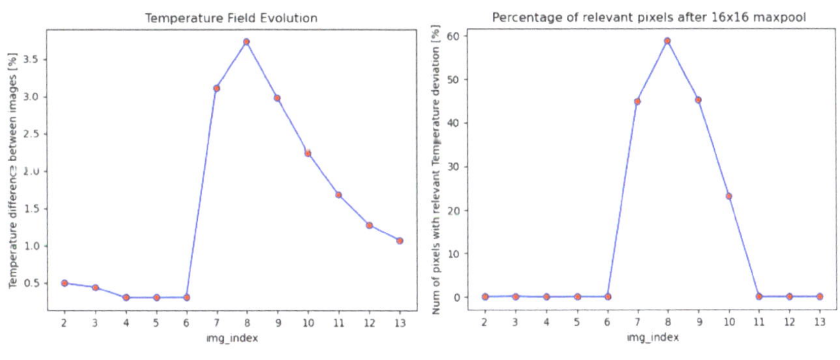

Figure 3. Evolution of consecutive frames over the course of an experiment. (**Left**): Mean pixel value change compared to the first steady-state condition. (**Right**): The percentage of pixels with a deviation larger than 3%.

2.2. Dataset

The training of the digital twin model necessitates a substantial amount of data. In this study, we performed 323 experiments, with each experiment saved as an individual HDF-file. The dataset was split into an 87.5/12.5% training-validation split and the frames were captured at a fixed rate of 1 image per 30 s. Each frame is stored as a grayscale image. The selection of the frame rate was based on preliminary experiments aimed at identifying the system's thermal inertia and response time. A higher frame rate would yield negligible differences between the images, making it challenging for the model to capture the temperature field's evolution. Conversely, longer time intervals may result in the loss of crucial information, such as heat propagation mechanisms and the formation and dissipation of local hot spots.

Within each experiment, the first six frames (2 min and 30 s) represent the initial steady state, denoted as s_0. This allows for the use of up to six frames as an input sequence, ensuring that all subsequent frames after thermal disturbances can be utilized as the ground truth at least once, maximizing the information within the dataset. Furthermore, to cover the parameter space for heating and cooling loads, we randomly sampled fan settings from a 0 to 100% workload with 20% increments and heating strip loads from 0 to 100% workload with 25% increments. In other words, fan settings and heating loads were randomly sampled from a pool of 6^3 and 5^3 possible configurations, respectively. These settings are also saved in the labels of the HDF5-files for post-processing purposes.

It is important to note that different initial conditions, heat loads, and fan settings influence the behavior of the system. Consequently, each configuration requires a varying amount of time to reach a steady-state operation, leading to variations in the sequence lengths across different experiments. Table 1 summarizes the distribution of experiment durations in the dataset.

Table 1. Summary of Experiment Duration in the Dataset.

Duration in Frames	Number of Experiments
8	32
9	103
10	85
11	48
12	35
13	16
14	4

2.3. *Digital Twin*

2.3.1. Model Architecture

The digital twin serves as the fundamental component of the proposed MPC pipeline. Hence, an extensive parametric study was conducted to identify an appropriate architecture and training protocol (see Appendix A for details). The model is based on Convolutional Long Short-Term Memory (ConvLSTM) cells [6]. Given the thermal inertia and slow evolution of the temperature field, it is anticipated that a smaller kernel size would yield better results. This hypothesis was confirmed through numerical experiments, where models utilizing a 3×3 kernel outperformed those employing a 5×5 kernel. Hence, the standard ConvLSTM cell with a 3×3 convolutional kernel is employed as the fundamental building block of the model. Following the lead of prior studies implementing ConvLSTM-based models, we adopt an auto-encoder structure. This choice offers two significant advantages. Firstly, it allows for the extraction of rich semantic information at a relatively low computational cost. Secondly, the learned compression of input data can considerably reduce the workload associated with the genetic programming-based optimization process, while enabling a high accuracy (mean absolute percentage error, Equation (1)). The architecture of the model is depicted in Figure 4.

The encoder is constructed by stacking seven convolutional layers with an increasing number of channels. Semantic information is extracted and the spatial dimension of the input is compressed by each layer. Various compression strategies, such as max pooling, average pooling, and strided convolution, were compared in the preliminary tests. The best results were achieved using a strided convolution with a stride of two. The structure of a single convolutional layer consists of (i) a ConvLSTM cell with a 3×3 kernel, (ii) a stride of two, (iii) L2 weight regularization and (iv) batch normalization. This structure enables the compression of the input image of size $n \times 512 \times 640 \times 1$ to a $n \times 4 \times 5 \times 256$ tensor, which contains rich semantic features. The parameter n represents the number of frames in the input sequence. The feature tensor is subsequently flattened into a vector for further processing.

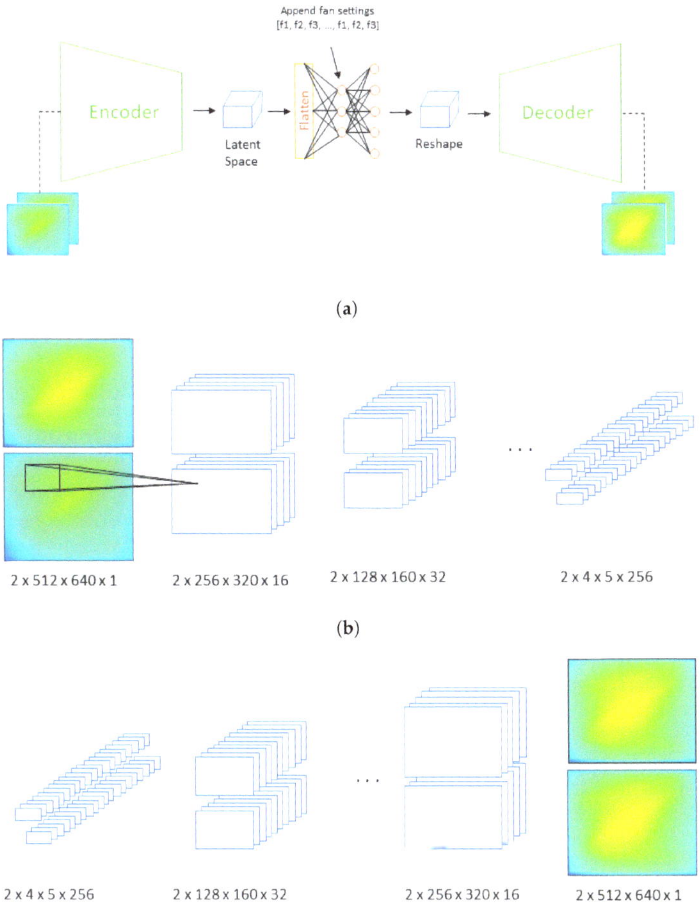

(c)

Figure 4. Deployed digital twin model architecture. (**a**) The next sequence predictor architecture with input and output sequence length of two. The fan settings vector is appended to the output of the first dense layer. (**b**) A detailed view of the encoder architecture. The input sequence is compressed to a latent state representation through 7 convolutional layers with (16, 32, 64, 64, 128, 128, 256) channels, respectively. (**c**) A detailed view of the decoder. The output of the second dense layer is reshaped into a $2 \times 4 \times 5 \times 256$ tensor. The reconstruction is conducted through 7 consecutive deconvolutional layers with (256, 128, 64, 32, 16, 8, 1) channels, respectively.

Following the encoder, a small fully connected network comprising two dense layers is employed. Due to the limited size of the training dataset, the number of dense layers is restricted to avoid overfitting, as supported by the parametric study conducted. Each dense layer includes (i) a dense layer with ReLU activation, (ii) a normal initializer, (iii) dropout regularization and (iv) batch normalization. The first dense layer consists of 2048 nodes and employs a dropout rate of 0.2. The optimal parameters were determined experimentally, considering the trade-off between computational burden and model performance. Next, the fan settings vector obtained from the experiment filename is appended. We select this point to introduce the meta-parameters since this is the layer containing the densest representation of the inputs. Hence, it is an ideal concatenation point that can serve as an input to the GP-based controller. The fan settings vector comprises one hundred repetition of the duty cycle values for each fan. This extension is necessary since the original vector contains only three entries, one for each fan. By appending the initial vector to itself, its relevance to the output of the neural network is increased. This enables the model to learn the impact of the ventilators on the plate's temperature distribution. The size of the second dense layer is predetermined as $m \times 5120$, where m represents the length of the predicted sequence. This ensures that the output is rescaled to $m \times 4 \times 5 \times 256$ to initiate the upscaling of the prediction. To accurately capture the influence of the fans, dropout is disabled in this layer. The activation and initializer used are the same as in the first dense layer.

The final component of the model is the decoder, which mirrors the structure of the encoder. It consists of seven "deconvolutional" layers with a decreasing number of channels. Unlike the encoder, the deconvolutional blocks in the decoder upscale their inputs. Therefore, non-strided convolution and an upsampling layer, which doubles the height and width of the input, are utilized. The structure of the block includes (i) ConvLSTM cell (same as the encoder cell but with a stride of 1), (ii) batch normalization and (iii) upsampling layer. The decoder output has the shape $m \times 512 \times 640 \times 1$ and represents the prediction for the next "m" frames in the sequence.

It is pertinent to highlight that the digital twin model operates as a functional approximator. In essence, this model facilitates the mapping of the temperature distribution across a defined spatial region, over a specific time interval. This mapping takes the form of predicting the temperature field for the upcoming minute based on the temperature distribution observed in the preceding minute—a configuration often referred to as a sequence-to-sequence prediction. It is crucial to emphasize that this mapping encompasses not only the intricate temporal relationships but also the intricate spatial correlations within the field. These predictions are executed on a grid whose spatial resolution mirrors the input dimensions (512 × 640), preserving the structured nature of the grid and facilitating a seamless translation of insights between the physical domain and the digital representation. This framework, driven by the principles of neural networks, extends the familiar principles of function approximation to the realm of dynamic systems, such as the multi-mode heat transfer setup developed in this work.

2.3.2. Training Protocol

Determining optimal hyperparameters for training neural networks can pose a challenge and often necessitates an empirical approach. In our case, extensive testing was conducted, leading to the derivation of the following list of hyperparameters:

- The batch size was set to 16.
- The optimizer employed was Adam, utilizing a default initial learning rate of 0.001.
- A learning rate decay scheme was employed, wherein $lr_t = lr_{t-1} \times 0.99$ was initiated after the tenth epoch, with decay continuing until a minimum value of 0.000001 was reached.
- Training was conducted for 800 epochs on an NVIDIA GeForce RTX 3080 GPU. Early stopping was implemented with a patience of 100 epochs.
- One hundred copies of the fan settings vector were utilized.

The selection of an appropriate loss function significantly influences the performance of the model. In this study, the mean absolute percentage error (MAPE) was adopted, with the following conventions: $\frac{0}{0} = 0$ and $\frac{a}{0} = \infty$ for all $a \neq 0$ [39]. Equation (1) demonstrates the calculation of the MAPE loss, where n denotes the number of pixels in the image, p represents the predicted value for a given pixel, and gt signifies the ground truth value.

$$LOSS_{MAPE} = \frac{1}{n} \sum_{i=1}^{n} \frac{(p_i - gt_i)}{gt_i} * 100 \quad (1)$$

Preliminary tests indicated that utilizing MAPE as the loss function yielded significantly improved the performance in comparison to the mean absolute error (MAE) or mean squared error (MSE) for both the training and validation datasets.

To maximize the utilization of all available data, the sequence length was limited to two, considering the duration of the experiments in the dataset as described in Table 1. For instance, an experiment comprising 8 frames contributed a single input-ground truth sequence pair, while 9 frames resulted in 2 pairs, and so forth. To prevent the model from memorizing the order of entries in the dataset, all sequence pairs were randomly shuffled.

2.4. Control Policy Generation Using Genetic Programming

The subsequent component of the pipeline involves the utilization of genetic programming (GP) to generate control policies for the fans. GP is a variant of Genetic Algorithms (GA) developed by John R. Koza, where the solution is encoded in a tree structure instead of a string [40–42]. Similar to GA, GP draws inspiration from nature and mimics the evolutionary process by iteratively applying a set of genetic operations on an initially randomly selected pool of candidate solutions [41,43,44]. However, unlike GA, which aims to solve specific optimization tasks, genetic programming focuses on creating a model with a predefined objective [45].

In this study, the controller population is designed with two primary objectives. Firstly, it aims to adjust the fans to achieve a homogeneous temperature field. Secondly, it strives to prevent the occurrence of local hot spots. Evaluating these phenomena can be challenging, and relying solely on a single metric may be insufficient. To address this issue, we propose a combination of three metrics to assess the performance of the controller. The first metric targets the homogeneity of the temperature field by minimizing the standard deviation of the pixel values. A lower standard deviation indicates a more uniform temperature distribution. However, relying solely on this metric is inadequate for effectively penalizing hot spot formation. Hence, we introduce a second loss, referred to as the hot spot loss, which calculates the sum of all positive pixel values after subtracting the mean temperature from each pixel. This loss function encourages strong cooling and discourages the formation of regions with temperatures significantly higher than the system's average temperature. Additionally, we incorporate an auxiliary loss function to penalize excessive fan usage:

$$
\begin{aligned}
Loss_{STD} &= \sqrt{\frac{\sum_{i=1}^{n}(x_i-\mu)^2}{n}} \\
Loss_{hotspot} &= \sum_{i=1}^{m} x_i - \mu \\
Loss_{fanload} &= \frac{1}{300}\sum_{i=1}^{3} f_i
\end{aligned}
\tag{2}
$$

where μ represents the mean value, n corresponds to the total number of pixels, and m corresponds to the number of pixels with values larger than μ. To ensure an appropriate evaluation, we scale these three losses to the same order of magnitude and assign weights to emphasize their relative importance. The assigned weights are 5, 5, and 1, respectively. This weight distribution ensures that the fan load loss only becomes relevant when different control laws produce similar temperature distributions.

Control Model Architecture

The integration of the controller into the pipeline requires a trained next-sequence predictor. As explained in Section 2.3.1, the predictive model is compiled as two parts, separated at the output of the initial dense layers. This separation offers a significant advantage: it allows the entire $2 \times 512 \times 640 \times 1$ input sequence to be compressed into a vector consisting of only 2048 data points. This compressed vector is used as the input for the GP-based controllers. By employing this compression technique, the entire input space can be spanned by deeper trees, enabling the generation of solutions based on the complete temperature field, rather than randomly selected local regions of interest.

Control laws in the form of a 3D vector are generated by each candidate in the population (Figure A1). To align with the expected input dimensions of the second part of the predictor, the vector is duplicated 100 times. Next, the proposed fan settings vector is appended, and predictions are generated using the decoder component of the digital twin model. These predictions are then evaluated against a predefined fitness function, and the corresponding fitness scores are assigned to the respective individuals (Figure A1).

The GP controller undergoes evolutionary training for 5 generations on each training experiment, amounting to a total of 1410 generations. Limiting the training to only 5 generations per sequence prevents overfitting to a specific problem, allowing for the transmission of genes that exhibit generalization capabilities across various heating loads. This can be considered similar to the early stopping policies in NN training. For additional information on the GP controller's configuration and the reasoning behind the chosen approaches, refer to Appendix B. Appendix C further presents the details of the MPC experiment design for a population of control laws.

3. Results

3.1. Testing Digital Twin as a Predictive Model

Before implementing with the GP-based controller on the real experimental setup, the performance of the digital twin is first assessed in two distinct aspects. First, it should be able to accurately predict the next two frames given a certain set of inputs. Second, it should be able to capture the impact of the fan loads on the temperature distribution within a virtual experiment, even if it is not part of its training set. In other words, the learnt model representation of the problem in NN parameters should be able to answer "what if" questions in a reasonable way.

Figures 5 and 6 illustrate some good and bad predictions of the digital twin model on new test experiments with pre-set heat load changes and fan settings. It is worth note here that the digital twin typically performed well for experiment trajectories with around 10 snapshots, while failing to capture the extreme hot spots in very short experiments, which were underrepresented in the training set (see Table 1). For instance, the first experiment in Figure 6 consists of only one executable sequence. As a result, the model never received information regarding the new heat load on the system. Consequently, the prediction is an informed guess, based on the last steady state reached. Similar behavior can be observed in the first predictions for experiments (a) and (b) in Figure 5. Hence, weaker performance is to be expected in such cases. This indicates that input sequences containing only the frames, depicting the steady state reached from the previous experiment, may have a negative influence on the model's predictive capabilities on hot spot risk estimation. Fortunately, we do not parse two consecutive steady-state frames as input to the controller, thus mitigating the effect of such outliers when we evaluate the MPC performance. The reason for the inaccurate predictions for the second experiment in Figure 6 is not clearly identifiable. While it manages to capture the structural evolution of the temperature field, it misses the hot spot formation. One reasonable explanation for this is the effect of sampling through a sparsely populated set of fan settings. Increasing the number of training and validation examples and sampling from a set with smaller intervals may remedy this behavior. In either case, however, the MAPE score was less than 5%, which would still be relatively informative enough to decide upon the best MPC policy given the input sequence.

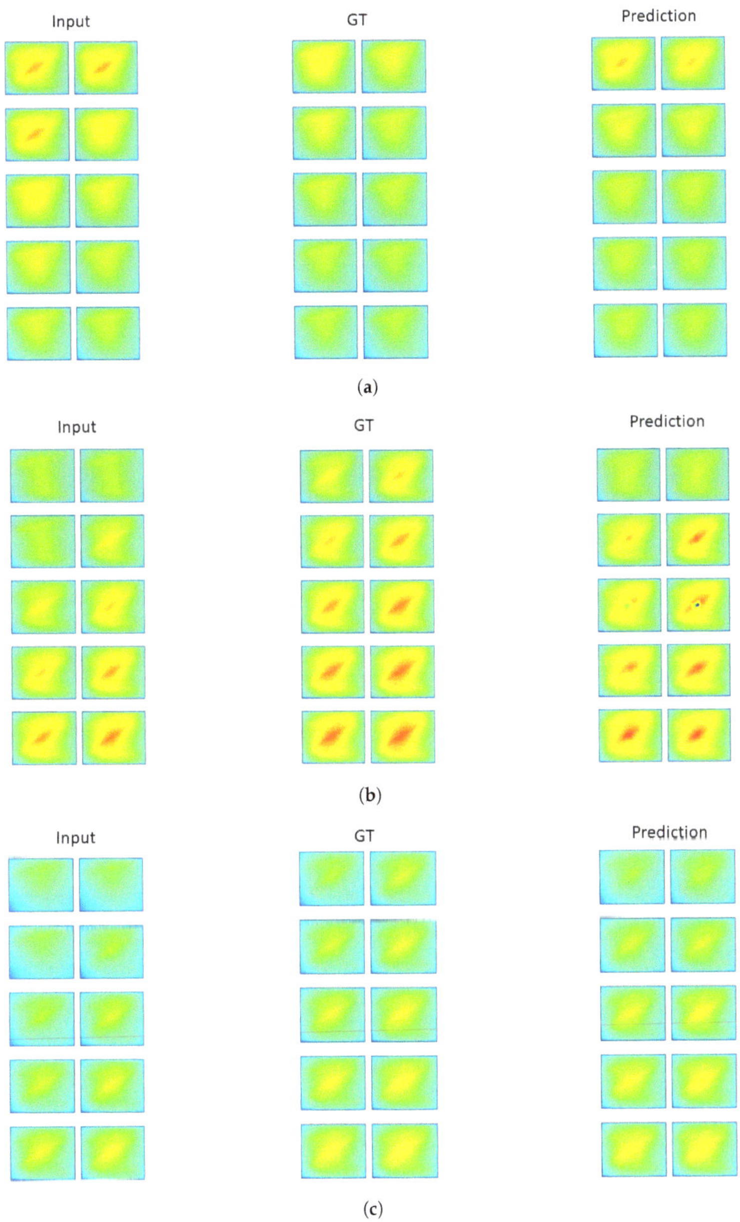

Figure 5. Examples of successful digital twin predictions. GT refers to the ground truth (i.e., experiments). (**a**) Fans [0, 40, 60]; Heating Strips [75, 0, 25]. (**b**) Fans [0, 40, 40]; Heating Strips [75, 100, 100]. (**c**) Fans [60, 80, 100]; Heating Strips [75, 75, 100].

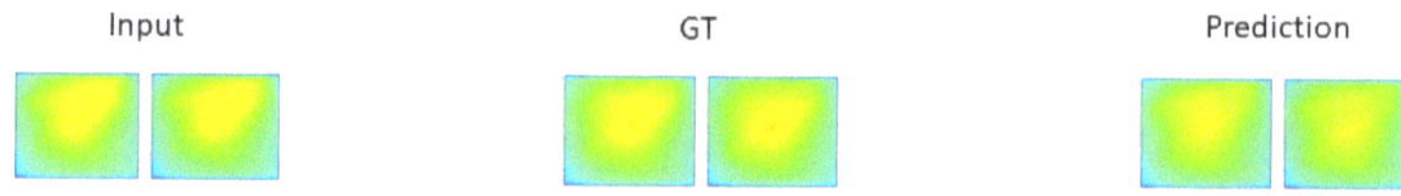

(a)

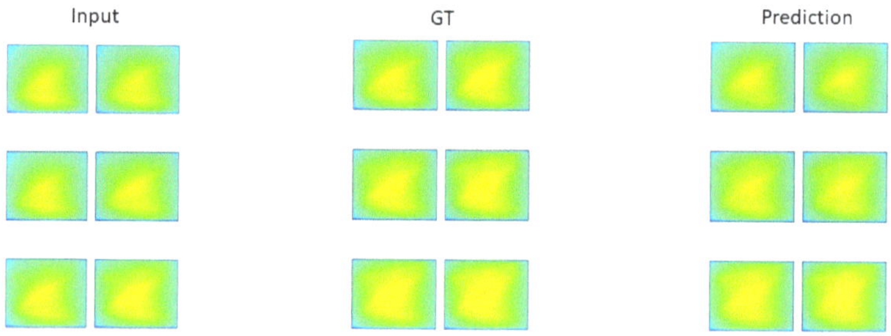

(b)

Figure 6. Digital twin predictions missing the hot spot formations. GT refers to the ground truth (i.e., experiments). (**a**) Fans [60, 20, 20]; Heating Strips [25, 100, 25]. (**b**) Fans [80, 0, 40]; Heating Strips [100, 75, 75].

The second assessment for the digital twin is related to its ability to capture the physical relationship between the fan settings and the evolution of the temperature field, as "understanding" the fans' impact is crucial for the performance of the controller. For that purpose, we conducted a set of parametric analysis. Given a sequence of inputs, the digital twin first makes a prediction of the next one minute for a given fan setting (e.g., [0%, 40%, 60%]), for which the ground truth measurements exist. After checking model accuracy (MAPE < 2%), the DT is used to estimate how the temperature field would be if the fans were fully open ([100%, 100%, 100%]), or fully closed ([0%, 0%, 0 %]). Some examples of the DT predictions are shown in Figure 7. While it is difficult to judge the extent to which the model perceives the impact of cooling on the temperature field distribution, one may conclude that it adequately shifts the prediction with changing fan loads. If they are fully opened, there is an increased cooling effect, while turning the fans off leads to the emergence of some hot spots.

It is worth noting here that changing the way the fan settings are parsed to the model can further improve its ability to capture the effect of the fan loads on the temperature distribution. In the current architecture, we clone the fan settings vector 100 times to increase its relative importance. Although this strategy achieves satisfactory results, it may not be the optimum approach. An alternative way would be to append each of the three fan loads as a channel to the input images. In this way, we would allow the encoder to "learn" the impact the fan settings have on the temperature field evolution. For the current implementation, however, it is considered to be unnecessary as the model already performs with high accuracy (mean absolute percentage error, Equation (1)).

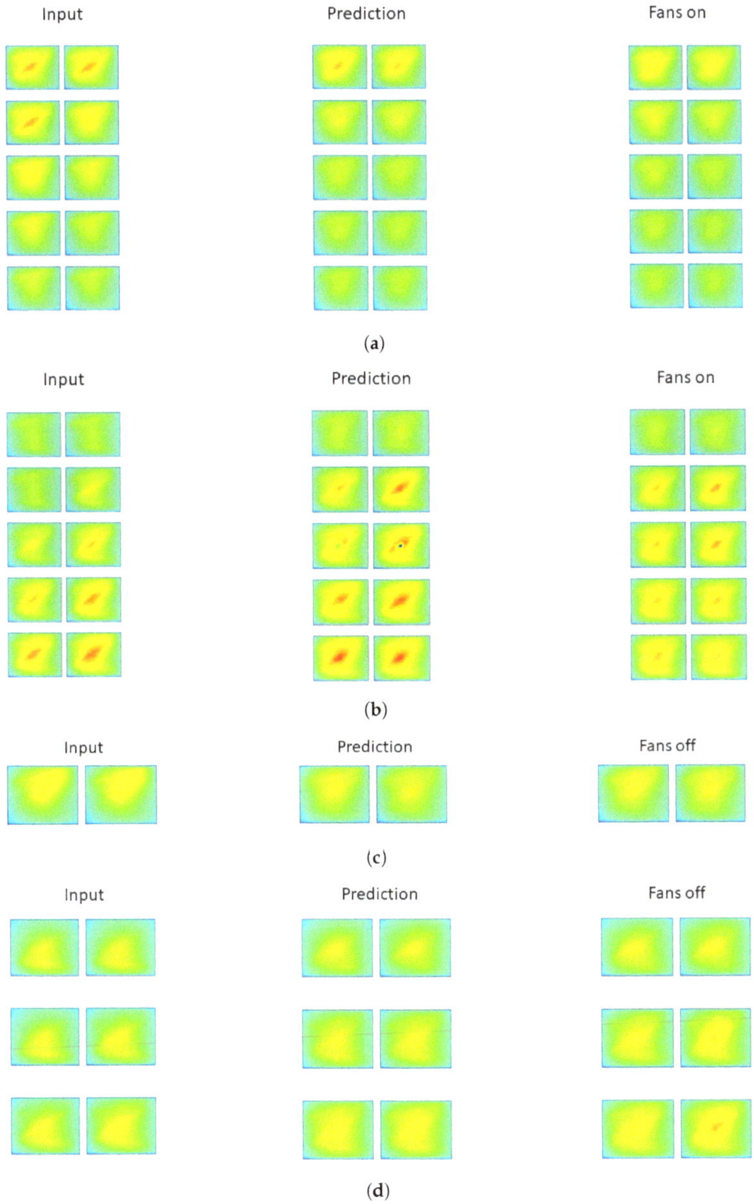

Figure 7. Capabilities of the digital twin model for extrapolation of the fan settings. (**a**) Prediction: Fans [0, 40, 60]; Fans on [100, 100, 100]. (**b**) Prediction: Fans [0, 40, 40]; Fans on [100, 100, 100]. (**c**) Prediction: Fans [60, 20, 20]; Fans off [0, 0, 0]. (**d**) Prediction: Fans [80, 0, 40]; Fans off [0, 0, 0].

3.2. Model Predictive Controller Performance

After validating the accuracy of the digital twin model, the performance of the control law population is investigated via following the experimental protocol described in Appendices B and C. The metrics used to evaluate the controller's performance are the same as the loss functions defined in Equation (2).

The greatest advantage of the intelligent controller is that it can leverage the speed of the NN-based predictive model to select the best control law policy among the alternatives for the current state trajectory in real time. Figure 8 portrays the change in the temperature field caused by a significant and sudden increase in the thermal load applied to the system, while Figure 9 shows the temporal evolution of performance metrics. In all GP-based tests, a control law population of 10 is deployed. In both figures, the term "Specialist" denotes a subset of controls particularly trained to handle high load disturbances. "General" refers to control laws learned for the entire operating range. The category labeled as "Random" corresponds to the benchmark case, where fan settings are randomly assigned (for further details, refer to Appendix C). It is clearly observed in Figure 9 that both GP controllers (Specialist, General) significantly outperform the random controller. Interestingly, the General population achieves a reasonably similar performance to the Specialist at significantly lower energy consumption.

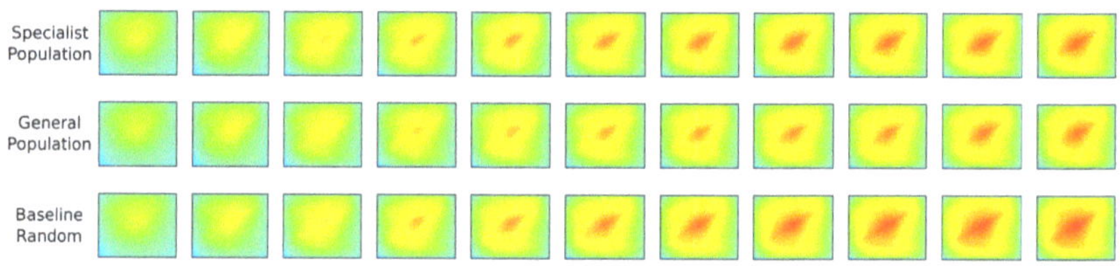

Figure 8. From left to right—Evolution of the temperature field during the experiment: Specialist (**top** row), General (**middle** row) and Random Control (**bottom** row).

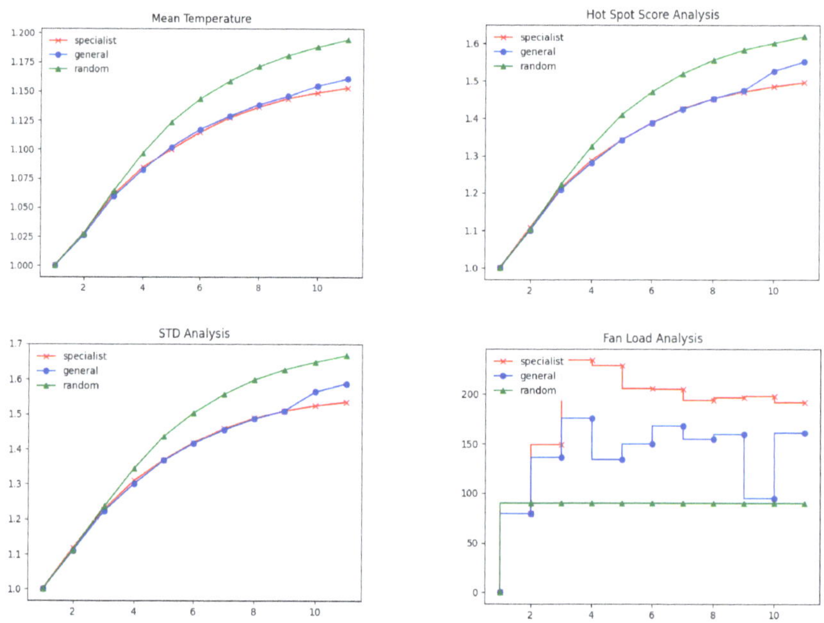

Figure 9. Performance metrics of MPC with 10 individuals at high thermal loads. The x-axis denotes the time, while the y-axis shows the metric.

When the the heat load is raised to medium range from low loads (Figure 10), the Specialist population was found to outperform both the General control law population and the Random cooling, despite the fact that the fan load of the Random case is much higher (Figure 11). If just the fan settings are considered, Specialist MPC is at a disadvantage to eliminate the hot spots on the surface, compared to the random controller. Yet it was found in repeated experiments that Specialist population-based control outperforms the others with less power usage for the fans. The performances of the GP-based controller were also tested in the settings where the heat load is reduced (Figures 12 and 13). As expected, the Specialist population is the best performer. However, its energy consumption is also higher. A possible explanation is that since a homogeneous temperature field is currently prioritized over efficiency, individuals that perform better on the hot-spot and standard deviation metrics are overtaken, albeit at a higher energetic cost.

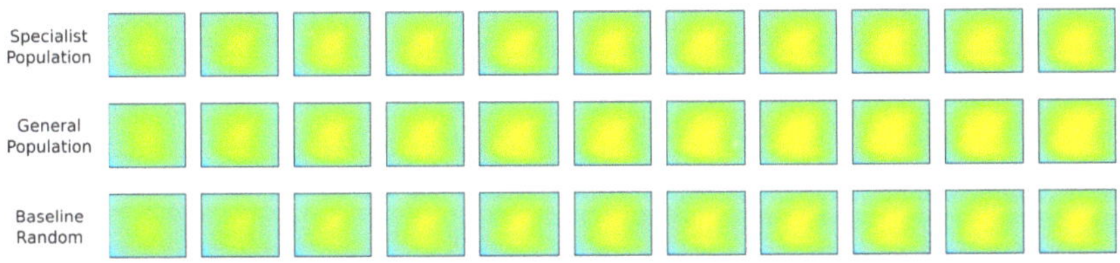

Figure 10. From left to right—Evolution of the temperature field during the experiment: Specialist (**top** row), General (**middle** row) and Random Control (**bottom** row).

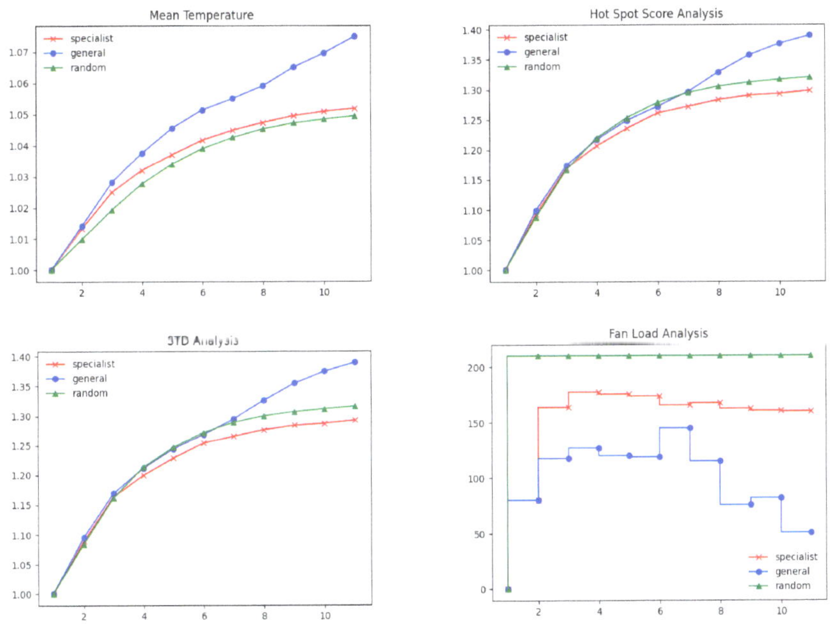

Figure 11. Performance metrics of MPC with 10 individuals at medium thermal loads. The x-axis denotes the time, while the y-axis shows the metric.

Figure 12. From left to right—Evolution of the temperature field during the experiment: Specialist (**top** row), General (**middle** row) and Random Control (**bottom** row).

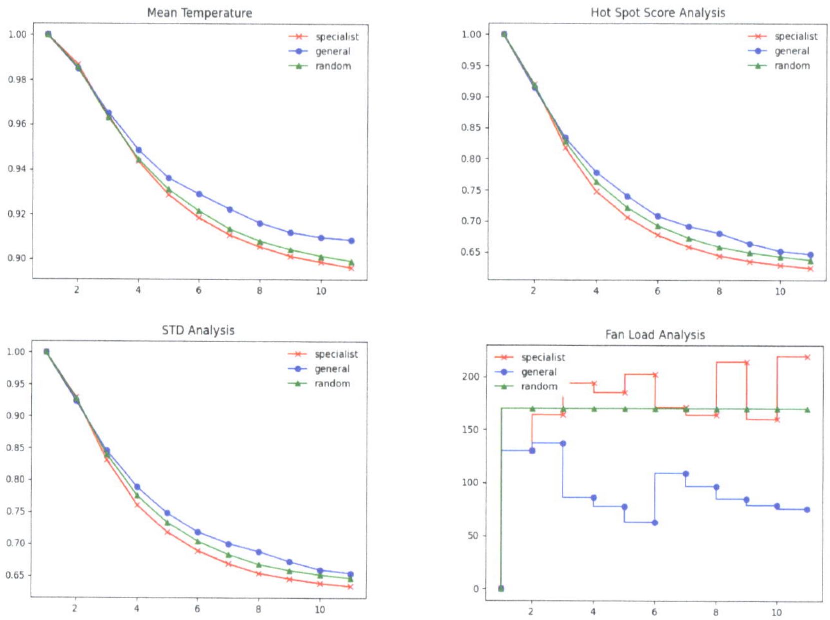

Figure 13. Performance metrics of MPC with 10 individuals at low thermal loads. The x-axis denotes the time, while the y-axis shows the metric.

4. Discussions

Many critical processes of a technical nature occur at high temperatures, leading to the heating of structurally and functionally important components. This heat can significantly deteriorate their properties, especially when coupled with an uneven distribution of temperatures that creates local stresses and deformations. Such processes are often characterized by nonlinearity and stochasticity, making analytical modeling challenging. Fortunately, recent advances in machine learning have provided new opportunities for modeling dynamic systems, even in the absence of precise mathematical descriptions. Consequently, it has become feasible to design controllers that exhibit robust performance and fast response times, even for systems that are stochastic and nonlinear in nature. The objective of this work is to establish a population-based model predictive controller, which tests alternative cooling policies via a virtually trained digital twin on a generic multi-mode heat transfer test rig. The practical aim is to minimize the hot spot formations on the surface, while simultaneously minimizing the overall surface temperature. In accordance, the controlled variables are taken from IR camera measurements, which creates an extremely large input space with more than half a million dimensions. Furthermore, the sudden changes in the heat load distributions on the surface leads to complex, nonlinear transient heat transfer processes, resulting in a significant variation in the time and length scales in the thermal state. In accordance, the controller should be complex enough to respond the drifts in both the system state and the measured variable characteristics. In this work, we propose to use a population of control models within an MPC scheme to respond to these demands. Moreover, the control models in the population were not assumed a priori, but rather learnt via an evolutionary algorithm on measured data. The same training database of experiments were also used to create a digital twin of the process, with which virtual control experiments can be conducted to speed up the evolutionary process. For the studied problem type of image sequence prediction, ConvLSTM-based autoencoder enabled the extraction of a latent representation of the past and current state by using IR camera measurements. More importantly, when fan settings are appended to the vector representation in the latent space, the autoencoder was shown to learn and interpret the impact of fan settings on the future state trajectories, which is of critical importance for a dynamic MPC problem. The robustness of the population-based controller is one of the key properties of the proposed digital-twin-assisted MPC pipeline. In order to demonstrate its added value, the same high, medium and low heat load tests were also conducted by picking one individual control model from the converged population pool, instead of 10 for the Specialist and the General sub-groups (Appendix D). While selecting one individual from the gene pool led to a better control when the heat load was suddenly decreased to medium and low load range, it resulted in a worse performance in hot spot formation when the load suddenly increased from a low to high range. It should be pointed out at this point that 323 experiments were conducted in the study to create a train/validation dataset, and the whole MPC pipeline was tested on randomly generated disturbances out of 27,000 possible configurations (data density was 1.2%). As a result of this sparsity, it is likely that the state dynamics may not be captured with a single control law, particularly if both the DT and the controller model is learnt from data. However, deploying an ensemble of controller models with a DT enables the testing of alternative control policies virtually and deploys the best approach. Furthermore, with an evolutionary approach, it is also possible to trigger the creation of new offspring models, if the current population starts to fail in suppressing the hot spot formations. In the current work, we only deployed 10 of the best individuals from the whole gene pool around 300 converged solutions, based on their performance on a small subset of the state space (<1%). Although the performance of 10 individuals was better than the benchmark case, utilizing the whole population within MPC would lead to much better performance. In MPC experiments, the time interval to make a decision after testing the controller models was set to be less than 30 s. In the current code implementation, the tree model compiling of the GP model was run in a serial mode, hence it limited the application to a maximum of 10 individuals. Therefore, it is strongly recommended to parallelize the controller testing for a more robust implementation. The task of speeding up the candidate evaluation problem and sampling from a larger pool of candidates remains open for future work.

Enhancing the accuracy of the predictive model is a paramount objective for future contributors. Expanding the size of the training and validation datasets is imperative to comprehensively evaluate the architecture's potential. Moreover, refining the data-cleaning process and incorporating experiments with longer durations could booster the model's performance and reliability. Tailoring the pipeline to the specific requirements of the problem at hand is another crucial aspect to consider. For instance, another potential improvement is to extend the length of the sequence for the ConvLSTM autoencoder to fully take advantage of the long-term memory capacity of the model, particularly if the proposed methodology is applied to a different problem. Additionally, we investigate the integration of fan settings as channels within the input images and explore the utilization of symmetric skip connections.

Overall, the results strongly suggest that taking advantage of the ability to test multiple control laws in real-time leads to a significant improvement in the controller's performance. The results clearly indicate that DT-assisted MPC produces effective and efficient control laws even with sparse training data. The fact that the specialist populations consistently outperform random controllers, highlights the potential for the application to more sophisticated problems.

5. Conclusions

This study highlights the significant potential that emerges from combining a population-based control strategy with neural networks to construct a robust and dynamic *Model Predictive Control* framework suitable for addressing complex and nonlinear challenges. The effectiveness of our approach is demonstrated through extensive real-time experiments conducted within a multi-mode heat transfer scenario, where the measured variable vector encompasses high-dimensional infrared camera measurements organized as a sequence (655,360 inputs). We utilize evolutionary algorithms to generate a diverse set of control laws from empirical data, allowing for adaptability to complex and transient heat transfer dynamics. Importantly, our digital twin-enhanced population-based MPC outperforms individual control models, particularly in scenarios involving sudden and stochastic shifts in localized thermal loads. The digital twin, engineered through ConvLSTM-based spatiotemporal pattern extraction, assumes a pivotal role in virtually testing alternative control policies, thereby substantially heightening the controller's responsiveness, even when confronted with limited data availability. Differentiating from traditional methods constrained by the nonlinear and stochastic aspects of complex systems, our data-driven approach harmonizes the capabilities of neural networks, genetic programming and digital twin technology. This blend not only demonstrates the practical efficacy of our contribution, but also highlights the broader potential of these methods across various domains.

Author Contributions: Conceptualization, C.A. and D.B.; methodology, C.A., D.B., J.A. and R.Y.; software, C.A., D.B. and R.Y.; formal analysis, C.A., D.B., J.A. and R.Y.; writing—original draft preparation, C.A., D.B. and R.Y.; writing—review and editing, J.A., R.K. and H.-J.B.; visualization, C.A., D.B. and R.Y.; supervision, C.A., R.K. and H.-J.B.; project administration, C.A. and H.-J.B.; funding acquisition, C.A. and H.-J.B. All authors have read and agreed to the published version of the manuscript.

Funding: This research received no external funding.

Data Availability Statement: Data will be available upon request. The code can be accessed via https://github.com/cihan-ates/model_predictive_control (accessed on 1 August 2023).

Acknowledgments: We acknowledge support by the KIT-Publication Fund of the Karlsruhe Institute of Technology. The authors also thanks Patrick Zengerle and particularly Michael Lahm from ITS Workshop for their support in building the experimental test rig.

Conflicts of Interest: The authors declare no conflict of interest. The funders had no role in the design of the study; in the collection, analyses, or interpretation of data; in the writing of the manuscript; or in the decision to publish the results.

Nomenclature

The following abbreviations are used in this manuscript:

ARIMA	Autoregressive moving average model
CNN	Convolutional neural network
ConvLSTM	Convolutional Long Short-Term Memory
DT	Digital twin
FSP	Fixed set-point
GA	Genetic algorithm
GP	Genetic programming
HDF	Hierarchical data format
HVAC	Heating, ventilation and air conditioning
LIDAR	Light detection and ranging
MAE	Mean absolute error
MAPE	Mean absolute percentage error
MSE	Mean squared error
MPC	Model predictive control
NARIMAX	Nonlinear Autoregressive moving average model with exogenous inputs
NN	Neural networks
PID	Proportional–integral–derivative controller
PSO	Particle swarm optimization
RNN	Recurrent neural network
ReLU	Rectified linear unit
STD	Standard deviation

Appendix A. Background of the Deployed Digital Twin Model

While data-driven methods have an impressive potential for application in the field of digital twin creation, it is important to note that the architecture and performance are heavily dependent on the nature of the problem to be solved. Thus, a thorough understanding of the system and the underlying fundamental physical laws could contribute to a more precise problem formulation. In turn, this can facilitate the selection of a more adequate architecture for the approximation of the system. The problem that the model used in this paper is going to solve falls within the subcategory of the image sequence prediction.

Given that the system's state is represented by infrared (IR) camera images, the predictive task undertaken by the digital twin becomes a challenging task of estimating conditioned image sequences. This entails the need to capture both the spatial structures within the images and the temporal relationships between consecutive frames. When working with image data, CNNs are widely regarded as the preferred choice due to their strong performance and efficiency. Conversely, RNNs have demonstrated success in handling time-series data. Thus, a combination of CNN and RNN architectures is necessary to address the image sequence prediction problem effectively. In recent years, architectures incorporating the *Convolutional Long Short-Term Memory* (ConvLSTM) module have emerged as successful solutions for such tasks [6,46,47]. The ConvLSTM memory cell has a very similar structure to the standard LSTM. However, the fully connected matrix multiplications are replaced by convolutional operators [47]. This simple modification has two significant implications. First, it reduces the redundancy in the model. Second, by setting the convolutional kernel to a value larger than one, one can capture complex "spatiotemporal motion patterns" [6]. An interesting point to highlight here is the robustness of LSTM-based temporal modeling. For instance, in a recent work, the concept has been further extended to a reversed sequence-to-sequence mapping technique that is applicable for long time-horizon forecasting in dynamical systems [48]. The applicability of the approach was also shown to model spiking (biological) pyramidal neurons in hippocampal CA1 [48].

The typical ConvLSTM architecture resembles an Encoder-Decoder architecture. In the original implementation of this architecture, Shi et al. [6] try out several models with varying depths and widths. This approach consistently outperforms the fully connected LSTM. In another example, ref. [49] construct a next-frame prediction model adopting ConvLSTM. The encoder extracts high-level features and encodes them into a fixed-size vector, while the decoder reads the vector and transforms it into the prediction for the next frame's state [49].

Considering the practical importance of multivariate time series prediction, several improvements to the original ConvLSTM architecture have been proposed. Ref. [50] demonstrated that symmetric skip connections between the encoder and decoder parts of the model can significantly improve its image restoration capabilities. Others try to combine ConvLSTM cells with conventional convolutional modules. For instance, ref. [51] applied a ConvLSTM network to the fully compressed feature map of a five-layer convolutional encoder to predict subsurface flows. This allows them to extract rich features through the convolutional encoder alongside the long-term temporal evolution of the flow with a relatively compact model. Alternatively, ref. [52] applied a standard 2D convolution in parallel with a ConvLSTM layer. In this way, he preserves the original ConvLSTM implementation where the input dimensions remain constant, while simultaneously compressing the inputs through a standard convolutional encoder. This architecture allows the addition of more layers, and thus extracts more features, without a dramatic increase in the number of total parameters. As a result, the model can generalize better and process longer sequences. Ref. [53] adopted a similar approach, however, they argued that separating the convolutional autoencoder from the ConvLSTM network may further increase the network's performance. Furthermore, they proposed an improved training protocol. The autoencoder was first trained independently. Consequently, latent space representations are used for the training of the ConvLSTM network. As a last step, the entire network was trained together for fine-tuning [53]. Finally, ref. [47] proposed an inception-inspired ConvLSTM, where each convolution was implemented with a different kernel size, thus extracting features at different scales. Overall, the previous work indicates that ConvLSTM-based models can achieve good results for image sequence prediction. Furthermore, the architecture can be optimized according to the task at hand.

In this work, a relatively simpler design approach was considered. The image space of the case of interest was found to be relatively homogeneous, and the duration of the experiments ranged between three and five minutes. As a result, the main objectives could be identified as follows: (i) accurate predictions of the next frames, (ii) low computational cost to be useful to the controller, and (iii) avoidance of information loss during image reconstruction. Consequently, a ConvLSTM-based approach was deemed sufficient due to its adequate performance, flexibility, and straightforward implementation. Details of the deployed architecture are provided in the next section.

Appendix B. GP Controller Hyperparameters and Operators

Table A1. Hyperparameters of the deployed genetic programming approach.

Parameter/Operator	Value/Policy	Argument
Mutation Probability	0.05	To prevent the loss of good solutions while maintaining diversity in the gene pool.
Crossover Probability	0.85	To avoid unnecessary population shrinkage and prevent excessively fast convergence.
Tree Depth	15–25	Shallow trees would only utilize a small portion of the inputs and would be insufficient for generating sophisticated control laws. Deeper trees, however, require longer computational times for evaluation.
Selection Strategy	Tournament selection	This strategy is widely used and has shown acceptable results. According to [41], all selection strategies can generate satisfactory outcomes, except for roulette, which is not suitable for minimization tasks.
Tournament Size	2	A smaller tournament size preserves greater variety in the gene pool.
Population Size	300	A larger initial population ensures a more diverse gene pool. However, it also leads to longer training times. To capitalize on the processing power of our GPU unit, we explore a broader set of initial candidates.
Output Filter	Sigmoid	The outputs of the trees are scaled to values between 0 and 1 using the sigmoid function.

Furthermore, we selected the following mathematical operations for the nodes of the trees:

- Linear operations—summation, addition, subtraction, multiplication and negation;
- Trigonometric operations—sine and cosine—these operators are used to scale the floating point numbers in the tree. This prevents an "explosion" of the values in either direction (positive or negative), resulting in only two possible modes of operation for the fans—either 0% or 100% load;
- Regrouping operations—create a 3D vector from three values—this is a hard-coded function for the output of the tree, which should result in a 3D vector with one value for the duty cycle of each fan.

Appendix C. MPC Experiment Design

The next step is to transfer the controller from the virtual to the physical domain and assess its performance on the experimental setup. Figure A2 depicts the final procedure for the MPC experiments with one, or multiple control models.

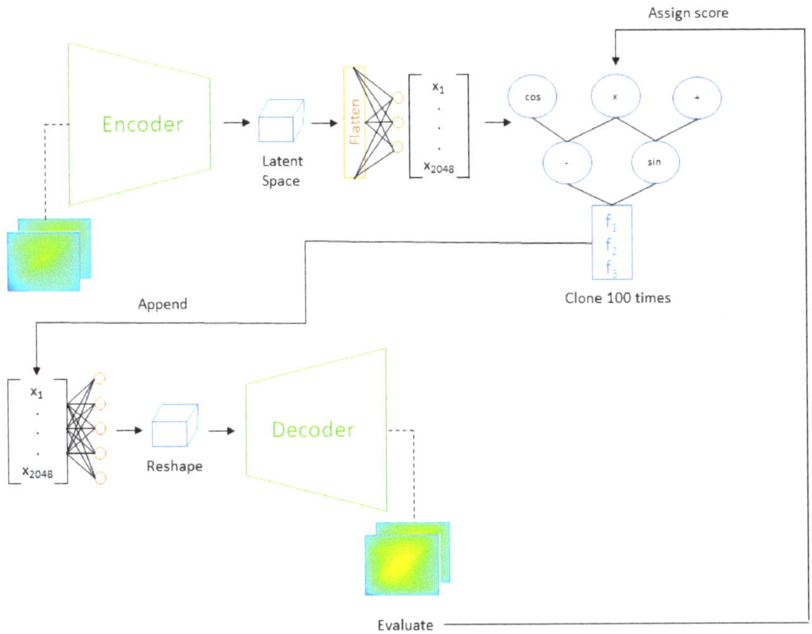

Figure A1. The training pipeline for the GP controller.

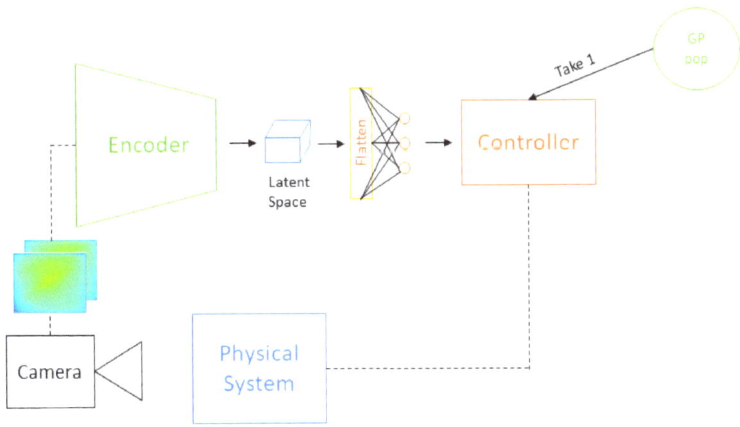

(a)

Figure A2. *Cont.*

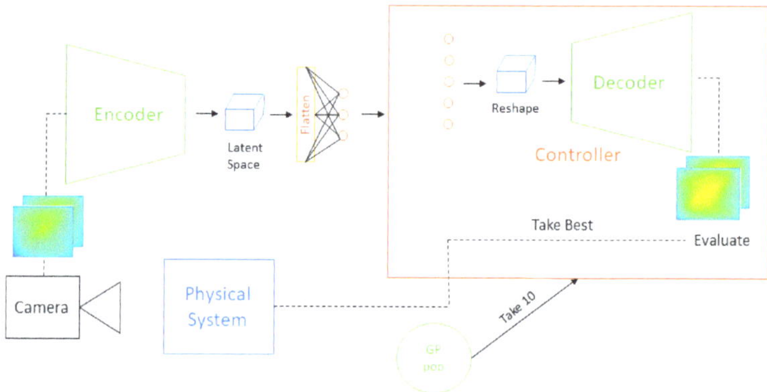

(**b**)

Figure A2. Experimental protocol for MPC. (**a**) Experiment pipeline with a single individual. (**b**) Experiment pipeline with population-based MPC.

MPC tests were conducted using three distinct control policies: (i) specialist control models based on heat loading, (ii) general-purpose control models, and (iii) a simple control model utilized as a benchmark. The specialist groups were formed by selecting the top 10 performers from the final population in experiments with low (total load < 100), medium (100 < total load < 200), and high heat load conditions (200 < total load < 300). As a result, three specialist populations were created, each corresponding to one of the heating load groups. The general group consisted of randomly chosen individuals from the final population.

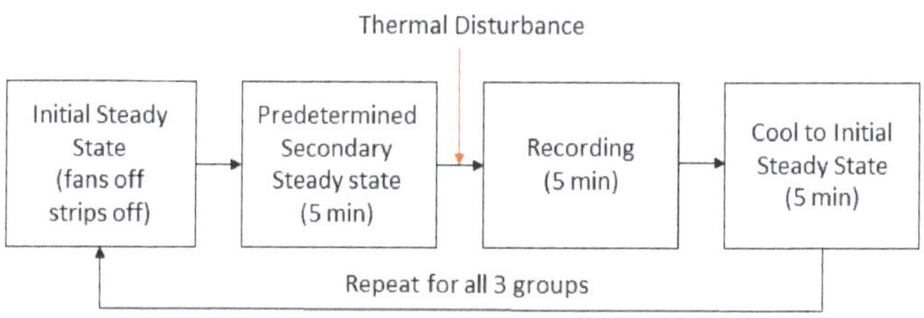

Figure A3. Standardized protocol for the Performance Evaluation Experiments.

To ensure a proper evaluation of the controller's performance, it is essential to maintain comparability among experiments within each group. To achieve this, a standardized workflow is followed, as depicted in Figure A3. The workflow includes the following steps:

1. Cooling to the initial state: All experiments begin from the same starting point by cooling the system to the initial state. This step ensures consistency across experiments.
2. Recreating a predetermined steady state: To simulate the control of a dynamic system and replicate a realistic scenario, the system is preheated to a predetermined secondary steady state. This step further enhances the reliability of the evaluation.
3. Fixed experiment duration: Each experiment is conducted for a fixed duration of 5 min, with a frame captured every 30 s. This extended monitoring period allows for a comprehensive observation of the evolution of the temperature field.

In the MPC tests, three different thermal load scenarios are investigated:

- High heat loading: the load on the heating strips was suddenly increased from [50%, 25% and 0%] to [75%, 100% and 75%], while the fans were open at [20%, 40% and

20%]. The benchmark control law resulted in a fan setting for the cooling experiment of [70%, 0% and 20%] after the set point change.

- Medium heat loading: the heating strip loads were suddenly raised from [25%, 0% and 50%] to [25%, 50% and 70%], while the fans were open at [30%, 20% and 30%] during the second steady state. In this situation, the benchmark control law adjusted the fan settings to [30%, 80% and 100%].
- Low heat loading: the thermal load was abruptly reduced from [75%, 75% and 50%] to [0%, 25% and 25%], while the fans were open at [50%, 80% and 0%]. In this case, the benchmark controller set the fan settings to [80%, 50% and 40%].

Finally, the number of candidates to be evaluated in real-time before applying the control laws needs to be determined. Given our objective of achieving quick response times, it is crucial to strike a balance between evaluation accuracy and computational efficiency. To address this, we employ two different strategies, as illustrated in Figure A2. In the first strategy, a single individual is evaluated. For the specialist populations, the best individual is selected, while for the general populations, a single individual is randomly chosen. This approach ensures a focused evaluation while minimizing computational overhead. In the second strategy, ten individuals are selected for real-time evaluation. Similar to the first strategy, individuals are randomly chosen from the general populations. However, for the specialist populations, the entire population is included in the evaluation. This expanded evaluation allows for a more comprehensive assessment of the control laws. Regardless of the chosen strategy, the randomly generated fan settings remain constant throughout the entire duration of the control experiment. This ensures consistency and eliminates any potential bias introduced by varying fan settings.

Appendix D. Single Individual Tests

Appendix D.1. High Load Test Case

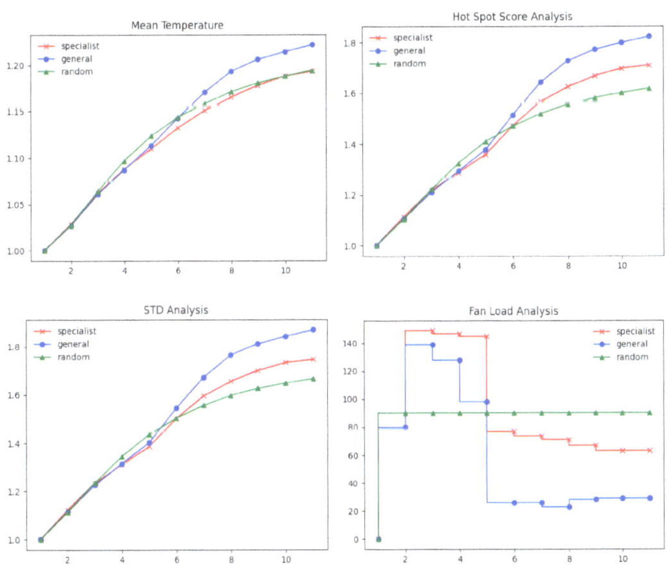

Figure A4. Performance metrics of MPC with 1 individual at high thermal loads. The x-axis denotes the time, while the y-axis shows the metric.

Appendix D.2. Medium Load Test Case

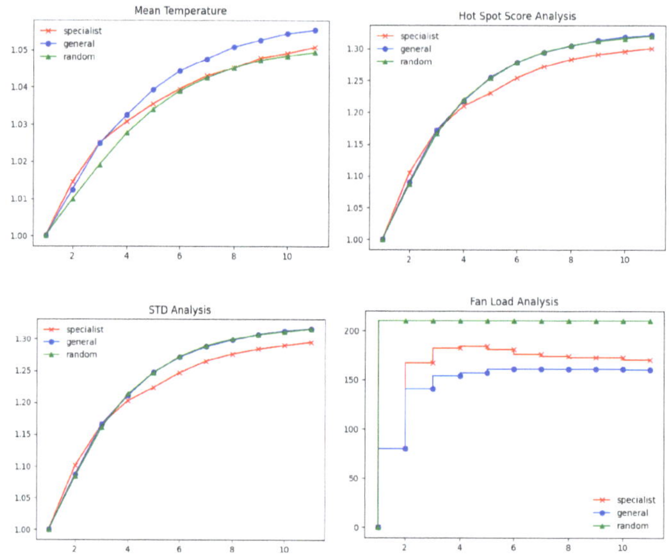

Figure A5. Performance metrics of MPC with 1 individual at medium thermal loads. The x-axis denotes the time, while the y-axis shows the metric.

Appendix D.3. Low Load Test Case

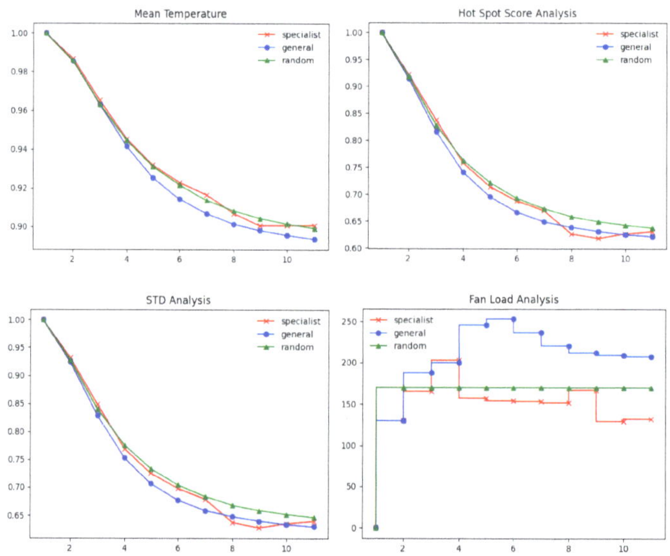

Figure A6. Performance metrics of MPC with 1 individual at low thermal loads. The x-axis denotes the time, while the y-axis shows the metric.

References

1. Marusak, P.M. Numerically Efficient Fuzzy MPC Algorithm with Advanced Generation of Prediction—Application to a Chemical Reactor. *Algorithms* **2020**, *13*, 143. [CrossRef]
2. Nebeluk, R.; Ławryńczuk, M. Tuning of Multivariable Model Predictive Control for Industrial Tasks. *Algorithms* **2021**, *14*, 10. [CrossRef]
3. Domański, P.D. Performance Assessment of Predictive Control—A Survey. *Algorithms* **2020**, *13*, 97. [CrossRef]
4. Wright, L.; Davidson, S. How to tell the difference between a model and a digital twin. *Adv. Model. Simul. Eng. Sci.* **2020**, *7*, 13. [CrossRef]
5. Sun, C.; Shi, V.G. PhysiNet: A combination of physics-based model and neural network model for digital twins. *Int. J. Intell. Syst.* **2022**, *37*, 5443–5456. [CrossRef]
6. Shi, X.; Chen, Z.; Wang, H.; Yeung, D.Y.; Wong, W.K.; Woo, W.C. Convolutional LSTM network: A machine learning approach for precipitation nowcasting. In Proceedings of the Advances in Neural Information Processing Systems 28 (NIPS 2015), Montreal, QC, Canada, 7–12 December 2015; pp. 1–9 .
7. Liu, C.; Atkeson, C.G. Standing balance control using a trajectory library. In Proceedings of the 2009 IEEE/RSJ International Conference on Intelligent Robots and Systems, St. Louis, MO, USA, 10–15 October 2009; pp. 3031–3036. [CrossRef]
8. Koller, T.; Berkenkamp, F.; Turchetta, M.; Krause, A. Learning-Based Model Predictive Control for Safe Exploration. In Proceedings of the 2018 IEEE Conference on Decision and Control (CDC), Miami Beach, FL, USA, 17–19 December 2018; pp. 6059–6066. [CrossRef]
9. Tavakoli, M.; Shokridehaki, F.; Marzband, M.; Godina, R.; Pouresmaeil, E. A two stage hierarchical control approach for the optimal energy management in commercial building microgrids based on local wind power and PEVs. *Sustain. Cities Soc.* **2018**, *41*, 332–340. [CrossRef]
10. Maddalena, E.T.; Müller, S.A.; dos Santos, R.M.; Salzmann, C.; Jones, C.N. Experimental data-driven model predictive control of a hospital HVAC system during regular use. *Energy Build.* **2022**, *271*, 112316. [CrossRef]
11. McKinnon, C.D.; Schoellig, A.P. Learn Fast, Forget Slow: Safe Predictive Learning Control for Systems with Unknown and Changing Dynamics Performing Repetitive Tasks. *IEEE Robot. Autom. Lett.* **2019**, *4*, 2180–2187. [CrossRef]
12. Wang, H.; Chen, Y.; Kang, J.; Ding, Z.; Zhu, H. An XGBoost-Based predictive control strategy for HVAC systems in providing day-ahead demand response. *Build. Environ.* **2023**, *238*, 110350. [CrossRef]
13. Ay, M.; Stemmler, S.; Schwenzer, M.; Abel, D.; Bergs, T. Model Predictive Control in Milling based on Support Vector Machines. *IFAC-PapersOnLine* **2019**, *52*, 1797–1802.
14. Piche, S.; Sayyar-Rodsari, B.; Johnson, D.; Gerules, M. Nonlinear model predictive control using neural networks. *IEEE Control. Syst. Mag.* **2000**, *20*, 53–62. [CrossRef]
15. Mu, J.; Rees, D. Approximate model predictive control for gas turbine engines. In Proceedings of the 2004 American Control Conference, Boston, MA, USA, 30 June–2 July 2004; Volume 6, pp. 5704–5709. [CrossRef]
16. Afram, A.; Janabi-Sharifi, F.; Fung, A.S.; Raahemifar, K. Artificial neural network (ANN) based model predictive control (MPC) and optimization of HVAC systems: A state of the art review and case study of a residential HVAC system. *Energy Build.* **2017**, *141*, 96–113. [CrossRef]
17. Li, S.; Jiang, P.; Han, K. RBF Neural Network based Model Predictive Control Algorithm and Its Application to a CSTR Process. In Proceedings of the 2019 Chinese Control Conference (CCC), Guangzhou, China, 27–30 July 2019; pp. 2948–2952. [CrossRef]
18. Maddalena, E.; Moraes, C.D.S.; Waltrich, G.; Jones, C. A Neural Network Architecture to Learn Explicit MPC Controllers from Data. *IFAC-PapersOnLine* **2020**, *53*, 11362–11367.
19. Nubert, J.; Köhler, J.; Berenz, V.; Allgöwer, F.; Trimpe, S. Safe and Fast Tracking on a Robot Manipulator: Robust MPC and Neural Network Control. *IEEE Robot. Autom. Lett.* **2020**, *5*, 3050–3057. [CrossRef]
20. Shin, Y.; Smith, R.; Hwang, S. Development of model predictive control system using an artificial neural network: A case study with a distillation column. *J. Clean. Prod.* **2020**, *277*, 124124. [CrossRef]
21. Núñez, F.; Langarica, S.; Díaz, P.; Torres, M.; Salas, J.C. Neural Network-Based Model Predictive Control of a Paste Thickener Over an Industrial Internet Platform. *IEEE Trans. Ind. Inform.* **2020**, *16*, 2859–2867. [CrossRef]
22. Pan, Y.; Wang, J. Model predictive control of unknown nonlinear dynamical systems based on recurrent neural networks. *IEEE Trans. Ind. Electron.* **2012**, *59*, 3089–3101. [CrossRef]
23. Pon Kumar, S.S.; Tulsyan, A.; Gopaluni, B.; Loewen, P. A Deep Learning Architecture for Predictive Control. *IFAC-PapersOnLine* **2018**, *51*, 512–517. [CrossRef]
24. Shahnazari, H.; Mhaskar, P.; House, J.M.; Salsbury, T.I. Modeling and fault diagnosis design for HVAC systems using recurrent neural networks. *Comput. Chem. Eng.* **2019**, *126*, 189–203. [CrossRef]
25. Wu, Z.; Tran, A.; Rincon, D.; Christofides, P.D. Machine learning-based predictive control of nonlinear processes. Part I: Theory. *AIChE J.* **2019**, *65*, e16729. [CrossRef]
26. Wu, Z.; Rincon, D.; Christofides, P.D. Real-Time Adaptive Machine-Learning-Based Predictive Control of Nonlinear Processes. *Ind. Eng. Chem. Res.* **2020**, *59*, 2275–2290. [CrossRef]
27. Huang, K.; Wei, K.; Li, F.; Yang, C.; Gui, W. LSTM-MPC: A Deep Learning Based Predictive Control Method for Multimode Process Control. *IEEE Trans. Ind. Electron.* **2022**, *70*, 11544–11554. [CrossRef]
28. Zarzycki, K.; Ławryńczuk, M. Advanced predictive control for GRU and LSTM networks. *Inf. Sci.* **2022**, *616*, 229–254. [CrossRef]

29. Zheng, Y.; Zhao, T.; Wang, X.; Wu, Z. Online learning-based predictive control of crystallization processes under batch-to-batch parametric drift. *AIChE J.* **2022**, *68*, e17815. [CrossRef]
30. Cho, M.; Ban, J.; Seo, M.; Kim, S.W. Neural network MPC for heating section of annealing furnace. *Expert Syst. Appl.* **2023**, *223*, 119869. [CrossRef]
31. Jung, M.; da Costa Mendes, P.R.; Önnheim, M.; Gustavsson, E. Model Predictive Control when utilizing LSTM as dynamic models. *Eng. Appl. Artif. Intell.* **2023**, *123*, 106226. [CrossRef]
32. Meng, J.; Li, C.; Tao, J.; Li, Y.; Tong, Y.; Wang, Y.; Zhang, L.; Dong, Y.; Du, J. RNN-LSTM-Based Model Predictive Control for a Corn-to-Sugar Process. *Processes* **2023**, *11*, 1080. [CrossRef]
33. Achirei, S.D.; Mocanu, R.; Popovici, A.T.; Dosoftei, C.C. Model-Predictive Control for Omnidirectional Mobile Robots in Logistic Environments Based on Object Detection Using CNNs. *Sensors* **2023**, *23*, 4992. [CrossRef] [PubMed]
34. Sands, T. Comparison and Interpretation Methods for Predictive Control of Mechanics. *Algorithms* **2019**, *12*, 232. [CrossRef]
35. Rosolia, U.; Zhang, X.; Borrelli, F. Data-Driven Predictive Control for Autonomous Systems. *Annu. Rev. Control. Robot. Auton. Syst.* **2018**, *1*, 259–286. [CrossRef]
36. Rawlings, J.B.; Maravelias, C.T. Bringing new technologies and approaches to the operation and control of chemical process systems. *AIChE J.* **2019**, *65*, e16615. [CrossRef]
37. Schwenzer, M.; Ay, M.; Bergs, T.; Abel, D. Review on model predictive control: An engineering perspective. *Int. J. Adv. Manuf. Technol.* **2021**, *117*, 1327–1349. [CrossRef]
38. Schweidtmann, A.M.; Esche, E.; Fischer, A.; Kloft, M.; Repke, J.U.; Sager, S.; Mitsos, A. Machine Learning in Chemical Engineering: A Perspective. *Chemie-Ingenieur-Technik* **2021**, *93*, 2029–2039. [CrossRef]
39. De Myttenaere, A.; Golden, B.; Le Grand, B.; Rossi, F. Mean absolute percentage error for regression models. *Neurocomputing* **2016**, *192*, 38–48. [CrossRef]
40. Nazmul Siddique, H. *Intelligent Control: A Hybrid Approach Based on Fuzzy Logic, Neural Networks and Genetic Algorithms*; Springer: Cham, Switzerland, 2013.
41. Ahvanooey, M.T.; Li, Q.; Wu, M.; Wang, S. A Survey of Genetic Programming and Its Applications. *KSII Trans. Internet Inf. Syst.* **2019**, *13*, 1765–1794.
42. Zheng, C.; Eskandari, M.; Li, M.; Sun, Z. GA-Reinforced Deep Neural Network for Net Electric Load Forecasting in Microgrids with Renewable Energy Resources for Scheduling Battery Energy Storage Systems. *Algorithms* **2022**, *15*, 338. [CrossRef]
43. Koza, J.R.; Keane, M.A.; Yu, J.; Bennett, F.H.; Mydlowec, W. Automatic creation of human-competitive programs and controllers by means of genetic programming. *Genet. Program. Evolvable Mach.* **2000**, *1*, 121–164. [CrossRef]
44. Grosman, B.; Lewin, D.R. Automated nonlinear model predictive control using genetic programming. *Comput. Chem. Eng.* **2002**, *26*, 631–640. [CrossRef]
45. Vyas, R.; Goel, P.; Tambe, S.S. Genetic programming applications in chemical sciences and engineering. In *Handbook of Genetic Programming Applications*; Springer: Cham, Switzerland, 2015, pp. 99–140.
46. Lotter, W.; Kreiman, G.; Cox, D. Deep predictive coding networks for video prediction and unsupervised learning. *arXiv* **2016**, arXiv:1605.08104.
47. Hosseini, M.; Maida, A.S.; Hosseini, M.; Raju, G. Inception-inspired lstm for next-frame video prediction. *arXiv* **2019**, arXiv:1909.05622.
48. Plaster, B.; Kumar, G. Data-Driven Predictive Modeling of Neuronal Dynamics Using Long Short-Term Memory. *Algorithms* **2019**, *12*, 203. [CrossRef]
49. Desai, P.; Sujatha, C.; Chakraborty, S.; Ansuman, S.; Bhandari, S.; Kardiguddi, S. Next frame prediction using ConvLSTM. *J. Phys. Conf. Ser.* **2022**, *2161*, 012024. [CrossRef]
50. Hong, S.; Kim, S.; Joh, M.; Song, S.K. Psique: Next sequence prediction of satellite images using a convolutional sequence-to-sequence network. *arXiv* **2017**, arXiv:1711.10644.
51. Tang, M.; Liu, Y.; Durlofsky, L.J. A deep-learning-based surrogate model for data assimilation in dynamic subsurface flow problems. *J. Comput. Phys.* **2020**, *413*, 109456. [CrossRef]
52. Kakka, P.R. Sequence to sequence AE-ConvLSTM network for modelling the dynamics of PDE systems. *arXiv* **2022**, arXiv:2208.07315.
53. Mukherjee, S.; Ghosh, S.; Ghosh, S.; Kumar, P.; Roy, P.P. Predicting video-frames using encoder-convlstm combination. In Proceedings of the ICASSP 2019—2019 IEEE International Conference on Acoustics, Speech and Signal Processing (ICASSP), Brighton, UK, 12–17 May 2019; pp. 2027–2031.

algorithms

MDPI

Article

Improvement of Ant Colony Algorithm Performance for the Job-Shop Scheduling Problem Using Evolutionary Adaptation and Software Realization Heuristics

Pavel V. Matrenin

Ural Power Engineering Institute, Ural Federal University named after the first President of Russia B.N. Yeltsin, 620002 Ekaterinburg, Russia; p.v.matrenin@urfu.ru

Abstract: Planning tasks are important in construction, manufacturing, logistics, and education. At the same time, scheduling problems belong to the class of NP-hard optimization problems. Ant colony algorithm optimization is one of the most common swarm intelligence algorithms and is a leader in solving complex optimization problems in graphs. This paper discusses the solution to the job-shop scheduling problem using the ant colony optimization algorithm. An original way of representing the scheduling problem in the form of a graph, which increases the flexibility of the approach and allows for taking into account additional restrictions in the scheduling problems, is proposed. A dynamic evolutionary adaptation of the algorithm to the conditions of the problem is proposed based on the genetic algorithm. In addition, some heuristic techniques that make it possible to increase the performance of the software implementation of this evolutionary ant colony algorithm are presented. One of these techniques is parallelization; therefore, a study of the algorithm's parallelization effectiveness was made. The obtained results are compared with the results of other authors on test problems of scheduling. It is shown that the best heuristics coefficients of the ant colony optimization algorithm differ even for similar job-shop scheduling problems.

Keywords: job-shop scheduling problem; ant colony optimization; multiphasic systems; genetic algorithm; parallel computing

1. Introduction

1.1. Job-Shop Scheduling Problem

In all cases of human activity to achieve the desired result, as a rule, plans and schedules are drafted. The complexity of task scheduling along with the continuous improvement of automation tools for such activities has led to increased interest in scheduling synthesis theory and calendar planning. The tasks of calendar planning reflect the process of the distribution over time of a limited number of resources assigned to the project, which includes a list of related works.

Problems of scheduling theory belong to the class of problems of combinatorial optimization or ordering. The active research and development of scheduling theory began in the 1950s. One of the main issues of scheduling theory was the classification of tasks and the establishment of their complexity. Reviews of problems in scheduling theory are presented in the works of Gary and Johnson, Lower, Brucker, Xie, Leusin, and Xiong, et al. [1–6].

The scheduling problem of the "job-shop" class is NP-hard if there are more than two devices [5,7]. The survey [6] shows that the job-shop scheduling (JSS) problem is one of the most difficult among all NP-class problems even from the point of view of task formulation. As shown in [8], the number of combinations for a job-shop task with n jobs and m devices (each job contains m stages) is proportional to the value $(n!)^m$. At the same time, JSS problems are important for many fields: manufacturing, semiconductors, pharmaceuticals, supply chains, rail-bound transportation, mining, healthcare, etc. [6].

Since planning tasks are very important in practice and have high complexity and variety, a wide variety of methods are used to solve them, including artificial intelligence methods [5,9,10]. Although classical optimization methods are also used, such as the branch and bound method [11,12], dynamic programming [7], and methods based on heuristics and rules [13–16].

Among the methods of artificial intelligence, the most commonly used is the genetic algorithm (GA) [5,17–19] and other population-based algorithms such as the Particle Swarm Optimization [20,21] and ant colony optimization (ACO) algorithms [22]. All these stochastic population optimization algorithms (evolutionary or swarm) provide high flexibility and solve scheduling problems not with 100% accuracy but with sufficient accuracy in a reasonable time. In addition, population algorithms can be used to create hybrids with other, deterministic approaches [7,17–19,23]. Additionally worthy of note is the use of stochastic algorithms that are faster than population algorithms and based on Simulated Annealing [10,24].

Despite a large number of solution methods, none of them can be called dominant. Besides the usual reasons typical for NP-hard problems [25], the variability of planning problems even within the same class should also be noted.

Most scheduling tasks are associated with the concept of multi-stage service systems. These include systems in which servicing requirements consist of several stages. Despite the diversity of production systems, the formalized description of the JSS problem can be considered basic for a large class of multi-stage systems. The job-shop problem can be formulated as follows.

1. There is a finite set $N = \{1, 2, \ldots, n\}$ of requirements (works, jobs, orders) and a finite set $M = \{1, 2, \ldots, m\}$ of devices (machines, executors, workstations, etc.).

The service process for requirement $\underline{i}$ includes r_i stages. At the same time, each requirement i and each stage q ($1 \leq q \leq r_i$) of its service is associated with some subset of machines $M^i q$ from the set M. It is assumed that each machine can simultaneously serve no more than one requirement. In such systems with successive servers, each job i is assigned its own, characterizing for this job the sequence L_i of its servicing by machines: $L_i = (L_1{}^i, L_2{}^i, \ldots, L_{ri}{}^i)$.

The requirement i is served first by the machine $L_1{}^i$, then by $L_2{}^i$, and so on. Service sequences may be different for different requirements and may contain instrument repetitions. If the requirement i at stage q must be serviced by machine l, then the duration t_{liq} of its servicing by this machine is assumed to be given. The system operation process can be described by setting a schedule (calendar plan), i.e., some set of indications as to whether particular requirements are served at each moment of time.

Figure 1 shows a Gantt chart of an example of a JSS problem with jobs A (blue), B (green), C (red), and D (yellow) and machines R, S, T, and Q. For example, job A has three stages that require the consistent use of machines R (8 h), S (5 h), and Q (2 h).

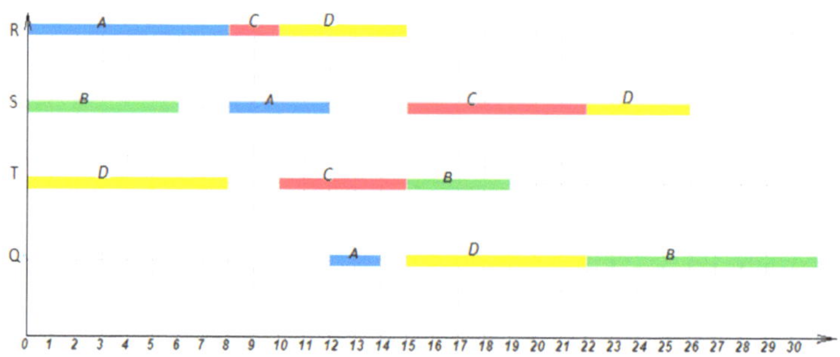

Figure 1. An example of a JSS problem solution (Gantt chart).

Under the assumptions made above, the schedule can be considered a vector $\{s_1(t), s_1(t), \ldots, s_m(t)\}$, whose components are piecewise constant left continuous functions. Each of them is given on the interval $0 \le t < \infty$ and takes a value of $0, 1, \ldots, n$.

$$s = \{s_1(t), s_2(t), \ldots, s_m(t)\}. \quad (1)$$

If $(t') = i, l \in M, i \in N$, then at the time t', the device l serves the requirement i. When setting the schedule, all conditions and restrictions arising from the formulation of the problem under consideration must be observed, which means the schedule must be permissible.

If there are several permissible schedules, it is necessary to choose the best of them, which means setting some selection criterion (quality criterion). In the classical scheduling theory, such a criterion is the completion time of all requirements (makespan); that is, the completion time of the last requirement. Each admissible schedule s uniquely determines the vector of time points for completing the service of all jobs:

$$T(s) = (T_1(s), T_2(s), \ldots, T_n(s)). \quad (2)$$

If some valid, non-decreasing in each of the variables function $F(x)$ is given,

$$F(x) = F(x_1, x_2, \ldots, x_n), \quad (3)$$

then the quality of the schedule s is estimated by the value of this function at $x = T(s)$:

$$F(x) = \max\{x_i\}, i = 1,2, \ldots, n. \quad (4)$$

In this case,

$$F(T(s)) = T_{\max}(s), \text{ where } T_{\max}(s) = \max\{T_i(s)\}, i = 1, 2, \ldots, n, \quad (5)$$

From this statement of the problem, the main difficulties are noticeable:

- Discreteness;
- Multivariance;
- Multifactorialism;
- The inability to construct an objective function in the form of an algebraic expression, since the objective function is calculated only algorithmically.

Mathematically, the JSS problem can be divided into several subtypes according to their constrictions, criteria, and other features. The review [6] identifies 37 subtypes of the JSS problem. It also provides mathematical formulations for various subtypes and a review of solution methods. A variety of tasks and methods and the fact that research on this issue does not stop indicate both the relevance and high complexity of the JSS problem.

1.2. Ant Colony Optimization Algorithm

Ants solve pathfinding problems using chemical regulation [26]. Each ant leaves a trail of special substances on the ground (named pheromones). Another ant, sensing a footprint on the ground, rushes along it. The more ants have passed along one path, the more noticeable the trace for them, and the more noticeable the trace, the greater the desire to go in the same direction arises in ants. Since the ants that find the shortest path to the "feeder" spend less time traveling back and forth, their trail quickly becomes the most visible. It attracts more ants, so the process of finding a shorter path is completed quickly. Other, less-used paths gradually disappear. It is possible to formulate the basic principles of interaction between ants: stochastic; multiplicity; positive feedback.

Since each ant performs primitive actions, the algorithm turns out to be very simple and boils down to multiple traversals of some graph, the edges of which have not only weight but also an additional, dynamically changing quantitative characteristic, called the amount of pheromone or simply pheromone.

The ACO algorithm is inherently the most suitable for solving optimization problems related to graphs and routes [26–29]. Currently, research related to the ACO algorithm is aimed at solving problems such as finding an efficient starting point [28,29], hybridization with other methods that solve subproblems (local search [30,31], exact large neighborhood search [32], etc.), the usage of adaptation methods, and the meta-optimization of the algorithm [33,34]. The application of the local search and neighborhood search [30–32] is difficult for JSS problems because of their non-trivial formulation [6].

Research in which the ACO algorithm would be applied to scheduling problems began as soon as ACO algorithms became known; for example, the application of ACO to single-machine scheduling problems [35,36] or JSS problems in general [37]. In particular, authors use techniques for combining the ACO algorithm and specialized methods for solving JSS problems; for example, to perform local searches [38,39]. The JSS problem differs significantly from route search problems and other problems on graphs. In studies, the process of schedule creation is presented as moving along a schedule-based graph [40,41], which imposes some restrictions on the capabilities of the ACO algorithm [42]. In addition, it is not clear how best to assign weights to edges with the JSS problem.

The issue of setting the ACO algorithm parameters requires separate research. It is important to understand how the best algorithm parameters differ for different JSS problems, and whether they depend on the dimension of the problem (numbers of jobs, stages, and machines). The studies cited above do not address this issue in detail. The authors of papers [37,41,42] used the same parameters for all tasks, and the parameters' values were selected experimentally. In the works [38,43], the parameters were tuned using only one JSS problem instance. The number of ants and a parameter influencing the pheromone updating were studied in [40]; it was shown that different values should be chosen for different JSS problem instances.

1.3. Meta-Optimization Approach

Genetic algorithm (GA) usage in conjunction with other (heuristic, as a rule) algorithms is a common practice [44,45]. Most often, the GA is used as the main algorithm for solving the problem with a local search additional algorithm. Studies [5,16,19,46] applied this approach to the JSS problem. In [18], another approach is presented wherein a heuristic algorithm is used to determine the initial population of the GA.

Finally, the third approach is using the GA as a meta-optimizer [18,47]. The GA adjusts the hyper-parameters of another optimization algorithm. This approach is relatively rarely used because it requires large computational costs.

In this paper, a new way of representing the graph along which ants move is proposed for solving the scheduling problem. It is distinguished by simplicity, versatility, and, at the same time, flexibility. In particular, it can be used in case of dynamic changes in constraints or initial data (for example, replacing stages in jobs or changing their execution time). Some techniques are given to improve the performance in software implementation. To study the parameters of the ACO algorithm in the JSS problem, meta-optimization was implemented using the GA. As noted above, this evolutionary meta-optimization approach has not been used previously for the ACO algorithm and JSS problem because of the high computational complexity. However, in scheduling problems and with long-term production processes, the high computational complexity is not a critical flaw.

The structure of the paper is as follows. Section 2 presents, first, the proposed method for constructing the pheromone graph and traversing it, suitable for applying the ACO algorithm; second, the method of adjusting the coefficients of the ACO algorithm; third, techniques for improving software implementation performance. Section 3 presents the results of computational experiments and their analysis. The conclusion summarizes the results.

2. Materials and Methods

2.1. Proposed Application of the ACO Algorithm for the JSS Problem

To solve the JSS problem by using the ACO algorithm, it is necessary to:

1. Present the problem as a directed graph;
2. Determine the heuristics of the behavior of ants when constructing a solution;
3. Adjust the algorithm parameters.

The iterative ACO algorithm includes building a solution by all ants, improving the solution using the local search method, and updating the pheromone. Building a solution starts with an empty partial solution, which is expanded by adding a new, permissible solution component to it.

Based on the algorithm and formulas proposed in [26], in this study, the calculation relations presented below, which are used when adapting the method to the problems of JSS, have been written down. The choice of the solution component is carried out according to the rules of probabilistic choice at each step of constructing the solution in accordance with:

$$P_k = \frac{(f_k)^{\alpha}}{\sum_i (f_i)^{\alpha}} \tag{6}$$

The coefficient α determines the influence of the amount of pheromone on the k-th edges (f_k) on the probability that the ant will choose this edge. The denominator is the sum over all edges accessible from the node. The proposed approach does not use any heuristic information; for example, the duration of the selected stage or the duration of the job to which the selected stage belongs. Preliminary experiments have shown that it does not improve accuracy. For the traveling salesman problem, a route does not include all edges. Therefore, it makes sense to increase the probability of choosing a shorter graph edge for each step. For the scheduling problem, a route must include all stages in any case.

Pheromone renewal is necessary to increase it on the best (short) path and to decrease its amount on paths corresponding to bad decisions. Pheromone evaporation is also used in order to avoid the too-fast convergence of the algorithm.

If F is the value of the objective function on the route, then the amount of pheromone applied by the ant to all edges of the route Δf can be determined:

$$\Delta f = \left(\frac{\gamma}{F}\right)^{\beta} \tag{7}$$

Here β and γ are the intensity coefficients of pheromone release. The coefficient β was introduced in this work in order to make the dependence of applying the pheromone on the graph more flexible (not necessarily linear).

The coefficient ρ characterizes the pheromone evaporability. Here, it is considered that a certain minimum non-zero amount of pheromone should always remain on the edges. Otherwise, the probability of choosing an edge may be zero and it will be "ignored" by the ants. The maximum value is also limited, which prevents the convergence of the algorithm to a solution far from the optimal one. The coefficient takes values from 0 (no evaporation) to 1 (evaporates to a minimum level).

$$f' = \begin{cases} f(1-\rho), \; f_{\min} < f(1-\rho) < f_{\max} \\ f_{\min}, \; f(1-\rho) \leq f_{\min} \\ f_{\max}, \; f(1-\rho) \geq f_{\min} \end{cases} \tag{8}$$

During the experimental studies, an improvement in results was revealed with an increase in the significance of the current best solution. To do this, on all edges of the path corresponding to the best result at each iteration, a certain amount of pheromone is added, which is determined by the coefficient λ:

$$f_{best} = \begin{cases} f_{best} \cdot \lambda, \; f_{best} \cdot \lambda < f_{\max} \\ f_{\max}, \; f_{best} \cdot \lambda \geq f_{\max} \end{cases} \tag{9}$$

Thus, the limit on the maximum amount of pheromone is taken into account here as well.

It is possible to present the search for a solution to the JSS problem as follows.

In order to completely set the schedule, it is enough to determine which job to load on the device it needs at each i-th step, $I = 1, 2, \ldots, C_s$, where C_s is the total number of stages of all jobs from the set N. Then, the graph will have C_s+1 vertexes, with the first vertex connected only to the second, the second to the first and third, the third to the second and fourth, and so on (the graph is direct). The vertex numbered C_s+1 is connected only to the vertex C_s. The edges connecting the vertices correspond to jobs.

Passing along the graph, the ant remembers its path—in this case, the sequence of jobs. As soon as job j enters into this sequence as many times as it has stages (r_j), the ant starts ignoring the edges corresponding to it until the end of the path.

For example, there are three requirements, $N = \{A, B, C\}$, $n = 3$. Requirement A has two stages and requirements B and C each have three stages. Figure 2 shows the graph.

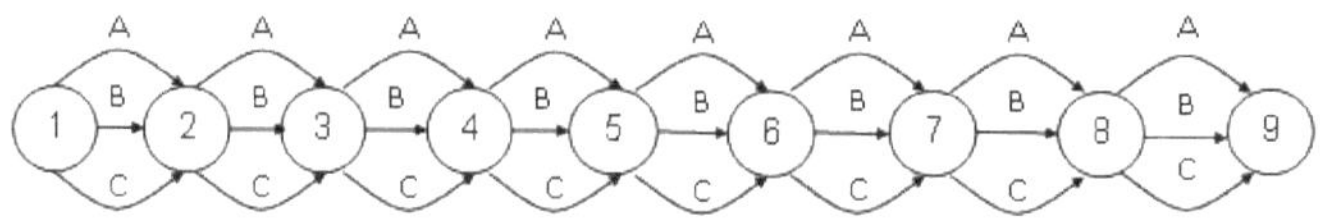

Figure 2. The JSS graph for the proposed ACO application scheme.

For example, an ant in the first step chose requirement A, then B, and again A. Requirement A has two stages, so the ant will ignore its remaining edges in the next steps (shown by the dotted line in Figure 3). Then, let the ant select requirements C, C, B, and C in succession, then only edge B remains valid at the 8th node. Because of the above pass, a sequence of requirements $\{A, B, A, C, C, B, C, B\}$ will be obtained. Using this sequence, it is easy to obtain the stage selection sequence vector:

$$L^{**} = \{l_1{}^A, l_1{}^B, l_2{}^A, l_1{}^C, l_2{}^C, l_2{}^B, l_3{}^C, l_3{}^B\}.$$

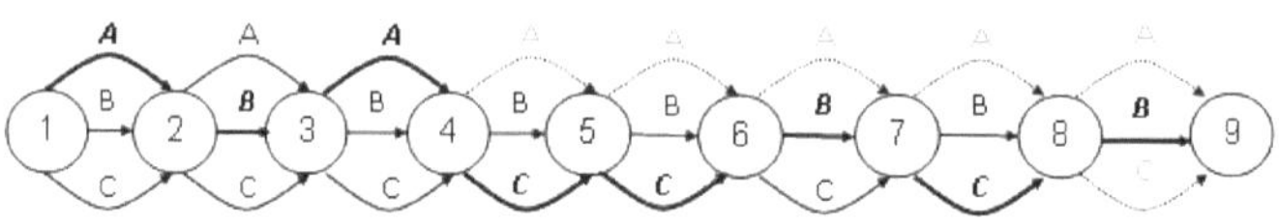

Figure 3. An example of passing through a graph.

Figure 3 shows the path of the ant along the graph for this example. The selected edges are shown with thicker lines. The dotted line shows the edges that were ignored by the particle based on the selections made.

Thus, the problem under consideration differs from the weighted undirected graph traversal problem. However, to adapt the algorithm to these conditions, it is enough to place the leftmost vertex in the list of vertices of the graph that are allowed to start the bypass. The graph is not weighted; this is equivalent to the unit weight of all graph edges.

This approach to graph representation is universal, as it allows for considering various additional requirements. For example, in the classical formulation of the JSS problem, there are no dependencies between different stages of different jobs (all jobs are independent). For the proposed approach, it is easy to take into account such a modification of the problem. In addition, it becomes possible to solve scheduling problems that dynamically change. For example, when, after the plan is drawn up and the execution begins, the order of stages or the duration of stages change, or new works appear.

A more formalized description of the algorithm is given in Algorithms 1 and 2. Algorithm 1 presents the algorithm in general; Algorithm 2 shows the traversal of the graph by one ant.

Algorithm 1. Pseudocode for the ACO Algorithm Application for JSS Problem

Input: $N, M, I_{aco}, C_{ant}, f_{\min}, f_{\max}, \alpha, \beta, \gamma, \rho, \lambda$
Output: T, *makespan*
Auxiliary Variables: f, C_s, *routes, makespans, best_route, best_makespan*
Initialization: $C_s = Count\_stages(N), f = I[n \times C_s] \cdot f_{\min}$,
$best\_makespan = \infty$
Begin ***ACO-JSS Algorithm***
1 ***for*** $(i = 1, \ldots, I_{aco})$ ***do***
2   ***for*** $(a = 1, \ldots, C_{ant})$ ***do***
3         $makespanes_a, routes_a = Ant\_route(N, M, C_s, f, \alpha, \beta)$
4   ***end for***
5   ***for*** $(a = 1, \ldots, C_{ant})$ ***do***
6   ***for*** $(s = 1, \ldots, C_s)$ ***do***
7             $j = routes_{a,s}$
8             $f_{s,j} = f_{s,j} + (\gamma / makespanes_a)^{\beta}$
9   ***end for***
10   ***end for***
11     $a = \text{argmin}_a(makespanes_a)$
12   ***if*** $(makespanes_a < best\_makespan)$ ***then***
13         $best\_makespan = makespanes_a$
14         $best\_route = routes_a$
15   ***end if***
16   ***for*** $(s = 1, \ldots, C_s)$ ***do***
17         $j = best\_route_s$
18         $f_{s,j} = \lambda \cdot f_{s,j}$
19   ***end for***
20   ***for*** $(\varphi \in f)$ ***do***
21     $\varphi = \max(\min(\varphi \cdot (1 - \rho), f_{\max}), f_{\min})$
22   ***end for***
23 ***end for***
24 $T = JSS(best\_route)$
25 $makespan = best\_makespan$
26 ***return*** T, *makespan*
End ***ACO-JSS Algorithm***

In Algorithm 1 the following designations are introduced: I_{aco} is the number of ACO algorithm iterations; C_{ant} is the number of ants; C_s is the total number of all stages of all jobs; $I[A \times B]$ is an identity matrix $A \times B$.

Each ant traverses the graph at each algorithm iteration (rows 2–4). After that, the application of the pheromone is performed in accordance with Equations (7) (rows 5–10), (9) (rows 11–19), and (8) (rows 20–22). The schedule obtained with the best-found route is the output result of the algorithm (rows 24–26).

In Algorithm 2, the following designations are introduced: *tabu_list* is the list of job numbers for which all stages are added to the schedule; *stage_counters* is the vector of the counters of added stages for each job; *stages* is the vector of the number of stages in each job.

During the traversal, the ant at each step chooses an edge. Edge selection means job selection, as shown in Figures 2 and 3. The next stage of the selected job will be added to the schedule with the start of execution as soon as possible. Edge selection probabilities are calculated according to Equation 6 (rows 3–15). The probabilistic choice is made using roulette wheel simulation (rows 16–17). If the selected stage is the last stage for the corresponding job, then the stages of this job can no longer be selected (rows 18–21).

Algorithm 2. Pseudo Code for the Ant_route

```
Input: N, M, C_s, α, f
Output: makespan, route
Auxiliary Variables: p, sp, tabu_list, stage_counters, stages
Initialization: route = 0[C_s], tabu_list = {}, stage_counters = 0[n]
stages_i = Count_stages(N_i), i = 1, ... , n
Begin Ant_route Algorithm
for (s = 1, ... , C_s) do
    sp = 0
    for (j = 1, ... , n) do
        if (j ∉ tabu_list) then
            p_j = (f_{s,j})^α
            sp = sp + p_j
        else
            p_j = 0
        end if
    end for
    for (j = 1, ... , n) do
        if (j ∉ tabu_list) then
            p_j = p_j / sp
        end if
    end for
    j = Roulette_Selection(p)
    route_s = j
    stage_counters_j + = 1
    if (stage_counters_j = stages_j) then
        tabu_list = tabu_list ∪ j
    end if
end for
T = JSS(route)
makespan = max(T)
return makespan, route
End Ant_route Algorithm
```

2.2. Adaptive Selection of Algorithm Parameters

As noted in [26,27,33,34,40,43], the quality of the solutions obtained using the ACO algorithm strongly depends on the coefficients (parameters) used in it. In the above algorithm, such coefficients are α, β, γ, ρ, λ (Equations (6)–(9). Since each of the coefficients can take an infinite number of values, the question arises of choosing the coefficients that make it possible to obtain a solution that is closest to the optimal one. Selecting coefficients manually is inefficient because of the large range of their values and the lack of methods for their selection. In this study, it is proposed to select coefficients using their evolutionary selection. The most common method for implementing such a selection is a genetic algorithm.

Algorithm 3 presents the GA application for tuning ACO parameters.

The ACO parameters selection is carried out according to the scheme described below:

1. Generation of a random initial state. The first generation is created from randomly selected solutions (chromosomes), where the parameters α, β, γ, ρ, λ are used as genes (initialization in Algorithm 3).
2. Calculation of the coefficient of survival (fitness). Each solution (chromosome) is assigned a certain numerical value, depending on its proximity to the value of the fitness function (rows 2–12).
3. Reproduction. Chromosomes with greater fitness are more likely to pass to offspring, roulette selection, and a single-point crossover operation is performed (rows 13–25).
4. Mutation. If it is randomly determined that it is necessary to carry out a mutation, then the chromosome is changed to a new random chromosome (rows 21–31).

5. If the specified number of iterations is completed, then the problem is solved. Otherwise, steps 2–4 are repeated.

In Algorithm 3, the following designations are introduced: I_g—the number of GA iterations; C_g—the number of chromosomes; and *population*—the population of GA chromosomes.

Algorithm 3. Pseudo Code for the ACO Algorithm with GA Adaptation

Input: $N, M, I_g, C_g, I_{aco}, C_{ant}, f_{\min}, f_{\max}$
Output: T, *makespan*, $\alpha, \beta, \gamma, \rho, \lambda$
Auxiliary Variables: *population*, *prob*, *fitnesses*, *best_parameters*, *best_fitness*, P_m
Initialization: *population* = $I[C_g \times 5] \cdot Random[C_g \times 5]$, *fitnesses* = [], *prob* = $0[C_g]$
best_fitness = ∞, $P_m = 0.05$
Begin ***ACO-GA Algorithm***
  for $(i = 1, \ldots, I_g)$ ***do***
    for $(g = 1, \ldots, C_g)$ ***do***
      $\alpha, \beta, \gamma, \rho, \lambda$ = *Scale*($population_g$)
      T, *makespane* = *ACO_JSS*($N, M, I_{aco}, C_{ant}, f_{\min}, f_{\max}, \alpha, \beta, \gamma, \rho, \lambda$)
      $fitnesses_g$ = *makespane*
    end for
    for $(g = 1, \ldots, C_g)$ ***do***
      if ($fitnesses_g$ < *best_fitness*) ***do***
        best_fitness = $fitnesses_g$
        best_parameters = $population_g$
      end if
    end for
    next_population = *population*
    for $(j = 1, \ldots, C_g/2)$ ***do***
      prob = 1/*fitnesses*
      a = *Roulette_Selection*(*prob*)
      b = *Roulette_Selection*(*prob*)
      x = *round*(*Random*()·4)
      $next\_population_{2j-1} = population_{a,1 \ldots x} \,\|\, population_{b,\,x+1 \ldots 5}$
      $next\_population_{2j} = population_{b,\,1 \ldots x} \,\|\, population_{a,x+1 \ldots 5}$
    end for
    for $(j = 1, \ldots, C_g)$ ***do***
      if (*Random*() < P_m)***do***
        $next\_population_j$ = *Random* [5]
      end if
    end for
    population = *next_population*
  end for
  $\alpha, \beta, \gamma, \rho, \lambda$ = *Scale*(*best_parameters*)
  T, *makespane* = *ACO_JSS*($N, M, I_{aco}, C_{ant}, f_{\min}, f_{\max}, \alpha, \beta, \gamma, \rho, \lambda$)
  return T, *makespan*, $\alpha, \beta, \gamma, \rho, \lambda$
End ***ACO-GA Algorithm***

The operation of the genetic algorithm is an iterative process until a stopping criterion is met, such as a number of generations. In this case, we consider the problem of continuous optimization:

$$\min F(x),\ D = \{x_1, x_2, x_3, x_4, x_5 | x_i \in [a_i, b_i]\}, \tag{10}$$

where $F(x)$ is the objective function to be minimized (in this work, it is the function calculated by Equation (5)), D is the search area, and $x = \{\alpha, \beta, \gamma, \rho, \lambda\}$. The results of the implementation of the adaptive properties of the ACO algorithm are given below, in Section 3. In this work, a genetic algorithm with a single-point crossover of two parents, 95% crossover probability, and 10% mutation probability is used. During mutation, one randomly selected coefficient is changed to a random number in the allowable range.

2.3. Improving the Performance of the Software Implementation of the Algorithm

With the approach described above, the solution search time increases dramatically, since the solution of the problem by the ACO algorithm is launched many times. The search speed can be significantly increased by parallelizing calculations by dividing the population into parts and distributing the computational load for working with these parts between processors.

The mutation and calculation of the fitness function of individuals can be easily parallelized since they occur independently for each individual. At the same time, data common to all individuals is used only for reading, so there are no difficulties with the need to synchronize these stages and waste time on blocking processes while waiting for resources to be released.

Crossover is more difficult to parallelize since during this stage there is an interaction between individuals from different parts of the population. However, there is no need for parallelization, since this stage takes negligible time compared to other calculations.

However, the higher the efficiency of parallelization, the higher the level at which it is performed. Since the ACO algorithm is stochastic, it seems reasonable to simply run multiple independent instances of the algorithm at the same time. Since this paper uses meta-optimization based on a genetic algorithm, then parallelization is performed at the level of calculating the GA fitness function. In Algorithm 3, row 4 occupies the vast majority of the running time of the entire algorithm and, at the same time, the loop in rows 2–6 is easily parallelized.

Since the algorithm requires multiple traversals of the graph and changing the pheromone on edges, the choice of the graph structure and the mechanism for applying the pheromone is very important. At first glance, it might seem that an implementation of a graph would be a set of nodes containing a list of edges, each of which contains a pointer to a neighboring node and quantitative characteristics (weight and amount of pheromone). However, the graph can be represented as a matrix of weights and a pheromone matrix. It is, first, easier to implement; second, lesser in terms of the amount of memory required (no need to store lists of pointers in each node); and, third, it works faster.

The following method is especially effective: apply the pheromone to the matrix representing the graph, not at the end of each iteration (after the graph has been traversed by all ants), but create a copy of the matrix and, after each ant has traversed, increase the value of the pheromone in this copy, and after the traversal stage is over, perform a reverse replacement.

Using this method (let us designate two pheromone graphs as *fGraph* and *fTmpGraph*) allows us to significantly increase the speed of calculations by applying the following trick. Within one iteration, the number of pheromones on each edge remains unchanged; therefore, the f_k^{α} values from Equation (6) also do not change within one iteration. In this case, there is no need to calculate them for each ant again. Then, at the initialization stage, the *fTmpGraph* edges receive the initial value of the pheromone, and the *fGraph* edges receive the initial value to the power of α. At each iteration, the ants, bypassing the graph, are guided by *fGraph* (it is no longer necessary to calculate f_k^{α}—it is the essence of increasing the speed), and the pheromone is deposited on *fTmpGraph*. After all the ants traverse the graph and the pheromone evaporates from the graph *fTmpGraph*, each k-th branch of fGraph receives a pheromone value equal to $fTmpGraph_k = (fTmpGraph_k)^{\alpha}$.

Equation (6) contains the operations of exponentiation. Depending on the compiler, raising a number to the power of e and calculating the natural logarithm may be faster than raising a number to an arbitrary power, so in the first case, the operation f^{α} should be replaced as follows: $f^{\alpha} = e^{\alpha \ln(f)}$. It should be noted that there are ways to quickly calculate the exponent and the natural logarithm. If there is a high probability that the coefficient α will be an integer, especially 1 or 2, then for this case it is possible to add a variant of the algorithm in which multiplication will replace the exponentiation functions.

3. Results and Discussion

The software implementation of the proposed algorithm has been tested on the well-known model JSS problems from [48–50] and the real-life manufacturing problems from [51]. Table 1 shows the values of the ACO algorithm's coefficients, which were selected by the GA as the best for test tasks.

Table 1. Examples of the best sets of coefficients obtained using the genetic algorithm.

Problem	I_z	L_{min}	L_{avg}	I_{aco}	C_{ant}	α	β	ρ	γ	λ
abz6	40	948	977.333	1000	100	0.63	2.0	0.696	28	1.3
abz6	40	945	982.524	1000	100	1.1	1.0	0.499	900	1.3
ft10	40	950	995.866	1000	100	0.63	1.2	0.7	1000	1.1
ft10	20	951	1006.1	1000	50	0.3781	1.711	0.97	1108.7	2.277
la17	20	784	805.4	1000	100	0.392	2.7701	0.2998	425.5387	1.9615
la17	20	785	798.25	1000	100	0.0341	1.7968	0.5461	949.1535	4.5589
la15	20	1207	1215.45	1000	100	0.531	1.72	0.663	1032	1.2
3_Plates	10	657.55	662.075	30	10	0.2782	0.4251	0.4919	296.61	2.5373
3_Plates	10	657.55	662.3275	30	10	0.1754	0.5705	0.3836	326.05	2.5083
la01	10	666	670.2	200	20	0.2262	0.8665	0.6883	903.3459	2.0363
la01	10	666	669.4	200	20	0.3542	0.6527	0.8001	120.8012	2.1305
la21	10	1107	1150.9	2000	100	0.7478	1.1134	0.3488	790.57	2.2236
6_Plates	20	107	111.45	30	10	0.6218	2.7953	0.6995	335.6241	1.2376
6_Plates	20	107	111.5	30	10	0.6204	0.2863	0.0775	137.6017	1.479

In Table 1 and the next two tables, the following designations are introduced:

- *Iz* is the number of runs over which averaging was carried out (with the same coefficients);
- L_{min} is the best-obtained solution;
- L_{avg} is the solution averaged over I_z launches;
- *Iaco* is the number of ACO iterations;
- C_{ant} is the number of ants;
- α is the degree of significance of the pheromone when choosing the graph edge (Equation (6));
- β is the non-linear pheromone deposition coefficient (Equation (7));
- ρ is the pheromone evaporation coefficient (Equation (8));
- γ is the linear coefficient of pheromone application (Equation (7));
- λ is the accounting factor for the best current solution (Equation (9)).

It follows from the data obtained that the best-found sets of coefficients differ even when solving the same problem. The search for the relationship between the coefficients and their correlation is a direction for further research.

The experiments showed a significant improvement in the results compared to those obtained earlier without the evolutionary selection of coefficients (best and average results were determined by 40 runs), which is reflected in Table 2.

Table 2. Examples of the best sets of coefficients obtained using the genetic algorithm.

Problem	L_{m1}	L_{a1}	L_g	L_{ga}	L_{m2}	L_{a2}	I_{aco}	C_{ant}
abz6	980	1005.3	945	977.33	948	985.26	1000	100
ft06	55	55.16	55	55	55	55.16	30	10
ft10	1017	1038.8	950	995.87	975	1013.84	1000	100
la01	666	673.08	666	669.4	666	673.08	30	10
la10	958	958	958	958	958	958	1000	100
la15	1211	1220.6	1207	1215.45	1207	1220.62	1000	100
la17	796	809.32	784	798.25	787	809.32	1000	100
la21	1121	1168.1	1107	1150.9	1118	1154.06	1000	100
3_Plates	657.55	664.782	657.55	662.08	657.55	664.782	30	10
6_Plates	109	113.22	107	111.45	108	112.12	30	10

In Table 2, in addition to those already described, the following notations are used:

- L_{m1} is the best solution that was recorded before using the GA (the coefficients were selected manually);
- L_{a1} is the average value of the solutions that were recorded before using the GA;
- L_g is the best solution that was obtained using the GA;
- L_{ga} is the average value of the solutions that were obtained using the coefficients found by the GA;
- L_{m2} is the best solution that was obtained using the coefficients found by averaging over other solved problems;
- L_{a2} is the average value of the solutions that were obtained using the coefficients found by averaging over other solved problems (except for the coefficient γ).

Here, averaged coefficients are understood as a set of coefficients found as the arithmetic means among the best-found coefficients for problems of similar dimensions.

To assess the improvement in the quality of schedules compiled with the adaptation of the method parameters, quasi-optimal solutions to test problems were used [52]. The results are shown in Table 3. For the problem of processing plates, the result 657.55 [51] is given, which also coincides with the solution obtained in this paper.

Table 3. Comparison of results.

Problem	L_{m1}	L_{a1}	L_{gm}	L_{ga}	I_{aco}	C_{ant}	Best known
abz6	980	1005.3	945	977.33	1000	100	943
ft06	55	55.16	55	55	30	10	55
ft10	1017	1038.8	950	995.87	1000	100	930
la01	666	673.08	666	669.4	30	10	666
la10	958	958	958	958	1000	100	958
la15	1211	1220.6	1207	1215.45	1000	100	1207
la17	796	809.32	784	798.25	1000	100	784
la21	1121	1168.1	1107	1150.9	1000	100	1048
3_Plates	657.55	664.782	657.55	662.08	30	10	657.55
6_Plates	109	113.22	107	111.45	30	10	107

The experiments showed a significant improvement in the results (up to 12%) compared to those found earlier (without the adaptation of the coefficients).

The solutions obtained by the proposed adaptive algorithm for many problems from [47–49] turned out to be no worse than the known quasi-optimal solutions for these problems. The deviation from the known quasi-optimal solutions does not exceed 6% (in the work of the founders of the ACO algorithm [27], they state the 10% deviation in their results to job-shop problems). At the same time, the adaptive method makes it possible to obtain guaranteed solutions of the specified quality at each run with enough iterations.

Figure 4 shows experimental data on the increase in the speed of parallel calculations compared to sequential operation, depending on the number of processors (cores) used.

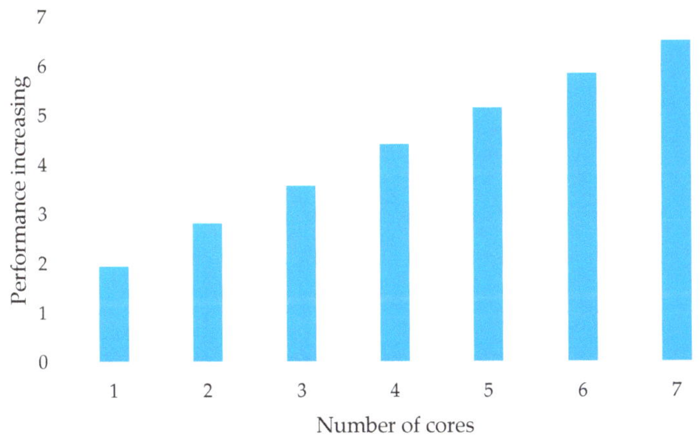

Figure 4. The parallelization effect.

It can be seen from the figure that the proposed approach can significantly reduce the computation time. The greater the effect of parallelization, the greater the number of calculations in solving the problem by the ACO algorithm, i.e., the greater the dimension of the problem, the number of ants, and the number of iterations. Indeed, according to Amdahl's law, parallel computing is more effective the greater the proportion of calculations performed in parallel. In the test examples under consideration, the proportion of such calculations was 3–5%.

The greater the gain from the above technique of using two graphs, the greater the number of ants and the size of the graph. In test tasks of scheduling with 10 requirements in five stages, the calculation time was reduced by about four times; in tasks with 10 requirements in 10 stages—five times; in tasks with 50 requirements in 10 stages—seven times.

4. Conclusions

This study considers ways to improve the speed, accuracy, and flexibility of the ant colony optimization algorithm for solving scheduling problems. A new way of representing the problem as a problem of finding the shortest path on a graph is proposed, which is distinguished by a high level of universality and flexibility. At the same time, its use allows for obtaining acceptable job-shop scheduling problem solutions. It is shown that the use of the Genetic Algorithm as a meta-optimizer for tuning the parameters of the ACO algorithm simplifies the study, makes the algorithm adaptive to the problem being solved, and improves the resulting plans. It is determined that the sets of the best parameters of the algorithm differ from task to task.

For the next steps, we plan to conduct a study on a larger basis of scheduling instances, while covering not only job-shop scheduling problems but also open-shop scheduling (OSS) problems and flexible JSS and OSS problems [6,41,53,54] and considering the advantages of the proposed approach for planning problems with dynamically changing conditions [54–56]. In addition, the study of dependencies between the properties of the scheduling problem, the best values of the parameters of the ACO algorithm, and the efficiency of the solutions will be continued.

Funding: The research funding from the Ministry of Science and Higher Education of the Russian Federation (Ural Federal University Program of Development within the Priority-2030 Program) is gratefully acknowledged.

Data Availability Statement: Not applicable.

Conflicts of Interest: The authors declare no conflict of interest.

References

1. Johnson, S.M. Optimal two- and three-stage production schedules with setup times included. *Nav. Res. Logist. Q.* **1954**, *1*, 61–68. [CrossRef]
2. Lawler, E.L.; Lenstra, J.K.; Rinnooy Kan, A.H.G.; Shmoys, D.B. *Sequencing and Scheduling: Algorithms and Complexity*; Technische Universiteit Eindhoven: Eindhoven, The Netherlands, 1989.
3. Brucker, P.; Knust, S. *Complex Scheduling*; Springer: Berlin, Germany, 2012.
4. Xie, J.; Gao, L.; Peng, K.; Li, X.; Li, H. Review on flexible job shop scheduling. *IET Collab. Intell. Manuf.* **2019**, *1*, 67–77. [CrossRef]
5. Leusin, M.E.; Frazzon, E.M.; Uriona Maldonado, M.; Kück, M.; Freitag, M. Solving the Job-Shop Scheduling Problem in the Industry 4.0 Era. *Technologies* **2018**, *6*, 107. [CrossRef]
6. Xiong, H.; Danni, S.S.; Hu, R.J. A survey of job shop scheduling problem: The types and models. *Comput. Oper. Res.* **2022**, *142*, 105731. [CrossRef]
7. Gonçalves, J.F.; de Magalhães Mendes, J.J.; Resende, M.G. A hybrid genetic algorithm for the job shop scheduling problem. *Eur. J. Oper. Res.* **2005**, *167*, 77–95. [CrossRef]
8. Gromicho, J.A.S.; Hoorn, J.J.; Timmer, G.T. Exponentially better than brute force: Solving the job-shop scheduling problem optimally by dynamic programming. *Comput. Oper. Res. Arch.* **2012**, *39*, 2968–2977. [CrossRef]
9. Çaliş, B.; Bulkan, S. A research survey: Review of AI solution strategies of job shop scheduling problem. *J. Intell. Manuf.* **2015**, *26*, 961–973. [CrossRef]
10. Matrenin, P.V.; Manusov, V.Z. The cyclic job-shop scheduling problem: The new subclass of the job-shop problem and applying the simulated annealing to solve it. In Proceedings of the IEEE 2nd International Conference on Industrial Engineering, Applications and Manufacturing (ICIEAM), Chelyabinsk, Russia, 19–20 May 2022.
11. Brucker, P.; Jurisch, B.; Sievers, B. A branch and bound algorithm for job shop scheduling problem. *Discret. Appl. Math.* **1994**, *49*, 107–127. [CrossRef]
12. Baptiste, P.; Flamini, M.; Sourd, F. Lagrangian bounds for just-in-time job shop scheduling. *Comput. Oper. Res.* **2008**, *35*, 906–915. [CrossRef]
13. Canbolat, Y.B.; Gundogar, E. Fuzzy priority rule for job shop scheduling. *J. Intell. Manuf.* **2004**, *15*, 527–533. [CrossRef]
14. Klein, R. Bidirectional planning: Improving priority rule-based heuristic for scheduling resource-constrained projects. *Eur. J. Oper. Res.* **2000**, *127*, 619–638. [CrossRef]
15. Stastny, J.; Skorpil, V.; Balogh, Z.; Klein, R. Job Shop Scheduling Problem Optimization by Means of Graph-Based Algorithm. *Appl. Sci.* **2021**, *11*, 1921. [CrossRef]
16. Ziaee, M.; Mortazavi, J.; Amra, M. Flexible job shop scheduling problem considering machine and order acceptance, transportation costs, and setup times. *Soft Comput.* **2022**, *26*, 3527–3543. [CrossRef]
17. Asadzadeh, L. A local search genetic algorithm for the job shop scheduling problem with intelligent agents. *Comput. Ind. Eng.* **2015**, *85*, 376–383. [CrossRef]
18. Kundakcı, N.; Kulak, O. Hybrid genetic algorithms for minimizing makespan in dynamic job shop scheduling problem. *Comput. Ind. Eng.* **2016**, *96*, 31–51. [CrossRef]
19. Gao, J.; Gen, M.; Sun, L.Y. A hybrid of genetic algorithm and bottleneck shifting for multiobjective flexible job shop scheduling problems. *Comput. Ind. Eng.* **2007**, *53*, 149–162. [CrossRef]
20. Matrenin, P.V.; Sekaev, V.G. Particle Swarm optimization with velocity restriction and evolutionary parameters selection for scheduling problem. In Proceedings of the IEEE International Siberian Conference on Control and Communications (SIBCON), Omsk, Russia, 21–23 May 2015.
21. Liu, B.; Wang, L.; Jin, Y.H. An effective hybrid PSO-based algorithm for flow shop scheduling with limited buffers. *Comput. Oper. Res.* **2008**, *35*, 2791–2806. [CrossRef]
22. Xiang, W.; Lee, H.P. Ant colony intelligence in multi-agent dynamic manufacturing scheduling. *Eng. Appl. Artif. Intell.* **2008**, *21*, 73–85. [CrossRef]
23. Matrenin, P.; Myasnichenko, V.; Sdobnyakov, N.; Sokolov, S.; Fidanova, S.; Kirillov, L.; Mikhov, R. Generalized swarm intelligence algorithms with domain-specific heuristics. *IAES Int. J. Artif. Intell.* **2021**, *10*, 157–165. [CrossRef]
24. Zhang, C.Y.; Li, P.G.; Rao, Y.Q. A very fast TS/SA algorithm for the job shop scheduling problem. *Comput. Oper. Res.* **2008**, *35*, 82–294. [CrossRef]
25. Wolpert, D.H.; Macready, W.G. No free lunch theorems for optimization. *IEEE Trans. Evol. Comput.* **1997**, *1*, 67–82. [CrossRef]
26. Dorigo, M.; Blum, C. Ant colony optimization theory: A survey. *Theor. Comput. Sci.* **2005**, *344*, 243–278. [CrossRef]
27. Dorigo, M.; Stützle, T. Ant colony optimization: Overview and recent advances. In *Handbook of Metaheuristics*; Springer: Cham, Switzerland, 2019; pp. 311–351.
28. Neroni, M. Ant Colony Optimization with Warm-Up. *Algorithms* **2021**, *14*, 295. [CrossRef]
29. Xu, Q.; Zhang, L.; Yu, W. A Localization Method of Ant Colony Optimization in Nonuniform Space. *Sensors* **2022**, *22*, 7389. [CrossRef] [PubMed]

30. Wu, Y.; Gong, M.; Ma, W.; Wang, S. High-order graph matching based on ant colony optimization. *Neurocomputing* **2019**, *328*, 97–104. [CrossRef]
31. Al-Shourbaji, I.; Helian, N.; Sun, Y.; Alshathri, S.; Abd Elaziz, M. Boosting Ant Colony Optimization with Reptile Search Algorithm for Churn Prediction. *Mathematics* **2022**, *10*, 1031. [CrossRef]
32. D'andreagiovanni, F.; Krolikowski, J.; Pulaj, J. A fast hybrid primal heuristic for multiband robust capacitated network design with multiple time periods. *Appl. Soft Comput.* **2015**, *26*, 497–507. [CrossRef]
33. Li, S.; Wei, Y.; Liu, X.; Zhu, H.; Yu, Z. A New Fast Ant Colony Optimization Algorithm: The Saltatory Evolution Ant Colony Optimization Algorithm. *Mathematics* **2022**, *10*, 925. [CrossRef]
34. Chen, X.; Dai, Y. Research on an Improved Ant Colony Algorithm Fusion with Genetic Algorithm for Route Planning. In Proceedings of the 4th IEEE Information Technology, Networking, Electronic and Automation Control Conference (ITNEC), Electr Network, Chongqing, China, 12–14 June 2020; pp. 1273–1278.
35. Bauer, A.; Bullnheimer, B.; Richard, F.H.; Strauss, C. An Ant Colony Optimization Approach for the Single Machine Total Tardiness Problem. In Proceedings of the Congress on Evolutionary Computation-CEC99, Washington, DC, USA, 6–9 July 1999; pp. 1445–1450.
36. M'Hallah, R.; Alhajraf, A. Ant colony systems for the single-machine total weighted earliness tardiness scheduling problem. *J. Sched.* **2016**, *19*, 191–205. [CrossRef]
37. Purism, A.; Bello, R.; Trujillo, Y.; Nowe, A.Y.; Martínez, Y. Two-Stage ACO to Solve the Job Shop Scheduling Problem. In Proceedings of the 12th Iberoamericann Congress on Pattern Recognition (CIARP), Valparaiso, Chile, 13–16 November 2007; pp. 447–456.
38. Chaouch, I.L.; Driss, O.B.; Ghedira, K. A Modified Ant Colony Optimization algorithm for the Distributed Job shop Scheduling Problem. *Procedia Comput. Sci.* **2017**, *112*, 296–305. [CrossRef]
39. Eswaramurthy, V.; Tamilarasi, A. Hybridizing tabu search with ant colony optimization for solving job shop scheduling problems. *Int. J. Adv. Manuf. Technol.* **2009**, *40*, 1004–1015. [CrossRef]
40. Tran, L.V.; Huynh, B.H.; Akhtar, H. Ant Colony Optimization Algorithm for Maintenance, Repair and Overhaul Scheduling Optimization in the Context of Industrie 4.0. *Appl. Sci.* **2019**, *9*, 4815. [CrossRef]
41. Wang, L.; Cai, J.; Li, M.; Liu, Z. Flexible Job Shop Scheduling Problem Using an Improved Ant Colony Optimization. *Sci. Program.* **2017**, 9016303. [CrossRef]
42. Blum, C.; Sampels, M. An Ant Colony Optimization Algorithm for Shop Scheduling Problems. *J. Math. Model. Algorithms* **2004**, *3*, 285–308. [CrossRef]
43. Da Silva, A.R. Solving the Job Shop Scheduling Problem with Ant Colony Optimization. Available online: https://arxiv.org/abs/2209.05284 (accessed on 20 November 2022).
44. Blum, C.; Ermeev, A.; Zakharova, Y. Hybridizations of evolutionary algorithms with Large Neighborhood Search. *Comput. Sci. Rev.* **2022**, *46*, 100512. [CrossRef]
45. Grosan, C.; Abraham, A. Hybrid Evolutionary Algorithms: Methodologies, Architectures, and Reviews. *Stud. Comput. Intell.* **2007**, *75*, 1–7.
46. Bramm, A.M.; Khalyasmaa, A.I.; Eroshenko, S.A.; Matrenin, P.V.; Papkova, N.A.; Sekatski, D.A. Topology Optimization of the Network with Renewable Energy Sources Generation Based on a Modified Adapted Genetic Algorithm. *Energ. Proc. CIS High. Educ. Inst. Power Eng. Assoc.* **2022**, *65*, 341–354. [CrossRef]
47. Sipper, M.; Fu, W.; Ahuja, K.; Moore, J. Investigating the parameter space of evolutionary algorithms. *BioData Min.* **2018**, *11*, 2. [CrossRef]
48. Adams, J.; Balas, E.; Zawack, D. The shifting bottleneck procedure for job shop scheduling. *Manag. Sci.* **1991**, *34*, 391–401. [CrossRef]
49. Fisher, H.; Thompson, G. *Probabilistic Learning Combination of Local Job-Shop Scheduling Rules in Industrial Scheduling*; Prentice-Hall: Englewood Cliffs, NJ, USA, 1963.
50. Lawrence, S. *Supplement to Resource Constrained Project Scheduling: An Experimental Investigation of Heuristic Scheduling Techniques*; Tech. rep., GSIA; Carnegie Mellon University: Pittsburgh, PA, USA, 1984.
51. Sekaev, V.G. Using algorithms for combining heuristics in constructing optimal schedules. *Inf. Technol.* **2009**, *10*, 61–64.
52. Beasley, J.E. OR-Library: Distributing test problems by electronic mail. *J. Oper. Res. Soc.* **1990**, *41*, 1069–1072. [CrossRef]
53. Ahmadian, M.M.; Khatami, M.; Salehipour, A.; Cheng, T.C.E. Four decades of research on the open-shop scheduling problem to minimize the makespan. *Eur. J. Oper. Res.* **2021**, *295*, 399–426. [CrossRef]
54. Luo, S.; Zhang, L.; Fan, Y. Real-Time Scheduling for Dynamic Partial-No-Wait Multiobjective Flexible Job Shop by Deep Reinforcement Learning. *IEEE Trans. Autom. Sci. Eng.* **2022**, *19*, 3020–3038. [CrossRef]
55. Romanov, A.M.; Romanov, M.P.; Manko, S.V.; Volkova, M.A.; Chiu, W.-Y.; Ma, H.-P.; Chiu, K.-Y. Modular Reconfigurable Robot Distributed Computing System for Tracking Multiple Objects. *IEEE Syst. J.* **2021**, *15*, 802–813. [CrossRef]
56. Wan, Y.; Zuo, T.-Y.; Chen, L.; Tang, W.-C.; Chen, J. Efficiency-Oriented Production Scheduling Scheme: An Ant Colony System Method. *IEEE Access* **2020**, *8*, 19286–19296. [CrossRef]

algorithms

MDPI

Article

Correlation Analysis of Factors Affecting Firm Performance and Employees Wellbeing: Application of Advanced Machine Learning Analysis

Jozsef Pap [1], Csaba Mako [2], Miklos Illessy [3], Zef Dedaj [4], Sina Ardabili [5], Bernat Torok [2] and Amir Mosavi [5,6,*]

1 Szechenyi University Doctoral School of Management (SzEEDSM), Szechenyi Istvan University, 9026 Gyor, Hungary
2 Institute of the Information Society, National University of Public Service, 1083 Budapest, Hungary
3 Center for Social Sciences, Eotvos Lorand Research Network, 1097 Budapest, Hungary
4 Doctoral School of Business Administration, University of Pecs, 7622 Pecs, Hungary
5 Institute of Information Engineering, Automation and Mathematics, Slovak University of Technology in Bratislava, 81243 Bratislava, Slovakia
6 John von Neumann Faculty of Informatics, Obuda University, 1034 Budapest, Hungary
* Correspondence: amirhosein.mosavi@stuba.sk

Abstract: Given the importance of identifying key performance points in organizations, this research intends to determine the most critical intra- and extra-organizational elements in assessing the performance of firms using the European Company Survey (ECS) 2019 framework. The ECS 2019 survey data were used to train an artificial neural network optimized using an imperialist competitive algorithm (ANN-ICA) to forecast business performance and employee wellbeing. In order to assess the correctness of the model, root mean square error (RMSE), mean absolute percentage error (MAPE), mean square error (MSE), correlation coefficient (r), and determination coefficient (R2) have been employed. The mean values of the performance criteria for the impact of internal and external factors on firm performance were 1.06, 0.002, 0.041, 0.9, and 0.83, and the value of the performance metrics for the impact of internal and external factors on employee wellbeing were 0.84, 0.0019, 0.0319, 0.83, and 0.71 (respectively, for MAPE, MSE, RMSE, r, and R2). The great performance of the ANN-ICA model is indicated by low values of MAPE, MSE, and RMSE, as well as high values of r and R2. The outcomes showed that "skills requirements and skill matching" and "employee voice" are the two factors that matter most in enhancing firm performance and wellbeing.

Keywords: organizational performance; machine learning; big data; imperialist competitive algorithm; employee wellbeing; artificial neural networks; firm performance; artificial intelligence; deep learning; data science

1. Introduction

One of the top goals that today's firms are searching for is a competitive edge. They attempt to achieve this by providing high-quality goods or services. As a result, performance review and quality enhancement seem crucial [1]. Monitoring organizational performance is one of the responsibilities of managers. However, it may be claimed that organizational performance is a wide notion that encompasses both the products and interactions a firm has. Actually, organizational efficiency can be related to the effectiveness of the organization's mission, assignments, and organizational actions, as well as the quality of its outcomes [2]. One of the challenges that the business and academic sectors have given a significant deal of interest to is organizational performance evaluation [3]. In order to achieve the objective of the business with the highest level of performance and to serve the needs of the workforce, there is a need to employ performance evaluation using the effective instruments and methods of human resource management. An efficient evaluation system that also makes use of its findings is necessary for the organization's growth and the quality of its personnel. Naturally, by enhancing employee effectiveness, formulating and having a performance evaluation process in place can help companies achieve their objectives [3].

The literature contains evidence that one of the elements impacting the performance of firms is management factors. The organizational ideals and mission are defined by managers who also make them accessible, develop the values necessary for long-term success, and put those values into practice through proper action and behavior. These elements may have a direct or indirect impact on how well a company performs and how it conducts business [4]. Another element whose influence on businesses' success has been researched and verified is human resources [5,6]. Making people productive in the production and service sectors is crucial for joining international markets and building an economy in the current period of intense market rivalry. Quality, affordability, and speed are the three competitive advantages. In order to improve their innovation culture, several firms opt for a command and control culture [7]. Another factor that significantly affects how well businesses succeed is organizational structure. Synchronizing organizational performance with employee welfare is crucial for improving organizational performance. In recent years, machine learning (ML) techniques have provided valuable tools for evaluating systems [8,9], modeling proper frameworks [10,11] and increasing system accuracy [12]. ML-based techniques can successfully link the dependent and independent variables to provide a practical mapping of a system. Fredström et al. (2022) suggested that using ML techniques improves business success, and companies should communicate using terms connected to AI, particularly when discussing innovation and teamwork [13]. Shaaban et al. (2022) employed association rule algorithms, Apriori algorithm, and chi-square automatic interaction detection analysis tree to enhance business performance. This enhancement also provides considerable wellbeing [14]. Ahmed et al. (2022) employed ML techniques for boosting business performance [15]. As is clear from the literature, ML provides a promising output for analyzing firm performance and employee wellbeing. In the present study, an advanced ML was employed to provide a conceptual framework of firm performance and employee wellbeing. In the following, the provided framework was employed to identify the most effective parameters for firm performance and employee wellbeing. The ECS (2019) conceptual framework is used to assess firm performance [16]. The two outputs of this model are the effectiveness of the company and the happiness of the employees. Two levels of variables, organizational features and the external environment, are said to have an impact on these outcomes. Organizational features include job organization, skills availability and skill development, and employee voice, according to Eurofound and Cedefop (2020) [17], Valeyre et al. (2009) [18], and Haapakorpi and Alasoini (2018) [19]. Accordingly, the present study has three main layers. The first layer presents the characteristics of the dataset, the second layer presents the modeling phase, and the last layer is a description of the results and findings for proper policy making in the field.

2. Materials and Methods

2.1. Dataset Description

The dataset was prepared according to the 2019 European Company Survey (ECS). In the 2019 ECS, 3073 employee representatives and 21,869 management representatives from 27 EU Member States participated in an interview-based representative sample survey [17]. The data must first be unified since various data types utilize distinct units of measurement before being subjected to quantitative analysis. For instance, the ESC model assesses "work organization" using the two variables "collaboration and outsourcing" and "job complexity and autonomy". There are eight questions that have been created to gauge complexity and autonomy, and each question has a yes/no response option. The respondent must select one of the two alternatives in order to respond to two of the eight questions. The work of quantitative data analysis is made challenging by the discrepancy in the units of measurement of the inquiries. As a result, the questions were originally changed and combined, and each was rewritten such that the responses may be either zeros or ones.

For instance, for yes or no questions and questions where the respondent had to select an alternative, one was provided for a yes response and zero for a no response. The option that was not chosen received a score of 0, whereas the chosen option received a score of 1.

Figure 1 presents the variables employed in the study and their definitions. According to Table 1, each area contains factors that have been extracted from the questionary. Employee wellbeing and firm performance are two dependent factors. Work organization was evaluated using collaboration and outsourcing and job complexity and autonomy. Skills use and skills strategies was evaluated using "skills requirements and skills match" and "training and skill development". Employee voice was evaluated using "direct employee participation" and "indirect employee participation". The external environment was evaluated using "innovation", "digitalization", and "product market strategy". All these parameters had an effect on the "employee wellbeing" and "firm performance" as the two outputs of the system.

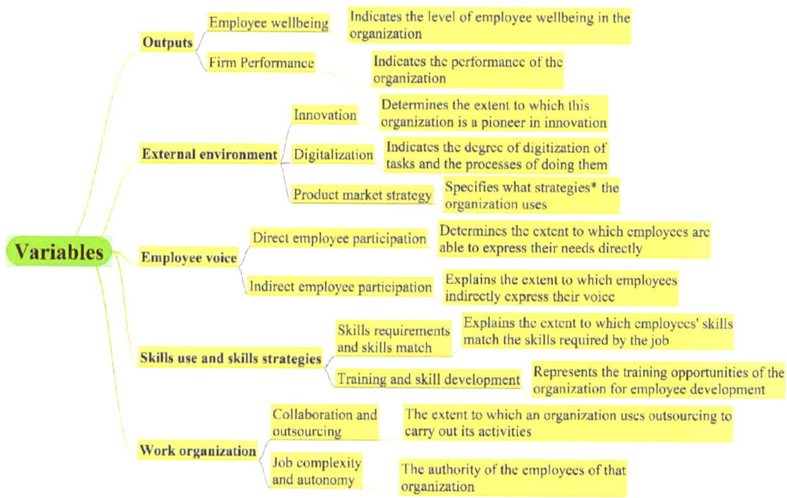

Figure 1. The explanation of the variables. The stared strategies are listed related to product market guideline.

2.2. Machine Learning Method

The present study developed an advanced multi-layered perceptron (MLP) integrated with the imperialist competitive algorithm (ICA) (called ANN-ICA) [20] to analyze the factors affecting firm performance and employee wellbeing. MLP is one of the most popular multilayer feeder networks [21,22]. This network processes existing data using activation functions in tandem layers. In this network, the input signals in each step by forwarding transmit the error signal for each node in the output layer [23,24]. The resulting error rate moves backward, and the weights and biases of the network change. Several activation functions are applied to the input to produce the neuron output. The outputs are then transmitted as input to the neurons in the next layer. Sigmoid transfer functions may be used when dealing with nonlinear situations.

Atashpaz-Gargari and Lucas [25] developed the imperialist competitive algorithm (ICA) as a solution for optimization problems. A random population solution initiates ICA. In ICA, the individuals are referred to as countries. The best solution is for the countries with the maximum power to be identified as imperialists. Figure 2 presents the main algorithm for the ICA optimization.

Table 1. Training MAPE for the effect of work organization on outputs.

Order	Neuron Arrangements for Hidden Layer	No. of Countries	No. of ITERATIONS	Prodvol_68	Profit_69	Profplan_70	Chempfut_71	Sickleave_59	Lowmot_60	Retainemp_62	Qwprel_63
1	20-10	100	1000	7.314	6.706	5.304	6.903	5.801	5.756	7.423	8.123
2	20-10	200	1000	6.001	5.804	5.112	6.209	5.111	5.569	7.057	7.912
3	20-10	300	1000	5.905	5.586	4.920	6.017	5.765	5.554	6.929	7.178
4	20-10-5	100	1000	5.271	5.002	5.000	5.343	5.887	5.021	6.045	6.213
5	20-10-5	200	1000	4.364	4.632	4.323	5.009	5.521	4.982	5.944	5.965
6	20-10-5	300	1000	4.133	4.895	3.903	4.522	5.108	4.020	5.420	5.651
7	30-20	100	1000	4.199	4.555	3.429	4.043	4.822	3.858	5.010	5.400
8	30-20	200	1000	3.906	4.004	3.005	3.788	4.011	3.201	4.831	5.187
9	30-20	300	1000	3.819	3.777	2.487	3.115	3.333	2.871	4.338	4.876
10	30-20-10	100	1000	3.542	3.008	1.999	2.911	2.024	2.006	3.999	4.077
11	30-20-10	200	1000	2.788	2.001	1.461	2.700	1.211	1.458	3.503	3.522
12	*30-20-10*	*300*	*1000*	*2.033*	*1.366*	*1.103*	*2.231*	*0.899*	*0.700*	*3.114*	*2.900*

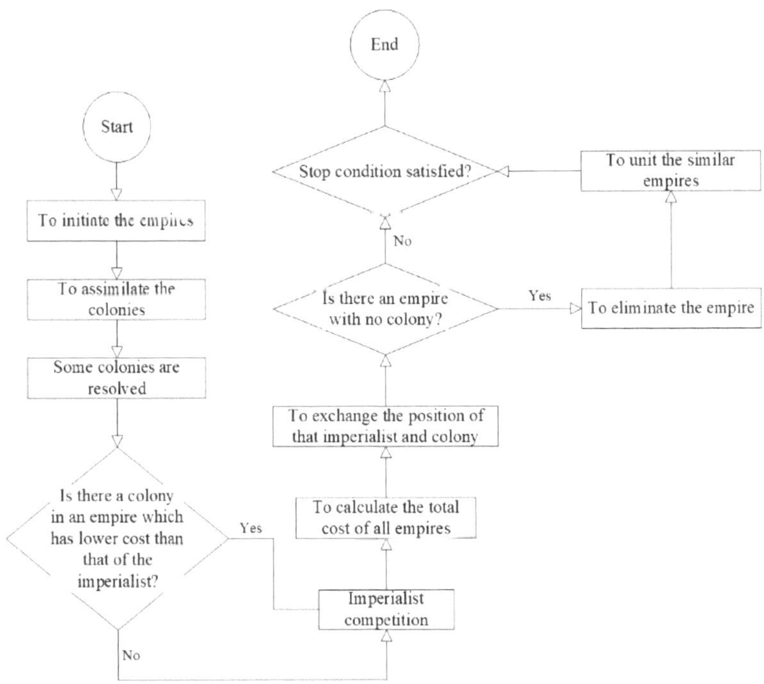

Figure 2. A schematic representation of the ICA algorithm.

The capabilities of the MLP network can be improved with meta-heuristic algorithms such as ICA [26]. These algorithms can replace the learning algorithm in the MLP network and adjust the weight and bias values to reduce the network output error. In this study, a combination of the MLP network with ICA (called MLP-ICA) investigated the correlation analysis of the factors affecting firm performance and employee wellbeing. The network was implemented based on the study of different treatments in terms of the number of hidden layers, the number of neurons in each layer, and the number of populations in a fixed number of iterations. This method was performed in the network training phase, and the analyses were performed using different indices to find the best network configuration. The results of this step are shown in Tables 1–4 for the various outputs based on mean absolute percentage error (MAPE). Equations (1)–(4) present the evaluation metrics for comparing the model's output with the target values [27–31].

$$\text{Mean square error (MSE)} = \frac{1}{t \times o} \sum_{i=1}^{o} \sum_{j=1}^{t} (T_{ij} - O_{ij})^2 \tag{1}$$

$$\text{Root mean square error (RMSE)} = \sqrt{\frac{1}{t \times o} \sum_{i=1}^{o} \sum_{j=1}^{t} (T_{ij} - O_{ij})^2} \tag{2}$$

$$\text{Correlation coefficient (r)} = \sqrt{\frac{\Sigma_{i=1}^{n}\left[\left(O_i - O\right)\left(T_i - T\right)\right]}{\Sigma_{i=1}^{n}\left[\left(O_i - O\right)^2 \Sigma_{i=1}^{n}\left(T_i - T\right)^2\right]}} \tag{3}$$

$$\text{Mean absolute percentage error (MAPE)} = 100 \times \frac{1}{o \times t} \sum_{i=1}^{o} \sum_{j=1}^{t} \left|\frac{T_{ij} - O_{ij}}{T_{ij}}\right| \tag{4}$$

$$\text{Determination coefficient (R2)} = \frac{\Sigma_{i=1}^{n}\left[\left(O_i - O\right)\left(T_i - T\right)\right]}{\Sigma_{i=1}^{n}\left[\left(O_i - O\right)^2 \Sigma_{i=1}^{n}\left(T_i - T\right)^2\right]} \tag{5}$$

where O refers to the output values, T refers to the target values, o refers to the number of output values, t refers to the number of target values, and n refers to the number of data.

Table 2. Training MAPE for the effect of skill requirements on outputs.

Order	Neuron Arrange-ments for Hidden Layer	No. of Countries	No. of Iterations	Prodvol_68	Profit_69	Profplan_70	Chempfut_71	Sickleave_59	Lowmot_60	Retainemp_62	Qwprel_63
1	20-10	100	1000	7.113	0.899	4.161	2.100	1.422	4.198	0.0500	0.903
2	20-10	200	1000	6.001	0.702	3.604	1.912	1.310	3.698	0.048	0.803
3	20-10	300	1000	5.434	0.732	3.169	1.808	1.278	3.121	0.031	0.800
4	20-10-5	100	1000	5.005	0.693	2.234	1.721	1.162	2.891	0.020	0.731
5	20-10-5	200	1000	4.777	0.613	1.906	1.600	1.001	2.400	0.008	0.605
6	20-10-5	300	1000	4.100	0.501	1.333	1.449	0.912	2.005	0.006	0.500
7	30-20	100	1000	3.356	0.412	1.125	1.228	0.900	1.977	0.004	0.389
8	30-20	200	1000	2.988	0.290	0.996	0.991	0.787	1.822	0.003	0.201
9	30-20	300	1000	2.401	0.056	0.721	0.620	0.422	1.701	0.003	0.142
10	30-20-10	100	1000	1.889	0.014	0.506	0.399	0.211	1.498	0.002	0.099
11	30-20-10	200	1000	0.987	0.0009	0.422	0.100	0.098	1.032	0.001	0.049
12	*30-20-10*	*300*	*1000*	*0.301*	*0.0005*	*0.297*	*0.0403*	*0.014*	*0.432*	*0.0000*	*0.013*

Table 3. Training MAPE for the effect of employee voice on outputs.

Order	Neuron Arrangements for Hidden Layer	No. of Countries	No. of Iterations	Prodvol_68	Profit_69	Profplan_70	Chempfut_71	Sickleave_59	Lowmot_60	Retainemp_62	Qwprel_63
1	20-10	100	1000	5.014	6.891	2.093	3.618	2.948	2.094	3.577	2.051
2	20-10	200	1000	4.194	5.792	1.999	3.321	2.431	1.901	3.113	1.901
3	20-10	300	1000	3.900	5.299	1.891	2.965	2.131	1.872	2.976	1.878
4	20-10-5	100	1000	3.564	5.014	1.700	2.432	1.990	1.789	2.667	1.750
5	20-10-5	200	1000	3.109	4.842	1.509	2.006	1.776	1.609	2.067	1.450
6	20-10-5	300	1000	2.942	4.511	1.400	1.891	1.540	1.430	1.645	1.251
7	30-20	100	1000	2.777	3.888	1.294	1.603	1.345	1.202	1.236	1.051
8	30-20	200	1000	2.001	3.001	1.010	1.590	1.223	1.029	1.069	0.905
9	30-20	300	1000	1.666	2.118	0.822	1.333	1.005	0.999	0.907	0.850
10	30-20-10	100	1000	1.213	1.542	0.555	1.003	0.899	0.621	0.700	0.502
11	30-20-10	200	1000	0.801	1.002	0.282	0.872	0.567	0.328	0.699	0.200
12	***30-20-10***	***300***	*1000*	*0.488*	*0.719*	*0.099*	*0.444*	*0.302*	*0.121*	*0.586*	*0.099*

Table 4. Training MAPE for the effect of the external environment on outputs.

Order	Neuron Arrangements for Hidden Layer	No. of Countries	No. of Iterations	Prodvol_68	Profit_69	Profplan_70	Chempfut_71	Sickleave_59	Lowmot_60	Retainemp_62	Qwprel_63
1	20-10	100	1000	7.5194	5.9298	5.4228	4.9581	5.268	5.142	7.074	6.141
2	20-10	200	1000	6.944	5.268	5.005	4.101	4.811	4.992	6.714	5.800
3	20-10	300	1000	6.532	4.999	4.898	3.911	4.333	4.215	6.001	5.150
4	20-10-5	100	1000	6.001	4.708	4.451	3.526	4.089	4.000	5.704	4.845
5	20-10-5	200	1000	5.823	4.277	4.021	3.051	3.698	3.482	5.048	4.101
6	20-10-5	300	1000	5.104	3.810	3.709	2.508	3.064	3.100	4.571	3.811
7	30-20	100	1000	4.601	3.021	3.202	1.968	2.939	2.777	4.061	3.112
8	30-20	200	1000	3.904	2.987	2.658	1.501	2.282	2.452	3.379	2.642
9	30-20	300	1000	3.101	2.892	2.202	1.331	2.008	2.012	3.005	2.465
10	30-20-10	100	1000	2.400	2.598	2.002	1.111	1.841	1.723	2.893	2.001
11	30-20-10	200	1000	2.000	2.220	1.777	1.032	1.570	1.404	2.500	1.555
12	***30-20-10***	***300***	*1000*	*1.999*	*1.872*	*1.383*	*0.876*	*1.380*	*1.130*	*2.170*	*1.132*

Based on the results presented in Tables 1–4, increasing the number of hidden layers, the number of neurons, and the number of countries increased the model's accuracy. Model No. 12 was selected as the best model for the prediction of firm performance and employee wellbeing with the lowest MAPE. The best architecture was obtained to be 11-30-20-10-2. It should be noted that the modeling and analysis were performed using MATLAB software (version R2022a, The MathWorks, Inc. New York, NY, USA) on hardware consisting of an Intel® Core™ i7-8557U CPU @ 1.70 GHz and 16 GB RAM in the presence of the 70% of the dataset as the training dataset and 30% of the dataset as the testing dataset. The increasing number of layers and neurons and the number of countries require more processing time and power due to the huge number of datasets. Figure 3 also shows the implementation algorithm of the desired network.

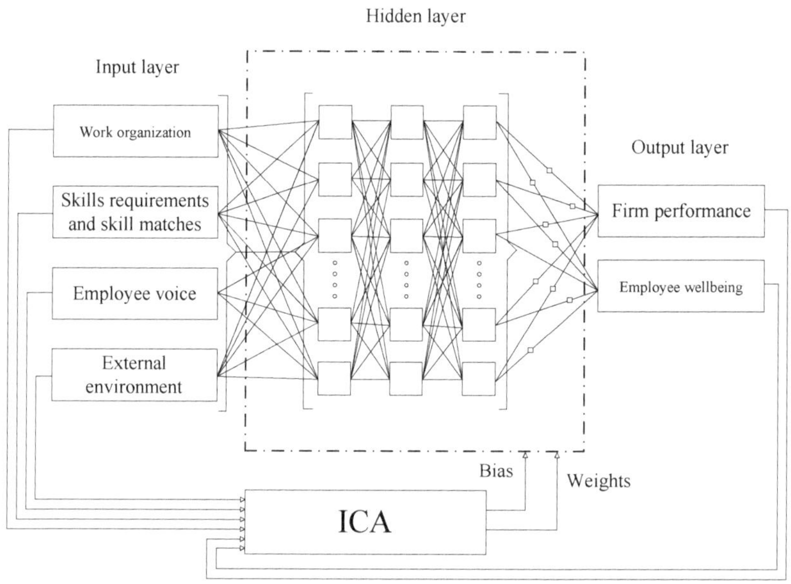

Figure 3. The architecture of the proposed method.

According to Figure 3, ICA adjusts the bias and weights using the relations of input and output values and provides a training algorithm for the MLP method. Work organization, skills requirements and skill matches, employee voice, and external environment are considered as the independent variables, and firm performance and employee wellbeing are considered as the dependent variables. The next step presents the results and discussion section.

3. Results

This section has two main categories. The first phase presents the analytical results for the nature of the dataset and the second phase provides the modeling results.

3.1. Mean Value Analysis

This section presents the mean value analysis for the target values. This analysis provides a simple and accurate sight of the dataset's range, min, max, and average values for better discussion (Table 5).

3.2. Modeling Results

This section presents the testing phase modeling results. Accordingly, the highest correlation can refer to the highest impact of that parameter on the output value. Tables 6–13 refer to the testing results for work organization, skills requirements and skill matches, employee voice, and external environment, and their impact on the firm performance, and employee wellbeing, respectively. Each table also presents the average values for better justification.

Table 5. Descriptive statistics for the effect of results on the dataset.

Parameter	Minimum	Maximum	Mean	Std. Deviation
sickleave_59	1	2	1.745542	0.435606
lowmot_60	1	2	1.78235	0.412695
retainemp_62	1	2	1.3123	0.463484
qwprel_63	1	2	1.859625	0.347415
prodvol_68	1	2	1.501143	0.500056
profit_69	1	2	1.714906	0.451511
profplan_70	1	2	1.807727	0.394131
chempfut_71	1	2	1.322359	0.467433

Table 6. Testing results for the effect of work organization on firm performance.

Work Organization	Prodvol_68	Profit_69	Profplan_70	Chempfut_71	Average
MAPE	2.217	1.546	1.230	2.857	1.962
MSE	0.004	0.003	0.003	0.004	0.004
RMSE	0.064	0.058	0.057	0.063	0.060
R	0.893	0.876	0.831	0.852	0.863
R2	0.797	0.767	0.691	0.727	0.745

Table 7. Testing results for the effect of work organization on employee wellbeing.

Work Organization	Sickleave_59	Lowmot_60	Retainemp_62	Qwprel_63	Average
MAPE	0.727	0.842	3.209	1.045	1.456
MSE	0.002	0.001	0.006	0.002	0.003
RMSE	0.044	0.036	0.078	0.047	0.051
R	0.904	0.797	0.682	0.821	0.801
R2	0.818	0.635	0.464	0.673	0.648

Table 8. Testing results for the effect of skills requirements and skill matches on firm performance.

Skills Requirements and Skill Matches	Prodvol_68	Profit_69	Profplan_70	Chempfut_71	Average
MAPE	0.0084	0.7622	0.0000	0.0293	0.2000
MSE	0.0001	0.0010	0.0001	0.0001	0.0002
RMSE	0.0004	0.0310	0.0001	0.0038	0.0088
R	0.9996	0.9426	0.9997	0.9992	0.9854
R2	0.9999	0.8885	0.9999	0.9983	0.9717

Table 9. Testing results for the effect of skills requirements and skill matches on employee wellbeing.

Skills Requirements and Skill Matches	Sickleave_59	Lowmot_60	Retainemp_62	Qwprel_63	Average
MAPE	0.3338	0.0002	0.4586	0.0330	0.2064
MSE	0.0012	0.0001	0.0023	0.0004	0.0010
RMSE	0.0351	0.0001	0.0482	0.0209	0.0260
R	0.9183	0.9996	0.7196	0.9531	0.8978
R2	0.8433	0.9999	0.5178	0.9085	0.8174

Table 10. Testing results for the effect of employee voice on firm performance.

Employee Voice	Prodvol_68	Profit_69	Profplan_70	Chempfut_71	Average
MAPE	0.5149	0.8209	0.0990	0.1306	0.3914
MSE	0.0008	0.0013	0.0000	0.0001	0.0005
RMSE	0.0284	0.0356	0.0046	0.0071	0.0189
R	0.9708	0.9229	0.9983	0.9971	0.9723
R2	0.9425	0.8517	0.9967	0.9942	0.9462

Table 11. Testing results for the effect of employee voice on employee wellbeing.

Employee Voice	Sickleave_59	Lowmot_60	Retainemp_62	Qwprel_63	Average
MAPE	0.3384	0.2290	0.6067	0.0500	0.3060
MSE	0.0003	0.0005	0.0010	0.0003	0.0005
RMSE	0.0185	0.0219	0.0316	0.0179	0.0225
R	0.9775	0.9205	0.8755	0.9649	0.9346
R2	0.9556	0.8474	0.7665	0.9311	0.8752

Table 12. Testing results for the effect of the external environment on firm performance.

External Environment	Prodvol_68	Profit_69	Profplan_70	Chempfut_71	Average
MAPE	2.5194	1.9298	1.4228	0.9581	1.7075
MSE	0.0081	0.0130	0.0031	0.0027	0.0067
RMSE	0.0898	0.1139	0.0560	0.0516	0.0778
R	0.8296	0.6417	0.8629	0.9206	0.8137
R2	0.6883	0.4118	0.7447	0.8475	0.6731

Table 13. Testing results for the effect of the external environment on employee wellbeing.

External Environment	Sickleave_59	Lowmot_60	Retainemp_62	Qwprel_63	Average
MAPE	1.268	1.142	2.074	1.141	1.4062
MSE	0.004	0.004	0.003	0.003	0.0033
RMSE	0.061	0.061	0.052	0.053	0.0569
R	0.787	0.481	0.845	0.688	0.7003
R2	0.619	0.232	0.714	0.474	0.5096

Figures 4–11 present the plot diagrams for the testing phase separately for firm performance and employee wellbeing. These figures evaluate the linearity of target values against the output values. These figures also present the trendline, including the determination coefficient, for better analysis.

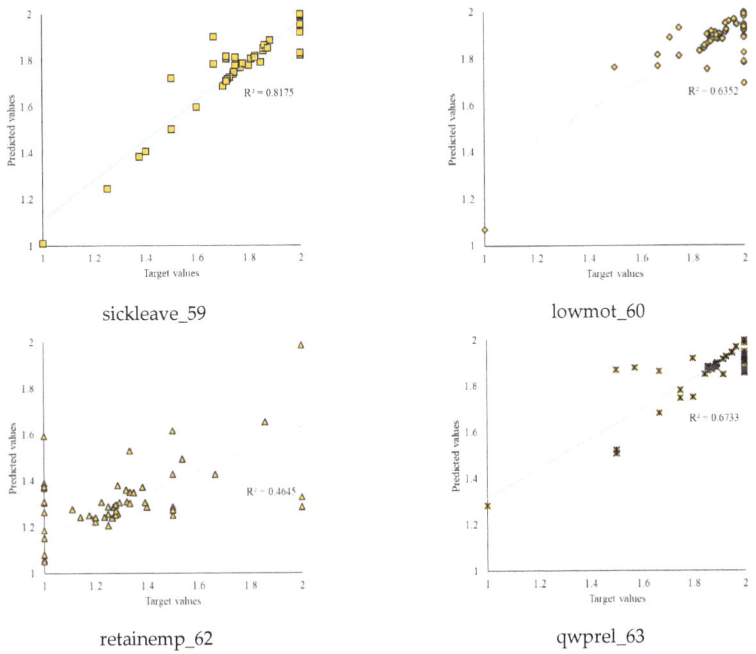

Figure 4. Plot diagrams for the effects of work organization on output values of employee wellbeing.

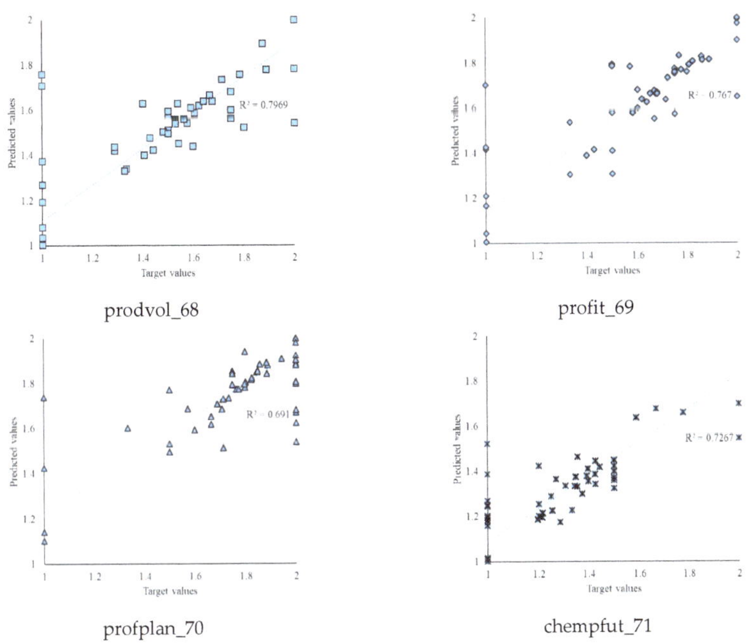

Figure 5. Plot diagrams for the effects of work organization on output values of firm performance.

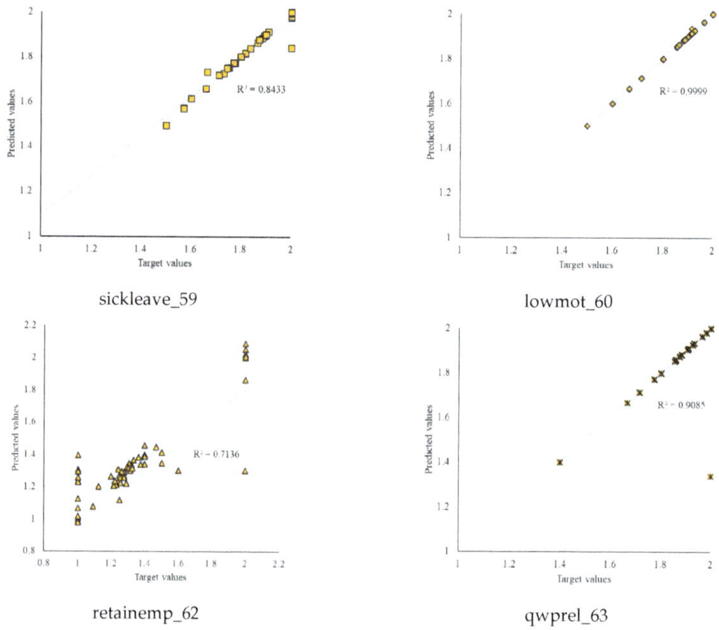

Figure 6. Plot diagrams for the effects of skills requirements and skill matches on output values of employee wellbeing.

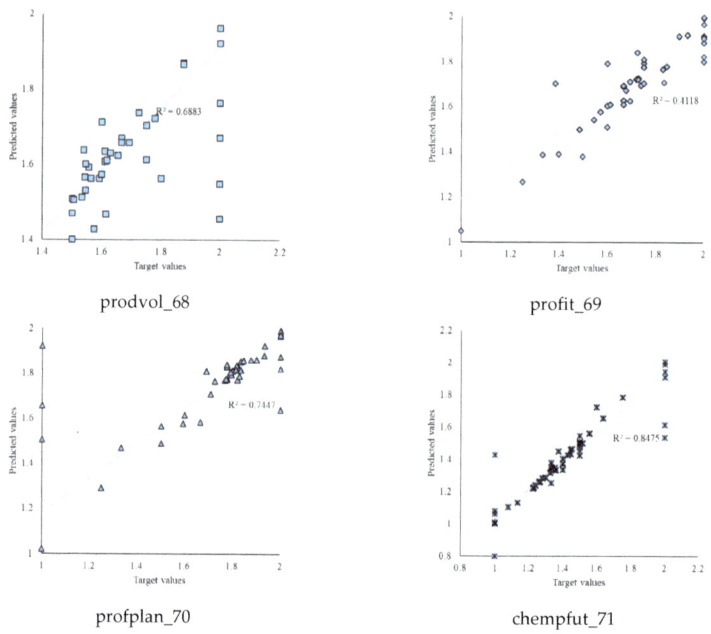

Figure 7. Plot diagrams for the effects of skills requirements and skill matches on output values of firm performance.

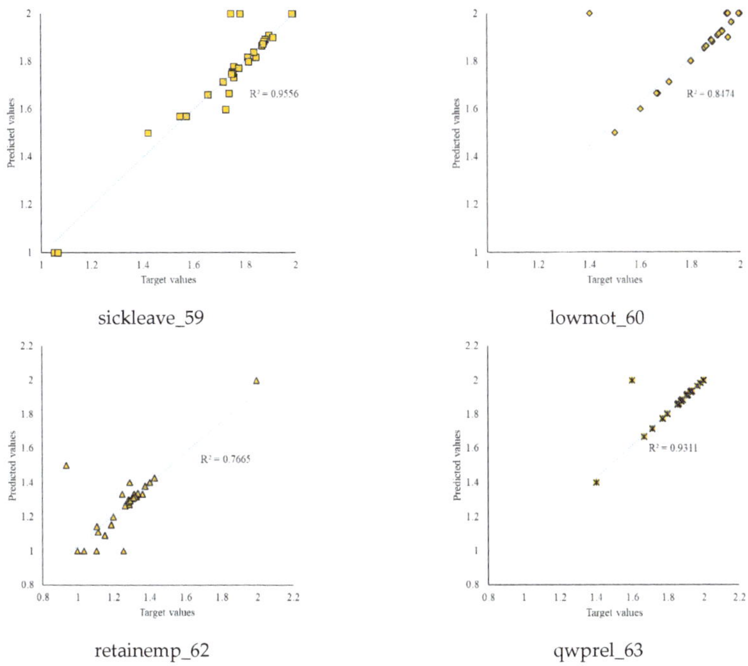

Figure 8. Plot diagrams for the effects of employee voice on output values of employee wellbeing.

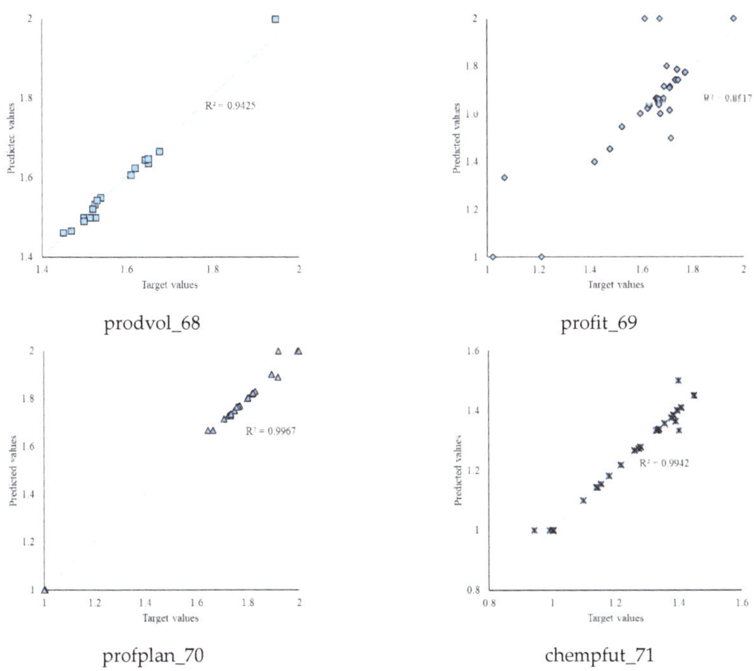

Figure 9. Plot diagrams for the effects of employee voice on output values of firm performance.

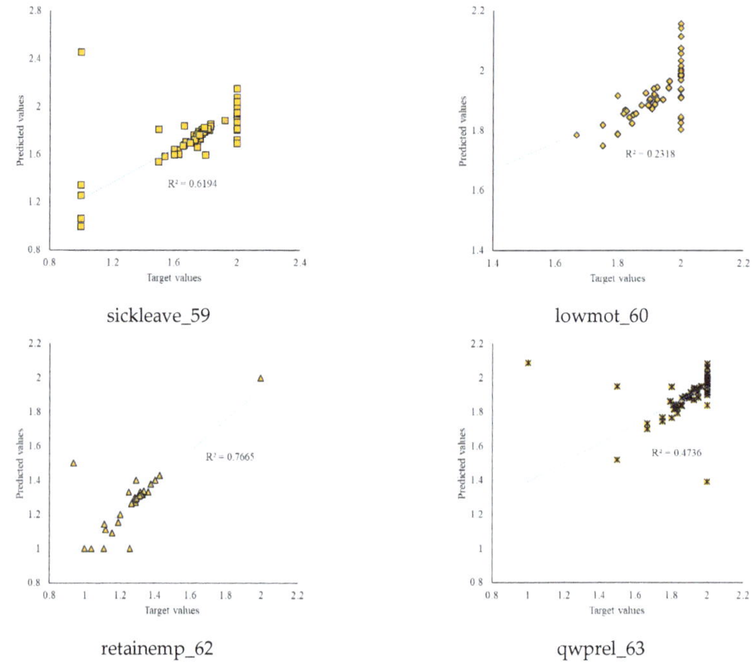

Figure 10. Plot diagrams for the effects of the external environment on output values of employee wellbeing.

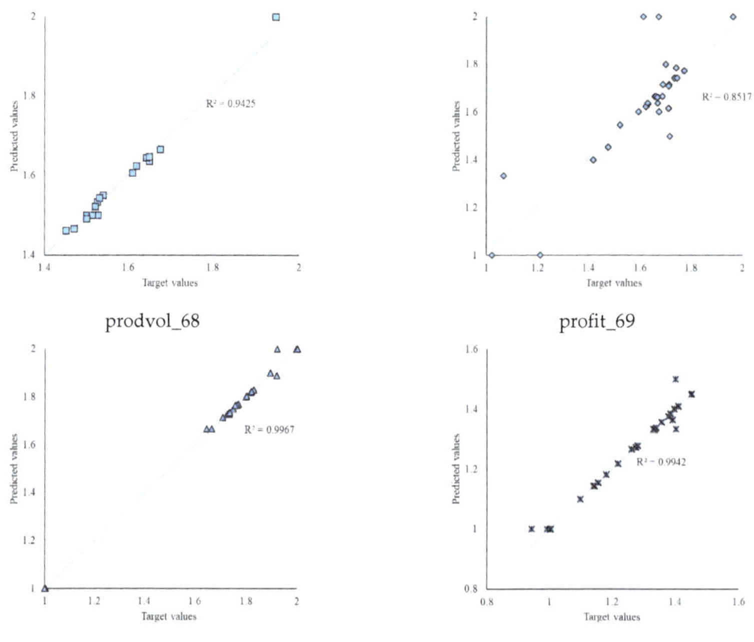

Figure 11. Plot diagrams for the effects of the external environment on output values of firm performance.

According to Figure 4, the mean value of linearity for predicting employee wellbeing using a working organization is about 64%. Figure 5 presents the effect of working organization on firm performance. As is clear from Figure 5, the mean value of linearity for predicting firm performance using a working organization is about 74%, which is about 10% higher than that for predicting employee wellbeing. This trend describes that the effect of work organization-related factors on firm performance is about 15% higher than that of the effect of work organization-related factors on employee wellbeing.

The mean value of linearity for forecasting employee wellbeing using skills requirements and skill matches-related factors is approximately 86%, as shown in Figure 6. The impact of skills requirements and skill matches-related factors on firm performance is shown in Figure 7.

The mean value of linearity for predicting firm performance using skills requirements and skill matches is approximately 67%, which is about 19% lower than that for predicting employee wellbeing. According to this tendency, the impact of skills requirements and skill matches-related characteristics on firm performance is around 22% lower than the impact of those same factors on employee wellbeing.

According to characteristics connected to employee voice, the mean value of linearity for predicting employee wellbeing is roughly 87%, as shown in Figure 8. Figure 9 illustrates how factors related to employee voice affect firm performance.

Figure 9 shows that the mean value of linearity for forecasting firm performance based on employee voice is around 94%, which is about 7% higher than that for predicting employee wellbeing. This pattern indicates that the influence of employee voice-related features on firm performance is around 8% higher than the influence of the same qualities on employee wellbeing.

Figures 10 and 11 present the effects of the external environment-related factors on output values of employee wellbeing and firm performance, respectively. Figure 10 illustrates the mean value of linearity for forecasting employee wellbeing based on factors related to the external environment, which is around 52%. The impact of parameters connected to the external environment on firm performance is seen in Figure 11.

Figure 11 demonstrates that the average linearity for predicting firm performance using the external environment is around 94%, which is roughly 42% higher than that for predicting employee wellbeing. This trend suggests that the impact of external environment-related characteristics on firm performance is approximately 80% greater than the impact of the same characteristics on employee wellbeing.

Figure 12 presents the main findings from the previous sections for describing the effects of the independent parameters on the output values. As is clear from Figure 8, skill requirements and skill matches have the highest correlation with firm performance. However, in the case of employee wellbeing, the highest correlation refers to the employee voice. It can be mentioned that skill requirements and skill matches and employee voice have the highest impact on firm performance and employee wellbeing, respectively.

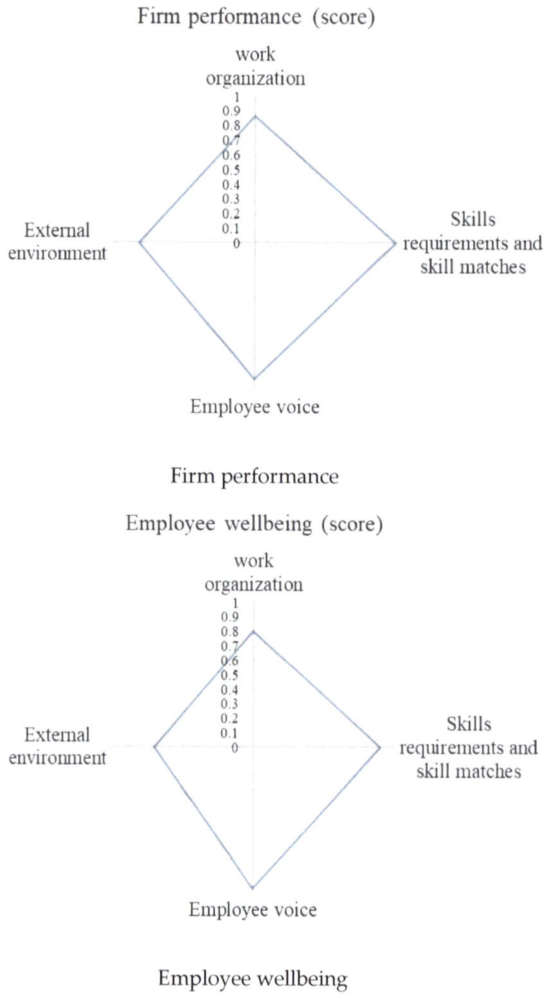

Figure 12. Analyzing the effects of independent parameters on output values.

4. Conclusions

This study was employed for the evaluation of the firm performance and employee wellbeing parameters using the ANN-ICA technique. Outputs of the models have been compared using evaluation criteria with the target values. In the second phase, the effect of each independent category was considered compared to the output values to find the most effective variables. According to the findings, the model architecture of 11-30-20-10-2 (11 inputs interconnected with 30 neurons in the first hidden layer, 20 neurons in the second hidden layer, 10 neurons in the third hidden layer, and 2 outputs) was selected as the best model for the prediction of the firm performance and employee wellbeing with the lowest MAPE. According to the findings, it can be mentioned that, when predicting company success (firm performance) using working organizations, the mean value of linearity was around 74%, which is about 10% higher than that for predicting employee wellbeing. This pattern showed that the impact of work organization-related characteristics on firm performance was around 15% greater than the impact of these same factors on employee wellbeing. The mean value of linearity, on the other hand, was around 67% for forecasting firm performance using skill needs and skill matches, which was roughly 19% lower than that for predicting employee wellbeing. This tendency indicates that the influence of the qualities linked to the skills needed and skill matching on firm performance was approximately 22% less than the impact of the same characteristics on employee wellbeing. Additionally, based on employee feedback, the mean linearity for predicting firm performance was about 94%, which was around 7% higher than that for predicting employee wellbeing. This trend showed that the impact of characteristics linked to employee voice on firm performance was around 8% more than the impact of the same characteristics on employee wellbeing. Furthermore, the average linearity for forecasting firm performance using the external environment was about 94%, which was roughly 42% higher than that for forecasting employee wellbeing. According to this pattern, the influence of factors connected to the external environment on a company's success was almost 80% bigger than its influence on employee wellbeing. It would be exciting to use this method (ANN-ICA) to identify the cross-country differences covering EU-27 countries involved in the ECS 2019 survey. It would be exciting to locate country group differences (e.g., Nordic countries, continental countries, Mediterranean countries, etc.).

Author Contributions: Conceptualization, A.M., C.M. and M.I.; methodology, S.A.; software, S.A. and A.M.; validation, S.A. and A.M.; formal analysis, S.A. and A.M.; investigation, S.A., C.M. and A.M.; resources, M.I., J.P. and Z.D.; data curation, S.A., J.P. and A.M.; writing—original draft preparation, S.A., J.P. and A.M.; writing—review and editing, S.A., C.M. and A.M.; visualization, S.A. and A.M.; supervision, S.A., B.T. and A.M.; project administration, J.P. and Z.D.; All authors have read and agreed to the published version of the manuscript.

Funding: The research was supported by the European Union within the framework of the RRF-2.3.1-21-2022-00004 Artificial Intelligence National Laboratory Program.

Institutional Review Board Statement: Not applicable.

Informed Consent Statement: Not applicable.

Data Availability Statement: Not applicable.

Conflicts of Interest: The authors declare no conflict of interest.

References

1. Farzianpour, F.; Aghababa, S.; Delgoshaei, B.; Haghgoo, M. Performance evaluation a teaching hospital affiliated to Tehran University of medical sciences based on baldrige excellence model. *Am. J. Econ. Bus. Adm.* **2011**, *3*, 277. [CrossRef]
2. Chang, W.J.A.; Huang, T.C. Relationship between strategic human resource management and firm performance. *Int. J. Manpow.* **2005**, *26*, 434–449. [CrossRef]
3. Marr, B.; Schiuma, G. Business performance measurement–past, present and future. *Manag. Decis.* **2003**, *41*, 680–687. [CrossRef]
4. Morgan, A.; Colebourne, D.; Thomas, B. The development of ICT advisors for SME businesses: An innovative approach. *Technovation* **2006**, *26*, 980–987. [CrossRef]
5. Maranto-Vargas, D.; Rangel, R.G.-T. Development of internal resources and capabilities as sources of differentiation of SME under increased global competition: A field study in Mexico. *Technol. Forecast. Soc. Change* **2007**, *74*, 90–99. [CrossRef]
6. Lee, H.; Kim, J.; Kim, J. Determinants of success for application service provider: An empirical test in small businesses. *Int. J. Hum. Comput. Stud.* **2007**, *65*, 796–815. [CrossRef]
7. Zare, M. The relationship between commanding leadership style and personality traits of nursing managers of hospitals affiliated to Tehran Medical Sciences Universities in 2014–2015. *Med. Sci. J. Islam. Azad Univ.-Tehran Med. Branch* **2016**, *26*, 238–247.
8. Jacobs, G.; Hoste, V.J.L.R. SENTiVENT: Enabling supervised information extraction of company-specific events in economic and financial news. *Comput. Humanit.* **2022**, *56*, 225–257. [CrossRef]
9. Elsharkawy, M.; Sharafeldeen, A.; Soliman, A.; Khalifa, F.; Ghazal, M.; El-Daydamony, E.; Atwan, A.; Sandhu, H.S.; El-Baz, A.J.D. A novel computer-aided diagnostic system for early detection of diabetic retinopathy using 3D-OCT higher-order spatial appearance model. *Diagnostics* **2022**, *12*, 461. [CrossRef]
10. Meng, Y.; Shao, C.J.M.S.; Processing, S. Physics-informed ensemble learning for online joint strength prediction in ultrasonic metal welding. *Mech. Syst. Signal Process.* **2022**, *181*, 109473. [CrossRef]
11. Sargent, B.; Jafari, M.; Marquez, G.; Mehta, A.S.; Sun, Y.-H.; Yang, H.-y.; Zhu, K.; Isseroff, R.R.; Zhao, M.; Gomez, M. A machine learning based model accurately predicts cellular response to electric fields in multiple cell types. *Sci. Rep.* **2022**, *12*, 9912. [CrossRef]
12. Song, W.; Zou, S.; Tian, Y.; Fong, S. Classifying 3D objects in LiDAR point clouds with a back-propagation neural network. *Human-Centric Comput. Inf. Sci.* **2018**, *8*, 29. [CrossRef]

13. Fredström, A.; Parida, V.; Wincent, J.; Sjödin, D.; Oghazi, P.J.T.F.; Change, S. What is the Market Value of Artificial Intelligence and Machine Learning? The Role of Innovativeness and Collaboration for Performance. *Technol. Forecast. Soc. Chang.* **2022**, *180*, 121716. [CrossRef]
14. Shaaban, A.G.; Khafagy, M.H.; Elmasry, M.A.; El-Bei, H.H.; Ibrahim, M.H. Knowledge discovery in manufacturing datasets using data mining techniques to improve business performance. *Indones. J. Electr. Eng. Comput. Sci.* **2022**, *26*, 1736–1746. [CrossRef]
15. Ahmed, A.A.A.; Agarwal, S.; Kurniawan, I.G.A.; Anantadjaya, S.P.; Krishnan, C. Business boosting through sentiment analysis using Artificial Intelligence approach. *Int. J. Syst. Assur. Eng. Manag.* **2022**, *13*, 699–709. [CrossRef]
16. Van Houten, G.; Russo, G. *European Company Survey 2019: Workplace Practices Unlocking Employee Potential*; Eurofound: Brussels, Belgium, 2020.
17. Eurofound; Cedefop. *European Company Survey 2019 Series*; Publications Office of the European Union: Luxembourg, 2020; ISBN 978-92-897-2107-3. Available online: https://www.cedefop.europa.eu/en/publications/2228 (accessed on 12 April 2022).
18. Valeyre, A.; Lorenz, E.; Cartron, D.; Csizmadia, P.; Gollac, M.; Illéssy, M.; Makó, C. Munkaszervezeti modellek Európában és az emberierőforrás-gazdálkodás néhány jellemzője Kísérlet a munkaszervezetek nemzetközi paradigmatérképének elkészítésére (II. rész). *Vez. Bp. Manag. Rev.* **2009**, *40*, 36–51. [CrossRef]
19. Haapakorpi, A.; Alasoini, T. Work organization and technology: Introduction to the theme of the special issue. *Nord. J. Work. Life Stud.* **2018**, *8*, S3. [CrossRef]
20. Khosravi, A.; Syri, S.J.J.o.C.P. Modeling of geothermal power system equipped with absorption refrigeration and solar energy using multilayer perceptron neural network optimized with imperialist competitive algorithm. *J. Clean. Prod.* **2020**, *276*, 124216. [CrossRef]
21. Pham, D.T.; Sagiroglu, S. Training multilayered perceptrons for pattern recognition: A comparative study of four training algorithms. *Int. J. Mach. Tools Manuf.* **2001**, *41*, 419–430. [CrossRef]
22. Plunkett, K.; Marchman, V. U-shaped learning and frequency effects in a multilayered perceptron: Implications for child language acquisition. *Cognition* **1991**, *38*, 487–526. [CrossRef]
23. Shepherd, A.J. *Second-Order Methods for Neural Networks: Fast and Reliable Training Methods for Multi-Layer Perceptrons*; Springer Science & Business Media: Berlin/Heidelberg, Germany, 2012.
24. Taud, H.; Mas, J. Multilayer perceptron (MLP). In *Geomatic Approaches for Modeling Land Change Scenarios*; Springer: Berlin/Heidelberg, Germany, 2018; pp. 451–455.
25. Atashpaz-Gargari, E.; Lucas, C. Imperialist competitive algorithm: An algorithm for optimization inspired by imperialistic competition. In Proceedings of the 2007 IEEE Congress on Evolutionary Computation, Singapore, 25–28 September 2007; pp. 4661–4667.
26. Zadeh Shirazi, A.; Mohammadi, Z. A hybrid intelligent model combining ANN and imperialist competitive algorithm for prediction of corrosion rate in 3C steel under seawater environment. *Neural Comput. Appl.* **2017**, *28*, 3455–3464. [CrossRef]
27. Kim, G.G.; Choi, J.H.; Park, S.Y.; Bhang, B.G.; Nam, W.J.; Cha, H.L.; Park, N.; Ahn, H.-K. Prediction model for PV performance with correlation analysis of environmental variables. *IEEE J. Photovolt.* **2019**, *9*, 832–841. [CrossRef]
28. Ahmad, T.; Chen, H.J.E. Short and medium-term forecasting of cooling and heating load demand in building environment with data-mining based approaches. *Energy Build.* **2018**, *166*, 460–476. [CrossRef]
29. Roy, S.S.; Samui, P.; Nagtode, I.; Jain, H.; Shivaramakrishnan, V.; Mohammadi-Ivatloo, B. Forecasting heating and cooling loads of buildings: A comparative performance analysis. *J. Ambient Intell. Humaniz. Comput.* **2020**, *11*, 1253–1264. [CrossRef]
30. Roy, S.; Banerjee, R.; Bose, P.K. Performance and exhaust emissions prediction of a CRDI assisted single cylinder diesel engine coupled with EGR using artificial neural network. *Appl. Energy* **2014**, *119*, 330–340. [CrossRef]
31. Kertész, G.; Szénási, S.; Vámossy, Z. Comparative analysis of image projection-based descriptors in Siamese neural networks. *Adv. Eng. Softw.* **2021**, *154*, 102963. [CrossRef]

algorithms

MDPI

Article

Calibration of an Adaptive Genetic Algorithm for Modeling Opinion Diffusion

Kara Layne Johnson * and Nicole Bohme Carnegie

Department of Mathematical Sciences, Montana State University, Bozeman, MT 59717, USA; nicole.carnegie@montana.edu

* Correspondence: kara.johnson4@montana.edu

Abstract: Genetic algorithms mimic the process of natural selection in order to solve optimization problems with minimal assumptions and perform well when the objective function has local optima on the search space. These algorithms treat potential solutions to the optimization problem as chromosomes, consisting of genes which undergo biologically-inspired operators to identify a better solution. Hyperparameters or control parameters determine the way these operators are implemented. We created a genetic algorithm in order to fit a DeGroot opinion diffusion model using limited data, making use of selection, blending, crossover, mutation, and survival operators. We adapted the algorithm from a genetic algorithm for design of mixture experiments, but the new algorithm required substantial changes due to model assumptions and the large parameter space relative to the design space. In addition to introducing new hyperparameters, these changes mean the hyperparameter values suggested for the original algorithm cannot be expected to result in optimal performance. To make the algorithm for modeling opinion diffusion more accessible to researchers, we conduct a simulation study investigating hyperparameter values. We find the algorithm is robust to the values selected for most hyperparameters and provide suggestions for initial, if not default, values and recommendations for adjustments based on algorithm output.

Keywords: genetic algorithm; hyperparameters; control parameters; opinion diffusion; parameter estimation; social networks

1. Introduction

Genetic algorithms, developed by John Holland in the 1970s, mimic the process of natural selection to solve optimization or search problems and are particularly useful when the objective function lacks continuity, differentiability, or convexity or has local optima on the search space [1–6]. These algorithms represent a solution to the optimization problem as a chromosome consisting of genes. The chromosomes undergo biologically-inspired operators, modifying the genes to identify progressively better solutions. Hyperparameters or control parameters govern the behavior of these operators; however, specifying these hyperparameters is a barrier to use of genetic algorithms, particularly for researchers outside of the field of machine learning who are applying genetic algorithms in their research [7,8].

We developed a genetic algorithm to fit DeGroot opinion diffusion models using limited data on small social networks specifically for use in network and social science research [9]. While there were existing algorithms for the closely-related Stochastic Opinion Dynamics Model (SODM), both the maximum-likelihood-based algorithm and the particle learning algorithm were developed for online social networks and require far more data than are practical to obtain in the public health and social science applications for which we developed our method [10,11]. Though other bio-inspired algorithms may be viable options for fitting the DeGroot model–for example, bacterial foraging optimization (BFO) or particle swarm optimization (PSO)–these algorithms have a tendency to identify local as opposed to global optima: a concern motivating our choice of a genetic algorithm

[12–14]. Using adaptive modifications of these algorithms, such as the self-adaptive chemotaxis strategy for bacterial foraging optimization (SCBFO), is a potential solution, but the performance of a genetic algorithm has already been demonstrated on the related problem of design of constrained mixture experiments with the structure of the design matrix and the matrix of parameters for the DeGroot model having a similar structure and the same sum-to-one constraint across rows [2,14]. Further, we demonstrated the performance of the genetic algorithm under the conditions expected in the intended application of this method [15].

While we adapted the operators from the genetic algorithm for design of mixture experiments, substantial changes to the operators were necessary due to model assumptions and the large parameter space relative to the design space. As such, the suggested hyperparameter values for the original algorithm cannot be expected to result in optimal performance. While research exists on either optimizing or removing hyperparameters from genetic algorithms in general, the algorithms and objective functions used bear even less resemblance to our algorithm because of the features specific to the opinion diffusion application [7,16]. To make the algorithm for modeling opinion diffusion more accessible to applied researchers, we conduct a simulation study investigating hyperparameter values, removing a barrier for researchers applying this methodological development to their applied research.

We begin by providing an overview of the model for opinion diffusion, detailing the genetic algorithm, and describing our approach and procedures for calibrating the algorithm in Section 2. We then present the results of the simulation study, addressing the performance of the algorithm in terms of parameter recovery and efficiency for the different hyperparameter values considered in Section 3. Finally, we conclude by tying the results back to the hyperparameters considered, providing specific suggestions for hyperparameter values and paying particular attention to hyperparameters that can negatively affect performance if poorly calibrated in Section 4.

2. Materials and Methods

In this section, first, we explain our model for opinion diffusion, focusing on the features that inform our decisions regarding the genetic algorithm. Then, we detail the genetic algorithm, highlighting the purposes of the operators and how the hyperparameters govern their behavior. Lastly, we describe the hyperparameters, procedures, and measures used in the simulation study.

2.1. Opinion Diffusion Modeling

In this section we provide an overview of the approach we take to opinion diffusion modeling. We focus on the details of the model to be fit and the modifications necessary to work with ordinal opinion data. Finally, we detail the objective function, highlighting why a new method was appropriate for optimization and why suggestions on hyperparameter values from the algorithm we adapted are not expected to be informative.

2.1.1. DeGroot Model

The DeGroot model for opinion diffusion is a deterministic model that describes the process through which individuals or *agents* update their opinions from time t, through the influence of their social network contacts, to their opinions at time $t+1$ using

$$X(t+1) = WX(t), \tag{1}$$

where $X(t)$ is an $N \times 1$ vector of opinions and W is an $N \times N$ weight matrix. Each element in $X(t)$, $x_i(t) \in [0,1]$, represents the opinion of agent i at time t and each element of W, $w_{ij} \in [0,1]$, represents the weight that agent i places on the opinion of agent j when updating their current opinion. The elements in W are restricted by $\sum_{j=1}^{N} w_{ij} = 1$ so that w_{ij} can be interpreted as the proportion of the total influence on agent i exerted by agent j. The model also incorporates the structure of the social network through an adjacency matrix A, where $a_{ij} = a_{ji} = 1$ if agents i and j can directly influence each other and $a_{ij} = a_{ji} = 0$ otherwise, with a link between i and j in the social network being the simplest definition of "ability to influence". The adjacency matrix constrains the weight matrix by forcing $w_{ij} \leq a_{ij}$, so the absence of influence implies zero weight. Though atypical for social network analysis, we include a self-link ($a_{ii} = 1$) so that agents update their opinions based on their own current opinions.

2.1.2. Transformations

The purpose of our method is to fit the above model, producing estimates for the parameters in the weight matrix W, using observed opinions across T time steps on a network of N agents. Ideally, we would be able to observe the continuous opinions, on the interval [0, 1], of all agents across T time steps $(X(0), X(1), ..., X(T-1))$. In practice, opinions are typically measured using a Likert or other ordinal scale in behavioral and social science research. As such, we assume the continuous opinions are shared with network contacts without error according to the DeGroot model, but researchers are only able to measure these opinions on an n-point ordinal scale $(Y(0), Y(1), ..., Y(T-1))$. To be consistent with the model, we assume these ordinal data possess interval properties. A common approach when using ordinal data, this is necessary to perform any mathematical operations and is implicit in the use of a composite scale. We convert between ordinal and continuous opinions using the following process:

Forward Transformation

1. Begin with data on an n-point ordinal scale, converting to a 1 to n scale if necessary.
2. Divide the interval $[0, 1]$ into n sub-intervals of equal width.
3. An opinion of y on the ordinal scale takes on the middle value, x, in the yth sub-interval on the continuous scale.

Back Transformation

1. Begin with data on a continuous $[0, 1]$ interval to be converted to an n-point ordinal scale.
2. Multiply the continuous opinion x by n.
3. Round the multiplied continuous opinion up to an integer (ceiling function) to produce an opinion on the ordinal scale. (This final step does not work for the edge case where $x = 0$, so any such values are automatically converted to an ordinal value of 1.)

This process is also presented graphically in Figure 1 using a 5-point ordinal scale. For example, an ordinal opinion of 4 is converted to a continuous opinion of 0.7, the center of the 4th sub-interval or *bin* from 0.6 to 0.8, and any continuous opinion on that sub-interval are converted back to an ordinal opinion of 4.

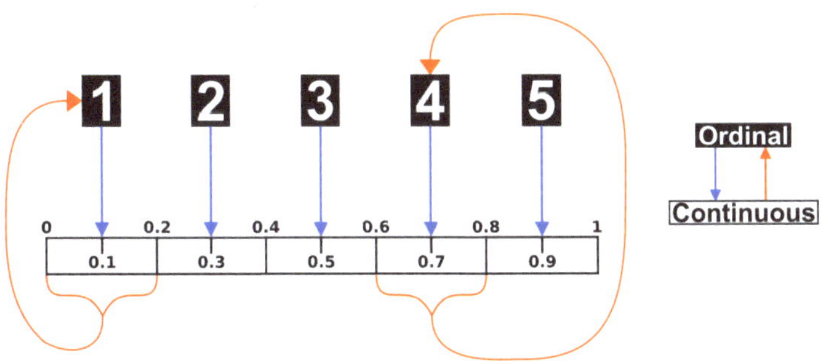

Figure 1. Transformation procedure for a 5-point ordinal scale.

2.1.3. Objective Function

Our selected objective function incorporates opinions on both the continuous and ordinal scales, accounting for an important feature of the back-transformation process: a range of continuous opinions map back to a single ordinal opinion. We use

$$f(\hat{X}, X) = \sum_{i=1}^{N} \sum_{t=0}^{T-1} B(\hat{x}_i(t), x_i(t)) |\hat{x}_i(t) - x_i(t)|, \tag{2a}$$

where N is the number of agents in the network and $B(\hat{x}_i(t), x_i(t))$ measures the absolute deviation between the observed and predicted opinions on the ordinal scale, measured in *bins*. This allows us to penalize deviation from the center of the correct interval on the continuous scale only if the observed and predicted opinions also differ on the ordinal scale ($B(\hat{x}_i(t), x_i(t)) \neq 0$). Though this objective function is well-suited for our goal of fitting a model based on observed ordinal opinions, the inclusion of $B(\hat{x}_i(t), x_i(t))$ presents problems for any optimization method requiring continuity or differentiability. We also expect many perfect solutions ($f(\hat{X}, X) = 0$) will fail to recover the parameters, particularly for less precise ordinal scales (ones with fewer points) and fewer time steps. This objective function can also be assessed on a chromosome or agent level by excluding the sum across agents:

$$f(\hat{x}_i, x_i) = \sum_{t=0}^{T-1} B(\hat{x}_i(t), x_i(t)) |\hat{x}_i(t) - x_i(t)|, \tag{2b}$$

which we leverage as part of the gene-swapping procedure in Section 2.2.1.

2.2. Genetic Algorithm

We use the genetic algorithm to identify the parameters of the DeGroot model, in the form of the weight matrix W, that minimize the objective function. A chromosome is defined as the weight matrix W and a gene as a row of W, denoted W_i and representing the sources and strength of influence on agent i. We begin with a population consisting of an odd number of chromosomes, consistent with any fixed values. These fixed values are usually zeros resulting from zeros in the adjacency matrix (See Section 2.1.1) but can be other known parameters. Though the user has the option to specify chromosomes, the default is a population of randomly generated chromosomes and an identity matrix. This population undergoes selection, blending, crossover, mutation, and survival operators, incorporating a gene-swapping procedure, to identify an optimal solution.

2.2.1. Gene Swapping

Since the objective function can be assessed on the individual– or gene–level, the fitness of a gene clearly does not directly depend on the other genes within the chromosome. Instead, the fitness of a gene W_i depends on the predicted opinions of the agents who influence agent i, as indicated by non-zero elements within W_i. Since these predicted opinions are a function of the genes corresponding to the agents who influence agent i, the fitness of a gene can be assessed independently of other genes within the chromosome but does depend those other genes. We use this ability to assess fitness at the gene level while accounting for dependencies in our gene-swapping process.

At any point in the algorithm where we identify the fittest chromosome, we assess the fitness of each gene within that chromosome and for all other chromosomes. If the overall fittest chromosome B contains a gene B_i which is less fit than the corresponding gene C_i in a less fit chromosome C, we swap B_i and C_i between the two chromosomes to produce B^* and C^*. We retain this change for both chromosomes if B^* is fitter than B and revert to B and C otherwise. In the case where the less fit population contains multiple chromosomes, we swap all fitter genes at once, either retaining all swaps or reverting to the original chromosome B. This helps prevent the loss of a fit gene in an otherwise unfit chromosome while ensuring the best solution identified so far is retained.

2.2.2. Operators

We apply selection, blending, crossover, mutation, and survival operators to our population of chromosomes. The application of all operators constitutes a single iteration of the algorithm and produces a new generation of chromosomes. We use "iteration" and "generation" interchangeably except where a distinction between the process of producing a new generation (in this case referred to as an iteration) and the generation itself is meaningful. We repeat the process until stopping criterion are met, modifying the behavior of the operators as the generations progress to shift from exploration of the parameter space to exploitation of existing solutions, making this an adaptive genetic algorithm as suggested by the literature [2,17–19]. Descriptions of the operators that include examples are available in Johnson et al. and the code is linked in the Data Availability Statement [9].

Selection: In order to preserve the best solution identified in any previous generation, we use selection with elitism: identifying the fittest chromosome (the chromosome producing the lowest value of the objective function), and exempting it from the remaining operators until the next generation. After identifying the elite chromosome, we attempt gene swapping between that chromosome and the remaining population of non-elite chromosomes. We exempt either the original elite chromosome or row-swapped elite chromosome, depending on the fitness of each, and proceed with either the original remaining population or the row-swapped remaining population as appropriate.

Blending: Using the even number of chromosomes remaining after the selection operator, we randomly pair all chromosomes. For each pair of chromosomes, blending occurs independently for each gene with probability p_b. For a pair of chromosomes B and C, if blending occurs for row i, a blending factor β is drawn from a $Unif(0,1)$ distribution. The new genes (B_i^* and C_i^*) are the weighted averages of the current genes and corresponding genes from the paired chromosome according to:

$$B_i^* = \beta B_i + (1-\beta)C_i \quad \text{and} \quad C_i^* = (1-\beta)B_i + \beta C_i. \tag{3}$$

While this can result in substantial changes to genes B_i and C_i when these genes are very different, we use the blending operator primarily to make slight changes to a population of similar chromosomes for later generations in order to refine a solution as we shift from exploration to exploitation, meaning we begin with a lower value of p_b and increase the probability over time.

Crossover: The within-parent crossover operator defined by Limmun, Borkowski, and Chomtee uses a crossover point after the decimal point, resulting in small changes to the genes [2]. Since both the blending and mutation operator either already accomplish this goal or can easily be modified in later generations to do so, we use a more drastic version of this operator to explore our much larger parameter space. Crossover occurs independently for each gene within each chromosome with probability p_c, with all values not fixed at zero randomly reshuffled within the gene, preserving the sum-to-one constraint and any fixed values. Since exploring the parameter space is desirable during early generations, but drastic changes to chromosomes are not helpful in later generations, we begin with a higher value of p_c which decreases over time.

Mutation: While the mutation operator is also used to make slight changes to genes for later generations, the primary purpose of this operator is to explore the boundaries of the parameter space: solutions where a gene contains a weight where $w_{ij} = 1$ and all others are zero (or with $w_{ij} = 1 - w_{fixed}$ where w_{fixed} is the sum of all fixed weights within the row). Since our method for generating the initial population of chromosomes–drawing each weight from a $Unif(0,1)$ distribution and scaling the rows to sum to one–will not result in any edge cases other than the identity matrix included in the initial population, this is necessary in order to consider edge cases as potential solutions. Mutation occurs independently for all genes within each chromosome with probability p_m. If mutation occurs, ε is drawn from a $N(0, \sigma^2)$ distribution and added to a randomly selected weight within the gene to produce $w^* = w + \varepsilon$, and all other non-fixed weights are scaled by $\frac{1}{1-w_{fixed}-w^*}$ to preserve the sum-to-one constraint. We handle edge cases as follows:

- If $w^* < 0$, w^* is set to 0, with scaling of other non-fixed weights as above.
- If $w^* > 1 - w_{fixed}$, w^* is set to $1 - w_{fixed}$. All other non-fixed weights in the row are set to 0.
- If the selected weight $w = 1 - w_{fixed}$, the excess weight of $1 - w_{fixed} - w^*$ is evenly distributed between all other non-fixed weights within the row.

Survival: After the preceding operators, our population of chromosomes includes the elite chromosome, the parent chromosomes (the chromosomes from the previous generation), and the offspring chromosomes (the chromosomes from the current generation, having undergone the selection, crossover, and mutation operators). For each pair of parent and offspring chromosomes, we identify the fittest chromosome and attempt gene swapping with the other chromosome. The fittest chromosome from each pair after the attempted gene swapping along with the elite chromosome constitute the current generation and become the parent chromosomes for the next generation.

2.2.3. Other Features

As discussed in the descriptions of the operators, we use an adaptive genetic algorithm where each operator becomes more or less important as the generations progress, and the mutation operator in particular can be modified to serve a different purpose. This allows us to begin with a focus on exploration of the parameter space and progressively move to refining existing solutions (exploitation). For the sake of clarity, we will refer to the values controlling behavior of the individual operators, the operator probabilities (p_b,p_c,p_m) and σ, as *control parameters* and reserve the term *hyperparameters* for the user-specified values that govern the overall behavior of the algorithm, including the way the control parameters are modified within the algorithm. We modify the control parameters by applying a multiplicative adjustment whenever a specified number of generations without improvement is reached. For example, $p_b^* = cp_b$ for the specified constant c where p_b^* is the new value of the probability of blending.

We apply a similar process with chromosome reintroduction: reintroducing either a clone of the elite chromosome or an identity matrix after a specified number of generations without improvement. Reintroducing a clone of the elite chromosome allows slight changes to the current best solution—facilitating exploitation—while still preserving this solution in the selection operator. Reintroducing an identity matrix reinforces a prior belief that agents place high weight on their own opinions. In either case, the reintroduced chromosome replaces the least fit chromosome in the population.

2.3. *Algorithm Calibration*

In this section, we explain all aspects of the simulation study to calibrate the algorithm, detailing the hyperparameters and our approach for condensing them into groups, describing the procedure for the simulation study, and presenting the measure used to assess algorithm performance. Though tuning approaches such as the Chess Rating System (CRS-tuning), Relevance Estimation and Value Calibration (REVAC), and F-race are available, the simulation study approach, overviewed in Figure 2, better suits our objectives [8,20]. The simulation study facilitates investigating the relationship between hyperparameter values and performance and providing accessible suggestions to algorithm users based on the results while acknowledging that both the relationship and suggestions may depend on network or dataset characteristics.

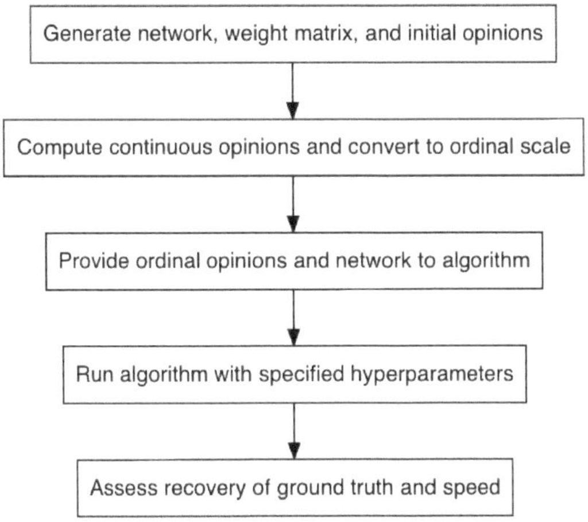

Figure 2. Procedure for algorithm calibration.

F-race identifies a set or sets of hyperparameters that are statistically significantly better than others; however, our goal is not to identify an ideal set of hyperparameters based on an arbitrary threshold but to characterize the behavior of the algorithm under various hyperparameter combinations [21]. While CRS-tuning does address the concerns of the binary include or exclude through the use of a ranking system, this raking does not contain the information necessary for users to develop intuition about how the different hyperparameters affect algorithm behavior [22]. Since REVAC identifies a marginal distribution of high-performing values for each hyperparameter that approximates the maximum Shannon entropy distribution, this approach produces a distribution of values instead of a single value, and the relevance of each parameter can be measured [23,24]. While these are both appealing, the simulation study allows for an assessment of relevance through the relationship between the values used and algorithm performance while also presenting this overall relationship in an accessible manner that incorporates network and dataset features.

2.3.1. Hyperparameters

Table 1 contains all of the hyperparameters used in the algorithm. Since most are considered in the simulation study, we highlight the ones that are not: `max_iter`, `min_improve`, `min_dev`, and `reintroduce`. In all simulations, we run the algorithm until we either reach 100,000 iterations (`max_iter=100,000`) or identify a perfect solution on the ordinal scale (`min_dev=0`). Note that this check is only applied every thousand generations. We do not specify a minimum change in the objective function that is considered an improvement (`min_improve=0`) and reintroduce the elite chromosome (`reintroduce="elite"`).

To reduce the simulation study to a manageable size, we condense some of these hyperparameters to a single value or otherwise group them. We consider 200, 1000, and 5000 generations without improvement before modifying control parameters or reintroducing a chromosome, using the same value for all relevant hyperparameters (`iterb`, `iterc`, `iterm`, `iters`, and `iterr`) within a run of the algorithm. The remaining hyperparameters are grouped into ProbSigma (`probb`, `probc`, `probm`, and `sigma`), MinMax (`maxb`, `minc`, `minm`, and `mins`), and MultFactor (`factorb`, `factorc`, `factorm`, `factors`). These groupings represent the starting values of the control parameters, the minimum or maximum values for the control parameters, and the factors for multiplicative adjustment to the control parameters, respectively. Since the hyperparameters within a group cannot reasonably be set to the same value, we instead define three levels for each group with differing values of each hyperparameter but consistent goals or concepts.

Table 1. Name and description of all hyperparameters used in the algorithm.

Hyperparameter	Description
`chromosomes`	Number of chromosomes
`probb`	Initial probability of blending (p_b)
`factorb`	Multiplicative factor for modifying p_b
`maxb`	Maximum value of p_b
`iterb`	Number of iterations with no improvement before modifying p_b
`probc`	Initial probability of crossover (p_c)
`factorc`	Multiplicative factor for modifying p_c
`minc`	Minimum value of p_c
`iterc`	Number of iterations with no improvement before modifying p_c
`probm`	Initial probability of blending (p_m)
`factorm`	Multiplicative factor for modifying p_m
`minm`	Minimum value of p_m
`iterm`	Number of iterations with no improvement before modifying p_m
`sigma`	Initial value of standard deviation σ of ε for mutation operator
`factors`	Multiplicative factor for modifying σ
`mins`	Minimum value of σ
`iters`	Number of iterations with no improvement before modifying σ
`max_iter`	Maximum number of iterations to run algorithm
`min_improve`	Minimum decrease in value of objective function considered an improvement
`min_dev`	Acceptable value of objective function for stopping algorithm
`reintroduce`	Type of chromosome to be reintroduced
`iterr`	Number of iterations with no improvement before reintroducing chromosome

For ProbSigma, we use *low*, *medium*, and *high* to indicate whether we use low, medium, or high initial values for the control parameters. Table 2 shows the specific hyperparameter values corresponding to each level for ProbSigma. For MinMax, we use *minimal*, *moderate*, and *extreme* to specify whether we applied minimal, moderate, or extreme restrictions on the minimum or maximum value of each control parameter. The specific values corresponding to each level for MinMax are in Table 3. Note that the *minimal* level imposes no restrictions on the probabilities beyond those either implied as probabilities or possible through a multiplicative adjustment. Finally, we use *slow*, *moderate*, and *rapid* levels for MultFactor, indicating whether the multiplicitive factors used will result in slow, moderate, or rapid changes to the control parameters, with specific values for each level in Table 4.

Table 2. Grouping levels and hyperparameter values for ProbSigma.

Level	`probb`	`probc`	`probm`	`sigma`
Low	0.01	0.05	0.05	0.2
Medium	0.1	0.1	0.1	0.5
High	0.2	0.2	0.2	1

Table 3. Grouping levels and hyperparameter values for MinMax.

Level	`maxb`	`minc`	`minm`	`mins`
Minimal	1	0	0	0
Moderate	0.5	0.01	0.01	0.01
Extreme	0.2	0.05	0.05	0.05

Table 4. Grouping levels and hyperparameter values for MultFactor.

Level	`factorb`	`factorc`	`factorm`	`factors`
Slow	2	0.5	0.5	0.5
Moderate	5	0.2	0.2	0.2
Rapid	10	0.1	0.1	0.1

2.3.2. Procedure

The hyperparameters and features of the social network and opinion diffusion process considered in the simulation study are in Table 5. We use each combination for ten runs of the algorithm, generating a new network, weight matrix, and dataset each time. First, we generate an Erdős–Rényi network, to represent a cluster within a larger network, of the specified size and target degree, rejecting any disconnected networks (networks that do not include a path between every pair of agents). We generate a weight matrix using a target self-weight of $w_{ii} = 0.5$, drawn from a beta distribution with $\kappa = \alpha + \beta = 4$, and draw all other weights from a $Unif(0,1)$ distribution, scaling all weights other than the self-weight to maintain the sum-to-one constraint. Note that this approach results in a ground truth that is biased against edge cases, as is the population of initial chromosomes other than the identity matrix. Then, we draw initial opinions ($X(0)$) from a $Unif(0,1)$ distribution, using these and the weight matrix to generate "true" opinions across the specified number of time steps ($X(1), ..., X(T-1)$). Finally, we convert the latent, continuous opinions to the appropriate ordinal scale to produce observed opinions ($Y(0), ..., Y(T-1)$), using the back-transformation process (See Section 2.1.2). We provide the adjacency matrix representing the generated network and the observed opinions to the algorithm, using the specified hyperparameter values.

Table 5. Inputs used in the hyperparameters simulation study.

Input	Values	Notes
Network Size	$N = 4, 20, 50$	reachability enforced
Mean Degree	$d = 2, 5, 9$	minimum degree $d = 1$ for all nodes
Self-weight	$w_{ii} = 0.5$	beta distribution with $\kappa = \alpha + \beta = 4$
Time Steps	$T = 2, 3, 6$	
Scale Bins	$n = 5, 7, 10, 20, 30$	
Chromosomes	5, 21, 51, 99	`chromosomes` hyperapramete r
ProbSigma	low, medium, high	(see Table 2)
MinMax	minimal, moderate, extreme	(see Table 3)
MultFactor	slow, moderate, rapid	(see Table 4)

2.3.3. Measures

Optimal hyperparameters would quickly identify a perfect solution in terms of the objective function. Ideally, this perfect solution would also result in good parameter recovery. Since how quickly the algorithm identifies a solution can be measured in both number of generations and time, we record the amount of time and the number of generations to reach a solution, both measured in thousand-generation increments. Simulations were run on a custom desktop with a Ryzen 9 3950X CPU with 64 GB of 3000 MHz RAM on Ubuntu Server 21.10 and Julia 1.5—using a single thread per run of the algorithm—and use `@elapsed` to time in thousand-generation increments [25]. We assess parameter recovery using root-mean-square-error (RMSE) according to

$$RMSE_{rec} = \sqrt{\frac{\sum_{i=1}^{N}\sum_{j=1}^{N}(w_{ij} - \hat{w}_{ij})^2}{\sum_{i=1}^{N}\sum_{j=1}^{N}a_{ij}}} = \sqrt{\frac{\sum_{i=1}^{P}(w_p - \hat{w}_p)^2}{P}}, \tag{4}$$

where P is the number of elements not fixed at zero in the weight matrix (the number of parameters to be estimated) and w_p is the pth non-structurally-zero element, with w_p and

$\hat{w}_p$ representing the true and estimated weights, respectively. Though we also assessed the ability of the algorithm to model the latent opinions on the observed time steps and predict future latent opinions in Johnson et al., parameter recovery implies the other outcomes and is not possible to measure in practical applications [15]. As such, selecting hyperparameters that improve parameter recovery is our priority.

3. Results

To provide context for this section, note that the existence of a perfect solution is guaranteed (the ground truth used to generate the data) but many "perfect" solutions that fail to recover the parameters are expected, particularly for runs with imprecise ordinal scales (i.e., few bins) and few time steps. Overall, the algorithm identified a perfect solution very quickly regardless of the hyperparameters used, with 67.7% of runs finding a solution within the first 1000 generations. Only 4.5% of runs failed to identify a perfect solution within 100,000 generations, though the largest value of the objective function for these runs was 0.02, representing a good—but imperfect—solution. Since we prioritize recovery over either measure of speed, we begin by assessing the hyperparameters that produce the best recovery. Informed by the results on recovery, we assess speed in number of iterations, the measure independent of the computer used. Finally, we present results on computation time to provide context on the trade-off between time per generation and number of generations.

3.1. Parameter Recovery

Figure 3 shows parameter recovery RMSE by number of generations without improvement before the control parameters are modified and the elite chromosome reintroduced, the only set of hyperparameters that produces a notable difference in parameter recovery. This plot includes only the subset of the data where a perfect solution was identified within the first 1000 generations to illustrate our next point, but the features seen in this plot hold for the full dataset. Clearly, using 200 generations without improvement results in the best parameter recovery. Nothing that the populations of chromosomes requiring either 1000 or 5000 generations without improvement could not possibly have begun the exploitation phase within 1000 generations, this initially seems intuitive since we would expect solutions resulting from the exploitation phase to be better. Unfortunately, this does not explain the results since all the solutions presented here are perfect in terms of the value of the objective function. Instead, we must explain why perfect solutions identified during the exploration phase have worse recovery that perfect solutions identified during the exploitation phase.

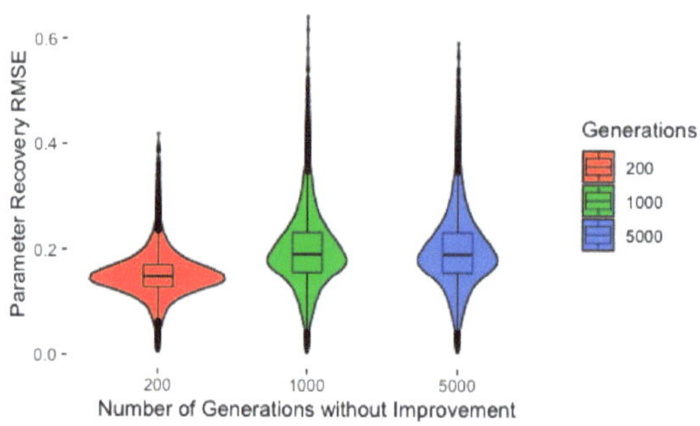

Figure 3. Boxplots and violin plots for root-mean-square-error for recovery by number of generations without improvement for runs that identified a solution with 1000 generations.

To do so, we revisit the intended purpose of the exploration process. During early iterations of the algorithm, we use control parameter values that result in drastic changes to the chromosomes and force—to varying degrees depending on the ProbSigma hyperparameters—the exploration of edge cases. As noted in our description of the procedures, our process for generating the true parameters is biased against edge cases. Consequently, populations forced to search the boundaries of the parameter space will identify solutions with poor recovery. Figure 4 supports this assertion by showing parameter recovery for 200, 1000, or 5000 generations without improvement by level of ProbSigma and number of time steps. For the purpose of transparency, this plot uses the full dataset. We use the number of time steps as a proxy for the prevalence of perfect solutions in the parameter space and include ProbSigma as it governs the extent to which early generations are forced to explore edge cases (The precision of the ordinal scale is also indicative of the ease of finding a perfect solution and demonstrates the same phenomenon seen in Figure 4. We selected number of time steps because the fewer levels of that factor improve readability of the plot).

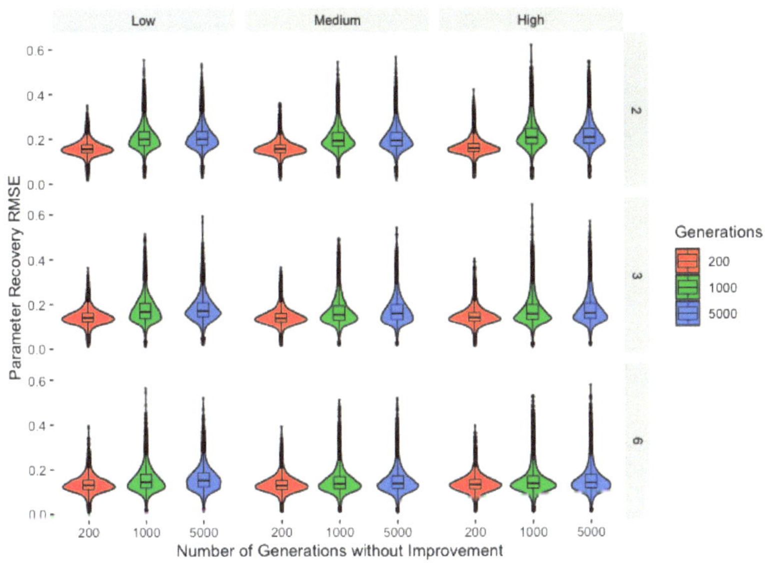

Figure 4. Boxplots and violin plots for root-mean-square-error for recovery by number of generations without improvement with ProbSigma hyperparameter levels (horizontal) and number of time steps (vertical) across facets.

Comparing across number of time steps, we see the difference in parameter recovery between different numbers of generations without improvement decreases as the number of time steps increases (decreasing the number of potential perfect solutions). This supports our assertion that the poor parameter recovery is the result of forcing the algorithm to search the boundaries, where any solutions identified will inherently result in poor recovery. When an increased number of time steps makes it more difficult to identify an edge-case solution, the threshold for number of generations without improvement can then be reached, starting the transition away from the exploration phase and pulling the chromosomes away from the boundary. As expected, high values for the hyperparameters in the ProbSigma group—corresponding to the *high* level—appear to exacerbate this difference since larger values of the control parameter σ apply stronger pressure to search the boundaries. It is much more difficult to assess any differences between the *low* and *medium* levels, but the level of ProbSigma also controls the values of p_b, p_c, and p_m, any of which could have a moderating effect on the value of σ.

3.2. Generations

While the poor parameter recovery with 1000 or 5000 generations without improvement when the ground truth is biased against edge cases does not necessarily imply they will perform poorly in practical applications, having $\frac{2}{3}$ of our runs identify a solution within 1000 generations does suggest lower values may be a better choice. Figure 5, showing the log-transformed number of generations to a solution by number of generations without improvement, further supports that 200 generations is a better choice. 200 generations consistently requires the fewest generations necessary to find a solution, though it also has the highest density of runs requiring 100,000 generations, suggesting a slight tendency to transition from the exploration phase too quickly and become stuck near a local minima that is not a perfect solution. We will consider only 200 generations without improvement for the remainder of these results.

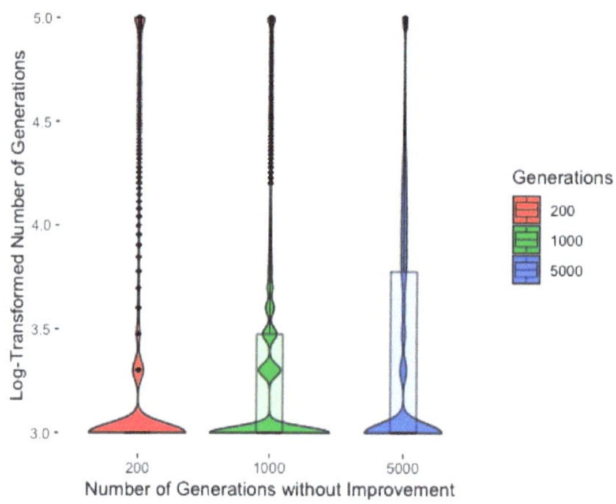

Figure 5. Boxplots and violin plots for log (base 10) number of generations to solution by number of generations without improvement. The absence of a box for 200 generations without improvement indicates that the median, first quartile, and third quartile are the same.

Figure 6 shows the log-transformed number of generations to a solution by number of chromosomes. Unsurprisingly, five chromosomes typically requires more generations to identify a solution and also has the most runs reaching 100,000 generations. Though each iteration would be completed more quickly with only five chromosomes, the iterations are much less efficient. Five chromosomes also resulted in slightly worse recovery overall, though this difference is barely discernible in a plot, so we remove five chromosomes from consideration. ProbSigma, MinMax, and MultFactor all showed minimal difference in number of iterations to find a solution across the varying levels.

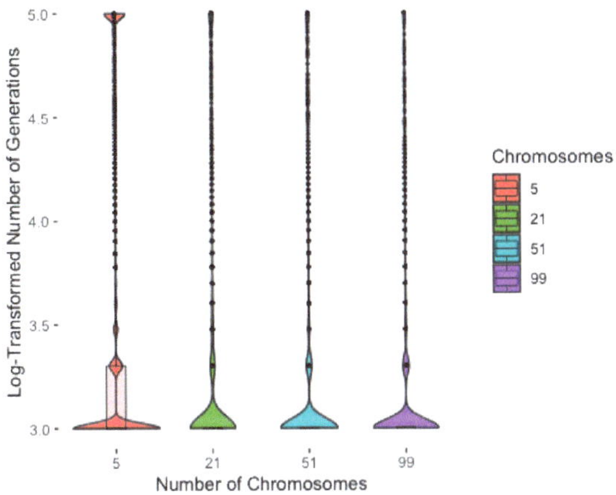

Figure 6. Boxplots and violin plots for log (base 10) number of generations to solution by number of chromosomes for 200 generations without improvement. The absence of a box for 21 or more chromosomes indicates that the median, first quartile, and third quartile are the same.

3.3. *Time*

Figure 7 shows the time to identify a solution on the log scale by number of chromosomes, with median times to identify a solution of 4.7 s, 11.0 s, and 19.3 s for 21, 51, and 99 chromosomes, respectively. This demonstrates that, for the computer used to conduct the simulation study, the efficiency of using fewer chromosomes outweighs any potential reduction in number of generations from using more chromosomes. Since the number of chromosomes used—after excluding 5—had little effect on the number of generations required to identify a solution, we expect this to be true for most users. It should also be noted that, while the magnitude of the differences in time are substantial on the scale used, these differences are fairly negligible in practice. The exception to this is for conditions that are known to increase computation time, such as large and high-degree networks. Since computational time scales roughly linearly with the number of chromosomes ($O(n)$ complexity), using a high number of chromosomes can substantially increase computation time under these conditions.

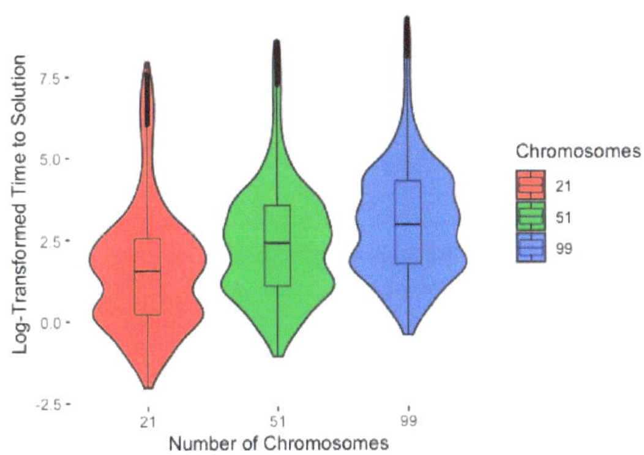

Figure 7. Boxplots and violin plots for log time to identify a solution (in seconds) by number of chromosomes for 200 generations without improvement.

4. Discussion

While we discuss the following specifically in the context of the opinion diffusion application, the hyperparameters of concern are the result of a parameter space with many perfect solutions other than the parameters used to generate the data. The behavior and suggestions for mitigation, along with the associated operator modifications, are relevant to other applications of genetic algorithms under similar conditions. Overall, the algorithm is fairly robust to the hyperparameter values selected, with number of generations without improvement (`iterb`, `iterc`, `iterm`, `iters`, and `iterr`) and number of chromosomes (`chromosomes`) being notable exceptions. We recommend using at least 21 chromosomes, though using more should have minimal practical impact on computation time, except in cases where the networks are large—increasing the size of the chromosomes—or more dense—making the chromosomes less sparse. For the hyperparameters in the ProbSigma, MinMax, and MultFactor groupings, we suggest values close to those in the *medium* and *moderate* levels simply because they fall roughly in the center of ranges of values demonstrated to perform well. The exception to this suggestion is when users may seek to use these hyperparameters to mitigate undesirable effects from the number of generations without improvement.

The results suggest using 200 generations without improvement is a good starting point for all relevant hyperparameters because of both the performance in recovering parameters and the low number of generations typically needed to find a solution. While the number of generations to identify a solution may increase in practical applications—without a guaranteed solution and with agents missing from the network—the user will receive this feedback and can adjust accordingly. We identified the bias against edge cases inherent in our weight matrix generation process as an explanation for the poor parameter recovery for runs using either 1000 or 5000 generations without improvement, pointing to `iters`—which triggers the change to the control parameter σ within the mutation operator—as the hyperparameter of concern. The choice of `itetrs` is the one decision where we encourage caution and careful consideration, particularly because the consequences are not just poor efficiency but also poor recovery.

While the bias against edge cases is clear in the networks used in this simulation study, the extent to which this is a concern for real-world opinion diffusion processes is unknown. Networks of stubborn individuals would be biased toward the boundary, while networks of highly receptive individuals could be biased either toward or away from the boundary, depending on whether they have preexisting opinions on the topic. Unfortunately, it is not possible to distinguish between these cases using the opinion data since consistent opinions across time could indicate either stubborn individuals or receptive individuals only connected to those with similar opinions. As such, it would be irresponsible to intentionally direct the algorithm toward or away from the boundaries using the hyperparameter. Instead, the user must find a balance between forcing the algorithm to search only the boundaries or beginning the exploitation phase without first exploring the boundaries. Recall that, since the method for generating the initial chromosomes is also biased against edge cases, setting the initial probability of mutation (`probm`) to zero or making the initial value of the control parameter σ (`sigma`) very small is not a viable solution, avoiding concerns about becoming stuck at the boundary by preventing the algorithm from exploring them at all.

As with the other hyperparameters controlling the number of generations without improvement before the control parameters are modified and the elite chromosome reintroduced, our recommendation for finding this balance for `iters` is to test different values and make modifications based on the feedback. Users can decrease the value of `iters` if the algorithm consistently identifies solutions at the boundary or increase `iters` to ensure they are being searched. A value closer to one for `factors` can also be used to control how quickly the algorithm moves away from the boundaries, mitigating the choice of an inappropriately low value of `iters`. Since the number of generations without improvement must be reached for `factors` to be relevant, this is not an option for correcting inappropriately high values of `iters`. Though not directly tied to the hyperparameters, using more time steps or a more precise scale can minimize the effect of `iters` by decreasing the prevalence of perfect solutions with poor recovery, which we already suggest as they improve overall performance of the method.

In summary, we suggest at least 21 chromosomes, values close to the *medium* and *moderate* levels for the ProbSigma, MinMax, and MultFactor groupings, and setting `iterb`, `iterc`, `iterm`, `iters`, and `iterr` to 200 as initial values. Users should assess performance with these values and make modifications as necessary. Since inappropriate values of `iters` inhibit a proper search of the parameter space, especially when used with a high value of `sigma`, we strongly recommend paying close attention to this hyperparameter. In cases where forcing a search of only the boundaries is of particular concern, such as datasets with limited time steps and imprecise ordinal scales, users can use a conservative (low) value of `iters`, mitigating concerns about failing to explore the edge cases by using values of `factors` closer to one. While all the discussion surrounding `iters` may seem intimidating, we want to highlight that the algorithm is robust to the choices of all but a few hyperparameter values, all of which are discussed here and for which initial, if not default, values are suggested.

Author Contributions: Conceptualization, K.L.J. and N.B.C.; methodology, K.L.J.; software, K.L.J.; validation, K.L.J.; formal analysis, K.L.J.; investigation, K.L.J.; data curation, K.L.J.; writing—original draft preparation, K.L.J.; writing—review and editing, K.L.J. and N.B.C.; visualization, K.L.J.; supervision, N.B.C.; project administration, N.B.C.; funding acquisition, N.B.C. All authors have read and agreed to the published version of the manuscript.

Funding: This work was partially funded by NIH grants R01AI147441 and R01NR017574.

Institutional Review Board Statement: Not applicable.

Informed Consent Statement: Not applicable.

Data Availability Statement: The data generated and analysed during the simulation study are available in the file "hyper.csv.zip" in the corresponding author's GitHub repository: https://github.com/karajohnson4/DeGrootGeneticAlgorithm. The genetic algorithm code is also available in the corresponding author's GitHub repository under the name Algorithm-Code The Algorithms-archive branch will serve as an archived version. The code is written in Julia, is platform independent, requires Julia 1.5 or higher, and uses the GNU GENERAL PUBLIC LICENSE [25].

Conflicts of Interest: The authors declare no conflict of interest. The funders had no role in the design of the study; in the collection, analyses, or interpretation of data; in the writing of the manuscript, or in the decision to publish the results.

Abbreviations

The following abbreviations are used in this manuscript:

SODM	stochastic opinion dynamics model
BFO	bacterial foraging optimization
PSO	particle swarm optimization
SCBFO	self-adaptive chemotaxis strategy bacterial foraging optimization
CRS	Chess Rating System
REVAC	Relevance Estimation and Value Calibration
RMSE	root-mean-square error

References

1. Haldurai, L.; Madhubala, T.; Rajalakshmi, R. A study on genetic algorithm and its applications. *Int. J. Comput. Sci. Eng.* **2016**, *4*, 139.
2. Limmun, W.; Borkowski, J.J.; Chomtee, B. Using a genetic algorithm to generate D-optimal designs for mixture experiments. *Qual. Reliab. Eng. Int.* **2013**, *29*, 1055–1068. [CrossRef]
3. Whitley, D. A genetic algorithm tutorial. *Stat. Comput.* **1994**, *4*, 65–85. [CrossRef]

4. Kumar, M.; Husain, M.; Upreti, N.; Gupta, D. Genetic Algorithm: Review and Application. 2010. Available online: https://ssrn.com/abstract=3529843 (accessed on 14 December 2021).
5. Holland, J.H. Genetic algorithms and adaptation. In *Adaptive Control of Ill-Defined Systems*; Springer: Berlin/Heidelberg, Germany, 1984; pp. 317–333.
6. Sampson, J.R. Adaptation in natural and artificial systems (John H. Holland). *SIAM Rev.* **1976**, *18*, 529–530. [CrossRef]
7. Harik, G.R.; Lobo, F.G. A parameter-less genetic algorithm. In Proceedings of the GECCO, Orlando FL, USA, 13–17 July 1999; Volume 99, pp. 258–267.
8. Eiben, A.E.; Smit, S.K. Parameter tuning for configuring and analyzing evolutionary algorithms. *Swarm Evol. Comput.* **2011**, *1*, 19–31. [CrossRef]
9. Johnson, K.L.; Walsh, J.L.; Amirkhanian, Y.A.; Borkowski, J.J.; Carnegie, N.B. Using a novel genetic algorithm to assess peer influence on willingness to use pre-exposure prophylaxis in networks of Black men who have sex with men. *Appl. Netw. Sci.* **2021**, *6*, 1–40. [CrossRef] [PubMed]
10. Castro, L.E.; Shaikh, N.I. Influence estimation and opinion-tracking over online social networks. *Int. J. Bus. Anal. (IJBAN)* **2018**, *5*, 24–42. [CrossRef]
11. Castro, L.E.; Shaikh, N.I. A particle-learning-based approach to estimate the influence matrix of online social networks. *Comput. Stat. Data Anal.* **2018**, *126*, 1–18. [CrossRef]
12. Salem, F.; Azab, M.; Mosaad, M. PV parameters estimation using different evolutionary algorithms. *J. Electr. Eng.* **2013**, *13*, 9–9.
13. Rini, D.P.; Shamsuddin, S.M.; Yuhaniz, S. Particle Swarm Optimization: Technique, System and Challenges. *Int. J. Comput. Appl.* **2011**, *1*. [CrossRef]
14. Chen, H.; Wang, L.; Di, J.; Ping, S. Bacterial foraging optimization based on self-adaptive chemotaxis strategy. *Comput. Intell. Neurosci.* **2020**, *2020*, 2630104. [CrossRef] [PubMed]
15. Johnson, K.L.; Walsh, J.L.; Amirkhanian, Y.A.; Carnegie, N.B. Performance of a Genetic Algorithm for Estimating DeGroot Opinion Diffusion Model Parameters for Health Behavior Interventions. *Int. J. Environ. Res. Public Health* **2021**, *18*, 13394. [CrossRef] [PubMed]
16. Grefenstette, J.J. Optimization of control parameters for genetic algorithms. *IEEE Trans. Syst. Man Cybern.* **1986**, *16*, 122–128. [CrossRef]
17. Tuson, A.L.; Ross, P. Adapting operator probabilities in genetic algorithms. Master's Thesis, Department of Artificial Intelligence, Univeristy of Edinburgh, Edinburgh, UK, 1995.
18. Črepinšek, M.; Liu, S.H.; Mernik, M. Exploration and exploitation in evolutionary algorithms: A survey. *ACM Comput. Surv. (CSUR)* **2013**, *45*, 1–33. [CrossRef]
19. Aleti, A.; Moser, I. A systematic literature review of adaptive parameter control methods for evolutionary algorithms. *ACM Comput. Surv. (CSUR)* **2016**, *49*, 1–35. [CrossRef]
20. Montero, E.; Riff, M.C.; Neveu, B. A beginner's guide to tuning methods. *Appl. Soft Comput.* **2014**, *17*, 39–51. [CrossRef]
21. Birattari, M.; Stützle, T.; Paquete, L.; Varrentrapp, K. A Racing Algorithm for Configuring Metaheuristics. In Proceedings of the Gecco, New York, NY, USA, 9–13 July 2002; Volume 2.
22. Veček, N.; Mernik, M.; Filipič, B.; Črepinšek, M. Parameter tuning with Chess Rating System (CRS-Tuning) for meta-heuristic algorithms. *Inf. Sci.* **2016**, *372*, 446–469. [CrossRef]
23. Nannen, V.; Eiben, A.E. Efficient relevance estimation and value calibration of evolutionary algorithm parameters. In Proceedings of the 2007 IEEE Congress on Evolutionary Computation, Singapore, 25–28 September 2007; pp. 103–110.
24. Rudolph, G.; Jansen, T.; Lucas, S.M.; Poloni, C.; Beume, N. *Parallel Problem Solving from Nature-PPSN X: 10th International Conference Dortmund, Germany, 13–17 September 2008*; Springer: Berlin/Heidelberg, Germany, 2008; Volume 5199.
25. Bezanson, J.; Edelman, A.; Karpinski, S.; Shah, V.B. Julia: A fresh approach to numerical computing. *SIAM Rev.* **2017**, *59*, 65–98. [CrossRef]

algorithms

MDPI

Article

Parameter Optimization of Active Disturbance Rejection Controller Using Adaptive Differential Ant-Lion Optimizer

Qibing Jin and Yuming Zhang *

College of Information Science and Technology, Beijing University of Chemical Technology, Beijing 100020, China; jinqb@mail.buct.edu.cn
* Correspondence: 2015400132@mail.buct.edu.cn; Tel.: +86-135-5276-0639

Abstract: Parameter optimization in the field of control engineering has always been a research topic. This paper studies the parameter optimization of an active disturbance rejection controller. The parameter optimization problem in controller design can be summarized as a nonlinear optimization problem with constraints. It is often difficult and complicated to solve the problem directly, and meta-heuristic algorithms are suitable for this problem. As a relatively new method, the ant-lion optimization algorithm has attracted much attention and study. The contribution of this work is proposing an adaptive ant-lion algorithm, namely differential step-scaling ant-lion algorithm, to optimize parameters of the active disturbance rejection controller. Firstly, a differential evolution strategy is introduced to increase the diversity of the population and improve the global search ability of the algorithm. Then the step scaling method is adopted to ensure that the algorithm can obtain higher accuracy in a local search. Comparison with existing optimizers is conducted for different test functions with different qualities, the results show that the proposed algorithm has advantages in both accuracy and convergence speed. Simulations with different algorithms and different indexes are also carried out, the results show that the improved algorithm can search better parameters for the controllers.

Keywords: antlion optimizer; heuristic algorithm; active disturbance rejection control

1. Introduction

Active disturbance rejection control (ADRC) is a promising and relatively new control technology, which was formally proposed by Han in 2009 [1], while the origin of ADRC could date back to the year of 1995 [2]. Its core idea is to treat both internal uncertainty and external disturbance as "generalized interference", estimate the generalized interference through a mechanism called "extended state observer (ESO)" in real time, and then compensate the generalized interference by a nonlinear feedback controller using the estimation of ESO. The greatest advantage of ADRC is that it only needs the relative order of the controlled object; thus, it is independent of a precise model of the controlled object. So far ADRC has been widely applied in many fields such as motion control [3], energy [4], chemical industry [5], power parafoil control [6], paper tension adjustment [7], and so on. ADRC has also shown broad commercial application value, one of the examples is InstaSPIN-MOTION motor control solution produced by Texas Instruments, which integrates ADRC inside to achieve high control performance.

Generally speaking, in the field of control engineering, how to obtain a set of controller parameters which can meet the specific performance index has always been a research topic. A set of optimized parameters can achieve better control performance, and this means a lot in industrial manufacturing, such as economic effects and even environment benefits. A properly designed and well-tuned ADRC can make the control system achieve good performance and robustness. However, in the design framework of origin ADRC, there are too many parameters that need to be adjusted, and the number of parameters will increase as the relative order of the controlled object increases. The number of parameters is one thing, the other complex thing is that these parameters interact with each other. Gao [8] proposed linear ADRC (LADRC) with scaling and a bandwidth parameterization method. The number of parameters of LADRC is successfully reduced to two, but the coupling effect between parameters still remains, and even becomes more obvious. Thus, it is rather difficult to analytically find the optimal parameters that can achieve good control performance. What's more, if LADRC is applied on industrial processes with time delay, due to the existence of time delay, the characteristic function of system is a pseudo polynomial, which makes it even impossible to have an analytical solution. Although it is easy to find a set of parameters that make the control system stable, how to find the optimal system performance parameters has always been a problem demanding prompt study.

On the other hand, the process of finding optimal parameters of a control system can be regarded as an optimization problem with system performance index as the objective function [9]. Usually, the optimization problem designed by this method is a non-convex optimization problem, and it is difficult to solve by conventional optimization methods, which urges researchers to find a new way to solve this kind of optimization problem. In recent years, with the development of digital computers, more and more researchers turned their attention to meta-heuristic algorithms to solve engineering and practical problems. Türk, Deveci, et al. [10] used a simulated annealing algorithm to improve an interval type-2 fuzzy sets and achieved an outstanding result for an electric charging station location problem. Demirel and Deveci [11] successfully optimized medium-scale airline crew pairing problems by a modified genetic algorithm. Meta-heuristic algorithms benefit from the use of random operators [12]. Random operators make these algorithms exhibit completely different behaviors from deterministic algorithms and that is the reason why meta-heuristic algorithms usually have stronger global search ability.

The ant-lion optimization (ALO) algorithm is a relatively new meta-heuristic algorithm developed by Mirjalili in 2015 [13], which is also a kind of bionics algorithm. The ant-lion algorithm simulates the unique behavior of antlion in the process of hunting, which is to build a funnel-shaped trap and throw sand at the prey after the prey enters the trap to accelerate its slide to the bottom of the pit, as shown in Figure 1. The significance of imitating this behavior is to accelerate the convergence rate of the algorithm. In addition, the idea of elitism is also introduced into ant-lion algorithm. By setting an elite antlion to affect all ants, the convergence speed of the algorithm is accelerated.

Figure 1. Pyramidal traps and predation behavior of antlions [13]. (**a**) Actual antlion traps; (**b**) Abstract drawing of antlion traps.

In recent years, ALO has attracted the attention of researchers and proved its success in many applications including feature selection [14,15], multi-layer perceptron optimization [16], optimal reactive power distribution power system [17], optimal reactive dispatch problem [18], system identification [19], distributed generation planning [20], networking [21] etc. The references mentioned here all indicate that ALO has impressive characteristics including fast convergence speed, good solution quality, easy implementation and small quantity of parameters. Motivated by these facts, we propose a modified ALO, known as differential step-scaling ant-lion algorithm (DSALO), to optimize the parameters of LADRC. This algorithm can explore the search space efficiently and has a promising accuracy by global and local exploration. To our knowledge, ALO has not been adopted to solve the parameter optimization problem of ADRC, so this literature can be a worthwhile exploration.

The main contributions of this literature are as follows:

- Differential evolution strategy is introduced into ALO to enhance the diversification of population in each iteration, which ensures the global exploration of the algorithm.
- A step-scaling method is integrated into ALO, which changes the step size according to the number of iterations. The step-scaling method can achieve a good balance of exploration and exploitation.
- DSALO algorithm is conducted on four representative test functions, compared with other algorithms to demonstrate its efficiency.
- DSALO is applied in the parameter optimization problem of ADRC. The results indicate that DSALO can search for better parameters.

The remainder of this work is organized as follows. Section 2 presents the original ALO briefly and proposes DSALO. Section 3 evaluates the proposed algorithm by using 4 test functions. In Section 4, DSALO algorithm is used to solve the parameter optimization problem of the active disturbance rejection controller. Finally, some conclusions and future directions are drawn in Section 5.

2. Differential Step-Scaling Antlion Algorithm

2.1. Antlion Algorithm

Ant-lion algorithm is a kind of meta-heuristic algorithm, which is inspired by the unique predation behavior of antlion, and it belongs to bionics algorithms. Antlions typically spend their larval years hunting and saving up energy, only reproducing as adults. As larvae, antlions use their jaws to dig a funnel-shaped sand pit and lie in wait for prey to appear. The edge of the pit is sharp enough to make it easy for the prey to fall into the pit. And when there's prey, the antlion will try to catch it. But the prey will do anything to get out of the pit, and that's where the antlion's unique hunting behavior comes in: it moves towards the prey and throws sand at the prey, stopping it from escaping and speeding it down to the bottom of the pit. When they get close enough to capture their prey, the antlion drags it underground to digest it, then returns to the surface, where it dumps the residue while repairing its sandpit and waiting for the next victim to arrive. The probability of an antlion catching prey is related to the size of the pit, and studies have shown that the size of the pit is positively correlated with the degree of hunger of the antlion [22]. The hungrier the antlion is, the larger the pit it digs, then the greater the chance of catching prey it has, which is what antlions have evolved to ensure the survival of the colony.

The ant-lion optimization algorithm is inspired by the interaction between predator antlion and prey ant in the sand pit. In order to describe this interaction, we need to first model the ant's walking route and the antlion's predation and reconstruction behavior respectively. Since ants typically conduct a random walk when searching for food, they can be modeled using the following vector:

$$X(t) = [0, cumsum(2r(t_1) - 1), cumsum(2r(t_2) - 1) \cdots cumsum(2r(t_{max}) - 1)] \quad (1)$$

where, *cumsum* represents the sum of the past time of the random function $r(t)$, and t_{max} represents the maximum number of iterations. $r(t)$ is a random function:

$$r(t) = \begin{cases} 1 & rand > 0.5 \\ 0 & rand \leq 0.5 \end{cases} \quad (2)$$

rand generates a random number evenly distributed between 0 and 1. Although the path of a single ant is random, reference [13] gives an example that this vector can ensure that the path of a colony of ants cover the entire search space.

It can be seen that for an individual ant, its walking route has already been determined when the algorithm is initialized. In addition, we need to define storage matrixes to store information about ants and antlions at each iteration:

$$M_A = \begin{bmatrix} A_{1,1} & A_{1,2} & \cdots & A_{1,d} \\ A_{2,1} & \vdots & \cdots & \vdots \\ \vdots & \vdots & \ddots & \vdots \\ A_{n,1} & \cdots & \cdots & A_{n,d} \end{bmatrix} \tag{3}$$

$$M_{AL} = \begin{bmatrix} AL_{1,1} & AL_{1,2} & \cdots & AL_{1,d} \\ AL_{2,1} & \vdots & \cdots & \vdots \\ \vdots & \vdots & \ddots & \vdots \\ AL_{n,1} & \cdots & \cdots & AL_{n,d} \end{bmatrix} \tag{4}$$

where $A_{i,j}$ represents the j-th dimension information of the i-th ant and $AL_{i,j}$ the corresponding information of the antlion. Each row in the two matrices represents a solution to the problem to be optimized. Moreover, we can define the position information of each ant and antlion as:

$$P_{A,i}(t) = [A_{i,1}, A_{i,2}, \ldots, A_{i,d}] \tag{5}$$

$$P_{AL,i}(t) = [AL_{i,1}, AL_{i,2}, \ldots, AL_{i,d}] \tag{6}$$

To evaluate the value of each solution, we need to calculate their fitness functions one by one and store the values of fitness functions in the following two matrices:

$$M_{OA} = \begin{bmatrix} f(A_{1,1}, A_{1,2}, \ldots, A_{1,d}) \\ f(A_{2,1}, A_{2,2}, \ldots, A_{2,d}) \\ \vdots \\ f(A_{n,1}, A_{n,2}, \ldots, A_{n,d}) \end{bmatrix} \tag{7}$$

$$M_{OAL} = \begin{bmatrix} f(AL_{1,1}, AL_{1,2}, \ldots, AL_{1,d}) \\ f(AL_{2,1}, AL_{2,2}, \ldots, AL_{2,d}) \\ \vdots \\ f(AL_{n,1}, AL_{n,2}, \ldots, AL_{n,d}) \end{bmatrix} \tag{8}$$

Thus, we can summarize the overall steps of the antlion algorithm:

The first step is the random walk of ants. All ants carry out the random walk according to Equation (1) and ensure that every dimension of ants carry out the random walk. In order to ensure that all ants are in the search space, the following formula is used to normalize the position of ants:

$$P^d_{A,n}(t) = \frac{\left(P^d_{A,n}(t) - minR\left(P^d_{A,n}\right)\right)\left(U^d(t) - L^d(t)\right)}{maxR\left(P^d_{A,n}\right) - \min R\left(P^d_{A,n}\right)} + L^d(t) \tag{9}$$

where $P^d_{A,n}(t)$ is defined as the d-th ant variable in the t-th iteration, $maxP\left(S^d_{A,n}\right)$ and $minP\left(S^d_{A,n}\right)$ represent the maximum and minimum value of the ant in the dimension respectively, $U^d(t)$ and $L^d(t)$ are the upper and lower limit of the dimension d in the t-th iteration.

The second step is to simulate the process of ants being trapped in the sand pit. In reality, the actions of ants will be affected by antlions. Therefore, in order to simulate this process, we need to use the following two expressions to update the upper and lower bounds of ants' random walk:

$$U_t^d(t) = \begin{cases} P_{AL}^d(t) + U_t^d & if\ rand > 0.5 \\ P_{AL}^d(t) - U_t^d & otherwise \end{cases} \tag{10}$$

$$L_t^d(t) = \begin{cases} P_{AL}^d(t) + L_t^d & if\ rand > 0.5 \\ P_{AL}^d(t) - L_t^d & otherwise \end{cases} \tag{11}$$

The third step is to simulate the antlion's trap-building process. To achieve this, a strategy called roulette wheel is introduced into the antlion algorithm. In the ant-lion algorithm, one ant can only correspond to one antlion, so roulette wheel strategy is used to determine which ant it can capture according to the fitness value of the antlion. This strategy has a high probability that a better-fit antlion will capture a better-fit ant.

The fourth step is to simulate the process of an antlion throwing sand to make its prey slide to the bottom of the pit. In the algorithm, we assume that antlions with better fitness build bigger traps. Although the ant is random, when it gets close to the antlion, the antlion throws sand at it and thus it slides to the bottom of the pit. From the perspective of mathematical model, it can be understood that the range of the ants' movements is getting smaller and smaller. Therefore, the algorithm uses the following conditions to update the upper and lower bounds of the ants' migration:

$$L^d(t) = \frac{L^d(t)}{I} \tag{12}$$

$$U^d(t) = \frac{U^d(t)}{I} \tag{13}$$

In Equations (12) and (13), the value of I is defined as $I = 10^w t_{current}/t_{max}$, where $t_{current}$ is the current iteration number, t_{max} is the maximum iteration number, and w is a value determined according to the current iteration number ($t_{current} > 0.1t_{max}$ then $w = 2$, $t_{current} > 0.5t_{max}$ then $w = 3$, $t_{current} > 0.7t_{max}$ then $w = 4$, $t_{current} > 0.9t_{max}$ then $w = 5$, $t_{current} > 0.95t_{max}$ then $w = 6$). By changing the value of w during different iterations, the accuracy of the algorithm search can be adjusted.

The fifth step is to simulate the process of the antlion capturing prey and rebuilding the trap. When the ant finally falls into the antlion's mouth and is captured by the antlion, the antlion burrows underground in its current position to digest the ant, and after digesting the antlion returns to the surface to reconstruct the trap. In the algorithm, this process is the updating of the fitness value of the antlion. Assuming that the antlion will only capture the ants with better fitness than itself, the position of the antlion after the capture is the same as that of the ant before. This process can be simulated by the following formula:

$$P_{AL,j}(t) = P_{A,i}(t),\ if\ f(P_{A,i}(t)) < f(P_{AL,j}(t)) \tag{14}$$

where $P_{AL,j}(t)$ is the position of the j-th antlion at t-th iteration, and $P_{A,i}(t)$ is the position of the i-th ant at t-th iteration. To achieve this behavior, it is needed to rank all $f(P_{AL,j}(t))$ and $f(P_{A,i}(t))$ in ascending order of their numeric value, then update the first N lines of $f(P_{AL,j}(t))$ to $f(P_{A,i}(t))$, and update the corresponding position information $P_{AL,j}(t)$ at the same time.

Finally, elitism is introduced into ant-lion algorithm. Elitism is an important feature of evolutionary algorithms, enabling them to maintain the best solution obtained at any stage of the optimization process. In ALO, the best antlions obtained so far in each iteration are saved and considered elite. Since elite is the most adaptable antlion, it should be able to influence the movement of all ants during the iteration. Therefore, the algorithm assumes that each ant simultaneously walks randomly around the selected colony via roulette wheel and elite, as shown below:

$$P^d_{(A,n)}(t) = \frac{R_A(t) + R_E(t)}{2} \tag{15}$$

2.2. Differential Step-Scaling Ant-Lion Algorithm

For a meta-heuristic algorithm based on swarm agents, the migration strategy of the agent has a crucial influence on the convergence, stability, and speed. The same is true for ant-lion algorithms. Although each ant walks randomly when the algorithm is initialized, with the increase of iterations, we can know that better fitness values cannot be obtained in some search domains, so gradually there is no need to let the random walk of ants fill the whole space. In other words, in some other areas, we need to pay more attention, because the near-optimal solution (an accepted common sense is that intelligent optimization algorithms cannot really achieve the global optimization of the problem but can only obtain a near-optimal solution in an infinitesimal neighborhood of the global optimization. But when the error is small enough, we can assume that the result returned by the algorithm is globally optimal) is probably in one of these regions. That is also the reason that the idea of elitism and boundary reduction is introduced in ant-lion algorithm.

However, although in the telocinesia of iterative we don't need to let the search bodies traverse the entire space, at the beginning of the iteration, the range that search bodies can reach is still the bigger the better. Although the introduction of elitism can guarantee strong searching ability near global optimal solution in the later period of iteration, it can be seen from the Equation (15) that in the iterative process of the ant-lion algorithm, the attraction of elite antlion to all ants is fixed, which weakens the initial global search ability of the algorithm. Therefore, this paper introduces the idea of step scaling. The change in "step size" here is not the step size of each ant as it migrates, but the change in the influence of the elite antlion on the entire ant population in each iteration. At the beginning of the algorithm, the influence of the elite antlion is loosened so that the ants can explore the whole parameter space more "freely". At the end of the algorithm, the influence of the elite antlion is restored to its original state, which ensures that the improved algorithm has the same global optimal searching ability as the original antlion algorithm. Therefore, $P^d_{(A,n)}(t)$ is redefined as:

$$P^d_{(A,n)}(t) = \frac{R_A(t) + R_E(t)}{2} \times \sin\left(\frac{current}{maxgen} \times \frac{\pi}{2}\right) \tag{16}$$

where $R_A(t)$ is the random walk around ants S_{sel}, $R_E(t)$ is the random walk around the elite antlion S_{elite}, *current* is the current iteration number, and *maxgen* is the maximum iteration number set.

The reason for choosing a sine trigonometric function as multiplier in Equation (16) is that although we need to enhance the wandering ability of search bodies in the early stage of the algorithm, we don't need to let them "indulge" for too long. The sinusoidal trigonometric function has a high rising speed in the initial stage and will change rapidly with the change of the independent variable, thus playing a role of scaling step size, and the whole scaling process is smooth.

In addition, in order to enrich the population diversity and further increase the global searching ability of the ant-lion algorithm, a method that can enhance the global searching ability of the ant-lion algorithm should be introduced. A differential evolution algorithm is a reasonable solution. The algorithm was originally proposed by Storn and Price on the basis of the evolutionary idea of a genetic algorithm [23]. It is essentially a multi-objective continuous variable optimization method, used to solve the global optimal solution in multi-dimensional space. Compared with a genetic algorithm, their common point is to randomly generate the initial population, respectively calculate the fitness value of each individual in the population and select individuals according to the value of fitness. Their main processes both include mutation, crossover, and selection. The difference is that a genetic algorithm uses the fitness value of individual population to control the parent population for hybridization, and then carries out a mutation operation to obtain the probability value of offspring being selected. In a differential evolution algorithm, each individual in the population is regarded as a vector. Through vector calculation, the parent vector is calculated by difference to generate a mutation vector, and then the mutation vector is hybridized with the parent vector to generate a new vector, which is regarded as the child and selected with the parent directly, as shown in Figure 2. Differential evolution algorithms have strong robustness, fast convergence speed, and the most important thing is that they are easy to implement. The calculation steps of a differential evolution algorithm mainly include three stages: mutation, crossover, and selection, and "DE/x/y/z" is usually used to distinguish and represent different evolution methods and operators. In "DE/x/y/z", x specifies how to choose a basis vector; y specifies the number of difference vectors in evolution; z is a way of crossing operations. In addition to selecting strategies for specific problems, the performance of a differential evolution algorithm is also related to three key parameters: population size NP, scaling factor F, and crossover probability CR. A reasonable evolutionary strategy and a set of appropriate key parameters can greatly improve the convergence speed and accuracy of the algorithm.

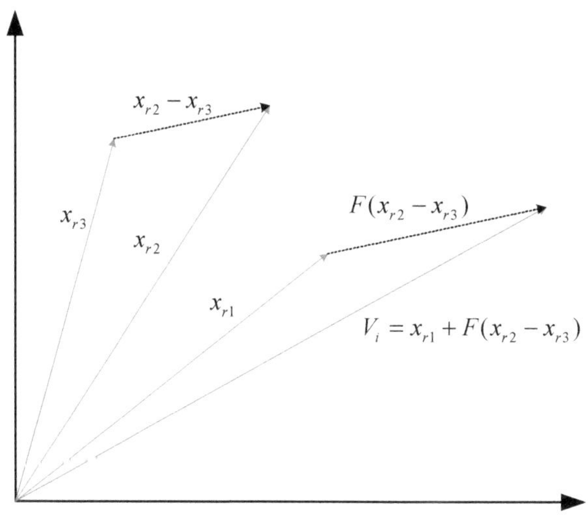

Figure 2. Basic idea of differential evolution algorithm.

In this paper, we choose the "DE/rand/1/binDE" mode, initialize all the individuals of the population into n-dimensional vectors, and then randomly generate individual positions in the search area. In the mutation stage, two vectors are randomly selected for difference operation to obtain the mutation vector, and then the mutation vector is scaled and added with a third parent vector to obtain a new child vector. The binomial crossover operator was used to ensure that at least one dimension of the final test individual comes from the mutant individual, so as to avoid being the same as the current individual and ensure the diversity of the population. A random number conforming to uniform 0–1 distribution is generated and compared value with the crossover probability CR. If the value of the random number is less than CR, the value of the mutant individual at this dimension is given to the test individual, or the value of the test individual at this dimension will come from the current individual. In the selection stage, the fitness values of the new individuals and the original individuals after mutation and crossover are compared, and the excellent ones are retained while the bad ones are discarded to ensure that the individuals in the population are currently optimal before entering the next iteration.

Specifically in this paper, the combination points of the differential evolution algorithm and the ant-lion algorithm are as follows:

In each iteration, after obtaining all antlions at the current iteration, the antlions were variated and differentiated.

Mutation: select several pairs of antlions randomly, regard them as the parent vector, calculate the difference between them and scale them according to the scaling factor, then add the scaled difference vector and the vector of the third antlion individual to obtain a new test body, the formula is defined as follows:

$$P'(t) = P^d_{AL,r1}(t) + F \cdot (P^d_{AL,r2}(t) - P^d_{AL,r3}(t)) \tag{17}$$

where F is the scaling factor, r_1, r_2, r_3 is the three different random numbers in the interval [1, N], $P'(t)$ is the test object obtained by mutation operation in the t-th iteration, and $P^d_{AL,r1}(t)$, $P^d_{AL,r2}(t)$, $P^d_{AL,r3}(t)$ is r_1-th, r_2-th, r_3-th antlion vector of this iteration. After that, in order not to make the test body run out of the search range, boundary condition judgment is also needed, and the formula is as follows:

$$P' = \begin{cases} L^d(t), & if\ S' < L^d(t) \\ U^d(t), & if\ S' \geq U^d(t) \end{cases} \tag{18}$$

where S' are the individual positions of antlions after mutation, $L^d(t)$ and $U^d(t)$ are the upper and lower bounds of all ants and antlions in the d-th dimension at t-th iteration.

Crossover: firstly, the crossover probability CR is determined, and the crossover operator is generated. In this work, we select the binomial operator to randomly generate a dimension identifier, then generate a random number with uniform distribution within the interval [0, 1], and compare its value with CR. Thus, a better individual can be selected:

$$U_i = \begin{cases} P', & if\ r_4 \leq CR \\ P, & otherwise \end{cases} \tag{19}$$

where $r_4 \in [0, 1]$ is a uniformly distributed random number, CR is crossover probability, also generated between 0 and 1; P' is a mutant, P_E is the elite antlion, U_i is a new individual retained from the crossover.

Selection: compare the fitness values of the elite antlion P_E with the fitness values of U_i in the previous step, discard those that do not meet the optimization requirements, and retain the better ones. The formula is as follows:

$$P_{AL} = \begin{cases} U_i, & if\ f(U_i) \leq f(P_E) \\ P_E, & otherwise \end{cases} \tag{20}$$

In this way, the population diversity of elite antlions is enriched, and the remaining antlion population is not weaker than the original antlion population, which further improves the searching ability of antlion algorithm.

2.3. Algorithm Idea and Specific Steps

The improvement of the algorithm mainly focuses on the enrichment of population diversity and improvement of local search ability. The pseudo-code corresponding to the Algorithm 1 is shown as follows:

Algorithm 1 Pseudo-Code of DSALO

```
Initialize the first population of ants and antlions randomly
Calculate the fitness of ants and antlions
Find the best ant or antlions, then set it as the initial elite antlion
While the maxmum iteration is not reached
  For each ant
  Select an antlion using Roulette wheel
  Update boundaries using Equations (12) and (13)
  Make a random walk using Equation (1)
  Normalize and update the position of ant using Equations (9) and (16)
  End for
  Calculate the fitness of all ants
  Replace an antlion if its corresponding ant becomes fitter
  Apply Mutation, Crossover, and Selection operator to antlions
  Update the elite antlion
End while
Return the elite antlion
```

3. Performance Evaluation of Differential Step-Scaling Ant-Lion Algorithm

3.1. Algorithm Evaluation Criteria

When we use a test function, the optimal value of each test function is already known. Because of the random walk strategy of the algorithm, the results of the algorithm in each run may be different. Considering the stability and accuracy of the algorithm, the mean value of fitness, standard deviation, maximum and minimum are selected as evaluation criteria of the algorithm.

For an algorithm, if it can obtain a fitter mean value closer to the optimal value, a smaller fitness standard deviation, a smaller fitness maximum value as well as a smaller fitness minimum value, it indicates that the algorithm is excellent, or better than other algorithms in the problems applied in this comparison.

3.2. Test Function

The test functions, corresponding solution intervals and optimal values used in this paper are shown in Table 1. Of the four test functions, F1 is a unimodal function, F2 and F3 are multimodal functions, and F4 is a composite function [13].

Table 1. Test functions.

	Functional Expression	Solution	The Optimal Value
F1	$f_1(x) = \sum_{i=1}^{n-1} [100(x_{i+1} - x_i^2)^2 + (x_i - 1)^2]$	$[-30, 30]$	0
F2	$f_2(x) = -20\exp\left(-0.2\sqrt{\frac{1}{n}\sum_{i=1}^{n} x_i^2}\right) - \exp\left(\frac{1}{n}\sum_{i=1}^{n}\cos(2\pi x_i)\right) + 20 + e$	$[-32, 32]$	0
F3	$f_3(x) = \frac{1}{4000}\sum_{i=1}^{n} x_i^2 - \prod_{i=1}^{n}\cos(\frac{x_i}{\sqrt{i}}) + 1$	$[-600, 600]$	0
F4	$f_1, f_2, \ldots, f_{10} = F_3$ $[\sigma_1, \sigma_2, \ldots \sigma_{10}] = [1, 1, \ldots, 1]$ $[\lambda_1, \lambda_2, \ldots, \lambda_{10}] = [0.05, 0.05, \ldots, 0.05]$	$[-5.12, 5.12]$	0

3.3. Analysis of Test Results

In this paper, DSALO is compared with ALO, PSO, and OEALO (Opposition based Exploratory differential Lion-based Optimization [24]). The dimension of test functions is set to 50. The test results are shown in Table 2. It can be seen from the table that

DSALO has significantly improved the search accuracy, which indicates that DSALO has some certain advantages. Since the original ant-lion algorithm randomly selects the initial value when the algorithm starts to run, the dependence of the ant-lion algorithm on the initial value is low, while the DSALO algorithm inherits this characteristic of the original ant-lion algorithm.

Table 2. Test results.

The Function Name	Algorithm	Mean Fitness	The Standard Deviation	Maximum Fitness	Minimum Fitness
F1	DSALO	6.19×10^{-1}	1.37×10^{1}	2.27	1.71×10^{-3}
	ALO	4.43×10^{1}	6.83×10^{2}	8.99×10^{2}	9.32
	PSO	3.73×10^{3}	1.12×10^{1}	6.64×10^{3}	8.93×10^{2}
	OEALO	8.34	2.64×10^{1}	7.38	1.67×10^{-3}
F2	DSALO	5.28×10^{-15}	9.46×10^{-3}	4.89×10^{-14}	8.73×10^{-16}
	ALO	2.65×10^{-5}	5.34×10^{-2}	3.92×10^{-5}	1.35×10^{-5}
	PSO	1.79	8.32×10^{-2}	3.17	1.01
	OEALO	4.74×10^{-5}	7.39×10^{-2}	1.44×10^{-5}	8.39×10^{-6}
F3	DSALO	1.06×10^{-15}	3.48	3.74×10^{-15}	8.88×10^{-16}
	ALO	9.15×10^{-2}	6.83×10^{1}	4.7×10^{-1}	7.63×10^{-2}
	PSO	4.36×10^{-2}	5.69×10^{-1}	7.97×10^{-2}	3.94×10^{-2}
	OEALO	3.47×10^{-9}	2.04×10^{-3}	2.56×10^{-9}	4.43×10^{-9}
F4	DSALO	3.39×10^{-4}	2.71×10^{-1}	3.78×10^{-4}	3.14×10^{-4}
	ALO	7.76×10^{-4}	1.04	8.67×10^{-4}	6.77×10^{-4}
	PSO	5.36×10^{-4}	5.82	7.08×10^{-4}	4.35×10^{-4}
	OEALO	3.57×10^{-4}	3.85×10^{-1}	3.86×10^{-4}	3.03×10^{-4}

The DSALO algorithm not only improves the accuracy, but also improves the convergence speed and stability. To intuitively demonstrate this point, the convergence curves of the DSALO algorithm, original ALO algorithm, PSO algorithm, and OEALO algorithm with 5 times of running on test functions F1 to F4 are shown in Figures 3–6 respectively. The test functions are all set as 100 dimensions and the maximum iteration is set to 800. It can be seen that, on the test function F1, the DSALO proposed in this paper has a relatively strong improvement in both convergence speed and accuracy. On the test function F2, the PSO algorithm falls into local optimum earlier. ALO can avoid falling into local optimum, but its optimization accuracy is not as good as DSALO. OEALO's effect is better than ALO but still has a disparity with DSALO. On the test function F3, both PSO and ALO fall into local optimum earlier. On the test function F4, DSALO and OEALO have similar performances and both of them are better than PSO and the origin ALO. From these results it can be concluded that DSALO has a significant performance improvement for multimodal functions, and has a similar performance with OEALO for unimodal and composite functions. Although DSALO has a similar effect to OEALO, it has a faster convergence speed. Since the four test functions in this section belong to different types of functions, so it can be shown that the DSALO algorithm has performs well in unimodal functions, multimodal functions, and composite functions.

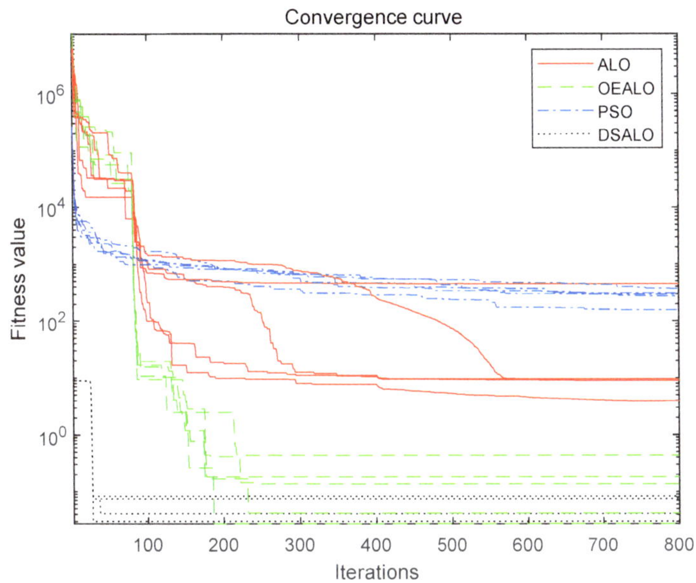

Figure 3. Convergence curve of algorithm optimization test function F1.

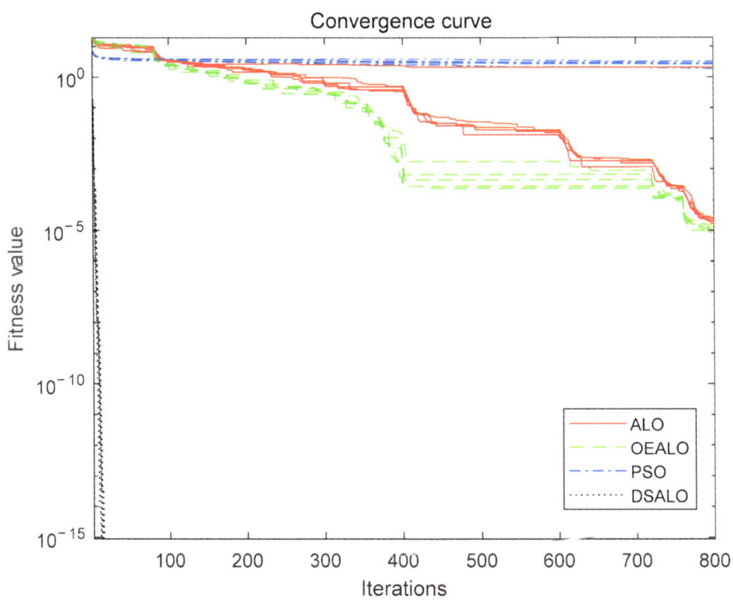

Figure 4. Convergence curve of algorithm optimization test function F2.

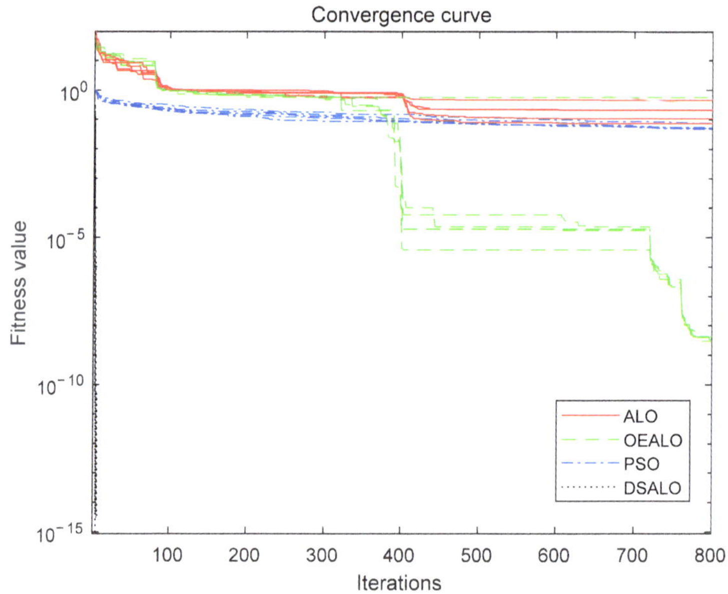

Figure 5. Convergence curve of algorithm optimization test function F3.

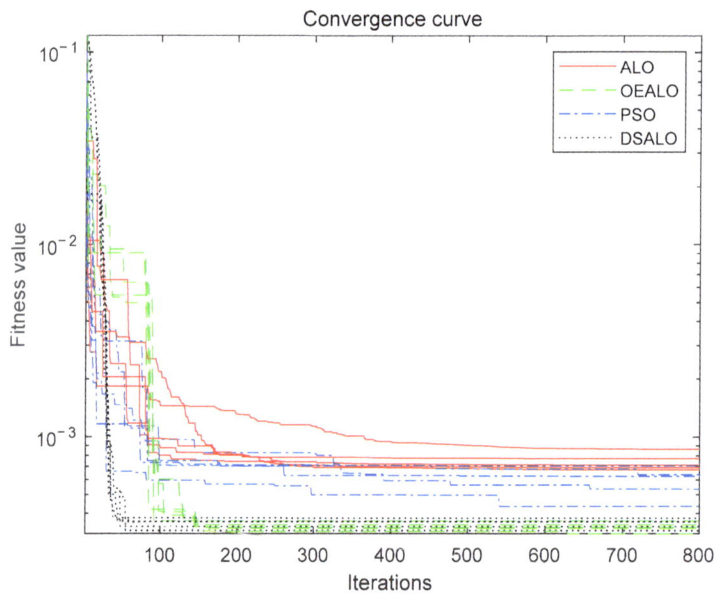

Figure 6. Convergence curve of test function F4 optimized by the algorithm.

4. Parameter Optimization of ADRC

In this section, the effectiveness of the DSALO algorithm is illustrated by examples. The controlled object is assumed to be a tank in industrial manufacture. In the parameter optimization problem of a linear active disturbance rejection controller, the structure used is shown in Figure 7:

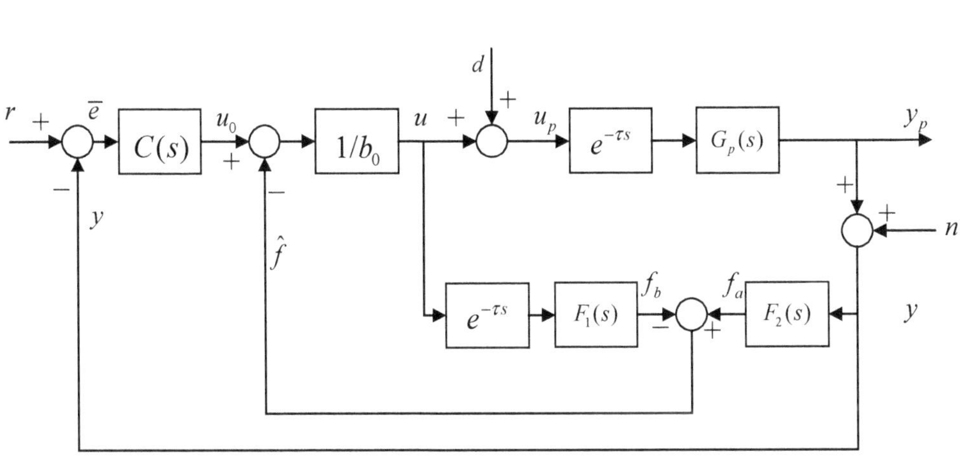

Figure 7. Control structure.

The controlled plant is a second-order system with time delay:

$$G_p(s) = \frac{e^{-6s}}{s^2 + 3s + 1} \tag{21}$$

The observer is designed as

$$F_1 = \frac{\omega_o^2}{(s + \omega_o)^2}, \quad F_2 = \frac{\omega_o^2 s^2}{(s + \omega_o)^2} \tag{22}$$

The controller takes the proportional controller ω_c.

Thus, we obtain a parameter set $\{\omega_o, \omega_c\}$ to be optimized.

There are two parameters optimization objectives: one is to minimize the IAE index of the system; the other is to reduce the overshoot of the system as much as possible while considering the IAE index. Since in this paper the performance of DSALO and OEALO has been verified in Section 3 that they are both better than the original ALO and PSO, only DSLAO and OEALO are considered for comparison in this section. Given the randomness of the algorithms, each algorithm is run 25 times, and only the best results are recorded.

The authors run the simulation of ADRC parameters optimization in the following hardware environment: Intel® Core™ I7-8700K, Nvidia GeForce GTX 1060, and 16GB memory. The software environment is a Windows 10 operating system and Matlab R2020b. According to statistics, when the number of populations is set to 50 and the algorithm iterates 100 times, the average time of running DSALO to optimize the active disturbance rejection controller is 32 min, and the average time of running OEALO is 34 min. Given the complexity of the algorithm and the long control cycle in the process industry, such operation time is acceptable. It is worth noting that due to the existence of uncertainty, parameter optimization usually needs to be run at regular intervals. A large number of iterations can obtain better parameters but is also time-consuming, which may lead to a phenomenon that the optimization time takes up too much ratio of running interval or even is longer than the running interval. This phenomenon may cause parameter updates to be delayed, which in turn has a negative impact on the effectiveness of control. So, in the problem of ADRC parameter optimization, it needs a compromise between the optimization effect and computation time. That is the reason why we choose to set the number of iterations to 100.

The search results of parameters under the two targets are listed in Table 3. Figures 8 and 9 show the corresponding output.

Table 3. Optimization results.

Performance Indicators	Methods	Index Number	ω_c	ω_o
IAE	DSALO	2.6116×10^3	1.1899	0.6133
	OEALO	2.6776×10^3	1.18026	0.57996
IAE + overshoot	DSALO	3.4860×10^3	0.99298	0.54947
	OEALO	3.5029×10^3	0.9577	0.5967

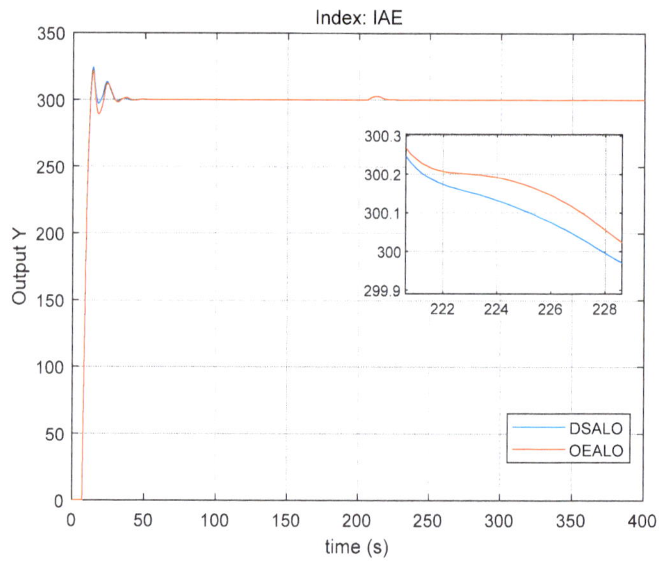

Figure 8. Using IAE as an indicator.

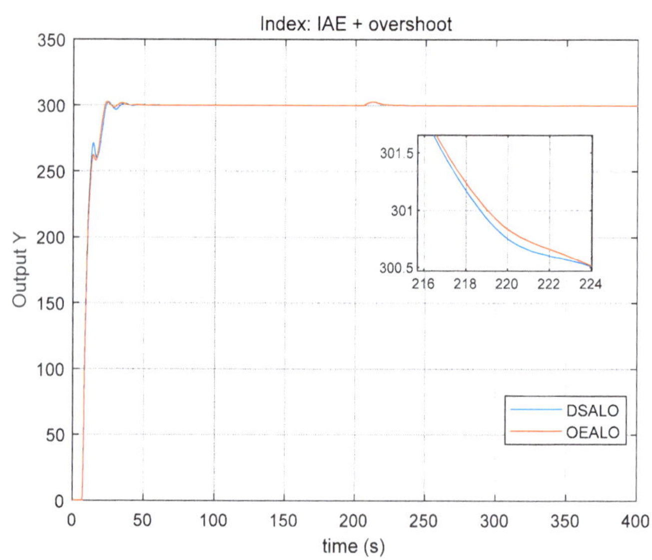

Figure 9. Using IAE+ overshoot as an indicator.

There is also one thing worth noting. The DSALO algorithm can be applied in industrial ADRC systems in this way: first collect input and output data of controlled plant to establish current model of the plant, then integrate the model in simulation software and take the control performance as objective function/fitness, finally run the simulation and DSALO simultaneously and the solutions of DSALO are the optimized parameters of ADRC.

It can be seen from the diagram, whichever kind of index or which kinds of optimization algorithm are used, the optimized performances of disturbance rejection (200 to 250 s) are very good. The difference mainly exists in the procedure of setpoint tracking (0 to 50 s). Using the parameters obtained by the DASLO algorithm can obtain smaller indexes. Combined with the meaning of IAE index, which is the corresponding energy consumption (coal, fuel, natural gas, etc.), the parameters obtained by DSALO have smaller performance metrics, which means better economy of the optimized system and better for the environment.

5. Conclusions and Future Perspectives

In this paper, an improved ant-lion algorithm called DSALO is proposed to solve the parameter optimization problem of ADRC. Because parameters of ADRC are directly related to the control performance, ulteriorly the economic effectiveness of the controlled object, finding an optimized set of parameters is of great importance. Specific to this work, a parameter set $\{\omega_o, \omega_c\}$ is optimized with two performance indexes: IAE and IAE + overshoot. These indexes are important because they can reflect the economic effectiveness of a controlled plant in industrial manufacturing. In order to improve search abilities of origin ALO, differential evolution strategy is introduced to improve global search ability and a step scaling method is used to enhance local search ability. Experiments on test functions show that the DSALO algorithm has a significant improvement in accuracy for multimodal functions and a significantly higher convergence speed for unimodal functions, multimodal functions, and composite functions. The experimental results show that the DSALO algorithm has a batter optimization effect, further show that DSALO is capable of an ADRC parameter optimization problem. Since this is the first time using an ant-lion based algorithm to optimize the ADRC parameter, this study can be a basis of future optimization work for different ADRC varieties and nonlinear ADRC.

It should be noted that, however, some aspects can be studied in future work. One aspect is that DSALO does not show significant accuracy improvement, though a small improvement exists, for unimodal functions and composite functions. This phenomenon needs more study and DSALO may need modification at a deeper level. On the other hand, the convergence speed of DSALO still needs further improvement. As stated in this paper, an industrial application of optimization algorithms usually inherently compromises between computation time and accuracy. It means that reducing computation time is of great importance. Additionally, a parallel version of DSALO should be developed for future work to deal with some complex cases, which can save the costs of computation time.

Author Contributions: Conceptualization, Q.J.; methodology, Y.Z.; software, Y.Z.; validation, Q.J.; formal analysis, Y.Z.; investigation, Y.Z.; resources, Q.J.; data curation, Q.J.; writing—original draft preparation, Y.Z.; writing—review and editing, Q.J.; visualization, Y.Z.; supervision, Y.Z.; project administration, Q.J. All authors have read and agreed to the published version of the manuscript.

Funding: This research received no external funding.

Institutional Review Board Statement: Not applicable.

Informed Consent Statement: Not applicable.

Data Availability Statement: Not applicable.

Conflicts of Interest: The authors declare no conflict of interest.

References

1. Han, J. From PID to active disturbance rejection control. *IEEE Trans. Ind. Electron.* **2009**, *56*, 900–906. [CrossRef]
2. Han, J. The "Extended State Observer" of a Class of Uncertain Systems. *Control Decis.* **1995**, *10*, 85–88.
3. Wang, C.; Quan, L.; Zhang, S.; Meng, H.; Lan, Y. Reduced-order model based active disturbance rejection control of hydraulic servo system with singular value perturbation theory. *ISA Trans.* **2017**, *67*, 455–465. [CrossRef] [PubMed]
4. Chang, X.; Li, Y.; Zhang, W.; Wang, N.; Xue, W. Active disturbance rejection control for a flywheel energy storage system. *IEEE Trans. Ind. Electron.* **2014**, *62*, 991–1001. [CrossRef]
5. Chen, Z.; Zheng, Q.; Gao, Z. Active disturbance rejection control of chemical processes. In Proceedings of the 2007 IEEE International Conference on Control Applications, Singapore, 1–3 October 2007; pp. 855–861.
6. Tao, J.; Sun, Q.L.; Tan, P.L.; Chen, Z.Q.; He, Y.P. Active disturbance rejection control (ADRC)-based autonomous homing control of powered parafoils. *Nonlinear Dynam* **2016**, *86*, 1461–1476. [CrossRef]
7. Hou, Y.; Gao, Z.; Jiang, F.; Boulter, B.T. Active disturbance rejection control for web tension regulation. In Proceedings of the 40th IEEE Conference on Decision and Control (Cat. No. 01CH37228), Orlando, FL, USA, 4–7 December 2001; pp. 4974–4979.
8. Gao, Z. Scaling and bandwidth-parameterization based controller tuning. In Proceedings of the American Control Conference, Minneapolis, MN, USA, 4–6 June 2003; pp. 4989–4996.
9. Kang, C.; Wang, S.; Ren, W.; Lu, Y.; Wang, B. Optimization design and application of active disturbance rejection controller based on intelligent algorithm. *IEEE Access* **2019**, *7*, 59862–59870. [CrossRef]
10. Türk, S.; Deveci, M.; Özcan, E.; Canıtez, F.; John, R. Interval type-2 fuzzy sets improved by Simulated Annealing for locating the electric charging stations. *Inf. Sci.* **2021**, *547*, 641–666. [CrossRef]
11. Demirel, N.Ç.; Deveci, M. Novel search space updating heuristics-based genetic algorithm for optimizing medium-scale airline crew pairing problems. *Int. J. Comput. Intell. Syst.* **2017**, *10*, 1082–1101. [CrossRef]
12. Bianchi, L.; Dorigo, M.; Gambardella, L.M.; Gutjahr, W.J. A survey on metaheuristics for stochastic combinatorial optimization. *Nat. Comput.* **2009**, *8*, 239–287. [CrossRef]
13. Mirjalili, S. The Ant Lion Optimizer. *Adv. Eng. Softw.* **2015**, *83*, 80–98. [CrossRef]
14. Emary, E.; Zawbaa, H.M.; Hassanien, A.E. Binary ant lion approaches for feature selection. *Neurocomputing* **2016**, *213*, 54–65. [CrossRef]
15. Zawbaa, H.M.; Emary, E.; Grosan, C. Feature selection via chaotic antlion optimization. *PLoS ONE* **2016**, *11*, e0150652. [CrossRef] [PubMed]
16. Yamany, W.; Tharwat, A.; Hassanin, M.F.; Gaber, T.; Hassanien, A.E.; Kim, T.-H. A new multi-layer perceptrons trainer based on ant lion optimization algorithm. In Proceedings of the 2015 Fourth International Conference on Information Science and Industrial Applications (ISI), Busan, Korea, 20–22 September 2015; pp. 40–45.
17. Rajan, A.; Jeevan, K.; Malakar, T. Weighted elitism based Ant Lion Optimizer to solve optimum VAr planning problem. *Appl. Soft Comput.* **2017**, *55*, 352–370. [CrossRef]
18. Mouassa, S.; Bouktir, T.; Salhi, A. Ant lion optimizer for solving optimal reactive power dispatch problem in power systems. *Eng. Sci. Technol. Int. J.* **2017**, *20*, 885–895. [CrossRef]
19. Tian, T.; Liu, C.; Guo, Q.; Yuan, Y.; Li, W.; Yan, Q. An improved ant lion optimization algorithm and its application in hydraulic turbine governing system parameter identification. *Energies* **2018**, *11*, 95. [CrossRef]
20. Li, Y.; Feng, B.; Li, G.; Qi, J.; Zhao, D.; Mu, Y. Optimal distributed generation planning in active distribution networks considering integration of energy storage. *Appl. Energy* **2018**, *210*, 1073–1081. [CrossRef]
21. Zainal, M.I.; Yasin, Z.M.; Zakaria, Z. Network reconfiguration for loss minimization and voltage profile improvement using ant lion optimizer. In Proceedings of the 2017 IEEE Conference on Systems, Process and Control (ICSPC), Meleka, Malaysia, 15–17 December 2017; pp. 162–167.
22. Grzimek, B.; Schlager, N.; Olendorf, D.; McDade, M.C. *Grzimek' s Animal Life Encyclopedia*; Gale Farmington Hills: Detroit, MI, USA, 2004.
23. Storn, R.; Price, K. Differential evolution—A simple and efficient heuristic for global optimization over continuous spaces. *J. Glob. Optim.* **1997**, *11*, 341–359. [CrossRef]
24. Wang, M.J.; Heidari, A.A.; Chen, M.X.; Chen, H.L.; Zhao, X.H.; Cai, X.D. Exploratory differential ant lion-based optimization. *Expert Syst. Appl.* **2020**, *159*, 113548. [CrossRef]

algorithms

MDPI

Article

Behavior Selection Metaheuristic Search Algorithm for the Pollination Optimization: A Simulation Case of Cocoa Flowers

Willa Ariela Syafruddin *, Rio Mukhtarom Paweroi and Mario Köppen

Department of Computer Science and System Engineering (CSSE), Graduate School of Computer Science and System Engineering, Kyushu Institute of Technology, 680-4 Kawazu, Fukuoka 820-8502, Japan; paweroi.rio-mukhtarom223@mail.kyutech.jp (R.M.P.); mkoeppen@ieee.org (M.K.)

* Correspondence: syafruddin.willa-ariela966@mail.kyutech.jp

Abstract: Since nature is an excellent source of inspiration for optimization methods, many optimization algorithms have been proposed, are inspired by nature, and are modified to solve various optimization problems. This paper uses metaheuristics in a new field inspired by nature; more precisely, we use pollination optimization in cocoa plants. The cocoa plant was chosen as the object since its flower type differs from other kinds of flowers, for example, by using cross-pollination. This complex relationship between plants and pollinators also renders pollination a real-world problem for chocolate production. Therefore, this study first identified the underlying optimization problem as a deferred fitness problem, where the quality of a potential solution cannot be immediately determined. Then, the study investigates how metaheuristic algorithms derived from three well-known techniques perform when applied to the flower pollination problem. The three techniques examined here are Swarm Intelligence Algorithms, Individual Random Search, and Multi-Agent Systems search. We then compare the behavior of these various search methods based on the results of pollination simulations. The criteria are the number of pollinated flowers for the trees and the amount and fairness of nectar pickup for the pollinator. Our results show that Multi-Agent System performs notably better than other methods. The result of this study are insights into the co-evolution of behaviors for the collaborative pollination task. We also foresee that this investigation can also help farmers increase chocolate production by developing methods to attract and promote pollinators.

Keywords: metaheuristic search algorithm; swarm intelligence; random search; multi-agent systems; optimization; behavior; pollination of cocoa flowers

1. Introduction

Pollination is a natural process that is required for most plants to produce fruit and seeds. Cocoa is one of the plants that depend on pollination for successful fruit formation [1]. The cacao plant (*Theobroma cacao*) grows almost everywhere globally, but it is most common in tropical areas such as West Africa, Indonesia, Central and South America, and Hawaii. This area issue creates a concern for chocolate production because cocoa flower pollinators prefer humid environments. Only a few fly genera, especially a tiny midge called *Forcipomyia Inornatipennis* (FP), can pollinate small flowers. The problem is because cacao flowers are unlike other flowers. Since the cacao flower is small and almost odorless, it does not attract the attention of many insects, especially not classical pollinators such as bees. FP wander to cacao flowers in order to obtain the nectar in bloom for food and egg maturation. The pollination process in cacao flowers can be summarized as follows: when the FP takes the nectar from the cacao flower, the FP inadvertently touches the bunch's head, causing pollen to be released and to stick to the FP. Pollination will occur by chance when the pollen picked up by FP on one flower meets the pollen on another cacao flower that the FP flies to.

Self-incompatible tree species are primarily cross-compatible, which means they can fertilize flowers on other trees, including those of the same variety. Cross-pollination is the only method to ensure successful fertilization because self-pollination is not suitable for cacao trees and will not result in successful fertilization [2]. This situation implies matching behaviors of the pollinators. We aim to investigate this process by pollination simulations on cocoa plants by using three methods of pollinator collaboration:

- Based on Swarm Intelligence Algorithms;
- Based on Individual Random Search;
- Based on Multi-Agent Systems differential search methods.

The study of optimization algorithm behavior to tackle pressing real-world problems has recently attracted many researchers' attention. Currently, new algorithms are set up and focused on achieving a pre-set desired optimization goal. While this can be useful and efficient in the short term, it is insufficient in the long run as it needs to be repeated for any new problem that occurs under potentially new specific difficulties. Therefore, one algorithm cannot be used for all real-world issues.

The development of optimization algorithms is essential because optimization problems can occur in various scientific fields such as economics, engineering, and medicine. There are still many researchers around the world working to solve problems in this field. Classical optimization algorithms are not very efficient at solving real-world problems because they cannot find the global optima or it requires massive efforts. Bn contrast, metaheuristic algorithms are more robust at avoiding local optima. They do not need a cost function gradient because the algorithm's main "trick" is also to exploit randomness and concurrency [3].

The paper focuses on theoretical and empirical research investigating approaches needed to analyze stochastic optimization algorithms and performance assessment concerning different criteria. Figure 1 shows the FP process to pollinate cocoa plants. The FP can use different search methods to ensure that the FP can collect enough nectar. However, if the tree pollination has occurred, the tree will no longer expose flowers and not produce nectar. Consequently, FP will have to seek out other trees that have not yet pollinated to obtain more nectar. This processing is then implemented in a 3D virtual environment to demonstrate and compare the effectiveness of the various cocoa pollination methods.

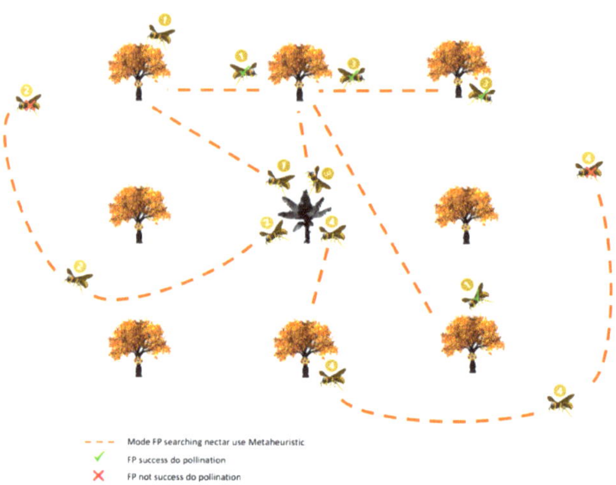

Figure 1. Process flow of *Forcipomyia* pollination.

This article is organized as follows. In Section 2, the real-world facts on cocoa pollination are introduced. Section 3 provides the material and methods used in this study.

Results are presented in Section 4, followed by discussions (Section 5) and conclusions (Section 6).

2. Real-World Pollination Optimization Problem

Cocoa flower pollination uses a different method of pollination compared to flower pollination in general. The flowers on these cacao plants are distinct from other plants since they are small (typical diameter of about 3 cm), which allows the flowers to be pollinated by only small-bodied insects (most excluding traditional pollinators such as bees). The flower's structure with the characteristic hooded petals enclosing the stamens favors neither self-pollination nor cross-pollination. However, there is considerable evidence from various sources that natural crossing occurs in a substantial amount. The reason is that the arrangement of cocoa flowers has distinctive veil petals which protect stamens that do neither prefer self-pollination nor cross-pollination, even though there are clear indications from several sources that natural cross-pollination occurs to a certain extent [4]. Based on the findings of Jones' (1912) experiments in Dominica, it is clear that small insects, whether ants, aphids, thrips, or a combination of the three, are the primary agents involved in the pollination of cocoa flowers [5].

Forcipomyia inornatipennis swarms can be classified into (1) normal and (2) mating swarms: [6]:

- Normal swarm: The standard FP flight has a 12 h cycle. Swarming activity affecting the highest number of insects occurs between 5 a.m. and 8 a.m., during which it rapidly declines to its lowest level, from about midday to around 2 p.m., where it starts to rise to a second high between 5 a.m. and 6:30 a.m. However, variation in the behavior of the insects depends on the light of the sun. If the sky is overcast, the dawn swarm will begin until after 9 a.m. A swarm that is 30–180 cm above the ground and consists of 4–80 individuals of both sexes may fly in either direction within a 100 cm radius. The higher the swarm, the more midges leave; thus, the remaining number of individuals is directly proportional to those engaged in the hive.
- Mating swarm: Almost 60% of mating swarm activities occur at dusk. The swarm has 2 to 30 individuals depending on the time of day and both hives have both sexes. In flight, males actively hunt for females and male mates in a swarm usually last around 15 min with three or four females. This habit is because the number of females taking part in flights is always smaller than males. If the swarm does not contain more than four or five pairs, the number of remaining midges will be determined by the mating swarm's size, as long as it exists.

Cocoa flowers have a different shapes compared to flowers in general, rendering them unattractive to specific potential pollinators. Cocoa flowers have different staminodes, as shown in Figure 2. These staminodes are similar to stamens, which is the male part of the flower, but they do not contain pollen and, thus, they are sterile. Only tiny insects at the flower's base can reach the pollen-producing anthers hidden beneath a hood. The research conducted by Frimpong-Anin [7] claimed that the variants of converging and parallel staminode flowers were the ideal types of staminode-style flowers for successful pollination.

(a) (b) (c)

Figure 2. Three variants of the Cocoa Flowers. (**a**) Converging. (**b**) Parallel. (**c**) Splay.

Flower pollination is a fascinating natural process that has captivated several authors who have researched it. The target of flower pollination is to ensure the survival of the most suitable and optimal plant reproduction in terms of both number and quality. All of the flower pollination factors and processes mentioned above interact to ensure that flowering plants reproduce optimally. Therefore, the author [8] introduced a new algorithm inspired by the perspective of flower pollination. The authors [9] developed a pollination simulation model and the results revealed that seed production is affected by pollinator and pollen carrier movement patterns. Another author [10] was inspired by the relationship between pollinating insects and flowering plants and presented an agent-based simulation to assess the potential impact of heterospecific pollen transfer by insects on two species of flowering plants in an environment that included a shared central region and specific-species refugia.

From the above description, the FP system for pollinating the flowers of the cocoa plant differs from the characteristics of the flowers in general. Therefore, three methods are proposed and then evaluated against the FP search method to observe how each method behaves. Many researchers have shown that eacg living creature in this world possess different selection behavior [11]. Based on this conclusion, a metaheuristic algorithm is proposed to assist FP in space exploration. The same can be said about another metaheuristic algorithm significantly inspired by animal behavior [12–17].

We have adopted the FP's pollination method based on ideas and concepts introduced in [6]. This process was implemented by using a simulation. Figure 3 shows the flowchart of our proposed methodology. We create an environment that follows the original scenario, such as a cocoa tree with tiny flowers with FP insects. As mentioned earlier, the FP and tree have a complicated relationship because the tree cannot self-pollinate and the FP only wants nectar from the cacao flower. Therefore, FP and tree concurrently follow different flowcharts. Figure 3a shows how the FP is looking for nectar, while Figure 3b shows how trees can be pollinated by FPs unintentionally by bringing pollen attached to their body from different trees. Pollinating conditions in this image indicate that pollination will occur when an is FP closer to the non-pollinated tree, the nectar amount of the FP increases, and the FP carries poll from that tree. If the FP already carries poll from another tree, the tree becomes pollinated.

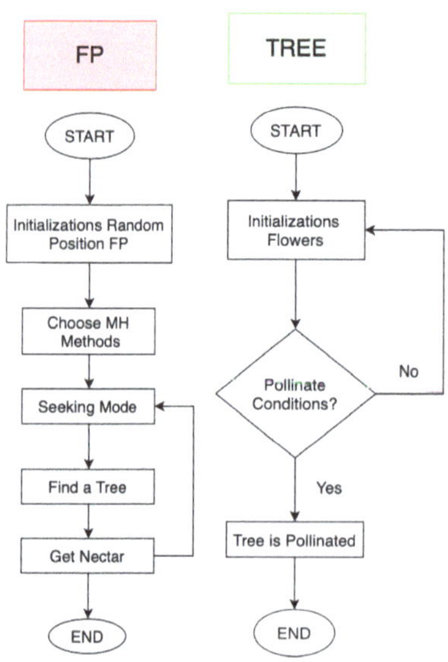

(a) (b)

Figure 3. Flowchart of the pollination model used here: (**a**) FP. (**b**) Tree.

3. Material and Methods

3.1. Material

For the simulation, a cloud-hosted instance of the OpenSimulator server (version 0.9.1) was used. This OpenSimulator provides a suitable environment for performing the study for offering various frameworks such as server-client architecture, grid architecture, avatar-based control, concurrency, and scripting support. Within the so-called hypergrid linking the different server simulations worldwide, it became possible to design an experimental framework for conducting simulations that can be tested, analyzed, and upgraded through multi-institutional collaboration [18].

All the experiments for this study were performed on Dual-Core Intel Core i5 MacBook @ 3.1 GHz with 8 GB 2133 MHz LPDDR3 of RAM running the viewer (client) software FirestormOS-Releasex64. The OpenSimulator server was running in the Metropolis Metaversum grid hosted by Hypergrid Virtual Solution UG, as illustrated in Figure 4.

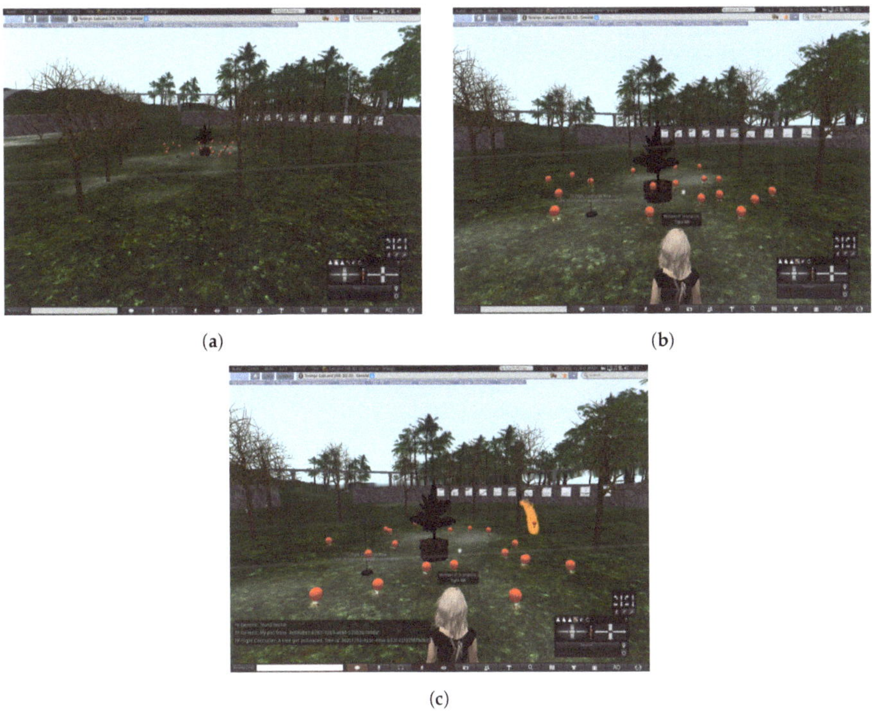

Figure 4. Implemented simulation in a 3D virtual environment. (**a**) FP randomly gathering around the breeding site. (**b**) FP starts searching trees. (**c**) A tree becomes pollinated.

Experimental Environment

The purpose of the experiment was to employ simulated creatures that comply with FP pollinating cocoa plant flowers by considering the use of the metaheuristics search algorithm. Utilizing various metaheuristic searches in this research study allows an almost identical real-life scenario, rendering it easy to observe surprising outcomes and to explore the benefits or drawbacks of each metaheuristic search used from different perspectives. In order to accomplish this goal and to calculate the efficiency of the studied metaheuristic search, the following scenarios are considered:

- FP foraging usually starts from dark moist places such as rotting banana trees, which is also the breeding site for FP;
- The starting point of the FP is random but is nearby its breeding site;

- Then, the follow three scenarios for a fixed period can occur: the first case where the number of reachable trees and the number of FP become the same; the second case where there are more reachable trees than FP; and the third case is where there are more FPs than reachable trees.

Table 1. Scenario of experiment.

	Experiment 1	Experiment 2	Experiment 3
FP	10	10	20
Tree	10	15	15
Time (minutes)	20	20	20
Number of Simulations	20	20	20

Table 1 and Figure 5 describe how the simulation works in each experiment. For additional information, the following explains how the simulation works in detail:

- The simulation occurs in circle space with a diameter of 90 m consisting of FP, tree, and FP breeding sites in the center of the circle space.
- The position of each tree is given in the Figure 5. Since each experiment had various trees, every tree was around 6 to 10 m apart.
- Before the simulation begins, the FP will be positioned at a random location within 5 m of the breeding site and will remain at the same height during the simulation, neither rising nor lowering.
- When the simulation begins, one of the algorithm methods is selected, and FP will start looking for trees in circle space for 20 min without crossing the boundary, with time steps of 1 s for Idle-Jaya, Idle-Cuckoo, Lévy, and DAG and 2 s for Idle-CSA.
- When an FP is closer than 3 m to a non-pollinated tree, the nectar amount of the FP increases and the FP carries poll from that tree. If the FP already carries poll from another tree, the tree become pollinated.
- Each tree exposes one flower. When the FP is near a tree, it will collect one nectar. The flower will then replicate nectar after 30 s and will not produce flowers again if pollination is successful.
- FP will fly around search for the trees till a time limit.

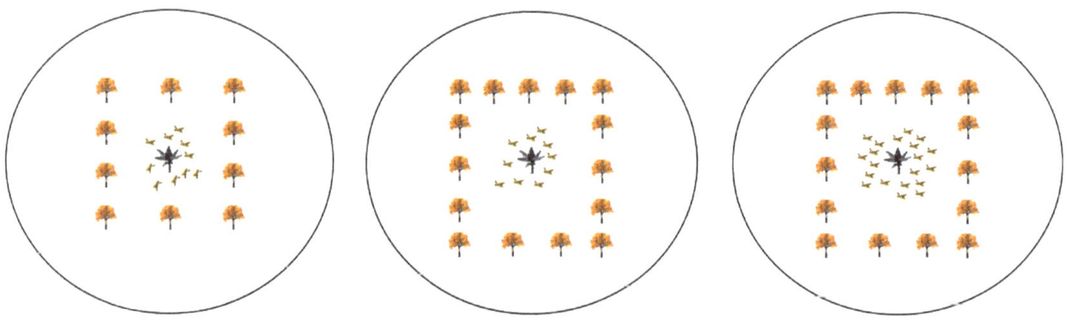

(a) (b) (c)

Figure 5. Search space environment of experiment. (**a**) Experiment 1. (**b**) Experiment 2. (**c**) Experiment 3.

3.2. Methodology

We use three different search methods: methods derived from Swarm Intelligence Algorithms, especially the Jaya algorithm [19], Crow Search Algorithm [20], and Cuckoo Search Algorithm [14]; the second method is the Individual Random Search method, Lévy flight [21]; and the last method is the Multi-Agent Systems differential search, i.e., Defender Aggressor Game (DAG). However, we did not use the original algorithms but had to modify them to fit deferred fitness. This means that we cannot use direct fitness evaluations, as they are needed especially for the Swarm Intelligence Algorithms. The FP also could not focus alone on maximizing nectar intake since this has no direct impact on the number of pollinated trees nor can the trees provide any means to maximize the number of pollinated trees themselves—they still require the FP for that to be possible. However, the Swarm Intelligence Algorithms can be redesigned to keep only their exploration components and so we used them in "idle-mode" for the exploration part only; fitness value evaluations were not utilized. The algorithm modification is for replacing all fitness-value based internal processing of those algorithms with random decisions. We will introduce it in the following subsection in more detail.

3.2.1. Swarm Intelligence Algorithm

This paper proposes three swarm algorithms that can solve the FP pollination problem. Such algorithms, which were inspired by the behavior of social insect colonies and other animal societies, are known as Swarm Intelligence (SI) and are one of the most widely used techniques by researchers to solve complex problems [22–24]. SI, in particular, is frequently used as an inspiration in natural biological systems, involving the collaborative study of the behavior of individuals from populations interacting with one another locally. However, as already explained, we do not use direct fitness evaluations on SI but, instead, a "idle-mode" variant.

Note that the algorithms operate in concurrent modes, each FP described is calculated at a new position on a periodic schedule within the simulation. There is no looping through all FP individuals or any central control of the algorithm. Moreover, generally all FP repositionings are clamped by not exceeding a maximum distance from the hives. A step *Pollination* in the following pseudo-codes is, according to the above descriptions, a tree is pollinated under the condition that current FP already carries poll picked up at a different tree in the preceding algorithm steps.

Method 1: Idle-Jaya

The Jaya Algorithm is one of the well-known algorithms used by researchers to solve complex optimization problems. Since this algorithm has no parameters to set, it is known as a simple algorithm. This Algorithm 1 concept is about the same as Particle Swarm Optimization (PSO) [25], but Jaya Algorithm tends toward the best and away from the worst rather than heading to the personal and global best. We used the Idle-Jaya formula in the pseudo-code below and by changing the concept mildly, we moved randomly towards the farther FP and away from the closer FP, which replaces the notion of the best and worst individual in the standard Jaya update formula:

$$X'_{j,k,l} = X_{j,k,l} + r_{1,j,i}\left(X_{j,best,i} - |X_{j,k,l}|\right) - r_{2,j,i}\left(X_{j,worst,i} - |X_{j,k,l}|\right) \quad (1)$$

Notation:

$X_{j,best,i}$	The value of the variable j for the best candidate;
$X_{j,worst,i}$	The value of the variable j for the worst candidate;
$X'_{j,k,l}$	The updated value of $X_{j,k,l}$;
$r_{1,j,i}$ and $r_{2,j,i}$	Random numbers i.i.d. from [0.1].

In this modification dubbed "Idle Jaya", two other FP are randomly selected and the closer one is taken as "worst" and the distant one "best".

Algorithm 1 The Idle-Jaya.

Initialize each FP position
Initialize each Tree position
while termination condition not satisfied:
  $FP_{current}$ choose two another random FP; FP_1 and FP_2.
  Repeat until $FP_1 \neq FP_2$.
  Get position of FP;
  $X_{current} = FP_{current}$ position, $X_1 = FP_1$ position, $X_2 = FP_2$ position.
  Calculate distance FP; $d_1 = d(X_{current} - X_1)$, $d_2 = d(X_{current} - X_2)$
  if $d_1 > d_2$:
    $X_{far} = X_1$; $X_{near} = X_2$.
  else
    $X_{far} = X_2$; $X_{near} = X_1$.
  end if
  if $r > 0.5$ (chance to move to new position):
    Normalized vector; $X_{towards} = X_{far} - X_{current}$.
    Normalized vector; $X_{away} = X_{near} - X_{current}$.
    Calculate new position using; $X_{new} = X_{current} + (r * X_{towards}) - (r * X_{away})$.
    Update new position.
  end if
  Calculate distance between FP and nearest Tree; $d_{tree} = d(X_{new} - X_{tree})$.
  if $d_{tree} \leq 3$ ($T_{nearest}$ found):
    if FP carry poll of $T_{poll} \neq T_{nearest}$:
      Pollination.
    end if
    FP carry poll of $T_{nearest}$; $T_{poll} = T_{nearest}$
  end if
end while

Method 2: Idle-CSA

Crow Search Algorithm (CSA) is a SI algorithm derived from the crow method to store food in a hiding place and to retrieve it when needed. The crow is considered an intelligent bird and Askarzadeh [20] has Stated that a foraging crow resembles an optimization process. In CSA, the concept of deception is incorporated in a SI algorithm. According to the pseudo-code in the Idle-CSA Algorithm 2, one FP can operate as both a position giver and a position receiver at the same time. The per iteration update formula in CSA is as follows.

$$X^{i,iter+1} = X^{i,iter} + r_i x f l^{i,iter} (m^{j,iter} - X^{i,iter}) \quad (2)$$

Notation:

$X^{i,iter}$	Position of crow i at time $iter$ in search space;
r_i	Random number with uniform distribution between 0 and 1;
$fl^{i,iter}$	Denotes the flight length of crow i at iteration $iter$;
$m^{j,iter}$	Denotes either the position of hiding place of crow j at time $iter$ or a random new location in search space (crows' deception).

Algorithm 2 The Idle-CSA.

```
Initialize each FP position
Initialize each Tree position
Set reach of step; reach.
Set base position; basepos.
Set radius; radius.
while termination condition not satisfied:
    Choose another FP randomly.
    Get a response from that FP.
    response = getResponse().
    <case: receive position>.
    Define target move; m = response
    Get current FP position; X_current.
    Calculate distance between target move and current FP position; d.
    Calculate new position; X_new = X_current + (m − X_current) ∗ r ∗ d
    Memorize position; X_memory = X_new
    Update new position.
    Calculate distance between FP and nearest Tree; d_tree = d(X_new − X_tree).
    if d_tree ≤ 3 (T_nearest found):
        if FP carry poll of T_poll ≠ T_nearest:
            Pollination.
        end if
        end if
    end if
    <case: give position>
    getResponse():
        X_memory = X_current.
        if r > awareness.
            response = X_memory.
        else
            response = basepos + r − radius.
        end if
    end getResponse
end while
```

Method 3: Idle-Cuckoo Search via Lévy Flights Algorithm

Cuckoo search is an algorithm that combines the breeding activity of a certain cuckoo species with Lévy flying behavior. Cuckoo search has two search modes: local search and global search, regulated by the redirect probability. As a result, the search space may be examined more effectively globally, increasing the probability of discovering the global optimum. This is because local searches use around one-quarter of the overall search time, whereas global searches use three-quarter of the total search time [26]. As an SI algorithm, the main difference compared to other SI algorithms is that a FP applies the position update of a different individual to itself instead of the other individual, resembling the parasitic habit of a cuckoo putting its eggs into another bird's nest.

$$X_i^{(t+1)} = X_j^t + \alpha \bigoplus L\acute{e}vy(\lambda) \tag{3}$$

Notation:

$X_i^{(t+1)}$	Generating new solutions $X^{(t+1)}$ for a cuckoo j; Lévy step is added to position of individual j;
$\alpha > 0$	The step size which should be related to the problem scale;
α	Weight factor of Lévy step;
$\bigoplus$	Entry-wise multiplications.

Furthermore, cuckoo search is more efficient since the global search uses Lévy flights rather than the typical random walk. In Algorithm 3, we used the recommended value of 0.1 for step size α to avoid too distant moves of FP. The details of the Lévy flight will be discussed in the following algorithm, as this uses the same concept.

Algorithm 3 The Idle-Cuckoo Search via Lévy Flights Algorithm.

Initialize each FP position
Initialize each Tree position
while termination condition not satisfied:
    $FP_{current}$ choose another one random FP, FP_1.
    Get position of FP; $X_1 = FP_1$ position.
    Calculate new position using Equation (3); $X_{new} = X_1 + RandomLevy() * 0.1$.
    Update new position
    Calculate distance between FP and nearest Tree; $d_{tree} = d(X_{new} - X_{tree})$.
    if $d_{tree} \leq 3$ ($T_{nearest}$ found):
        if FP carry poll of $T_{poll} \neq T_{nearest}$:
            Pollination.
        end if
        FP carry poll of $T_{nearest}$; $T_{poll} = T_{nearest}$
    end if
end while

3.2.2. Individual Random Search

Individual random search refers to an individual who conducts random investigations by themselves without referring to other FP location.

Method 4: Lévy Flight

Lévy flight is well known for solving diffuseness, scaling, and transmission problems related to optimization. According to numerous studies, researchers find that the Lévy technique is universal and many innovations have evolved to boost Lévy flight efficiency [27]. Lévy flight is essentially a random walk, with the arbitrary stride length drawn from the Lévy distribution which has infinite variance and infinite mean. According to Reynolds and Frye's research [28], the fruit flies influenced the Lévy flight style's intermittent free-scale search pattern or *Drosophila melanogaster* exploring their environment with a succession of straight flight routes interspersed by 90° sudden twists.

A random walk generates Lévy flights with a stride length drawn from the stable levy distribution, as shown in Algorithm 4. A simple power-law formula is then described using the Lévy probability distribution. Here, $0 < \beta \leq 2$ is the Index of Lévy distribution [29].

$$Lévy(s) \sim |S|^{-1-\beta} \tag{4}$$

Algorithm 4 Individual Lévy Flight.

Initialize each FP position
Initialize each Tree position
Set β.
Set list sigma value; $list\_sigma$.
Set reach of step; $reach$.
while termination condition not satisfied:
    if $0.5 < \beta < 1.95$:
        Calculate index; $i = (\beta/0.05) - 1$.
        Get sigma, $\sigma = list\_sigma[i]$.
        Choose random value; r_1, r_2.
        Calculate normal distribution 1; $nd_1 = \sqrt{log(r_1) * (-2)} * cos(2\pi r_2) * \sigma$
        Calculate normal distribution 2; $nd_2 = \sqrt{log(r_1) * (-2)} * cos(2\pi r_2)$
        Calculate random Lévy; $levy = nd_1 / |nd_2|^{(1/\beta)}$
    end if
    Calculate new position; $X_{new} = levy * reach * 0.1$
    Update new position.
    Calculate distance between FP and nearest Tree; $d_{tree} = d(X_{new} - X_{tree})$.
    if $d_{tree} \leq 3$ ($T_{nearest}$ found):
        if FP carry poll of $T_{poll} \neq T_{nearest}$:
            Pollination.
        end if
        FP carry poll of $T_{nearest}$; $T_{poll} = T_{nearest}$
    end if
end while

3.2.3. Multi-Agent System

A multi-agent system (MAS) is a system consisting of multiple interacting computing components known as agents. MAS appears to be a natural metaphor for understanding and building various types of what we can call an artificial social system. The concept of MAS is not reliant on a single application domain, but it seems to be prevalent across various application domains [30]. MAS is commonly used to model self-organizing systems and emerging behavior but has not been applied much to random searches and the immediate solution of optimization problems in a generic way. Since not tied to the direct evaluation of fitness functions, the Pollination Problem also offers MAS the prospect of an application.

Method 5: Defender-Aggressor-Game (DAG)

We used a basic participation game inspired the Defender-Aggressor-Game (DAG) in which each player chooses two other players at random. Assume that the selected players are player A and player B, as shown in Figure 6. Everyone in this game seeks to position themselves so that their A (the player's "Defender") is always between them and their particular B (the player's "Aggressor"). Everyone in this game tries to place herself with A and B in the same concurrent manner. This simple rule maintains the stable dynamics and keeps all agents moving around randomly, with a low chance that the pattern stabilizes to a line-like arrangement of all players [31].

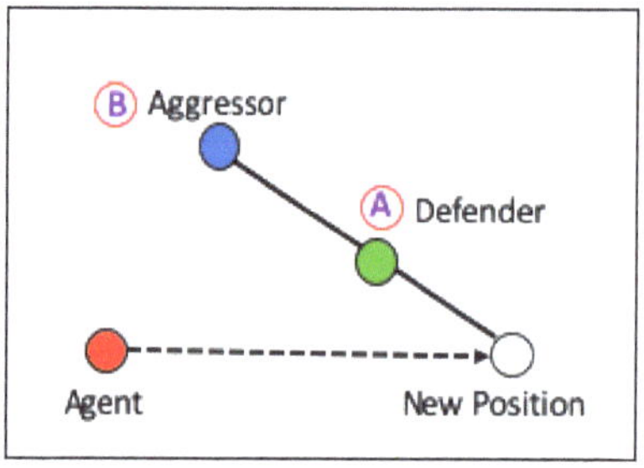

Figure 6. Rules for playing the Defender Aggressor Game.

It is stated in the Algorithm 5 that in order to obtain a new position, the position must be multiplied by the safety factor of 1.2. The safety factor is the parameter value that has been determined to move far enough behind the defender but not too far. A value above 1 but close to 1 is a common choice.

Algorithm 5 DAG.

Initialize each FP position
Initialize each Tree position
while termination condition not satisfied:
    $FP_{current}$ choose two another random FP; FP_1 and FP_2.
    Repeat until $FP_1 \neq FP_2$.
    Get position of FP; $X_1 = FP_1$ position, $X_2 = FP_2$ position.
    FP_1 as aggressor, FP_2 as defender.
    $X_{new} = X_1 + (X_2 - X_1) * 1.2$
    Update new position.
    Calculate distance between FP and nearest Tree; $d_{tree} = d(X_{new} - X_{tree})$.
    if $d_{tree} \leq 3$ ($T_{nearest}$ found):
        if FP carry poll of $T_{poll} \neq T_{nearest}$:
            Pollination.
        end if
        FP carry poll of $T_{nearest}$; $T_{poll} = T_{nearest}$
    end if
end while

4. Results

The experiment results using the metaheuristic algorithm method from the three different techniques vary depending on the method's behavior. Figure 7 represents the results of these variations by showing the average tree pollination. The time is represented on the x-axis, which ranges from 0 to 20 min. The first minute represented on the graph indicates that the average pollination happened between 0:00 and 0:59. Figure 7a indicates that DAG pollinated more trees at the first minute with an average value of 3.8. Lévy comes in second with an average value of 2.35, followed by Idle-CSA 2.2, Idle-Cuckco, and Idle-Jaya with the same average score of 0.95.

All simulations demonstrate a substantial difference in results when using the swarm algorithm, i.e., Idle-Jaya, Idle-CSA, and Idle-Cuckoo, compared to searches that do not use swarm behavior approaches such as Lévy flight and DAG; the average percentage results. Swarm search algorithms such as Idle-Jaya, Idle-CSA, and Idle-Cuckoo need some time to pollinate more trees, but Lévy flight and DAG require less time to pollinate more trees. This simulation indicates that the swarm method in pollination here requires a longer period of time since these algorithms are meant to work together in the search. However, if using multi-agent system search and individual random search method, more trees are pollinated in a not too long time period since the range of each FP is different. The FP acts independently without the need to stay together. In other words, in using SI algorithms, we could observe that the FP swarm all close to the same tree, where they can obtain all nectar but will not cross-pollinate before reaching another tree. Once the first FP arrives at the other tree, the tree becomes pollinated and the nectar will not be available to other FP anymore.

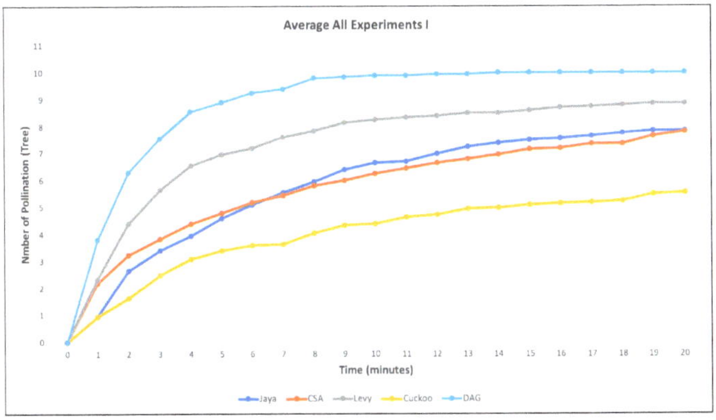

(**a**)

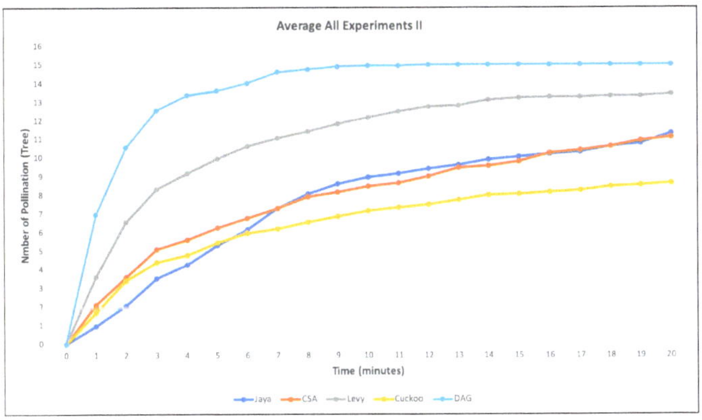

(**b**)

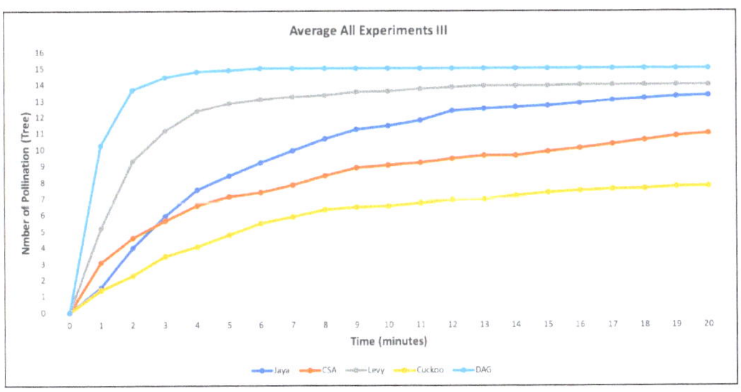

(**c**)

Figure 7. The average results from all simulation. (**a**) Experiment I. (**b**) Experiment II. (**c**) Experiment III.

Aside from the average tree pollination results shown above, this simulation also shows how much nectar FP collects during a tree search. The average results are shown in Table 2. The average amount of nectar collected from all simulations also shows that Lévy flight and DAG collect more nectar, even though the values of other Idle-SI are not significantly different from the results.

Table 2. The average nectar amount from all simulations.

Algorithm	Experiment 1	Experiment 2	Experiment 3
Idle-Jaya	9.55	12.10	15.50
Idle-CSA	10.10	13.20	13.95
Idle-Cuckoo	9.00	15.10	10.40
Levy Flight	10.50	18.80	15.50
DAG	11.70	17.70	16.80

According to Morgan and the researchers of [32], the Gini index is the single best measure of inequality. The Gini index is a well-known concentration index established by Corrado Gini [33] more than a century ago to measure the level of inequality in income distribution and wealth distribution. The Gini index is used here to describe whether FP nectar intake is spread throughout the FP population in a impartial and balanced manner, contrary to a situation where few FP pick most of the nectar alone. The Gini index values for the FP are shown in Table 3. The Gini index from all experiments revealed that FP distributed nectar equally because zero represents the Gini index of perfect equality. All values are the same, whereas 1 expresses maximal inequality among FP. However, an advantage of DAG against other algorithms is notable here.

Table 3. The Gini Index average of the simulated representation of FP distribution nectar.

Algorithm	Experiment 1	Experiment 2	Experiment 3
Idle-Jaya	0.53	0.47	0.63
Idle-CSA	0.47	0.39	0.55
Idle-Cuckoo	0.49	0.40	0.64
Lévy Flight	0.48	0.37	0.58
DAG	0.41	0.31	0.49

5. Discussion

After simulating the case of cocoa flower pollination by using various random search algorithms, the main finding is that Lévy Flight and DAG outperformed the selected SI search approaches, particularly Idle-Jaya, Idle-CSA, and Idle-Cuckoo Search (that also includes Lévy flight). Lévy flight and DAG could pollinate more trees than Idle-Jaya, Idle-CSA, and Idle-Cuckoo in the first several minutes of the simulation out of the three case simulations demonstrated. According to the paper [34], by comparing the search algorithm for neural architecture search (NAS), the evolutionary algorithm is better at handling optimization on NAS. Bn contrast, a random search may be faster but does not guarantee the best results in the case of the Pollination Problem.

The DAG method used here is not that different from general evolutionary methods. It can be related to a particular case of Differential Evolution (DE). The original DE procedure is summarized as follows: A simple differential mutation operation resulting from two different individuals chosen from the population to disturb a randomly selected individual as the base vector. Then generate progeny candidates and a one-to-one selection strategy to determine which individuals are still surviving [35]. The main point is that DE adds the difference vector between two other individuals to itself or a third randomly selected position for a new search candidate position. DAG essentially does the same by adding the difference vector of Defender and Aggressor to the Defender. Thus, it is a differential algorithm as well. DE is as known as a strong metaheuristic in many application cases while being easy to use and implement. Based on the results, we can conclude that DAG outperforms other Idle-SI algorithms. DE is also a favoured algorithm for solving real-valued continuous optimization problems [36–38].

In addition to DAG, Lévy flight produces good results in second place after DAG. This result also supports the author's [39] proposal to include Lévy flight in the Jaya basic algorithm to improve exploration and exploitation capabilities during the search process. In this paper, Lévy flight is proposed to be incorporated into Jaya basic algorithm to facilitate the global search in the initial stages and local stages of the last investigation, increasing the algorithm's exploration and local optima avoidance capabilities. However, Idle-Cuckoo search, a derived SI algorithm from Cuckoo Search, already includes a Lévy flight and the results show the worst performance among all algorithms studied here.

What is the main benefit of such studies? After all, we cannot consider a head-to-head competition among algorithms as is common in other studies on the application of metaheuristic algorithms, for example [40]. This is simply due to the lack of an immediately available fitness function. However, even when reducing such algorithms to their exploration component, it shows significant differences in the congruent goal of pollinating trees that are concomitant to nectar collection. We can observe that the three types of algorithms refer to cases of more general random search strategies:

- Individual strategies, such as Lévy flight, are such that each FP pursues its trajectory independent of the other FP. The case is most supported also by biological insights into insects flight patterns. We can testify that it is a good method but not the best quality method.
- The FP takes a reference to one or more other FP positions for deciding on the next move. This is basically implemented in all Swarm Intelligence algorithms. However, we can see that there is neither a significant advantage concerning nectar intake nor any gain in the number of pollinated trees. From a biological point of view, it also rests on the assumption that insects can recognize their species among other objects in the environment.
- A differential approach in which the FP decides the next step based on a reference to the offset between two objects in the environment. Our analysis clearly shows the advantage of this strategy: pollinating the most significant number of trees and including the fairest distribution of nectar within the population. Moreover, the pun is on "different objects" and not necessarily other FP to take as reference. It means that the same method might work as well, e.g., other insect species as reference points. This method is subject to further investigations.

Practically, the promotion of differential strategies can promote pollination, which would require related farm experiments. The other impact is on the study of related optimization problems from this class of deferred fitness problems. In fact, we can find numerous problems that have been hard to approach so far: the evolution of parasitism as an example from biology. Moreover, there are congruent constraints in the food supply chain, for example, producing farm goods to arrive in a new state at some consumer site.

6. Conclusions

Here, we studied the problem of Pollination optimization that came out to be a concurrent optimization problem with a deferred fitness evaluation. FP and trees act together in a seamless but also contingent way to achieve this objective.

We investigated three different random search methods: fitness-free versions of Swarm Intelligence Algorithm, i.e., Idle-Jaya, Idle-CSA, and Idle-Cuckoo Search; the Individual Random Search method, i.e., Lévy flight; and finally, the Multi-Agent Systems search method, i.e., Defender-Aggressor-Game (DAG). Those methods have been compared for simulating cocoa flower pollination.

We chose cocoa pollination as the simulation case because the flowers of the cocoa plant are unique from other plants. They are small (maximum diameter of 3 cm), allowing only small insects to pollinate them. Cross-pollination is the only method to ensure successful fertilization because the self-pollination of unsuitable varieties will not result in successful fertilization.

From the results of this study, we can observe the differences among random search strategies. Concerning the main objective and the ratio of pollinated trees, there is an apparent gain from the differential method DAG. There are no significant differences relative to nectar intake and distribution, while there is a better value tendency of DAG. Generally, we can conclude that there is no best method at all points. However, we can refer to the results of this simulation for multi-agent and random searches, which may be more suitable for cocoa pollination in the real world. The simulation approach is also expected to assist a farmer when it comes to the inadequate pollination of cocoa flowers. This can improve the cocoa plant's productivity, as the related setup and experiments can also be performed by farmers using the same simulation software to learn about the influence of the various factors in pollination. By utilizing this simulation, farmers can use this simulation to manage or design their tree or plant placement and the order of potential nests or breeding site for pollinator nests.

Author Contributions: Conceptualization, W.A.S. and M.K.; methodology, M.K.; software, M.K. and R.M.P.; validation, W.A.S. and M.K.; formal analysis, W.A.S. and M.K.; investigation, W.A.S. and M.K.; resources, W.A.S. and M.K.; data curation, W.A.S. and M.K.; writing—original draft preparation, W.A.S.; writing—review and editing, M.K.; visualization, W.A.S.; supervision, M.K. All authors have read and agreed to the published version of the manuscript.

Funding: This research received no external funding.

Data Availability Statement: No new data were created or analyzed in this study. Data sharing is not applicable to this article.

Acknowledgments: The authors of this article would like to thank the Kyushu Institute of Technology for their financial and educational support.

Conflicts of Interest: The authors declare that they have no known competing financial interests or personal relationships that could have appeared to influence the work reported in this paper.

References

1. Winder, J. Recent research on insect pollination of Cocoa. 1977. Available online: https://agris.fao.org/agris-search/search.do?recordID=XE20122002213 (accessed on 15 June 2021).
2. Claus, G.; Vanhove, W.; Van Damme, P.; Smagghe, G. Challenges in cocoa pollination: The case of Côte d'Ivoire. *Pollinat. Plants* **2018**, *39*.
3. Mousavirad, S.J.; Ebrahimpour-Komleh, H. Human mental search: A new population-based metaheuristic optimization algorithm. *Appl. Intell.* **2017**, *47*, 850–887. [CrossRef]
4. Bgrlbnd, S. Studies in cacao: Part I. The method of pollination. *Ann. Appl. Biol.* **1925**, *12*, 403–409. [CrossRef]
5. Jones, G. The structure and pollination of the cacao flower. *West Indian Bull* **1912**, *12*, 347–350.
6. Kaufmann, T. Behavioral biology of a cocoa pollinator, Forcipomyia inornatipennis (Diptera: Ceratopogonidae) in Ghana. *J. Kansas Entomol. Soc.* **1974**, 541–548.
7. Frimpong-Anin, K.; Adjaloo, M.K.; Kwapong, P.K.; Oduro, W. Structure and Stability of Cocoa Flowers and Their Response to Pollination. *J. Bot.* **2014**, *2014*, 513623. [CrossRef]
8. Yang, X.S. Flower pollination algorithm for global optimization. In Proceedings of the International Conference on Unconventional Computing and Natural Computation, Orléans, France, 3–7 September 2012; Springer: Berlin/Heidelberg, Germany, 2012; pp. 240–249.
9. Campbell, D.R. Predicting plant reproductive success from models of competition for pollination. *Oikos* **1986**, 257–266. [CrossRef]
10. Dorin, A.; Taylor, T.; Burd, M.; Garcia, J.; Shrestha, M.; Dyer, A.G. Competition and pollen wars: Simulations reveal the dynamics of competition mediated through heterospecific pollen transfer by non-flower constant insects. *Theor. Ecol.* **2020**, *14*, 207–218. [CrossRef]
11. Cho, S.H.; Kim, Y.H.; Park, I.W.; Kim, J.H. Behavior selection and memory-based learning for artificial creature using two-layered confabulation. In Proceedings of the RO-MAN 2007—The 16th IEEE International Symposium on Robot and Human Interactive Communication, Jeju, Korea, 26–29 August 2007; pp. 992–997.
12. Karaboga, D.; Basturk, B. A powerful and efficient algorithm for numerical function optimization: Artificial bee colony (ABC) algorithm. *J. Glob. Optim.* **2007**, *39*, 459–471. [CrossRef]
13. Krishnanand, K.; Ghose, D. Glowworm swarm optimization for simultaneous capture of multiple local optima of multimodal functions. *Swarm Intell.* **2009**, *3*, 87–124. [CrossRef]

14. Yang, X.S.; Deb, S. Cuckoo search via Lévy flights. In Proceedings of the 2009 World Congress on Nature & Biologically Inspired Computing (NaBIC), Coimbatore, India, 9–11 December 2009; pp. 210–214.
15. Wu, T.q.; Yao, M.; Yang, J.h. Dolphin swarm algorithm. *Front. Inf. Technol. Electron. Eng.* **2016**, *17*, 717–729. [CrossRef]
16. Cuevas, E.; Cienfuegos, M.; Zaldívar, D.; Pérez-Cisneros, M. A swarm optimization algorithm inspired in the behavior of the social-spider. *Expert Syst. Appl.* **2013**, *40*, 6374–6384. [CrossRef]
17. Yang, X.S. A new metaheuristic bat-inspired algorithm. In *Nature Inspired Cooperative Strategies for Optimization (NICSO 2010)*; Springer: Berlin/Heidelberg, Germany, 2010; pp. 65–74.
18. Delp, S.L.; Anderson, F.C.; Arnold, A.S.; Loan, P.; Habib, A.; John, C.T.; Guendelman, E.; Thelen, D.G. OpenSim: Open-source software to create and analyze dynamic simulations of movement. *IEEE Trans. Biomed. Eng.* **2007**, *54*, 1940–1950. [CrossRef]
19. Rao, R. Jaya: A simple and new optimization algorithm for solving constrained and unconstrained optimization problems. *Int. J. Ind. Eng. Comput.* **2016**, *7*, 19–34.
20. Askarzadeh, A. A novel metaheuristic method for solving constrained engineering optimization problems: Crow search algorithm. *Comput. Struct.* **2016**, *169*, 1–12. [CrossRef]
21. Yang, X.S. *Nature-Inspired Metaheuristic Algorithms*; Luniver Press: London, UK, 2010.
22. Abraham, A.; Das, S.; Roy, S. Swarm intelligence algorithms for data clustering. In *Soft Computing for Knowledge Discovery and Data Mining*; Springer: Boston, MA, USA, 2008; pp. 279–313.
23. Das, S.; Abraham, A.; Konar, A. Swarm intelligence algorithms in bioinformatics. In *Computational Intelligence in Bioinformatics*; Springer: Berlin/Heidelberg, Germany, 2008; pp. 113–147.
24. Kassabalidis, I.; El-Sharkawi, M.; Marks, R.; Arabshahi, P.; Gray, A. Swarm intelligence for routing in communication networks. In Proceedings of the GLOBECOM'01. IEEE Global Telecommunications Conference (Cat. No. 01CH37270), San Antonio, TX, USA, 25–29 November 2001; Volume 6, pp. 3613–3617.
25. Kennedy, J.; Eberhart, R. Particle swarm optimization. In Proceedings of the ICNN'95-International Conference on Neural Networks, Perth, WA, Australia, 27 November–1 December 1995; Volume 4, pp. 1942–1948.
26. Yang, X.S.; Deb, S. Cuckoo search: Recent advances and applications. *Neural Comput. Appl.* **2014**, *24*, 169–174. [CrossRef]
27. Kamaruzaman, A.F.; Zain, A.M.; Yusuf, S.M.; Udin, A. Levy flight algorithm for optimization problems-a literature review. In *Applied Mechanics and Materials*; Trans Tech Publications Ltd.: Stafa-Zurich, Switzerland, 2013; Volume 421, pp. 496–501.
28. Reynolds, A.M.; Frye, M.A. Free-flight odor tracking in Drosophila is consistent with an optimal intermittent scale-free search. *PLoS ONE* **2007**, *2*, e354. [CrossRef] [PubMed]
29. Chechkin, A.V.; Metzler, R.; Klafter, J.; Gonchar, V.Y. Introduction to the theory of Lévy flights. *Anomalous Transp.* **2008**, *1*, 129.
30. Wooldridge, M. *An Introduction to Multiagent Systems*; John wiley & Sons: Hoboken, NJ, USA, 2009.
31. Anderson, C. Linking micro-to macro-level behavior in the aggressor-defender-stalker game. *Adapt. Behav.* **2004**, *12*, 175–185. [CrossRef]
32. Morgan, J. The anatomy of income distribution. *Rev. Econ. Stat.* **1962**, *44*, 270–283. [CrossRef]
33. Gini, C. *I Fattori Demografici dell'evoluzione Delle Nazioni*; CreateSpace: Scotts Valley, CA, USA, 1912; Volume 8.
34. Liashchynskyi, P.; Liashchynskyi, P. Grid search, random search, genetic algorithm: A big comparison for nas. *arXiv* **2019**, arXiv:1912.06059.
35. Price, K.V. Differential evolution. In *Handbook of Optimization*; Springer: Berlin/Heidelberg, Germany, 2013; pp. 187–214.
36. Storn, R.; Price, K. Differential evolution—A simple and efficient heuristic for global optimization over continuous spaces. *J. Glob. Optim.* **1997**, *11*, 341–359. [CrossRef]
37. Price, K.V. Differential evolution: A fast and simple numerical optimizer. In Proceedings of the North American Fuzzy Information Processing, Berkeley, CA, USA, 19–22 June 1996; pp. 524–527.
38. Price, K.; Storn, R.M.; Lampinen, J.A. *Differential Evolution: A Practical Approach to Global Optimization*; Springer Science & Business Media: Berlin/Heidelberg, Germany, 2006.
39. Ingle, K.K.; Jatoth, R.K. An efficient JAYA algorithm with lévy flight for non-linear channel equalization. *Expert Syst. Appl.* **2020**, *145*, 112970. [CrossRef]
40. Baresel, A.; Sthamer, H.; Schmidt, M. Fitness function design to improve evolutionary structural testing. In Proceedings of the 4th Annual Conference on Genetic and Evolutionary Computation, New York, NY, USA, 9–13 July 2002; pp. 1329–1336.

algorithms

MDPI

Review

Generative Adversarial Network for Overcoming Occlusion in Images: A Survey

Kaziwa Saleh [1,*], Sándor Szénási [2,3] and Zoltán Vámossy [2]

1 Doctoral School of Applied Informatics and Applied Mathematics, Óbuda University, 1034 Budapest, Hungary
2 John von Neumann Faculty of Informatics, Óbuda University, 1034 Budapest, Hungary; szenasi.sandor@nik.uni-obuda.hu (S.S.); vamossy.zoltan@nik.uni-obuda.hu (Z.V.)
3 Faculty of Economics and Informatics, J. Selye University, 94501 Komárno, Slovakia
* Correspondence: kaziwa.saleh@uni-obuda.hu

Abstract: Although current computer vision systems are closer to the human intelligence when it comes to comprehending the visible world than previously, their performance is hindered when objects are partially occluded. Since we live in a dynamic and complex environment, we encounter more occluded objects than fully visible ones. Therefore, instilling the capability of amodal perception into those vision systems is crucial. However, overcoming occlusion is difficult and comes with its own challenges. The generative adversarial network (GAN), on the other hand, is renowned for its generative power in producing data from a random noise distribution that approaches the samples that come from real data distributions. In this survey, we outline the existing works wherein GAN is utilized in addressing the challenges of overcoming occlusion, namely amodal segmentation, amodal content completion, order recovery, and acquiring training data. We provide a summary of the type of GAN, loss function, the dataset, and the results of each work. We present an overview of the implemented GAN architectures in various applications of amodal completion. We also discuss the common objective functions that are applied in training GAN for occlusion-handling tasks. Lastly, we discuss several open issues and potential future directions.

Keywords: amodal completion; amodal content completion; amodal segmentation; amodal perception; order recovery; occlusion relationship; GAN; adversarial models

1. Introduction

Artificial intelligence has revolutionized the world. With the advent of deep learning and machine learning-based models, many applications and processes in our daily life have been automated. Computer vision is prominently essential in these applications, and while humans can effortlessly make sense of their surrounding, machines are far from achieving that level of comprehension. Our environment is dynamic, complex, and cluttered. Objects are usually partially occluded by other objects. However, our brain completes the partially visible objects without us being aware of it. The capability of humans to perceive incomplete objects is called amodal completion [1]. Unfortunately, this task is not as straightforward and easy for computers to achieve, because occlusion can happen in various ratios, angles, and viewpoints [2]. An object may be occluded by one or more objects, and an object may hide several other objects.

GAN is a structured probabilistic model that consists of two networks, a generator that captures the data distributions and a discriminator that decides whether the produced data come from the actual data distribution or from the generator. The two networks train in a two-player minimax game fashion until the generator can generate samples that are similar to the true samples, and the discriminator can no longer distinguish between the real and the fake samples.

Since its first introduction by Goodfellow et al. in 2014, numerous variants of GAN are proposed, mainly architecture variants and loss variants [3]. The modifications in the first category can either be in the overall network architecture such as progressive GAN (PROGAN) [4], in representation of the latent space such as conditional GAN (CGAN) [5], or in modifying the architecture toward a particular application as in CycleGAN [6]. The second category of variants encompasses modifications that are introduced to the loss functions and regularization techniques such as the Wasserstein GAN (WGAN) [7] and PatchGAN [8].

Despite the various modifications, GAN is challenging to train and evaluate. However, due to its generative power and outstanding performance, it has a significantly large number of applications in computer vision, bio-metric systems, medical field, etc. Therefore, there are a considerable number of reviews carried out on GAN and its application in different domains (shown in Section 3). There are a limited number of existing reviews that briefly mention overcoming occlusion in images with GAN. Therefore, in this survey we concentrate on the applications of GAN in amodal completion in detail. In summary, the contributions of this survey paper are:

1. We survey the literature for the available frameworks where they utilize GAN in one or more aspects of amodal completion.
2. We discuss in detail the architecture of existing works and how they have incorporated GAN in tackling the problems that occur from occlusion.
3. We summarize the loss function, the dataset, and the reported results of the available works.
4. We also provide an overview of prevalent objective functions in training the GAN model for amodal completion tasks.
5. Finally, we discuss several directions for the future research in tasks of occlusion handling wherein GAN can be utilized.

The term "occlusion handling" is polysemous in the computer vision literature. In object tracking, it mostly refers to the ability of the model to address occlusions and resume tracking the object once it re-appears in the scene [9]. In classification and detection tasks, the term indicates determining the depth order of the objects and the occlusion relationship between them [10]. Other works such as [11,12] define occlusion handling as the techniques that interpolate the blank patches in an object, i.e., content completion. However, we believe that, in order to enable a model to address occlusions, it needs the same tasks defined in amodal completion. Therefore, in this survey we use "amodal completion" and "occlusion handling" interchangeably.

As a limitation, we only focus on occlusion handling in a single 2D image. Therefore, occlusion in 3D images, stereo images, and video data are out of the scope of this work. Additionally, we emphasize on the GAN component of each architecture we reviewed. As GAN is applied for various tasks in different problems, it is difficult to carry out a systematic comparison of the existing models. Each model is evaluated on a different dataset using a different evaluation metric for a different task. In some cases, the papers do not assess the performance of GAN. In those cases, we present the result of the entire model.

The rest of this document is organized as follows: the methodology for conducting this survey is presented in Section 2. Next, Section 3 mentions the related available articles in the literature. Section 4 introduces the fundamental concepts about GAN and its training challenges, and the aspects of amodal completion. Afterward, Section 5 presents the problems in amodal completion and how GAN has been applied to address them. The common loss functions in GAN for amodal completion are discussed in Section 6. In Sections 7 and 8, future directions and key findings of this survey article are presented. Finally, conclusions are enunciated in Section 9.

2. Methodology

To perform a descriptive systematic literature review, we begin by forming the research questions which this survey attempts to answer. The questions are (1) what are the challenges in amodal completion? (2) how are GAN models applied to address the problems of amodal completion? Based on the formulated questions, the search terms are identified to find and collect relevant publications. The search keywords are "GAN AND occlusion", "GAN AND amodal completion", "GAN AND occlusion handling", "GAN for occlusion handling", and "GAN for amodal completion".

We inspect several research databases, such as IEEE Xplore, Google Scholar, Web of Science, and Scopus. The list of the returned articles from the search process is sorted and refined by excluding the publications that do not satisfy the research questions. The elimination criteria are as follows: the research article addresses aspects of occlusion handling but do not employ GAN; GAN is used in applications other than amodal completion; the authors have worked on occlusion in 3D data, or video frames. Subsequently, each of the remaining publications in the list is investigated and summarized. The articles are examined for the GAN architecture, the objective function, the dataset, the results, and the purpose of using GAN.

3. Related Works

Occlusion: Handling occlusion has been studied in various domains and applications. Table 1 shows the list of published surveys and reviews of occlusion in several applications. A survey of occlusion handling in generic object detection of still images is provided in [2], focusing on challenges that arise when objects are occluded. Similarly, the most recent survey article by the authors of [13] provides the taxonomy of problems in amodal completion from single 2D images. However, none of those review articles concentrate on the applications of GAN for overcoming occlusion particularly. Other works have focused on occlusion in specific scopes, such as object tracking [14,15], pedestrians [16,17], human faces [18–22], automotive environment [23,24], and augmented reality [25]. In contrary, we review the articles that address occlusion in single 2D images.

Table 1. Existing survey articles about occlusion that were published between 2017 and 2022.

#	Title	Pub.	Year
1	Multiple camera based multiple object tracking under occlusion: A survey [14]	IEEE	2017
2	Facial expression analysis under partial occlusion: A survey [18]	ACM	2018
3	Occlusion detection and restoration techniques for 3D face recognition: a literature review [19]	Springer	2018
4	Overcoming occlusion in the automotive environment—A review [23]	IEEE	2019
5	A comprehensive survey on multi object tracking under occlusion in aerial image sequences [15]	IEEE	2019
6	A Survey on Occluded Face recognition [26]	ACM	2020
7	Occlusion Handling in Generic Object Detection: A Review [2]	IEEE	2021
8	Occlusion Handling in Augmented Reality: Past, Present and Future [25]	IEEE	2021
9	A survey of face recognition techniques under occlusion [20]	Wiley	2021
10	Survey of pedestrian detection with occlusion [16]	Springer	2021
11	Occlusion Handling and Multi-scale Pedestrian Detection Based on Deep Learning: A Review [17]	IEEE	2022
12	Image Amodal Completion: A Survey [13]	arXiv	2022
13	A Literature Survey of Face Recognition Under Different Occlusion Conditions [21]	IEEE	2022

Generative Adversarial Network: Due to their power, GANs are ubiquitous in computer vision research. Due to the growing body of published works in GAN, there are several recent surveys and review papers in the literature investigating its challenges, variants, and applications. Table 2 contains a list of survey articles that have been published in the last five years. The list does not include papers that specifically focus on GAN applications outside the computer vision field.

The authors in [27–32] discuss the instability problem of GAN with the various techniques and improvisations that have been designed to stabilize its training. Adversarial attack can be carried out against machine learning models by generating an input sample that leads to unexpected and undesired results by the model. Sajeeda et al. [27] investigate the various defense mechanisms to protect GAN against such attacks. Li et al. [33] summarize the different models into two groups of GAN architectures: the two-network models and the hybrid models, which are GANs combined with an encoder, autoencoder, or variational autoencoder (VAE) to enhance the training stability. The authors of [34,35] explore the available evaluation metrics of GAN models. Other works have discussed the application of different GAN architectures for computer vision [36,37], image-to-image translation [38,39], face generation [40,41], medical field [29,42–44], person re-identification (ReID) [45], audio and video domains [29], generating and augmenting training data [46,47], image super-resolution [39,48], and other real-world applications [39,45,49,50]. Some of the mentioned review articles discuss the occlusion handling as an application of GAN very briefly, without detailing the architecture, loss functions, and the results.

Table 2. Available survey articles about GAN that were published between 2017 and 2022.

#	Title	Pub.	Year
1	Generative adversarial networks: introduction and outlook [37]	IEEE	2017
2	Comparative study on generative adversarial networks [51]	arXiv	2018
3	Generative adversarial networks: An overview [52]	IEEE	2018
4	Recent progress on generative adversarial networks (GANs): A survey [34]	IEEE	2019
5	How generative adversarial networks and their variants work: An overview [32]	ACM	2019
6	Generative adversarial networks (GANs): An overview of theoretical model, evaluation metrics, and recent developments [35]	arXiv	2020
7	Generative adversarial network technologies and applications in computer vision [36]	Hindawi	2020
8	Generative adversarial networks in digital pathology: a survey on trends and future potential [42]	Elsevier	2020
9	Deep generative adversarial networks for image-to-image translation: A review [38]	MDPI	2020
10	A Review on Generative Adversarial Networks: Algorithms, Theory, and Applications [50]	IEEE	2021
11	Generative adversarial network: An overview of theory and applications [49]	Elsevier	2021
12	The theoretical research of generative adversarial networks: an overview [33]	Elsevier	2021
13	Generative adversarial networks (GANs) challenges, solutions, and future directions [28]	ACM	2021
14	Generative adversarial networks: a survey on applications and challenges [31]	Springer	2021
15	A survey on generative adversarial networks for imbalance problems in computer vision tasks [46]	Springer	2021
16	Generative Adversarial Networks and their Application to 3D Face Generation: A Survey [41]	Elsevier	2021
17	Applications of generative adversarial networks (GANs): An updated review [45]	Springer	2021
18	Generative Adversarial Networks in Computer Vision: A Survey and Taxonomy [3]	ACM	2022
19	Exploring Generative Adversarial Networks and Adversarial Training [27]	Elsevier	2022
20	Generative Adversarial Networks for face generation: A survey [40]	ACM	2022
21	Generative Adversarial Networks: A Survey on Training, Variants, and Applications [30]	Springer	2022
22	Augmenting data with generative adversarial networks: An overview [47]	IOS	2022
23	A Survey on Training Challenges in Generative Adversarial Networks for Biomedical Image Analysis [43]	arXiv	2022
24	Attention-based generative adversarial network in medical imaging: A narrative review [44]	Elsevier	2022
25	Generative adversarial networks for image super-resolution: A survey [48]	arXiv	2022
26	Generic image application using GANs (Generative Adversarial Networks): A Review [39]	Springer	2022
27	A Survey on Generative Adversarial Networks: Variants, Applications, and Training [29]	ACM	2022

In this paper, we focus on the works that combine the two above-mentioned topics. Specifically, we want to present the works that have been carried out to tackle the problems that arise from occlusion using GAN. However, depending on the nature of the problems, the applicability of GAN varies. For example, in amodal appearance generation, GAN is the optimal choice of architecture. Comparably, in amodal segmentation and order recovery tasks, it is less used.

4. Background

4.1. Generative Adversarial Network

GAN is an unsupervised generative model that contains two networks, namely a generator and a discriminator. The two networks learn in an adversary manner similar to the min–max game between two players. The generator tries to generate a fake sample that the discriminator cannot distinguish from the real sample. On the other hand, the discriminator learns to determine whether the sample is real data or generated. The generator G takes a random noise z as input. It learns a probability distribution p_g over data x to generate fake samples that imitate the real data distribution (p_{data}). Then, the generated sample is forwarded to the discriminator D which outputs a single scalar that labels the data as real or fake (Figure 1). The classification result is used in training G as gradients of the loss. The loss guides G to generate samples that are less likely and more challenging to be labeled as fake by the D. Overtime, G becomes better in generating more realistic samples that would confuse D, and D becomes better at detecting fake samples. They both try to optimize their objective functions, in other words, G tries to minimize its cost value and D tries to maximize its cost value.

$$\min_G \max_D V(D, G) = \mathbb{E}_{x \sim p_{data}(x)}[logD(x)] + \mathbb{E}_{z \sim p_z(z)}[log(1 - D(G(z)))] \tag{1}$$

Equation (1) was designed by Goodfellow et al. [53] to compute the cost value of GAN where x is the real sample from the training dataset, $G(z)$ is the generated sample, and $D(x)$ and $D(G(z))$ are the discriminator's verdict that x is real and the fake sample $G(z)$ is real.

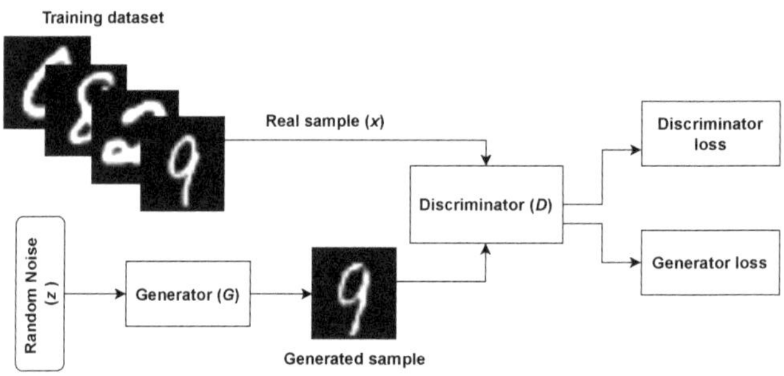

Figure 1. Architecture of the original GAN [53].

There are numerous variations of the original GAN. Among the most prominent ones are CGAN, WGAN, and Self-Attention GAN (SAGAN) [54]. CGAN extends the original GAN by taking an additional input which is usually a class label. The label conditions the generated data to be of a specific class. Therefore, the loss function in (1) becomes as follows:

$$\min_G \max_D V(D, G) = \mathbb{E}_{x \sim p_{data}(x)}[logD(x \mid c)] + \mathbb{E}_{z \sim p_z(z)}[log(1 - D(G(z \mid c)))] \tag{2}$$

where c is the conditional class label.

In order to prevent the vanishing gradient and mode collapse problems (discussed below), WGAN applies an objective function that implements the Earth-Mover (EM) [55] distance for comparing the generated and real data distributions. EM helps in stabilizing GAN's training and the equilibrium between the generator and the discriminator. If the gradient of the loss function becomes too large, WGAN will employ weight clipping. WGAN Gradient Penalty (WGAN-GP) [56] extends WGAN by introducing a penalty term instead of the weight clipping to enhance the training stability, convergence power, and output quality of the network. Moreover, SAGAN applies an attention mechanism to extract features from a broader feature space and capture global dependencies instead of the local neighborhoods. Thus, SAGAN can produce high-resolution details in data as it borrows cues from all feature locations in contrast to the original GAN that depends on only spatially local points.

In theory, both G and D are expected to converge at the Nash equilibrium point. However, in practice this is not as simple as it sounds. Training GANs is challenging, because they are unstable and difficult to evaluate. GANs are notorious for several issues, which are already covered intensively in the literature; therefore, we will only discuss them briefly below.

4.1.1. Achieving Nash Equilibrium

In game theory, Nash equilibrium is when none of the players will change their strategy no matter what the opponents do. In GAN, the game objective changes as the networks take turn during the training process. Therefore, it is particularly difficult to obtain the desired equilibrium point due to the adversarial behavior of its networks. Typically, gradient descent is used to find the minimum value of the cost function during training. However, in GAN, decreasing the cost of one network leads to the increase in the cost of the other network. For instance, if one player minimizes xy with regard to x and another player minimizes $-xy$ with regard to y, gradient descent reaches a stable sphere, but it does not converge to the equilibrium point which is $x = y = 0$ [57].

4.1.2. Mode Collapse

One of the major problems with GANs is that they are unable to generalize well. This poor generalization leads to mode collapse. The generator collapses when it cannot generate large diverse samples known as complete collapse, or it will only produce a specific type (or subset) of target data that will not be rejected by the discriminator as being fake, known as partial collapse [53,57].

4.1.3. Vanishing Gradient

GAN is challenging to train due to the vanishing gradient issue. The generator stops learning when the gradients of the weights of the initial layers become extremely small. Thus, the discriminator confidently rejects the samples produced by the generator [58].

4.1.4. Lack of Evaluation Metrics

Despite the growing progress in the GAN architecture and training, evaluating it remains a challenging task. Although several metrics and methods have been proposed, there is no standard measure for evaluating the models. Most of the available works propose a new technique to assess the strength and the limitation of their model. Therefore, finding a consensus evaluation metric remains an open research question [59].

4.2. *Amodal Completion*

Amodal completion is the natural ability of humans to discern the physical objects in the environment even if they are occluded. Our environment contains more partially visible or temporarily occluded objects than fully visible ones. Hence, the input to our visual system is mostly incomplete and segmented. Yet, we innately and effortlessly imagine the invisible parts of the object in our mind and perceive the object as complete [1]. For instance, if we only see a half of stripped legs in the zoo, we can tell that there is a zebra in that territory.

As natural and seamless this task is for humans, for computers it is challenging yet essential. This is because the performance of most computer vision-related real-world applications drop when objects are occluded. For example, in autonomous driving, the vehicle must be able to recognize and identify the complete contour of the objects in the scene to avoid accidents and drive safely.

Our environment is complex, cluttered, and dynamic. An object may be behind one or more other objects, or an object may hide one or more other objects. Thus, possible occlusion patterns between objects are endless. Therefore, the shape and appearance of occluded objects are unbounded.

Whenever a visual system requires de-occlusion, there are three sub-tasks involved in the process (Figure 2). Firstly, inferring the complete segmentation mask of the partially visible objects, including the hidden region. Secondly, predicting and reconstructing the RGB content of the occluded area based on the visible parts of the object and/or the image. Often, these two sub-tasks require the result of the third sub-task, which determines the depth order of the objects and the relationship between them, i.e., which object is the occluder and which one is the occludee. Several of the existing works address these sub-tasks simultaneously.

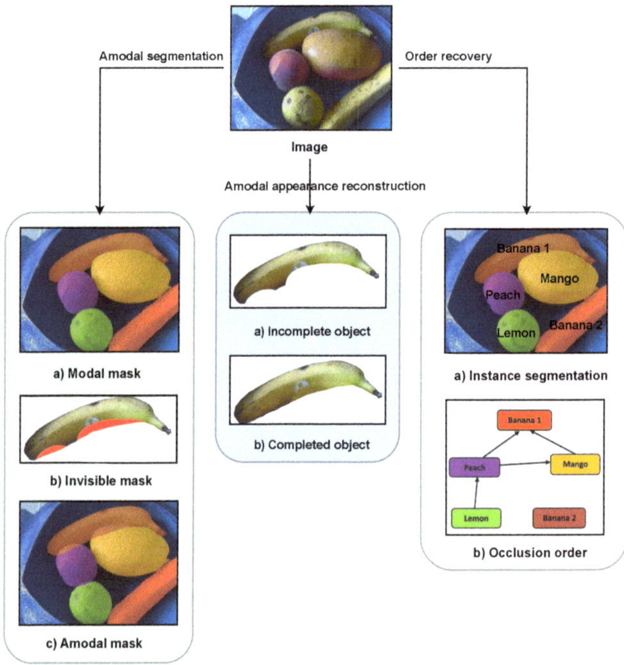

Figure 2. The three sub-tasks in amodal completion.

Designing and training a model that could perform any/all of the above-mentioned sub-processes presents several challenges. In the following section, we explore the existing works in the literature wherein a GAN architecture is implemented to address those obstacles.

5. GAN in Amodal Completion

The taxonomy of the challenges in amodal completion is presented by Ao et al. [13]. In the following sections, we present how GAN has been used to address each challenge. In exploring the existing research papers, we emphasized the aspects of amodal completion wherein GAN was utilized, not the original aim of the paper.

5.1. Amodal Segmentation

Image segmentation tasks such as semantic segmentation, instance segmentation, or panoptic segmentation solely predict the visible shape of the objects in a scene. Therefore, these tasks mainly operate with modal perception. Amodal segmentation, on the other hand, works with amodal perception. It estimates the shape of an object beyond the visible region, i.e., the visible mask (also called the modal mask) and the mask for the occluded region, from the local and the global visible visual cues (see Figure 3).

Amodal segmentation is rather challenging, especially if the occluder is of a different category (e.g., the occlusion between vehicles and pedestrians). The visible region may not hold sufficient information to help in determining the whole extent of the object. Contrariwise, if the occluder is an instance of the same category (e.g., occlusion between pedestrians), since the features of both objects are similar, it becomes difficult for the model to estimate where the boundary of one object ends and the second one begins. In either case, the visible region plays a significant role in guiding the amodal mask generation process. Therefore, most existing methods require the modal mask as input. To alleviate the need for a manually annotated modal mask, many works apply a pre-trained instance segmentation network to obtain the visible mask and utilize it as input.

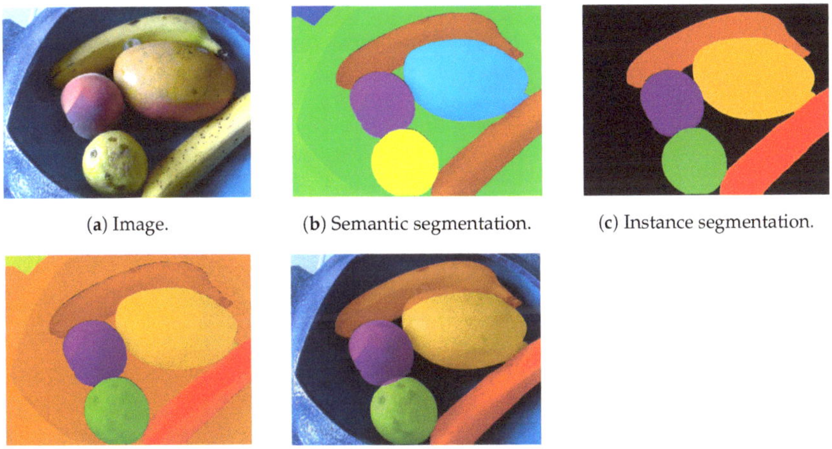

(**a**) Image. (**b**) Semantic segmentation. (**c**) Instance segmentation. (**d**) Panoptic segmentation. (**e**) Amodal segmentation.

Figure 3. Different types of image segmentation.

In the following, we describe the architecture of the GAN-based models that are used in generating the amodal mask of the occluded objects.

A two hourglass generator: Zhou et al. [60] apply a pre-trained instance segmentation network on the input image to obtain an initial mask and feeds it to a two-stage pipeline for human deocclusion. Given the initial mask, the generator implements two hourglass modules to refine and complete the modal mask to produce the amodal mask at the end. A discriminator enhances the quality of the output amodal mask. An additional parsing result accompanies the result of the generator, which is employed by a Parsing Guided Attention (PGA) module to reinforce the semantic features of body parts at multiple scales as a part of a parsing guided content recovery network. The latter uses a combination of UNet [61] and partial convolutions [62] in generating the content of the invisible area. The additional parsing branches add extra semantic guidance, which improves the final invisible mask.

A coarse-to-fine architecture with contextual attention: Xiong et al. [63] firstly employ a contour detection module to extract the visible contour of an object and then complete it through a contour completion network. The contour detection module uses DeepCut [64] to segment prominence objects, and performs noise removal and edge detection to extract the incomplete contour of the object from the segmentation map. Then, the contour completion network learns to conjecture the foreground contour. The contour completion network is composed of a generator and a discriminator. The generator has a coarse-to-fine architecture, each with a similar encoder–decoder structure, except that the refinement network employs a contextual attention layer [65]. Finally, the completed contour along with the ground-truth image are fed to the discriminator which produces a score map to indicate the originality of each region in the generated contour mask and can decide whether the mask aligns with the contour of the image. The discriminator is a fully convolutional PatchGAN [8] trained with a hinge loss. The results show that the contour completion step assists in the explicit modeling of the background and the foreground layer borders, which leads to less evident artifacts in the completed foreground objects.

A generator with priori knowledge: The authors of [66] also utilize a pre-trained instance segmentation model to obtain the visible human mask, which is fed with the input image into a GAN-based model to produce the amodal mask of occluded humans. The model predicts the mask of the invisible region through an hourglass network structure.

The local fine features and the higher-level semantic details are aggregated in the encoding stage, and they are added to each layer's feature maps in the decoding stage. The predicted amodal mask is evaluated by a Patch-GAN discriminator. To improve the amodal segmentation outcome, some typical human poses are concatenated with the feature maps as a priori information to be used in the decoding stage. Although the a priori knowledge enhances the predicted amodal masks, it restricts the application of the model to humans with specific poses.

A coarse-to-fine architecture with multiple discriminators: In the applications such as visual surveillance and autonomous driving, path prediction, and intelligent traffic control, detecting vehicles and pedestrians is essential. However, these are often obstructed by other objects which makes the task of learning the visual representation of intended objects more challenging. The model in [67] aims to recover the amodal mask of a vehicle and the appearance of its hidden regions iteratively. To tackle both tasks, the model is composed of two parts: a segmentation completion module and an appearance recovery module. The first network, follows an initial-to-refined framework. Firstly, an initial segmentation mask is generated by taking an input image with occluded vehicles through a pre-trained segmentation network. Then, the input image is fed again into the next stage after it is concatenated with the output from the initial stage. The second part, in contrary to a standard GAN, has a generator with an encoder–decoder structure, an object discriminator, and an instance discriminator. To assist the model in producing more realistic masks, an additional 3D model pool is employed. This provides silhouette masks as adversarial samples which motivates the model to learn the defining characteristics of actual vehicle masks. The object discriminator, which uses a Stack-GAN structure [68], enforces the output mask to be similar to a real vehicle, whereas the instance discriminator with a standard GAN structure aims at producing an output mask similar to the ground-truth mask. The recovered mask is fed to the appearance recovery module to regenerate the whole foreground vehicle. Both modules are trained with reconstruction loss (i.e., $\mathcal{L}1$ loss) and perceptual loss. Although using the 3D model pool and multiple discriminators produces better amodal masks, when the model is tested on synthetic images with different types of synthetic occlusions, it requires multiple iterations to progressively eliminate the occlusions. However, on real images with less severe occlusions, the model is unable to refine the results beyond three iterations and its performance declines.

5.2. Order Recovery

In order to apply any de-occlusion or completion process, it is essential to determine the occlusion relationship and identify the depth order between the overlapping components of a scene. Other processes such as amodal segmentation and content completion depend on the predicted occlusion order to accomplish their tasks. Therefore, vision systems need to distinguish the occluders from the occludees, and to determine whether an occlusion exists between the objects. Order recovery is vital in many applications, such as semantic scene understanding, autonomous driving, and surveillance systems.

The following works attempt to retrieve the depth order/layer order between the objects in a scene through utilizing a GAN-based architecture.

A generator with multiple discriminators: Dhamo et al. [69] present a method to achieve layered depth prediction and view synthesis. Given a single RGB image as input, the model learns to synthesize a RGB-D view from it and hallucinates the missing regions that were initially occluded. Firstly, the framework uses a fully-convolutional network to obtain a depth map and a segmentation mask for foreground and background elements from the input image. Depending on the predicted masks, the foreground objects are erased from the input image and the obtained depth map (RGB-D). Then, a Patch-GAN [8]-based network is used to refill the holes in the RGB-D background image that were created from removing the foreground objects. The network has a pair of discriminators to enforce inter-domain consistency. This method has data limitations, as it is difficult to obtain ground-truth layered depth images in real-world data.

Inferring the scene layout beyond the visible view and hallucinating the invisible parts of the scene is called amodal scene layout. MonoLayout, proposed in [70], provides the amodal scene layout in the form of bird's eye view (BEV) in real time. With a single input image of a road scene, the framework delivers a BEV of static (such as sidewalks and street areas) and dynamic (vehicles) objects in the scene, including the partially visible components. The model contains a context encoder, two decoders, and two discriminators. Given the input image, the encoder captures the multi-scale context representations of both static and dynamic elements. Then, the context features are shared with two decoders, an amodal static scene decoder and a dynamic scene decoder, to predict the static and dynamic objects in BEV. The decoders are regularized by two corresponding discriminators to encourage the predictions to be similar to the ground-truth representations. The context sharing within the decoders achieves better performance of amodal scene layout. MonoLayout can infer 19.6 M parameters in 32 fps. However, it needs generalization for unseen scenarios.

A single generator and discriminator: Zheng et al. [71] tackle the amodal scene understanding by creating a layer-by-layer pipeline (Completed Scene Decomposition Network (CSDNet)) to extract and complete RGB appearance of objects from a scene, and make sense of their occlusion relation. In each layer, CSDNet only separates the foreground elements that are without occlusion. This way, the system identifies and fills the invisible portion of each object. Then, the completed image is fed again to the model to segment the fully visible objects. In this iterative manner, the depth order of the scene is obtained, which can be used to recompose a new scene. The model is composed of a decomposition network and a completion network. The decomposition network follows Mask-RCNN [72] with an additional layer classification branch to estimate the instance masks, and determine whether an object is fully or partially visible. The predicted masks are forwarded to the completion network, which uses an encoder–decoder to complete the resultant holes in the masked image. By masking the fully visible objects in each step and the iterative completion of the objects in the scene, the earlier completion information is propagated to the later steps. Nonetheless, the model is trained on a rendered dataset; therefore, it cannot generalize well to real scenes that are unlike the rendered ones. In addition, the completion errors over the layers are accumulated, which leads to a drop in accuracy when the occlusion layers are too numerous.

On the other hand, Dhamo et al. [73] present an object-oriented model with three parts: object completion, layout prediction, and image re-composition, while the object completion unit attempts to fill the occluded area in the input RGBA image through an auto-encoder, the layout prediction uses a GAN architecture to estimate the RGBA-D (the RGBA and depth images) background, i.e., the object-free representation of the scene. The model infers the layered representation of a scene from a single image and produces a flexible number of output layers based on the complexity of the scene. However, the global and the local contexts, and the spatial relationship between the objects in the scene, are not considered.

5.3. Amodal Appearance Reconstruction

Recently, there has been a significant progress in image inpainting methods, such as the works in [65,74]. However, these models recover the plausible content of a missing area with no knowledge about which object is involved in that part. On the contrary, amodal appearance reconstruction (also known as amodal content completion) models require identifying individual elements in the scene, and recognizing the partially visible objects along with their occluded areas, to predict the content for the invisible regions.

Therefore, the majority of the existing frameworks follow a multi-stage process to address the problem of amodal segmentation and amodal content completion as one problem. Therefore, they depend on the segmentator to infer the binary segmentation mask for the occluded and non-occluded parts of the object. The mask is then forwarded as input to the amodal completion module, which tries to fill in the RGB content for the missing region indicated by the mask.

Among the three sub-tasks of amodal completion, GAN is most widely used in amodal content completion. In this section, we present the usage of GAN in amodal content completion for a variety of computer vision applications.

5.3.1. Generic Object Completion

GANs are unable to estimate and learn the structure in the image implicitly with no additional information about the structures or annotations regarding the foreground and background objects during training. Therefore, Xiong et al. [63] propose a model that is made up of a contour detection module, a contour completion module, and an image completion module. The first two modules learn to detect and complete the foreground contour. Then, the image completion module is guided by the completed contour to determine the position of the foreground and the background pixels. The incomplete input image, the completed contour, and the hole mask are fed to the image completion network to fill the missing part of the object. The network has a similar coarse-to-fine architecture as the contour completion module. However, the depth of the network weakens the effect of the completed contour. Therefore, the complete contour is passed to both the coarse network and the refinement network. The discriminator of the image completion network is a PatchGAN that is trained with hinge loss and requires the generated fake image or the ground-truth image with the hole mask. The experiments show that, under the guide of the contour completion, the model can generate completed images with less artifacts and complete objects with more natural boundaries. However, the model will fail to produce results without artifacts and color discrepancy around the holes due to implementing vanilla convolutions in extracting the features.

Therefore, Zhan et al. [75] use CGAN and partial convolution [62] to regenerate the content of the missing region. The authors apply the concept of partial completion to de-occlude the objects in an image. In the case of an object hidden by multiple other objects, the partial completion is performed by considering one object at a time. The model partially completes both the mask and the appearance of the object in question through two networks, namely Partial Completion Network-mask (PCNet-M) and Partial Completion Network-content (PCNet-C), respectively. A self-supervised approach is implemented to produce labeled occluded data to train the networks, i.e., a masked region is obtained by positioning a randomly selected occluder from the dataset on top of the concerned object. Then, the masked occludee is passed to the PCNet-M to reproduce the mask of the invisible area, which in turn is given to the PCNet-C. Although the self-supervised and partial completion techniques alleviate the need for annotated training data, the generated content contains the remaining of the occluder and its quality is not good if it has texture.

Ehsani et al. [76] trained a GAN-based model dubbed SeGAN. The model consists of a segmentator which is a modified ResNet-18 [77], and a painter which is a CGAN. The segmentator produces the full segmentation mask (amodal mask) of the objects including the occluded parts. On the other hand, the painter, which consists of a generator and a discriminator, takes in the output from the segmentator and reproduces the appearance of the hidden parts of the object based on the amodal mask. The final output from the generator is a de-occluded RGB image which is then fed into the discriminator. As a drawback, the model is trained on a synthetic dataset, which presents an inevitable domain gap between the training images and the real-world testing images.

Furthermore, Kahatapitiya et al. [78] aim to detect and remove the unrelated occluders, and inpaint the missing pixels to produce an occlusion-free image. The unrelated objects are identified based on the context of the image and a language model. Through a background segmentator and the foreground segmentator, the background and foreground objects are extracted, respectively. The foreground extractor produces pixel-wise annotations for the objects (i.e., thing class) and the background segmentator outputs the background objects (i.e., stuff class). Then, the relation predictor uses the annotations to estimate the relation of each foreground object to the image context based on a vector embedding of class labels trained with a language model. The result of the relation prediction can detect any unrelated objects which are considered as unwanted occlusion. Consequently, the relations and pixel annotations of the thing class are fed into the image inpainter to mask and recreate the pixels of the hidden object. The image inpainter is based on the contextual attention model by Yu et al. [65], which employs a coarse-to-fine model. In the first stage, the mask is coarsely filled in. Then, the second stage utilizes a local and a global WGAN-GP [56] to enhance the quality of the generated output from the coarse stage. A contextual attention layer is implemented to attend to similar feature patches from distant pixels. The local and global WGAN-GP enforce global and local consistency of the inpainted pixels [65]. The contextual information helps in generating a de-occluded image; however, the required class labels of the foreground and background objects limit the applicability of the method.

5.3.2. Face Completion

Occlusion is usually present in faces. The occluding objects can be glasses, scarf, food, cup, microphone, etc. The performance of biometric and surveillance systems can degrade when faces are obstructed or covered by other objects, which raises a security concern. However, compared to background completion, facial images are more challenging to complete since they contain more appearance variations, especially around the eyes and the mouth. In the following, we categorize the available works for face completion based on their architecture.

A single generator and discriminator: Cai et al. [79] present an Occlusion-Aware GAN (OA-GAN), with a single generator and discriminator, that alleviates the need for an occlusion mask as an input. Through using paired images with known mask of artificial occlusions and natural images without occlusion masks, the model learns in a semi-supervised way. The generator has an occlusion-aware network and a face completion network. The first network estimates the mask for the area where the occlusion is present, which is fed into the second network. The latter then completes the missing region based on the mask. The discriminator employs an adversarial loss, and an attribute preserving loss to ensure that the generated facial image has similar attributes to the input image.

Likewise, Chen et al. [80] depend on their proposed OA-GAN to automatically identify the occluded region and inpaint it. They train a DCGAN on occlusion-free facial images, and use it to detect the corrupted regions. During the inpainting process, a binary matrix is maintained, which indicates the presence of occlusion in each pixel. The detection of occluded region alleviates the need for any prior knowledge of the location and type of the occlusion masks. However, incorrect occlusion detection leads to partially inpainted images.

Facial Structure Guided GAN (FSG-GAN) [81] is a two-stage model with a single generator and discriminator. In the first part, a variational auto-encoder estimates the facial structure which is combined with the occluded image and fed into the generator of the second stage. The generator (UNet), guided by the facial structure knowledge, synthesizes the deoccluded image. A multi-receptive fields discriminator encourages a more natural and less ambiguous appearance of the output image. Nevertheless, the model cannot remove occlusion in a face image with large posture well, and it cannot correctly predict the facial structure under severe occlusions, which leads to unpleasant results.

Multiple discriminators: Several of the existing works employ multiple discriminators to ensure that the completed facial image is semantically valid and consistent with the context of the image. Li et al. [82] train a model with a generator, a local discriminator, a global discriminator, and a parsing network to generate an occlusion-free facial image. The original image is masked with a randomly positioned noisy square and fed into the generator which is designed as an auto-encoder to fill the missing pixels. The discriminators, which are binary classifiers, enhance the semantic quality of the reconstructed pixels. Meanwhile, the parsing network enforces the harmony of the generated part and the present content. The model can handle various masks of different positions, sizes, and shapes. However, the limitations of the model include the facts that (1) it cannot recognize the position/orientation of the face and its corresponding elements which leads to unpleasant generative content; (2) it fails to correctly recover the color of the lips; (3) it does not capture the full spatial correlations within neighboring pixels.

Similarly, Mathai et al. [83] use an encoder–decoder for the generator, a Patch-GAN-based local discriminator, and a WGAN-GP [56]-based global discriminator to address occlusions on distinctive areas of a face and inpaint them. Consequently, the model's ability in recognizing faces improves. To minimize the effect of the masked area on the extracted features, two convolutional gating mechanisms are experimented: hard gating mechanism known as partial convolutions [62] and a soft gating method based on sigmoid function.

Liu et al. [84] also follow the same approach by implementing a generator (autoencoder), a local discriminator, and a global discriminator. A self-attention mechanism is applied in the global discriminator to enforce complex geometric constrains on the global image structure, and model long-range dependencies. The authors report the results for the facial landmark detection only, without providing the experimental data.

Moreover, Cai et al. [85] present FCSR-GAN to create a high-resolution deoccluded image from a low-resolution facial image with partial occlusions. At first, the model is pre-trained for face completion to recover the missing region. Afterward, the entire framework is trained end-to-end. The generator comprises a face completion unit and a face super-resolution unit. The low-resolution occluded input image is fed into the face completion module to fill the missing region. The face completion unit follows an encoder–decoder layout and the overall architecture is similar to the generative face completion by Li et al. [82]. Then, the occlusion-free image is fed into the face super-resolution module which adopts a SRGAN [86]. The network is trained with a local loss, a global loss, and a perceptual loss to ensure that the generated content is consistent with the local details and holistic contextual information. An additional face parsing loss and perceptual loss are computed to produce more realistic face images.

Furthermore, face completion can improve the resistance of face identification and recognition models to occlusion. The authors in [87] propose a two-unit de-occlusion distillation pipeline. In the de-occlusion unit, a GAN is implemented to recover the appearance of pixels covered by the mask. Similar to the previously mentioned works, the output of the generator is evaluated by local and global discriminators. In the distillation unit, a pre-trained face recognition model is employed as a teacher, and its knowledge is used to train the student model to identify masked faces by learning representations for recovered faces with similar clustering behaviors as the original ones. This teaches the student model how to fill in the information gap in appearance space and in identity space. The model is trained with a single occlusion mask at a time; however, in real-world instances, multiple masks cover large discriminative regions of the face.

Multiple generators: In contrast to the OA-GAN presented by Cai et al. [79], the authors of [88] propose a two-stage OA-GAN framework with two generators and two discriminators. While the generators (G_1, and G_2) are made up of a UNet encoder–decoder architecture, PatchGAN is adopted in the discriminators. G_1 takes an occluded input image and disentangles the mask of the image to produce a synthesized occlusion. G_2 then takes the output from G_1 in order to remove the occlusions and generate a deoccluded image. Therefore, the occlusion generator (i.e., G_1) plays a fundamental role in the deocclusion process. The failure in the occlusion generator produces incorrect images.

Multiple generators and discriminators: While using multiple discriminators ensures the consistency and the validity of the produced image, some available works employ multiple generators, especially when tackling multiple problems. For example, Jabbar et al. [89] present a framework known as Automatic Mask Generation Network for Face Deocclusion using Stacked GAN (AFD-StackGAN) that is composed of two stages to automatically extract the mask of the occluded area and recover its content. The first stage employs an encoder–decoder in its generator to generate the binary segmentation mask for the invisible region. The produced mask is further refined with erosion and dilation morphological techniques. The second stage eliminates the mask object and regenerates the corrupted pixels through two pair of generators and discriminators. The occluded input image and the extracted occlusion mask are fed into the first generator to produce a completed image. The initial output from the first generator is enhanced by rectifying any missing or incorrect content in it. Two PatchGAN discriminators are implemented against the result of the generators to ensure that the restored face's appearance and structural consistency are retained. AFD-StackGAN can remove various types of occlusion masks in the facial images that cover a large area of the face. However, it is trained with synthetic data, and the incompatibility of the training images and the real-world testing images is likely.

In the same way, Li et al. [90] employ two generators and three domain-specific discriminators in their proposed framework called disentangling and fusing GAN (DF-GAN). They treat face completion as disentangling and fusing of clean faces and occlusions. This way, they remove the need for paired samples of occluded images and their congruent clean images. The framework works with three domains that correspond to the distribution of occluded faces, clean faces, and structured occlusions. In the disentangling module, an occluded facial image is fed into an encoder which encodes it to the disentangled representations. Thereafter, two decoders produce the corresponding deoccluded image and occlusion, respectively. In other words, the disentangling network learns how to separate the structured occlusions and the occlusion-free images. The fusing network, on the other hand, combines the latent representations of clean faces and occlusions, and creates the corresponding occluded facial image, i.e., it learns how to generate images with structured occlusions. However, real-world occlusions are of arbitrary shape and size, not necessarily structured.

Coarse-to-fine architecture: Conversely to the previously mentioned works where one output is generated, Jabbar et al. [91] propose a two-stage Face De-occlusion using Stacked Generative Adversarial Network (FD-StackGAN) model that follows the coarse-to-fine approach. The model attempts to remove the occlusion mask and fill in the affected area. In the first stage, the network produces an initial deoccluded facial image. The second stage refines the initial generated image to create a more visually plausible image that is similar to the real image. Similar to AF-StackGAN, FD-StackGAN can handle various regions in the facial images with different structures and surrounding backgrounds. However, the model is trained on a synthetic dataset but it is not tested on images with natural occlusions.

Likewise, Duan and Zhang [92] address the problem of deoccluding and recognizing face profiles with large-pose variations and occlusions through BoostGAN, which has a coarse-to-fine structure. In the coarse part, i.e., multi-occlusion frontal view generator, an encoder–decoder network is used for eliminating occlusion and producing multiple intermediate deoccluded faces. Subsequently, the coarse outputs are refined through a boosting network for photo-realistic and identity-preserved face generation. Consequently, the discriminator has a multi-input structure.

Since BoostGAN is a one-stage framework, it cannot handle de-occlusion and frontalization concurrently, which means that it loses the discriminative identity information. Furthermore, BoostGAN fails to employ the mask guided noise prior information. To address these, Duan et al. [93] perform face frontalization and face completion simultaneously. They propose an end-to-end mask guided two-stage GAN (TSGAN) framework. Each stage has its own generator and discriminator, while the first stage contains the face deocclusion module, the second one contains face frontalization module. Another module named mask-attention module (MAM) is deployed in both stages. The MAM encourages the face deocclusion module to concentrate more on missing regions and fills them based on the masked image input. The recovered image is fed into the second stage to obtain the final frontal image. TSGAN is trained with defined occlusion types and specified sizes, and multiple natural occlusions are not considered.

Table 3 provides an outline of the above-mentioned works, summarizing the type of GAN, the objective function, the dataset, and the results of each work.

Table 3. Summary of the face completion works, highlighting the types of GAN, loss functions, and the datasets that were used. The results are the reported results of the quality of the generated images (except for the ones marked with †). Results with * are the mean value of the published results. AL: Adversarial loss. PL: Perceptual loss. RL: Reconsturction loss. PSNR: Peak Signal-to-Noise Ratio ↑. SSIM: Structural Similarity ↑. ID: Identity Distance ↓. DIR@FAIR: Detection and Identification Rate at False Positive Rates ↑. MSE: Mean Square Error ↓. IS: Inception Score ↑. FID: Frechet Inception Distance ↓. NRMSE: Normalized Root MSE ↓.

#	Paper	Type of GAN	Loss Function	Dataset	Results
1.	Cai et al. [79]	OA-GAN	1. Training with synthetic occlusion: PL, style loss, pixel loss, smoothness loss, $\mathcal{L}2$ loss, and AL. 2. Training with natural images: smoothness loss, $\mathcal{L}2$ loss, and AL.	CelebA [94]	PSNR = 22.61, SSIM = 0.787
2.	Chen et al. [80]	DCGAN	AL.	LFW [95]	Equal Error Rate (EER) *† = 0.88
3.	Cheung et al. [81]	FSG-GAN	$\mathcal{L}1$ loss, identity-preserve loss, and AL.	CelebA, and LFW.	CelebA: PSNR * = 20.7513, SSIM = 0.8318; LFW: PSNR * = 20.8905, SSIM = 0.8527
4.	Li et al. [82]	GAN with two discriminators	Local and global AL, RL ($\mathcal{L}2$), and pixel-wise softmax loss.	CelebA, and Helen [96].	PSNR * = 19.60, SSIM * = 0.803, ID = 0.470
5.	Mathai et al. [83]	GAN (modified generator) with two discriminators	RL ($\mathcal{L}1$), global WGAN loss, and local PatchGAN loss.	1. Training the inpainter: CASIA WebFaces [97], VGG Faces [98], and MS-Celeb-1M [99]. 2. Testing the model: LFW, and LFW-BLUFR [100].	DIR@FAR † = 89.68
6.	Liu et al. [84]	GAN (modified generator) with two discriminators	RL ($\mathcal{L}2$), and AL.	CelebAMask-HQ [101]	NRMSE † = 6.96 (result of facial landmark detection)
7.	Cai et al. [85]	FCSR-GAN	MSE loss, PL, local and global AL, and face parsing loss.	CelebA, and Helen.	CelebA: PSNR = 20.22, SSIM = 0.780; Helen: PSNR = 20.01, SSIM = 0.761
8.	Li et al. [87]	GAN (modified generator) with two discriminators	Local and global AL, RL, and contextual attention loss.	CelebA, AR [102], and LFW.	Recognition accuracy † = 95.44%
9.	Dong et al. [88]	OA-GAN	AL and $\mathcal{L}1$ loss	CelebA, and CK+ [103], with additional occlusion images from the Internet.	PSNR * = 22.402, SSIM * = 0.753
10.	Jabbar et al. [89]	AFD-StackGAN (PatchGAN discriminators)	$\mathcal{L}1$ loss, RL ($\mathcal{L}1$, and SSIM), PL, and AL.	Custom dataset.	PSNR = 33.201, SSIM = 0.978, MSE = 32.435, NIQE (↓) = 4.902, BRISQUE (↓) = 39.872
11.	Li et al. [90]	DF-GAN	AL and cycle loss.	AR, Multi-PIE [104], Color FERET [105], and LFW.	AR: PSNR = 23.85, SSIM = 0.9168; Multi-PIE: PSNR = 28.21, SSIM = 0.9176; FERET: PSNR = 28.15, SSIM = 0.931; LFW: PSNR = 23.18, SSIM = 0.869
12.	Jabbar et al. [91]	FD-StackGAN	RL ($\mathcal{L}1$, and SSIM loss), PL, and AL.	Custom dataset.	PSNR = 32.803, SSIM = 0.981, MSE = 34.145, NIQE (↓) = 4.499, BRISQUE (↓) = 42.504
13.	Duan and Zhang. [92]	BoostGAN	AL, identity preserving loss, $\mathcal{L}1$ loss, symmetry loss, and total variation (TV) loss.	Multi-PIE and LFW.	Recognition rate † = 96.02
14.	Duan et al. [93]	TSGAN	AL, dual triplet loss, $\mathcal{L}1$ loss, symmetry loss, and TV loss.	Multi-PIE and LFW.	Recognition rate † = 96.87
15.	Cong and Zhou. [106]	DCGAN	Cycle consistency loss from CycleGAN, AL, and Wasserstain distance loss.	Wider Face [107].	IS = 10.36; FID = 8.85

5.3.3. Attribute Classification

With the availability of surveillance cameras, the task of object detection and tracking through its visual appearance in a surveillance footage has gained prominence. Furthermore, there are other characteristics of people that are essential to fully understand an observed scene. The task of recognizing the people attributes (age, sex, race, etc.) and the items they hold (backpacks, bags, phone, etc.) is called attribute classification.

However, occluding the person in question by another person may lead to incorrectly classifying the attributes of the occluder instead of the occludee. Furthermore, the quality of the images from the surveillance cameras is usually low. Therefore, Fabbri et al. [108] focus on the poor resolution and occlusion challenges in recognizing the attribute of people such as gender, race, clothing, etc., in surveillance systems. The authors propose a model based on DCGAN [109] to improve the quality of images in order to overcome the mentioned problems. The model has three networks, one for attribute classification from the full body images, and the other two networks attempt to enhance the resolution and recover from occlusion. Eliminating the occlusion produces an image without noise and the residual of other subjects that could result in misclassification. However, under severe occlusions, the reconstructed image still contains the remaining of the occluder and the model fails to keep the parts of the image that should stay unmodified.

Similarly, Fulgeri et al. [110] tackle the occlusion issue by implementing a combination of UNet and GAN architecture. The model requires as input the occluded person image and its corresponding attributes. The generator takes the input and restores the image. The output is then forwarded to three networks: ResNet-101 [77], VGG-16 [111], and the discriminator to calculate the loss. The loss is backpropagated to update the weights of the generator. The goal of the model is to obtain a result image of a person that (a) is not occluded, (b) is similar at the pixel level to a person shape, and (c) contains the similar visual features as the original image. The results show that the model can detect and remove occlusion without any additional information. However, the model fails to fully recover the pixels around the boundary of the body parts. The authors constraint the input images by not having occlusion of more than six-sevenths of the image height.

5.3.4. Miscellaneous Applications

In this section, we present the applications of GAN for amodal content completion in various categories of data.

Food: Papadopoulos et al. [112] present a compositional layer-based generative network called PizzaGAN that follows the steps of a recipe to make a pizza. The framework contains a pair of modules to add and remove all instances of each recipe component. A Cycle-GAN [6] is used to design each module. In the case of adding an element to the existing image, the module produces the appearance and the mask of the visible pixels in the new layer. Moreover, the removal module learns how to fill the holes that are left from the erased layer and generate the mask of the removed pixels. However, the authors do not provide any quantitative assessment of PizzaGAN.

Vehicles: Yan et al. [67] propose a two-part model to recover the amodal mask of a vehicle and the appearance of its hidden regions iteratively. To tackle both tasks, the model is composed of two parts: a segmentation completion module and an appearance recovery module. The first network is to complement the segmentation mask of the vehicle's invisible region. In order to complete the content of the occluded region, the appearance recovery module has a generator with a two-path network structure. The first path accepts the input image, the recovered mask from the segmentation completion module, and the modal mask, while learning how to fill in the colors of the hidden pixels. The other path requires the recovered mask and the ground-truth complete mask and learns how to use the image context to inpaint the whole foreground vehicle. The two paths share parameters, which increases the ability of the generator. To enhance the quality of the recovered image, it is taken through the whole model several times. However, the performance of the model degrades beyond three iterations for real images if occlusions are not severe.

Humans: The process of matching the same person in images taken by multiple cameras is referred to as Person re-identification (ReID). In surveillance systems where the purpose is to track and identify the individuals, ReID is essential. However, the stored images usually have low resolution and are blurry because they are from ordinary surveillance cameras [113]. Additionally, occlusion by other individuals and/or objects is most likely to occur since each camera has a different angle of view. Hence, some important features become difficult to recognize.

To tackle the challenge of person re-identification under occlusion, Tagore et al. [114] design a bi-network architecture with an Occlusion Handling GAN (OHGAN) module. An image with synthetic added occlusion is fed into the generator which is based on UNet architecture and produces an occlusion-free image by learning a non-linear project mapping function between the input image and the output image. Afterward, the discriminator computes the metric difference between the generated image and the original one. The ablation studies for the reconstruction task illustrate that the quality of completion is good for 10–20% occlusion and average for 30–40% occlusion. However, the quality of reconstruction degrades for occlusions higher than 50%.

On the other hand, Zhang et al. [66] attempt to complete the mask and the appearance of an occluded human through a two-stage network. First, the amodal completion stage predicts the amodal mask of the occluded person. Afterward, the content recovery network completes the RGB appearance of the invisible area. The latter uses a UNet architecture in the generator, with local and global discriminators to ensure that the output image is consistent with the global semantics while enhancing the clarity and contrast of the local regions. The generator adds a Visible Guided Attention (VGA) module to the skip connections. The VGA module computes a relational feature map to guide the low-level features to complete by concatenating the high-level features with the next-level features. The relational feature map represents the relation between the pixels inside and outside the occluded area. The process of extracting feature maps is similar to the self-attention mechanism in SAGAN by Zhang et al. [54]. Although incorporating VGA leads to a more accurate recovery of the content and texture, the model does not perform well on real images as it does on synthetic images.

5.4. Training Data

Supervised learning frameworks require annotated ground-truth data to train a model. These data can be either from a manually annotated dataset, a synthetic occluded data from 3D computer-generated images, or by superimposing a part of an object/image on another object. For example, Ehsani et al. [76] train their model (SeGAN) on a photo-realistic synthetic dataset, and Zhan et al. [75] apply a self-supervised approach to generate annotated training data. However, a model trained with synthetic data may fail when it is tested on real-world data, and human-labeled data are costly, time-consuming, and susceptible to subjective judgments.

In this section, we discuss how GAN is implemented to generate training data for several categories.

Generic objects: It is nearly impossible to cover all the probable occlusions, and the likelihood of appearance of some occlusion cases is rather small. Therefore, Wang et al. [115] aim to utilize the data to improve the performance of the object detection in the case of occlusions. They utilize an adversarial network to generate hard examples with occlusions, and use them to train a Fast-RCNN [116]. Consequently, the detector becomes invariant to occlusions and deformations. Their model contains an Adversarial Spatial Dropout Network (ASDN), which takes as input features from an image patch and predicts a dropout mask that is used to create occlusion such that it would be difficult for Fast-RCNN to classify.

Likewise, Han et al. [117] apply an adversarial network to produce occluded adversary samples to train an object detector. The model, named Feature Fusion and Adversary Networks (FFAN), is based on Faster RCNN [118] and consists of a feature fusion network and an adversary occlusion network, and while the feature fusion module produces a feature map of high resolution and high semantic information to detect small objects more effectively, the adversary occlusion module produces occlusion on the feature map of the object thus outputs an adversary training sample that would be hard for the detector to discriminate. Meanwhile, the detector becomes better in classifying the generated occluded adversary samples through self-learning. Over time, the detector and the adversary occlusion network learn and compete with each other to enhance the performance of the model.

The occlusions produced by adversary networks in [115,117] may lead to over-generalization, because they are similar to other class instances. For example, the occluded wheels of a bicycle results in misclassifying a wheel chair as a bike.

Humans: Zhao et al. [119] augment the input data to produce easy-to-hard occluded samples with different sizes and positions of the occlusion mask to increase the variation of occlusion patterns. They address the issue of ReID under occlusion through an Incremental Generative Occlusion Adversarial Suppression (IGOAS) framework. The network contains two modules, an incremental generative occlusion (IGO) block, and a global adversarial suppression (G&A) module. IGO takes the input data through augmentation and generates easy occluded samples. Then, it progressively enlarges the size of the occlusion mask with the number of training iterations. Thus, the model becomes more robust against occlusion as it learns harder occlusion incrementally rather than hardest ones directly. On the other hand, G&A consists of a global branch which extracts global features of the input data, and an adversarial suppression branch that weakens the response of the occluded region to zero and strengthens the response to non-occluded areas.

Furthermore, to increase the number of samples per identity for person ReID, Wu et al. [120] use a GAN network to synthesize labeled occluded data. Specifically, the authors impose block rectangles on the images to create random occlusion on the original person images which the model then tries to complete. The completed images that are similar but not identical to the original input are labeled with the same annotation as the corresponding raw image. Similarly, Zhang et al. [113] follow the same strategy to expand the original training set, expect that an additional noise channel is applied on the generated data to adjust the label further. Both approaches in [113,120] work with rectangular masks, but in real-world examples occlusions appear in free-form shapes.

Face images: Cong and Zhou [106] propose an improved GAN to generate occluded face images. The model is based on DCGAN with an added S-coder. The purpose of the S-coder is to force the generator to produce multi-class target images. The network is further optimized through Wasserstein distance and the cycle consistency loss from CycleGAN. However, only sunglasses and facial masks are considered as occlusive elements.

Figure 4 outlines of the discussed approaches for tackling the issues in overcoming occlusion through using GAN. Table 4 summarizes the GAN model, the loss function, and the datasets that were used in the discussed works in this section (except for the face completion works), it also shows the reported result for the tasks where GAN was applied.

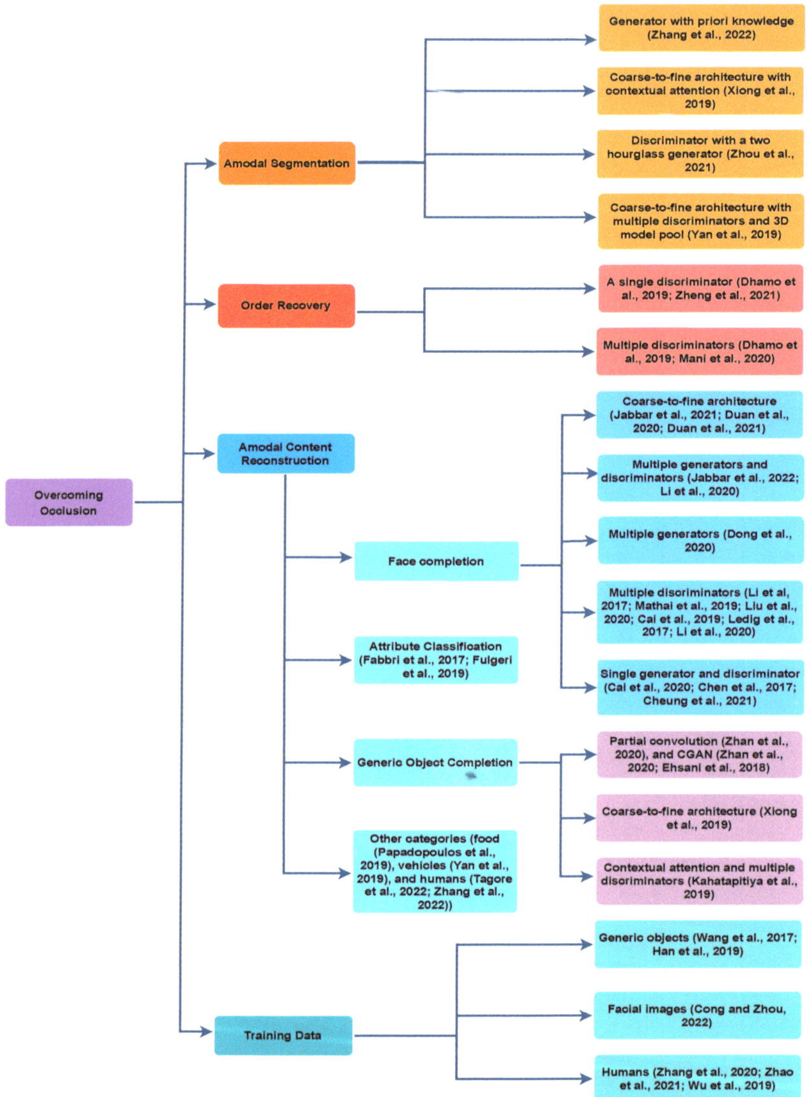

Figure 4. Outline of the approaches for addressing the challenges in overcoming occlusion through GAN. For amodal segmentation the implemented architecture are, a discriminator with a two hourglass generator [60], a coarse-to-fine architecture with contextual attention [63] or multiple discriminators [67], and a generator with priori knowledge [66]. For order recovery, GAN is designed as a generator with a single discriminator [71,73], or multiple discriminators [69,70]. To perform amodal content completion for facial images, the architectures include: a single generator and discriminator [79–81], multiple discriminators [82–87], multiple generators [88], multiple generators and discriminators [89,90], or a coarse-to-fine architecture [91–93]. Generic object completion is carried out through coarse-to-fine architecture [63], multiple discriminators with contextual attention [78], or partial convolution and CGAN [75,76]. Human completion for attribute classification is utilized in [108,110]. Other works use GAN to complete the images of food [112], vehicles [67], and humans [66,114]. GAN is also used to generate training data of generic objects [115,117], humans [113,119,120], and face images [106].

Table 4. Summary of the discussed works, highlighting the type of GAN, loss function, and the datasets that were used. The last two columns show the task that GAN was utilized for and its corresponding reported results. IoU: Intersection over Union ↑, R: Recall ↑, P: Precision ↑, ICP: Inception Conditional Probability ↑, SS: Segmentation Score ↑, Rel: Relative error ↓, RMSE: Root MSE ↓, MPE: Mean Pixel Error ↓, mIoU: mean IoU ↑, mAP: mean Average Precision ↑, mA: mean Accuracy ↑, AP: Average Precision ↑.

#	Paper	Model	Loss Function	Dataset	Task	Results
1.	Zhou et al. [60]	GAN with PGA	1. For mask generation: binary cross-entropy (BCE), adversarial loss, and $\mathcal{L}1$ loss. 2. For content completion: adversarial loss, $\mathcal{L}1$ loss, perceptual loss, and style loss.	AHP (custom dataset)	Amodal segmentation and content completion	For mask generation: IoU = 86.1/40.3, L1 = 0.1635; For content completion: FID = 19.49, L1 = 0.0617
2.	Xiong et al. [63]	Coarse-to-fine structure with a PatchGAN discriminator	1. For contour completion: a focal loss based content loss, and Hinge loss for adversarial loss. 2. For content completion: $\mathcal{L}1$ loss.	Places2 [121], and custom-designed dataset	Contour and content completion	L1 = 0.009327, L2 = 0.002329, PSNR = 29.86, SSIM = 0.9383, user study = 731 out of 1099 valid votes
3.	Zhang et al. [66]	GAN with multiple PatchGAN discriminators	1. For mask generation: adversarial loss, perceptual loss, and BCE loss. 2. For content generation: adversarial loss, $\mathcal{L}1$ loss, style loss, content loss, and TV loss.	Custom dataset	Amodal segmentation and content completion	For mask generation: mIoU = 0.82, L1 = 0.0638; For content completion: L1 = 0.0344, L2 = 0.0324, FID = 33.28
4.	Yan et al. [67]	GAN with multiple PatchGAN-based discriminators	$\mathcal{L}1$ loss, perceptual loss, and adversarial loss.	OVD (custom dataset)	Amodal segmentation and content completion	For mask generation: P = 0.9854, R = 0.8148, F1 = 0.8898, IoU = 0.8066, L1 = 0.0320, L2 = 0.0314; For content completion: ICP = 0.8350, SS = 0.9356, L1 = 0.0173, L2 = 0.0063
5.	Dhamo et al. [69]	PatchGAN-based	Adversarial loss and $\mathcal{L}1$ loss	SceneNet [122] and NYU depth v2 [123]	RGB-D completion	Rel = 0.017, RMSE = 0.095, SSIM = 0.903, RMSE = 19.76, PSNR = 22.22
6.	Dhamo et al. [73]	Original GAN	1. For object completion: $\mathcal{L}1$ loss 2. For layout prediction: reconstruction ($\mathcal{L}1$) loss, perceptual loss, and adversarial loss.	SunCG [124] and Stanford2D-3D [125]	RGBA-D completion	SunCG: MPE = 43.12, RMSE = 65.66; Stanford2D-3D: MPE = 42.45, RMSE = 54.92
7.	Mani et al. [70]	GAN with two discriminators	$\mathcal{L}2$ loss, adversarial loss, and the discriminator loss.	KITTI [126] and Argoverse [127]	Scene completion	KITTI object: mIoU = 26.08, mAP = 40.79; KITTI tracking: mIoU = 24.16, mAP = 36.83; Argoverse: mIoU = 32.05, mAP = 48.31
8.	Zheng et al. [71]	GAN with two discriminators	Reconstruction loss, adversarial loss, and perceptual ($\mathcal{L}1$) loss.	COCOA[128], KINS [129], and CSD (custom dataset)	Scene completion	RMSE = 0.0914, SSIM = 0.8768, PSNR = 30.45
9.	Zhan et al. [75]	PCNet with CGAN	1. For mask generation: BCE loss. 2. For content completion: losses in PC [62], $\mathcal{L}1$ loss, perceptual loss, and adversarial loss.	COCOA, and KINS	Content completion	KINS: mIoU = 94.76%; COCOA: mIoU = 81.35%
10.	Ehsani et al. [76]	SeGAN	1. For mask generation: BCE loss. 2. For content generation: Adversarial loss and $\mathcal{L}1$ loss.	DYCE (custom dataset)	Content completion	L1 = 0.07, L2 = 0.03, user study = 69.78%

Table 4. *Cont.*

#	Paper	Model	Loss Function	Dataset	Task	Results
11.	Kahatapitiya et al. [78]	Inpainter with contextual attention	Spatially discounted reconstruction $\mathcal{L}1$ loss, local and global WGAN-GP adversarial loss.	COCO-Stuff [130] and MS COCO [131]	Content completion	User study positive = 79.7%, negative = 20.3%
12.	Fabbri et al. [108]	DCGAN-based	1. For attribute classification: weighted BCE loss. 2. For content completion: reconstruction loss and adversarial loss of the generator.	RAP [132]	Content completion	mA = 65.82, accuracy = 76.01, P = 48.98, R = 55.50, F1 = 52.04
13.	Fulgeri et al. [110]	Modified GAN (one generator and three discriminators)	Adversarial loss, content loss, and attribute loss (weighted BCE).	RAP, and Aic (custom dataset)	Content completion	RAP: mA = 72.18, accuracy = 59.59, P = 73.51, R = 73.72, F1 = 73.62, SSIM = 0.8239, PSNR = 20.65; AiC: mA = 78.37, accuracy = 53.3, P = 55.73, R = 85.46, F1 = 67.46, SSIM = 0.7101, PSNR = 21.81
14.	Papadopoulos et al. [112]	PizzaGAN	Adversarial loss, classification loss, cycle consistency loss as in CycleGAN, mask regularization mask.	Custom dataset	Amodal segmentation and content completion	Mask generation mIoU = 29.30% (quantitative results are not reported for content generation)
15.	Zhang et al. [113]	CGAN	Adversarial loss.	Market-1501 [133]	Content completion	mAP = 90.42, Rank-1 = 93.35, Rank-5 = 96.87, Rank-10 = 97.92
16.	Tagore et al. [114]	OHGAN	BCE loss, and $\mathcal{L}2$ loss.	CUHK01 [134], CUHK03 [135], Market-1501, and DukeMTMC-reID [136]	Content completion	CUHK01: Rank-1 = 93.4, Rank-5 = 96.4, Rank-10 = 98.8; CUHK03: Rank-1 = 92.8, Rank-5 = 95.4, Rank-10 = 97.0; Market-1501: Rank-1 = 94.0, Rank-5 = 96.4, Rank-10 = 97.5, mAP = 86.4; DukeMTMC-reID: Rank-1 = 91.2, Rank-5 = 93.4, Rank-10 = 95.8, mAP = 82.4
17.	Wang et al. [115]	A custom-designed adversarial network	BCE loss.	VOC2007, VOC2012 [137], and MS COCO	Occlusion generation and deformation	VOC2007: mAP = 73.6; VOC2012: mAP = 69.0; MS COCO: AP^{50} = 27.1
18.	Han et al. [117]	Adversary occlusion module	BCE loss.	VOC2007, VOC2012, MS COCO, and KITTI	Occlusion generation	VOC2007: mAP = 78.1; VOC2012: mAP = 76.7; MS COCO: AP = 42.7; KITTI: mAP = 89.01
19.	Wu et al. [120]	Original GAN	Euclidean loss, and BCE loss.	CUHK03, Market-1501, and DukeMTMC-reID	Content completion	Market-1501: mAP = 90.36, Rank-1 = 93.29, Rank-5 = 96.96, Rank-10 = 97.68; DukeMTMC-reID: mAP = 82.81, Rank-1 = 86.35, Rank-5 = 92.87, Rank-10 = 94.56; CUHK03: mAP = 61.95, Rank-1 = 59.78, Rank-5 = 70.64

6. Loss Functions

In GAN, the generator G and the discriminator D play against each other in a two-player mini–max game until they reach Nash equilibrium through a gradient-based optimization method. The gradient of the loss value indicates the learning performance of the network. The loss value is calculated via a loss (objective) function. In fact, defining a loss function is one the fundamental elements of designing GAN. Consequently, numerous objective functions have been proposed to stabilize and regularize GAN. The following losses are the most common ones used in training GAN for amodal completion.

1. **Adversarial Loss**: The loss function used in training GAN is known as an adversarial loss. It measures the distance between the distribution of the generated sample and the real sample. Each of G and D have their dedicated loss function which together form the adversarial loss, as shown in Equation (1). However, G is trained as the term that reflects the distribution of the generated data ($\mathbb{E}_{z \sim p_z(z)}[log(1 - D(G(z)))]$). Extensions to the original loss function are the conditional loss and the Wasserstein loss defined in CGAN and WGAN, respectively.
2. **Content Loss**: In image generation, content loss [138] measures the difference between the content representation of the real and the generated images, to make them more similar in terms of perceptual content. If p and x are the original and the generated images, and p^l and X^l are their respective representations in layer l, the content loss is calculated as
$$\mathcal{L}_{content}(p, x, l) = \frac{1}{2} \sum_{i,j} (F^l_{ij} - P^l_{ij})^2 \tag{3}$$
3. **Reconstruction Loss**: The key idea behind reconstruction loss proposed by Li et al. [139] is to benefit from the visual features learned by D from the training data. The extracted features from the real data by D are fed to G to regenerate real data. By adding reconstruction loss to the GAN's loss function, G is encouraged to reconstruct from the features of D, which brings G closer to the configurations of the real data. The reconstruction loss equation is as follows:
$$\mathcal{L}^{\phi,\theta}_X = \mathbb{E}_{x \sim p_x}[||G^\theta(D^\phi_F(X)) - X||_1] \tag{4}$$
where D^ϕ_F is a part of the discriminator which encodes the data to features, and G^θ decodes the features to the training data.
4. **Style Loss**: The style loss, originally designed for image style transfer by Gatys et al. [138], is defined to ensure that the style representation of the generated image matches that of the input style image. It depends on the feature correlation between the feature maps, given by the Gram matrix (G^l). Let a and x be the original image and the generated image, respectively, and A^l and G^l their corresponding style representation in layer l. The style loss is computed by the element-wise mean square difference between A^l and G^l,
$$\mathcal{L}_{style}(a, x) = \sum_{l=0}^{L} w_l \frac{1}{4N_l^2 M_l^2} \sum_{i,j} (G^l_{ij} - A^l_{ij})^2 \tag{5}$$
where w^l is the weighting factor of each layer, and N and M represent the number and the size of the feature maps, respectively.
5. **$\mathcal{L}_1$ and $\mathcal{L}_2$ Loss**: $\mathcal{L}_1$ loss function is the absolute difference between the ground-truth and the generated image. On the other hand, $\mathcal{L}_2$ loss is the squared difference between the actual and the generated data. When used alone, these loss functions lead to blurred results [140]. However, when combined with other loss functions, they can improve the quality of the generated images, especially $\mathcal{L}_1$ loss. The generator is encouraged to not only fool the discriminator but also to be closer to the real data in $\mathcal{L}_1$ or $\mathcal{L}_2$ sense. Although these losses cannot capture high-frequency details, they

accurately capture low frequencies. $\mathcal{L}_1$ loss enforces correctness in low-frequency features; hence, it results in less blurred images compared to $\mathcal{L}_2$ [8]. Both losses are defined in Equations (6) and (7).

$$\mathcal{L}_1 = \mathbb{E}_{x,y,z}[||y - G(x,z)||_1] \quad (6)$$

$$\mathcal{L}_2 = \mathbb{E}_{x,y,z}[||y - G(x,z)||_2^2] \quad (7)$$

where x, y, and z are the ground-truth image, the generated image, and the random noise, respectively.

6. **Perceptual Loss**: The perceptual loss measures the high-level perceptual and semantic differences between the real and the fake images. Several works [141,142] introduce perceptual loss as a combination of the content loss (or feature reconstruction loss) and the style loss. However, Liu et al. [62] simply compute the L_1 distance between the real and the completed images. Others incorporate more similarity metrics into it [140].
7. **BCE Loss**: BCE loss measures how close the probability of the predicted data is to the real data. Its value increases as the predicted probability deviates from the real label. The BCE is defined as

$$\mathcal{L}_{BCE} = -\frac{1}{N}\sum_{i=1}^{N}(y_i log(D(i) + (1 - y_i) log(1 - D(i))) \quad (8)$$

where y_i is the label of i. y_i=0 and y_i=1 represents fake and real samples.
BCE is used in training the discriminator in amodal segmentation task [76], and in training the generator [110].

8. **Hinge Loss**: In GAN, Hinge loss is used to help the convergence to a Nash equilibrium. Proposed by Lim and Ye [143], the objective function for G is

$$\mathcal{L}_G = -\mathbb{E}_{z \sim p_z(z)}[D(G(z))] \quad (9)$$

and for D is

$$\mathcal{L}_D = \mathbb{E}_{x \sim p_{data}(x)}[max(0, 1 - D(x)] + \mathbb{E}_{z \sim p_z(z)}[max(0, 1 + D(G(z))] \quad (10)$$

where x and z are the ground-truth and the generated images, respectively.

As it can be seen from Tables 3 and 4, many of the previously mentioned loss functions are combined with others to train a GAN model. Adversarial loss is the base objective function for training the two networks of the GAN. However, with the original GAN's adversarial loss function, the model may not converge. Therefore, the Hinge loss is often implemented as an alternative objective function. In some works, global and local adversarial losses are used to train local and global discriminators to ensure that the generated data is semantically and locally coherent. In addition to this, $\mathcal{L}_1$ or $\mathcal{L}_2$ losses are frequently utilized to capture low-frequency features, and hence improve the quality of the generated images. Furthermore, the reconstruction loss is employed to encourage the generator to maintain the contents of the original input image. On the other hand, perceptual loss encourages the model to capture patch-level information when completing a missing patch in an object/image. Furthermore, to emphasize on the style match between the generated image and the input image, style loss is implemented.

The choice of the objective functions is an essential decision of designing a model. In amodal completion and inpainting, designing a loss function is still an active area of research. The ablation studies performed by the reviewed works show that there is no optimal objective function. For different tasks and data, a different set of loss terms produces the best results. In addition, using a complex loss function may lead to problems of instability, vanishing gradient, and mode collapse.

7. Open Challenges and Future Directions

Despite the significant progress of the research in GAN and amodal completion in the last decade, there remain a number of problems that can be considered as future directions.

1. **Amodal training data**: Up until now, there has been no fully annotated generic amodal dataset with sufficient ground-truth labels for the three sub-tasks in amodal completion. Most of the existing datasets are specific to a particular application or task. This not only makes training the models themselves more difficult, but verifying their learning capability as well. In many cases, there is no sufficient labeled amodal validation data to establish the accuracy of the model. We present the challenges related to each sub-task in amodal completion.
   For amodal segmentation, the current datasets do not contain sufficient occlusion cases between similar objects. Hence, the model cannot tell where the boundary of one object ends and the other one begins.
   The existing real (manually annotated) amodal datasets have no ground-truth appearance for the occluded region. This makes training and validating the model for amodal content completion more challenging.
   As for the case of order recovery, some occlusion situations are very rare in the existing datasets. On the other hand, it is impossible to cover all probable cases of occlusion in the real datasets. Nevertheless, in the future, the current datasets can be extended through generated occlusion to include more of those infrequent cases with varying degrees of occlusion.
2. **Evaluation metrics**: There are several quantitative and qualitative evaluation measures for GAN [59]. However, as it can be noticed from the results, there is no standard and unanimous evaluation metric for assessing the performance of GAN when it generates the occluded content. Many existing works depend on the human preference judgement which can be biased and subjective. Therefore, designing a consensus evaluation metric is of utmost importance.
3. **Reference data**: Existing GAN models fail to generate occluded content accurately if the hidden area is large. Particularly, when the occluded object is non-symmetric, such as the face or the human body. The visible region of the object may not hold sufficient relevant features to guide a visually plausible regeneration. As the next step, reference images can be used along the input image to guide the completion more effectively.

In addition to the above-mentioned problems, the challenges in the stability and convergence of GAN remain open issues [28].

8. Discussion

Current computational models approach the human capability of visible perception when performing visual tasks such as recognition, detection, and segmentation. However, our environment is complex and dynamic. Most of the objects we perceive are incomplete and fragmented. Therefore, the existing models that are designed and trained with a fully visible sample of instances do not perform well when tested on real-world scenes. Hence, overcoming occlusion is essential for leveraging the performance of available models. Amodal completion tasks address the occluded patches of an image to infer the occlusion relation between objects (i.e., order recovery), predict the full shape of the objects (i.e., amodal segmentation), and complete the RGB appearance of the missing pixels (i.e., amodal content completion). These tasks are usually interleaved and depend on each other. For example, amodal segmentation can benefit order recovery [144] and it is crucial for amodal content completion [76]. On the other hand, order recovery can guide the amodal segmentation [75].

Although GAN is notorious for its stability issues and is difficult to train, it is a popular approach for tasks that require generative capability. In handling occlusion, the initially incomplete representation needs to be extended to a complete representation with the missing region filled in. Therefore, GAN is the chosen architecture for processes/sub-processes involved in amodal completion. However, depending on the nature of the problems, the applicability of GAN varies. For example, in amodal appearance reconstruction, GAN is the ideal option of architecture and it produces superior results in comparison to other methods. Comparably, in amodal segmentation and order recovery tasks, GAN is less commonly used. Nevertheless, to take advantage of the potential of GAN, it can be combined with other architectures and learning strategies to tackle those tasks too.

In order to help GAN in learning implicit features from the visible regions of the image, various methods are used, which can be summarized as follows:

- **Architecture:** While the original GAN consists of a single generator and discriminator, several works utilize multiple generators and discriminators. The implementation of local and global discriminators is especially common, because it enhances the quality of the generated data. The generator is encouraged to concentrate on both the global contextual and local features, and produce images that are closer to the distribution of the real data. In addition to this, an initial-to-refined (also called coarse-to-fine) architecture is implemented in many models. The initial stage produces a coarse output from the input image, which is then further refined in the refinement step.
- **Objective function:** To improve the quality of the generated output and stabilize the training of the GAN, a combination of loss terms is used. While adversarial loss and Hinge loss are used in training the two networks in the GAN, other objective functions encourage the model to produce an image that is consistent with the ground-truth image.
- **Input:** Under severe occlusion, the GAN may fail to produce a visually pleasing output solely depending on the visible region. Therefore, providing additional input information guides GAN in producing better results. In the amodal shape and content completion, synthetic instances similar to the occluded object are useful, because they can be used as a reference by the model. A priori knowledge is also beneficial, as it can either be manually encoded (e.g., utilizing various human poses for human deocclusion) or transferred from a pre-trained model (e.g., using a pre-trained face recognition model in face deocclusion). In addition to these, employing the amodal mask and the category of the occluded object in the content completion task restricts the GAN model to focus on completing the object in question. For producing the amodal mask, a modal mask is needed as an input. If the input is not available, most of existing works depend on a pre-trained segmentation model to predict the visible segmentation mask.
- **Feature extraction:** The pixels in the visible region of an image are rather important and contain essential information for various tasks; hence, they are considered as valid pixels. Contrary to this, the invisible pixels are invalid ones; hence, they should not be included in the feature extraction/encoding process. However, the vanilla convolution process cannot differentiate between valid and invalid pixels, which generates images with visual artifacts and color discrepancies. Therefore, partial convolution and a soft gating mechanism are implemented to enforce the generator to focus only on valid pixels and eliminate/minimize the effect of the invalid ones. On the other hand, dilated convolution layers can replace the vanilla convolution layers to borrow information from relevant spatially distant pixels. Additionally, contextual attention layers and attention mechanism are added to the networks of the GAN to leverage the information from the image context and capture global dependencies.

Among the various architectures of GAN, three types are most commonly used in the reviewed works in this article, namely CGAN, WGAN-GP, and PatchGAN. The application of CGAN is mostly in amodal content completion tasks, because the GAN is encouraged to complete an object of a specific class. WGAN-GP stabilizes the training of GAN with an EM distance objective function and a weight clipping method. Therefore, it is a preferred architecture to ensure GAN convergence. On the other hand, PatchGAN is used in designing the discriminator, as it attempts to classify patches of the generated image as real or fake. Consequently, the image is penalized for style consistency between pixels that are spatially more than a patch diameter away from each other.

Finally, handling occlusion is fundamental in several computer vision tasks. For example, completing an occluded facial image helps in better recognizing the face and predicting the identity of the person. Similarly, inferring the full shape of pedestrians and vehicles as well as the occlusion relationship between them can lead to a safer autonomous driving. Furthermore, in surveillance cameras, amodal completion helps in target tracking and security applications.

9. Conclusions

GANs are considered the most interesting idea in machine learning since their invention. Due to their generative capability, they are extending the ability of artificial intelligence systems. The GAN-based models are creative instead of mere learners. In the challenging field of amodal completion, GAN has had a significant impact especially in generating the appearance of a missing region. This brings existing vision systems closer to the human capability in predicting the occluded area.

To help the researchers in the field, in this survey we have reviewed the available works in the literature wherein a GAN is applied in accomplishing tasks of amodal completion and resolving the problems that arise when addressing occlusion. We discussed the architecture of each model along with its strengths and limitations in detail. Then, we summarized the loss function and the dataset that was used in each work and presented their results. Then, we discussed the most common types of objective functions which are implemented in training the GAN models for occlusion handling. Finally, we provided a discussion of the key findings of our survey article.

However, after reviewing the current progress in overcoming occlusion using a GAN, we detected several key issues that remain an open challenge in the research of addressing occlusion. These issues pave the way for the future research direction. By addressing them, the field will progress significantly.

Author Contributions: Conceptualization, K.S., S.S. and Z.V.; methodology, K.S. and S.S.; investigation and data curation, K.S.; writing—original draft preparation, K.S. and S.S.; writing—review and editing, K.S., S.S. and Z.V.; visualization, K.S.; supervision, S.S. and Z.V. All authors have read and agreed to the published version of the manuscript.

Funding: This research received no external funding.

Institutional Review Board Statement: Not applicable.

Informed Consent Statement: Not applicable.

Data Availability Statement: The data will be made available upon request.

Acknowledgments: On behalf of the OHIOD project we are grateful for the possibility to use ELKH Cloud [145]. The authors would like to thank the High Performance Computing Research Group of Óbuda University for its valuable support. The authors also thank NVIDIA Corporation for their support.

Conflicts of Interest: The authors declare no conflict of interest.

References

1. Thielen, J.; Bosch, S.E.; van Leeuwen, T.M.; van Gerven, M.A.; van Lier, R. Neuroimaging findings on amodal completion: A review. *i-Perception* **2019**, *10*, 2041669519840047. [CrossRef] [PubMed]
2. Saleh, K.; Szénási, S.; Vámossy, Z. Occlusion Handling in Generic Object Detection: A Review. In Proceedings of the 2021 IEEE 19th World Symposium on Applied Machine Intelligence and Informatics (SAMI), Herl'any, Slovakia, 21–23 January 2021; pp. 477–484.
3. Wang, Z.; She, Q.; Ward, T.E. Generative adversarial networks in computer vision: A survey and taxonomy. *ACM Comput. Surv. (CSUR)* **2021**, *54*, 1–38. [CrossRef]
4. Karras, T.; Aila, T.; Laine, S.; Lehtinen, J. Progressive growing of gans for improved quality, stability, and variation. *arXiv* **2017**, arXiv:1710.10196.

5. Mirza, M.; Osindero, S. Conditional generative adversarial nets. *arXiv* **2014**, arXiv:1411.1784.
6. Zhu, J.Y.; Park, T.; Isola, P.; Efros, A.A. Unpaired image-to-image translation using cycle-consistent adversarial networks. In Proceedings of the IEEE International Conference on Computer Vision, Venice, Italy, 22–29 October 2017; pp. 2223–2232.
7. Arjovsky, M.; Chintala, S.; Bottou, L. Wasserstein generative adversarial networks. In Proceedings of the International Conference on Machine Learning, Sydney, Australia, 6–11 August 2017; pp. 214–223.
8. Isola, P.; Zhu, J.Y.; Zhou, T.; Efros, A.A. Image-to-image translation with conditional adversarial networks. In Proceedings of the IEEE Conference on Computer Vision and Pattern Recognition, Honolulu, HI, USA, 21–26 July 2017; pp. 1125–1134.
9. Yang, T.; Pan, Q.; Li, J.; Li, S.Z. Real-time multiple objects tracking with occlusion handling in dynamic scenes. In Proceedings of the 2005 IEEE Computer Society Conference on Computer Vision and Pattern Recognition (CVPR'05), San Diego, CA, USA, 21–23 September 2005; Volume 1, pp. 970–975.
10. Enzweiler, M.; Eigenstetter, A.; Schiele, B.; Gavrila, D.M. Multi-cue pedestrian classification with partial occlusion handling. In Proceedings of the 2010 IEEE Computer Society Conference on cOmputer Vision Furthermore, Pattern Recognition, San Francisco, CA, USA, 13–18 June 2010; pp. 990–997.
11. Benenson, R. Occlusion Handling. In *Computer Vision: A Reference Guide*; Ikeuchi, K., Ed.; Springer US: Boston, MA, USA, 2014; pp. 551–552. ._136. [CrossRef]
12. Tian, Y.; Guan, T.; Wang, C. Real-time occlusion handling in augmented reality based on an object tracking approach. *Sensors* **2010**, *10*, 2885–2900. [CrossRef]
13. Ao, J.; Ke, Q.; Ehinger, K.A. Image amodal completion: A survey. In *Computer Vision and Image Understanding*; Elsevier: Amsterdam, The Netherlands, 2023; p. 103661.
14. Anuj, L.; Krishna, M.G. Multiple camera based multiple object tracking under occlusion: A survey. In Proceedings of the 2017 International Conference on Innovative Mechanisms for Industry Applications (ICIMIA), Bengaluru, India, 21–23 February 2017; pp. 432–437.
15. Shravya, A.; Monika, K.; Malagi, V.; Krishnan, R. A comprehensive survey on multi object tracking under occlusion in aerial image sequences. In Proceedings of the 2019 1st International Conference on Advanced Technologies in Intelligent Control, Environment, Computing & Communication Engineering (ICATIECE), Bangalore, India, 19–20 March 2019; pp. 225–230.
16. Ning, C.; Menglu, L.; Hao, Y.; Xueping, S.; Yunhong, L. Survey of pedestrian detection with occlusion. *Complex Intell. Syst.* **2021**, *7*, 577–587. [CrossRef]
17. Li, F.; Li, X.; Liu, Q.; Li, Z. Occlusion Handling and Multi-scale Pedestrian Detection Based on Deep Learning: A Review. *IEEE Access* **2022**, *10*, 19937–19957. [CrossRef]
18. Zhang, L.; Verma, B.; Tjondronegoro, D.; Chandran, V. Facial expression analysis under partial occlusion: A survey. *ACM Comput. Surv. (CSUR)* **2018**, *51*, 1–49. [CrossRef]
19. Dagnes, N.; Vezzetti, E.; Marcolin, F.; Tornincasa, S. Occlusion detection and restoration techniques for 3D face recognition: A literature review. *Mach. Vis. Appl.* **2018**, *29*, 789–813. [CrossRef]
20. Zeng, D.; Veldhuis, R.; Spreeuwers, L. A survey of face recognition techniques under occlusion. *IET Biom.* **2021**, *10*, 581–606. [CrossRef]
21. Meena, M.K.; Meena, H.K. A Literature Survey of Face Recognition Under Different Occlusion Conditions. In Proceedings of the 2022 IEEE Region 10 Symposium (TENSYMP), Mumbai, India, 1–3 July 2022; pp. 1–6.
22. Biswas, S. Performance Improvement of Face Recognition Method and Application for the COVID-19 Pandemic. *Acta Polytech. Hung.* **2022**, *19*,1–21.
23. Gilroy, S.; Jones, E.; Glavin, M. Overcoming occlusion in the automotive environment—A review. *IEEE Trans. Intell. Transp. Syst.* **2019**, *22*, 23–35. [CrossRef]
24. Rosić, S.; Stamenković, D.; Banić, M.; Simonović, M.; Ristić-Durrant, D.; Ulianov, C. Analysis of the Safety Level of Obstacle Detection in Autonomous Railway Vehicles. *Acta Polytech. Hung.* **2022**, *1*, 187–205. [CrossRef]
25. Macedo, M.C.d.F.; Apolinario, A.L. Occlusion Handling in Augmented Reality: Past, Present and Future. *IEEE Trans. Vis. Comput. Graph.* **2021**, *29*, 1590–1609. [CrossRef]
26. Zhang, Z.; Ji, X.; Cui, X.; Ma, J. A Survey on Occluded Face recognition. In Proceedings of the 2020 The 9th International Conference on Networks, Communication and Computing, Tokyo, Japan, 18–20 December 2020; pp. 40–49.
27. Sajeeda, A.; Hossain, B.M. Exploring Generative Adversarial Networks and Adversarial Training. *Int. J. Cogn. Comput. Eng.* **2022**, *3*, 78–89. [CrossRef]
28. Saxena, D.; Cao, J. Generative adversarial networks (GANs) challenges, solutions, and future directions. *ACM Comput. Surv. (CSUR)* **2021**, *54*, 1–42. [CrossRef]
29. Jabbar, A.; Li, X.; Omar, B. A survey on generative adversarial networks: Variants, applications, and training. *ACM Comput. Surv. (CSUR)* **2021**, *54*, 1–49. [CrossRef]
30. Farajzadeh-Zanjani, M.; Razavi-Far, R.; Saif, M.; Palade, V. Generative Adversarial Networks: A Survey on Training, Variants, and Applications. In *Generative Adversarial Learning: Architectures and Applications*; Springer: Berlin/Heidelberg, Germany, 2022; pp. 7–29.
31. Pavan Kumar, M.; Jayagopal, P. Generative adversarial networks: A survey on applications and challenges. *Int. J. Multimed. Inf. Retr.* **2021**, *10*, 1–24. [CrossRef]

32. Hong, Y.; Hwang, U.; Yoo, J.; Yoon, S. How generative adversarial networks and their variants work: An overview. *ACM COmputing Surv. (CSUR)* **2019**, *52*, 1–43. [CrossRef]
33. Li, Y.; Wang, Q.; Zhang, J.; Hu, L.; Ouyang, W. The theoretical research of generative adversarial networks: An overview. *Neurocomputing* **2021**, *435*, 26–41. [CrossRef]
34. Pan, Z.; Yu, W.; Yi, X.; Khan, A.; Yuan, F.; Zheng, Y. Recent progress on generative adversarial networks (GANs): A survey. *IEEE Access* **2019**, *7*, 36322–36333. [CrossRef]
35. Salehi, P.; Chalechale, A.; Taghizadeh, M. Generative adversarial networks (GANs): An overview of theoretical model, evaluation metrics, and recent developments. *arXiv* **2020**, arXiv:2005.13178.
36. Jin, L.; Tan, F.; Jiang, S. Generative adversarial network technologies and applications in computer vision. *Comput. Intell. Neurosci.* **2020**, *2020*, 1459107. [CrossRef] [PubMed]
37. Wang, K.; Gou, C.; Duan, Y.; Lin, Y.; Zheng, X.; Wang, F.Y. Generative adversarial networks: Introduction and outlook. *IEEE/CAA J. Autom. Sinica* **2017**, *4*, 588–598. [CrossRef]
38. Alotaibi, A. Deep generative adversarial networks for image-to-image translation: A review. *Symmetry* **2020**, *12*, 1705. [CrossRef]
39. Porkodi, S.; Sarada, V.; Maik, V.; Gurushankar, K. Generic image application using GANs (Generative Adversarial Networks): A Review. *Evol. Syst.* **2022**, 1–15. [CrossRef]
40. Kammoun, A.; Slama, R.; Tabia, H.; Ouni, T.; Abid, M. Generative Adversarial Networks for face generation: A survey. *ACM Comput. Surv. (CSUR)* **2022**, *55*, 1–37. [CrossRef]
41. Toshpulatov, M.; Lee, W.; Lee, S. Generative adversarial networks and their application to 3D face generation: A survey. *Image Vis. Comput.* **2021**, *108*, 104119. [CrossRef]
42. Tschuchnig, M.E.; Oostingh, G.J.; Gadermayr, M. Generative adversarial networks in digital pathology: A survey on trends and future potential. *Patterns* **2020**, *1*, 100089. [CrossRef]
43. Saad, M.M.; O'Reilly, R.; Rehmani, M.H. A Survey on Training Challenges in Generative Adversarial Networks for Biomedical Image Analysis. *arXiv* **2022**, arXiv:2201.07646.
44. Zhao, J.; Hou, X.; Pan, M.; Zhang, H. Attention-based generative adversarial network in medical imaging: A narrative review. *Comput. Biol. Med.* **2022**, *149*, 105948. [CrossRef]
45. Alqahtani, H.; Kavakli-Thorne, M.; Kumar, G. Applications of generative adversarial networks (gans): An updated review. *Arch. Comput. Methods Eng.* **2021**, *28*, 525–552. [CrossRef]
46. Sampath, V.; Maurtua, I.; Aguilar Martín, J.J.; Gutierrez, A. A survey on generative adversarial networks for imbalance problems in computer vision tasks. *J. Big Data* **2021**, *8*, 1–59. [CrossRef]
47. Ljubić, H.; Martinović, G.; Volarić, T. Augmenting data with generative adversarial networks: An overview. *Intell. Data Anal.* **2022**, *26*, 361–378. [CrossRef]
48. Tian, C.; Zhang, X.; Lin, J.C.W.; Zuo, W.; Zhang, Y.; Lin, C.W. Generative adversarial networks for image super-resolution: A survey. *arXiv* **2022**, arXiv:2204.13620.
49. Aggarwal, A.; Mittal, M.; Battineni, G. Generative adversarial network: An overview of theory and applications. *Int. J. Inf. Manag. Data Insights* **2021**, *1*, 100004. [CrossRef]
50. Gui, J.; Sun, Z.; Wen, Y.; Tao, D.; Ye, J. A review on generative adversarial networks: Algorithms, theory, and applications. *IEEE Trans. Knowl. Data Eng.* **2021**, *35*, 3313–3332. [CrossRef]
51. Hitawala, S. Comparative study on generative adversarial networks. *arXiv* **2018**, arXiv:1801.04271.
52. Creswell, A.; White, T.; Dumoulin, V.; Arulkumaran, K.; Sengupta, B.; Bharath, A.A. Generative adversarial networks: An overview. *IEEE Signal Process. Mag.* **2018**, *35*, 53–65. [CrossRef]
53. Goodfellow Ian, J.; Jean, P.A.; Mehdi, M.; Bing, X.; David, W.F.; Sherjil, O.; Courville Aaron, C. Generative adversarial nets. In Proceedings of the 27th international Conference on Neural Information Processing Systems, Montreal, QC, Canada, 8–13 December 2014; Volume 2, pp. 2672–2680.
54. Zhang, H.; Goodfellow, I.; Metaxas, D.; Odena, A. Self-attention generative adversarial networks. In Proceedings of the International Conference on Machine Learning, Long Beach, CA, USA, 9–15 June 2019; pp. 7354–7363.
55. Rubner, Y.; Tomasi, C.; Guibas, L.J. The earth mover's distance as a metric for image retrieval. *Int. J. Comput. Vis.* **2000**, *40*, 99–121. [CrossRef]
56. Gulrajani, I.; Ahmed, F.; Arjovsky, M.; Dumoulin, V.; Courville, A.C. Improved training of Wasserstein GANs. *Adv. Neural Inf. Process. Syst.* **2017**, *30*, 5767–5777.
57. Salimans, T.; Goodfellow, I.; Zaremba, W.; Cheung, V.; Radford, A.; Chen, X. Improved techniques for training gans. *Adv. Neural Inf. Process. Syst.* **2016**, *29*, 2234–2242.
58. Arjovsky, M.; Bottou, L. Towards principled methods for training generative adversarial networks. *arXiv* **2017**, arXiv:1701.04862.
59. Borji, A. Pros and cons of gan evaluation measures. *Comput. Vis. Image Underst.* **2019**, *179*, 41–65. [CrossRef]
60. Zhou, Q.; Wang, S.; Wang, Y.; Huang, Z.; Wang, X. Human De-occlusion: Invisible Perception and Recovery for Humans. In Proceedings of the IEEE/CVF Conference on Computer Vision and Pattern Recognition, Nashville, TN, USA, 20–25 June 2021; pp. 3691–3701.
61. Ronneberger, O.; Fischer, P.; Brox, T. U-net: Convolutional networks for biomedical image segmentation. In *Proceedings of the International Conference on Medical Image Computing and Computer-Assisted Intervention, Munich, Germany, 5–9 October 2015*; Springer: Berlin/Heidelberg, Germany, 2015; pp. 234–241.

62. Liu, G.; Reda, F.A.; Shih, K.J.; Wang, T.C.; Tao, A.; Catanzaro, B. Image inpainting for irregular holes using partial convolutions. In Proceedings of the European Conference on Computer Vision (ECCV), Munich, Germany, 14–17 May 2018; pp. 85–100.
63. Xiong, W.; Yu, J.; Lin, Z.; Yang, J.; Lu, X.; Barnes, C.; Luo, J. Foreground-aware image inpainting. In Proceedings of the IEEE/CVF Conference on Computer Vision and Pattern Recognition, Long Beach, CA, USA, 15–20 June 2019; pp. 5840–5848.
64. Rajchl, M.; Lee, M.C.; Oktay, O.; Kamnitsas, K.; Passerat-Palmbach, J.; Bai, W.; Damodaram, M.; Rutherford, M.A.; Hajnal, J.V.; Kainz, B.; et al. Deepcut: Object segmentation from bounding box annotations using convolutional neural networks. *IEEE Trans. Med. Imaging* **2016**, *36*, 674–683. [CrossRef]
65. Yu, J.; Lin, Z.; Yang, J.; Shen, X.; Lu, X.; Huang, T.S. Generative image inpainting with contextual attention. In Proceedings of the IEEE Conference on Computer Vision and Pattern Recognition, Salt Lake City, UT, USA, 18–23 June 2018; pp. 5505–5514.
66. Zhang, Q.; Liang, Q.; Liang, H.; Yang, Y. Removal and Recovery of the Human Invisible Region. *Symmetry* **2022**, *14*, 531. [CrossRef]
67. Yan, X.; Wang, F.; Liu, W.; Yu, Y.; He, S.; Pan, J. Visualizing the invisible: Occluded vehicle segmentation and recovery. In Proceedings of the IEEE/CVF International Conference on Computer Vision, Seoul, Republic of Korea, 27 October–2 November 2019; pp. 7618–7627.
68. Zhang, H.; Xu, T.; Li, H.; Zhang, S.; Wang, X.; Huang, X.; Metaxas, D.N. Stackgan++: Realistic image synthesis with stacked generative adversarial networks. *IEEE Trans. Pattern Anal. Mach. Intell.* **2018**, *41*, 1947–1962. [CrossRef]
69. Dhamo, H.; Tateno, K.; Laina, I.; Navab, N.; Tombari, F. Peeking behind objects: Layered depth prediction from a single image. *Pattern Recognit. Lett.* **2019**, *125*, 333–340. [CrossRef]
70. Mani, K.; Daga, S.; Garg, S.; Narasimhan, S.S.; Krishna, M.; Jatavallabhula, K.M. Monolayout: Amodal scene layout from a single image. In Proceedings of the IEEE/CVF Winter Conference on Applications of Computer Vision, Snowmass Village, CO, USA, 1–5 March 2020; pp. 1689–1697.
71. Zheng, C.; Dao, D.S.; Song, G.; Cham, T.J.; Cai, J. Visiting the Invisible: Layer-by-Layer Completed Scene Decomposition. *Int. J. Comput. Vis.* **2021**, *129*, 3195–3215. [CrossRef]
72. He, K.; Gkioxari, G.; Dollár, P.; Girshick, R. Mask r-cnn. In Proceedings of the IEEE International Conference on Computer Vision, Venice, Italy, 22–29 October 2017; pp. 2961–2969.
73. Dhamo, H.; Navab, N.; Tombari, F. Object-driven multi-layer scene decomposition from a single image. In Proceedings of the IEEE/CVF International Conference on Computer Vision, Seoul, Republic of Korea, 27 October–2 November 2019; pp. 5369–5378.
74. Yu, J.; Lin, Z.; Yang, J.; Shen, X.; Lu, X.; Huang, T.S. Free-form image inpainting with gated convolution. In Proceedings of the IEEE/CVF International Conference on Computer Vision, Seoul, Republic of Korea, 27 October–2 November 2019; pp. 4471–4480.
75. Zhan, X.; Pan, X.; Dai, B.; Liu, Z.; Lin, D.; Loy, C.C. Self-supervised scene de-occlusion. In Proceedings of the IEEE/CVF Conference on Computer Vision and Pattern Recognition, Seattle, WA, USA, 14–19 June 2020; pp. 3784–3792.
76. Ehsani, K.; Mottaghi, R.; Farhadi, A. Segan: Segmenting and generating the invisible. In Proceedings of the IEEE Conference on Computer Vision and Pattern Recognition, Salt Lake City, UT, USA, 18–23 June 2018; pp. 6144–6153.
77. He, K.; Zhang, X.; Ren, S.; Sun, J. Deep residual learning for image recognition. In Proceedings of the IEEE Conference on Computer Vision and Pattern Recognition, Las Vegas, NV, USA, 27–30 June 2016; pp. 770–778.
78. Kahatapitiya, K.; Tissera, D.; Rodrigo, R. Context-aware automatic occlusion removal. In Proceedings of the 2019 IEEE International Conference on Image Processing (ICIP), Taipei, Taiwan, 22–25 September 2019; pp. 1895–1899.
79. Cai, J.; Han, H.; Cui, J.; Chen, J.; Liu, L.; Zhou, S.K. Semi-supervised natural face de-occlusion. *IEEE Trans. Inf. Forensics Secur.* **2020**, *16*, 1044–1057. [CrossRef]
80. Chen, Y.A.; Chen, W.C.; Wei, C.P.; Wang, Y.C.F. Occlusion-aware face inpainting via generative adversarial networks. In Proceedings of the 2017 IEEE International Conference on Image Processing (ICIP), Beijing, China, 17–20 September 2017; pp. 1202–1206.
81. Cheung, Y.M.; Li, M.; Zou, R. Facial Structure Guided GAN for Identity-preserved Face Image De-occlusion. In Proceedings of the 2021 International Conference on Multimedia Retrieval, Taipei, Taiwan, 21 August 2021; pp. 46–54.
82. Li, Y.; Liu, S.; Yang, J.; Yang, M.H. Generative face completion. In Proceedings of the IEEE Conference on Computer Vision and Pattern Recognition, Honolulu, HI, USA, 21–26 July 2017; pp. 3911–3919.
83. Mathai, J.; Masi, I.; AbdAlmageed, W. Does generative face completion help face recognition? In Proceedings of the 2019 International Conference on Biometrics (ICB), Crete, Greece, 4–7 June 2019; pp. 1–8.
84. Liu, H.; Zheng, W.; Xu, C.; Liu, T.; Zuo, M. Facial landmark detection using generative adversarial network combined with autoencoder for occlusion. *Math. Probl. Eng.* **2020**, *2020*, 1–8. [CrossRef]
85. Cai, J.; Hu, H.; Shan, S.; Chen, X. Fcsr-gan: End-to-end learning for joint face completion and super-resolution. In Proceedings of the 2019 14th IEEE International Conference on Automatic Face & Gesture Recognition (FG 2019), Lille, France, 14–18 May 2019; pp. 1–8.
86. Ledig, C.; Theis, L.; Huszár, F.; Caballero, J.; Cunningham, A.; Acosta, A.; Aitken, A.; Tejani, A.; Totz, J.; Wang, Z.; et al. Photo-realistic single image super-resolution using a generative adversarial network. In Proceedings of the IEEE Conference on Computer Vision and Pattern Recognition, Honolulu, HI, USA, 21–26 July 2017; pp. 4681–4690.
87. Li, C.; Ge, S.; Zhang, D.; Li, J. Look through masks: Towards masked face recognition with de-occlusion distillation. In Proceedings of the 28th ACM International Conference on Multimedia, Seattle, WA, USA, 12–16 October 2020; pp. 3016–3024.

88. Dong, J.; Zhang, L.; Zhang, H.; Liu, W. Occlusion-aware gan for face de-occlusion in the wild. In Proceedings of the 2020 IEEE International Conference on Multimedia and Expo (ICME), London, UK, 6–10 July 2020; pp. 1–6.
89. Jabbar, A.; Li, X.; Assam, M.; Khan, J.A.; Obayya, M.; Alkhonaini, M.A.; Al-Wesabi, F.N.; Assad, M. AFD-StackGAN: Automatic Mask Generation Network for Face De-Occlusion Using StackGAN. *Sensors* **2022**, *22*, 1747. [CrossRef]
90. Li, Z.; Hu, Y.; He, R.; Sun, Z. Learning disentangling and fusing networks for face completion under structured occlusions. *Pattern Recognit.* **2020**, *99*, 107073. [CrossRef]
91. Jabbar, A.; Li, X.; Iqbal, M.M.; Malik, A.J. FD-StackGAN: Face De-occlusion Using Stacked Generative Adversarial Networks. *KSII TRansactions Internet Inf. Syst. (TIIS)* **2021**, *15*, 2547–2567.
92. Duan, Q.; Zhang, L. Look more into occlusion: Realistic face frontalization and recognition with boostgan. *IEEE Trans. Neural Netw. Learn. Syst.* **2020**, *32*, 214–228. [CrossRef]
93. Duan, Q.; Zhang, L.; Gao, X. Simultaneous face completion and frontalization via mask guided two-stage GAN. *IEEE Trans. Circuits Syst. Video Technol.* **2021**, *32*, 3761–3773. [CrossRef]
94. Liu, Z.; Luo, P.; Wang, X.; Tang, X. Deep learning face attributes in the wild. In Proceedings of the IEEE International Conference on Computer Vision, Santiago, Chile, 7–13 December 2015; pp. 3730–3738.
95. Huang, G.B.; Mattar, M.; Berg, T.; Learned-Miller, E. Labeled faces in the wild: A database for studying face recognition in unconstrained environments. In Proceedings of the Workshop on faces in 'Real-Life' Images: Detection, Alignment, and Recognition, Marseille, France, 17 October 2008.
96. Le, V.; Brandt, J.; Lin, Z.; Bourdev, L.; Huang, T.S. Interactive facial feature localization. In *Proceedings of the European Conference on Computer Vision, Florence, Italy, 7–13 October 2012*; Springer: Berlin/Heidelberg, Germany, 2012; pp. 679–692.
97. Yi, D.; Lei, Z.; Liao, S.; Li, S.Z. Learning face representation from scratch. *arXiv* **2014**, arXiv:1411.7923.
98. Parkhi, O.M.; Vedaldi, A.; Zisserman, A. Deep Face Recognition In *Proceedings of the British Machine Vision Conference (BMVC), Swansea, UK, 7–10 September 2015*; BMVA Press, 2015; pp. 41.1–41.12.
99. Guo, Y.; Zhang, L.; Hu, Y.; He, X.; Gao, J. Ms-celeb-1m: A dataset and benchmark for large-scale face recognition. In *Proceedings of the European Conference on Computer Vision, Amsterdam, The Netherlands, 11–14 October 2016*; Springer: Berlin/Heidelberg, Germany, 2016; pp. 87–102.
100. Liao, S.; Lei, Z.; Yi, D.; Li, S.Z. A benchmark study of large-scale unconstrained face recognition. In Proceedings of the IEEE International Joint Conference on Biometrics, Clearwater, FL, USA, 29 September–2 October 2014; pp. 1–8.
101. Lee, C.H.; Liu, Z.; Wu, L.; Luo, P. Maskgan: Towards diverse and interactive facial image manipulation. In Proceedings of the IEEE/CVF Conference on Computer Vision and Pattern Recognition, Seattle, WA, USA, 13–19 June 2020; pp. 5549–5558.
102. Martinez, A.; Benavente, R. *The Ar Face Database: Cvc Technical Report, 24*; Universitat Autonoma do Barcelona: Barcelona, Spain, 1998.
103. Lucey, P.; Cohn, J.F.; Kanade, T.; Saragih, J.; Ambadar, Z.; Matthews, I. The extended cohn-kanade dataset (ck+): A complete dataset for action unit and emotion-specified expression. In Proceedings of the 2010 IEEE Computer Society Conference on Computer Vision and Pattern Recognition-Workshops, San Francisco, CA, USA, 13–18 June 2010; pp. 94–101.
104. Gross, R.; Matthews, I.; Cohn, J.; Kanade, T.; Baker, S. Multi-pie. *IMage Vis. Comput.* **2010**, *28*, 807–813. [CrossRef]
105. Phillips, P.J.; Moon, H.; Rizvi, S.A.; Rauss, P.J. The FERET evaluation methodology for face-recognition algorithms. *IEEE TRansactions Pattern Anal. Mach. Intell.* **2000**, *22*, 1090–1104. [CrossRef]
106. Cong, K.; Zhou, M. Face Dataset Augmentation with Generative Adversarial Network. *J. Phys. Conf. Ser.* **2022**, *2218*, 012035. [CrossRef]
107. Yang, S.; Luo, P.; Loy, C.C.; Tang, X. Wider face: A face detection benchmark. In Proceedings of the IEEE Conference on Computer Vision and Pattern Recognition, Las Vegas, NV, USA, 27–30 June 2016; pp. 5525–5533.
108. Fabbri, M.; Calderara, S.; Cucchiara, R. Generative adversarial models for people attribute recognition in surveillance. In Proceedings of the 2017 14th IEEE International Conference on Advanced Video and Signal Based Surveillance (AVSS), Lecce, Italy, 29 August–1 September 2017; pp. 1–6.
109. Radford, A.; Metz, L.; Chintala, S. Unsupervised representation learning with deep convolutional generative adversarial networks. *arXiv* **2015**, arXiv:1511.06434.
110. Fulgeri, F.; Fabbri, M.; Alletto, S.; Calderara, S.; Cucchiara, R. Can adversarial networks hallucinate occluded people with a plausible aspect? *Comput. Vis. Image Underst.* **2019**, *182*, 71–80. [CrossRef]
111. Simonyan, K.; Zisserman, A. Very deep convolutional networks for large-scale image recognition. *arXiv* **2014**, arXiv:1409.1556.
112. Papadopoulos, D.P.; Tamaazousti, Y.; Ofli, F.; Weber, I.; Torralba, A. How to make a pizza: Learning a compositional layer-based gan model. In Proceedings of the IEEE/CVF Conference on Computer Vision and Pattern Recognition, Long Beach, CA, USA, 15–20 June 2019; pp. 8002–8011.
113. Zhang, K.; Wu, D.; Yuan, C.; Qin, X.; Wu, H.; Zhao, X.; Zhang, L.; Du, Y.; Wang, H. Random Occlusion Recovery with Noise Channel for Person Re-identification. In Proceedings of the International Conference on Intelligent Computing. Springer, Shenzhen, China, 12–15 August 2020; pp. 183–191.
114. Tagore, N.K.; Chattopadhyay, P. A bi-network architecture for occlusion handling in Person re-identification. *Signal Image Video Process.* **2022**, *16*, 1–9. [CrossRef]
115. Wang, X.; Shrivastava, A.; Gupta, A. A-fast-rcnn: Hard positive generation via adversary for object detection. In Proceedings of the IEEE Conference on Computer Vision and Pattern Recognition, Honolulu, HI, USA, 21–26 July 2017; pp. 2606–2615.

116. Girshick, R. Fast r-cnn. In Proceedings of the IEEE International Conference on Computer Vision, Santiago, Chile, 7–13 December 2015; pp. 1440–1448.
117. Han, G.; Zhou, W.; Sun, N.; Liu, J.; Li, X. Feature fusion and adversary occlusion networks for object detection. *IEEE Access* **2019**, *7*, 124854–124865. [CrossRef]
118. Ren, S.; He, K.; Girshick, R.; Sun, J. Faster r-cnn: Towards real-time object detection with region proposal networks. *Adv. Neural Inf. Process. Syst.* **2015**, *28*, 91–99. [CrossRef]
119. Zhao, C.; Lv, X.; Dou, S.; Zhang, S.; Wu, J.; Wang, L. Incremental generative occlusion adversarial suppression network for person ReID. *IEEE Trans. Image Process.* **2021**, *30*, 4212–4224. [CrossRef]
120. Wu, D.; Zhang, K.; Zheng, S.J.; Hao, Y.T.; Liu, F.Q.; Qin, X.; Cheng, F.; Zhao, Y.; Liu, Q.; Yuan, C.A.; et al. Random occlusion recovery for person re-identification. *J. Imaging Sci. Technol.* **2019**, *63*, 30405. [CrossRef]
121. Zhou, B.; Lapedriza, A.; Khosla, A.; Oliva, A.; Torralba, A. Places: A 10 million image database for scene recognition. *IEEE Trans. Pattern Anal. Mach. Intell.* **2017**, *40*, 1452–1464. [CrossRef]
122. McCormac, J.; Handa, A.; Leutenegger, S.; Davison, A.J. Scenenet rgb-d: 5m photorealistic images of synthetic indoor trajectories with ground truth. *arXiv* **2016**, arXiv:1612.05079.
123. Silberman, N.; Hoiem, D.; Kohli, P.; Fergus, R. Indoor segmentation and support inference from rgbd images. In Proceedings of the European Conference on Computer Vision, Florence, Italy, 7–13 October 2012; pp. 746–760.
124. Song, S.; Yu, F.; Zeng, A.; Chang, A.X.; Savva, M.; Funkhouser, T. Semantic scene completion from a single depth image. In Proceedings of the IEEE Conference on Computer Vision and Pattern Recognition, Honolulu, HI, USA, 21–26 July 2017; pp. 1746–1754.
125. Armeni, I.; Sax, S.; Zamir, A.R.; Savarese, S. Joint 2d-3d-semantic data for indoor scene understanding. *arXiv* **2017**, arXiv:1702.01105.
126. Geiger, A.; Lenz, P.; Urtasun, R. Are we ready for autonomous driving? The kitti vision benchmark suite. In Proceedings of the 2012 IEEE Conference on Computer Vision and Pattern Recognition, Providence, RI, USA, 16–21 June 2012; pp. 3354–3361.
127. Chang, M.F.; Lambert, J.; Sangkloy, P.; Singh, J.; Bak, S.; Hartnett, A.; Wang, D.; Carr, P.; Lucey, S.; Ramanan, D.; et al. Argoverse: 3d tracking and forecasting with rich maps. In Proceedings of the IEEE/CVF Conference on Computer Vision and Pattern Recognition, Long Beach, CA, USA, 15–19 June 2019; pp. 8748–8757.
128. Zhu, Y.; Tian, Y.; Metaxas, D.; Dollár, P. Semantic amodal segmentation. In Proceedings of the IEEE Conference on Computer Vision and Pattern Recognition, Honolulu, HI, USA, 21–26 July 2017; pp. 1464–1472.
129. Qi, L.; Jiang, L.; Liu, S.; Shen, X.; Jia, J. Amodal instance segmentation with kins dataset. In Proceedings of the IEEE/CVF Conference on Computer Vision and Pattern Recognition, Long Beach, CA, USA, 15–20 June 2019; pp. 3014–3023.
130. Caesar, H.; Uijlings, J.; Ferrari, V. Coco-stuff: Thing and stuff classes in context. In Proceedings of the IEEE Conference on Computer Vision and Pattern Recognition, Salt Lake City, UT, USA, 18–23 June 2018; pp. 1209–1218.
131. Lin, T.Y.; Maire, M.; Belongie, S.; Hays, J.; Perona, P.; Ramanan, D.; Dollár, P.; Zitnick, C.L. Microsoft coco: Common objects in context. In Proceedings of the European Conference on Computer Vision, Zurich, Switzerland, 6–12 September 2014; pp. 740–755.
132. Li, D.; Zhang, Z.; Chen, X.; Ling, H.; Huang, K. A richly annotated dataset for pedestrian attribute recognition. *arXiv* **2016**, arXiv:1603.07054.
133. Zheng, L.; Shen, L.; Tian, L.; Wang, S.; Wang, J.; Tian, Q. Scalable person re-identification: A benchmark. In Proceedings of the IEEE International Conference on Computer Vision, Santiago, Chile, 7–13 December 2015; pp. 1116–1124.
134. Li, W.; Zhao, R.; Wang, X. Human reidentification with transferred metric learning. In Proceedings of the Computer Vision–ACCV 2012: 11th Asian Conference on Computer Vision, Daejeon, Republic of Korea, 5–9 November 2012; pp. 31–44.
135. Li, W.; Zhao, R.; Xiao, T.; Wang, X. Deepreid: Deep filter pairing neural network for person re-identification. In Proceedings of the IEEE Conference on Computer Vision and Pattern Recognition, Columbus, OH, USA, 23–28 June 2014; pp. 152–159.
136. Zheng, Z.; Zheng, L.; Yang, Y. Unlabeled samples generated by gan improve the person re-identification baseline in vitro. In Proceedings of the IEEE International Conference on Computer Vision, Venice, Italy, 22–29 October 2017; pp. 3754–3762.
137. Everingham, M.; Van Gool, L.; Williams, C.K.; Winn, J.; Zisserman, A. The pascal visual object classes (voc) challenge. *Int. J. Comput. Vis.* **2010**, *88*, 303–338. [CrossRef]
138. Gatys, L.A.; Ecker, A.S.; Bethge, M. Image style transfer using convolutional neural networks. In Proceedings of the IEEE Conference on Computer Vision and Pattern Recognition, Las Vegas, NV, USA, 27–30 June 2016; pp. 2414–2423.
139. Li, Y.; Xiao, N.; Ouyang, W. Improved generative adversarial networks with reconstruction loss. *Neurocomputing* **2019**, *323*, 363–372. [CrossRef]
140. Dosovitskiy, A.; Brox, T. Generating images with perceptual similarity metrics based on deep networks. *Adv. Neural Inf. Process. Syst.* **2016**, *29*, 658–666.
141. Gatys, L.A.; Ecker, A.S.; Bethge, M. A neural algorithm of artistic style. *arXiv* **2015**, arXiv:1508.06576.
142. Johnson, J.; Alahi, A.; Fei-Fei, L. Perceptual losses for real-time style transfer and super-resolution. In Proceedings of the Computer Vision—ECCV 2016: 14th European Conference, Amsterdam, The Netherlands, 11–14 October 2016; pp. 694–711.
143. Lim, J.H.; Ye, J.C. Geometric gan. *arXiv* **2017**, arXiv:1705.02894.

144. Li, K.; Malik, J. Amodal instance segmentation. In Proceedings of theComputer Vision—ECCV 2016: 14th European Conference, Amsterdam, The Netherlands, 11–14 October 2016; pp. 677–693.
145. Héder, M.; Rigó, E.; Medgyesi, D.; Lovas, R.; Tenczer, S.; Török, F.; Farkas, A.; Emődi, M.; Kadlecsik, J.; Mező, G.; et al. The past, present and future of the ELKH cloud. *Inform. Társadalom* **2022**, *22*, 128–137. [CrossRef]

MDPI AG
Grosspeteranlage 5
4052 Basel
Switzerland
Tel.: +41 61 683 77 34

Algorithms Editorial Office
E-mail: algorithms@mdpi.com
www.mdpi.com/journal/algorithms

www.ingramcontent.com/pod-product-compliance
Lightning Source LLC
Chambersburg PA
CBHW041416210926
51850CB00013B/3285
* 9 7 8 3 7 2 5 8 4 3 7 3 2 *